KV-511-789

Too Big To Fail – Brauchen wir ein Sonderinsolvenzrecht für Banken?

ILFS

Institute for Law and Finance Series

Edited by

Theodor Baums
Andreas Cahn

De Gruyter

Too Big To Fail – Brauchen wir ein Sonderinsolvenzrecht für Banken?

Herausgegeben von

Patrick S. Kenadjian

De Gruyter

ISBN 978-3-11-027220-8
e-ISBN 978-3-11-027251-2

Bibliografische Information der Deutschen Nationalbibliothek

Die Deutsche Bibliothek verzeichnet diese Publikation in der Deutschen Nationalbibliografie; detaillierte bibliografische Daten sind im Internet über http://dnb.ddb.de abrufbar.

Einbandabbildung: Medioimages/Photodisc
Datenkonvertierung/Satz: jürgen ullrich typosatz, Nördlingen
Druck und Bindung: Hubert & Co. GmbH & Co. KG, Göttingen
♾ Gedruckt auf säurefreiem Papier

Printed in Germany

www.degruyter.com

Vorwort

Ausgangspunkt der bereits seit mehr als drei Jahren anhaltenden Finanzkrise war der Bankensektor. Die Folgen der Insolvenz des Bankhauses Lehman Brothers und die Ungewissheit über die Konsequenzen einer Insolvenz „systemrelevanter" Banken für das globale Finanzsystem und damit auch für die Weltwirtschaft werfen die Frage auf, ob besondere Regeln für eine Insolvenz von Banken notwendig sind, um eine geordnete Abwicklung solcher Institute zu ermöglichen, ohne die Gefahren eines Dominoeffekts und eines allgemeinen Vertrauensverlustes in das Finanzsystem heraufzubeschwören.

Das Institute for Law and Finance hat sich am 5. November 2010 im Rahmen einer gemeinsam mit Rechtsanwalt Patrick S. Kenadjian und Prof. Dr. Peter v. Wilmowsky, organisierten ganztätigen Fachtagung zum Thema „Brauchen wir ein Sonderinsolvenzrecht für Banken?" der Frage angenommen, ob solche Sonderregeln notwendig sind und wie sie gegebenenfalls beschaffen sein sollten. Im Rahmen dieser Veranstaltung, die im House of Finance der Frankfurter Goethe-Universität stattfand, hat eine Reihe hochkarätiger Referenten aus dem In- und Ausland zu den in diesem Zusammenhang bedeutsamen Fragen Stellung genommen und mit dem Publikum diskutiert.

Der vorliegende Band aus der Reihe „Institute for Law and Finance Series" (ILFS) vereint die schriftlichen Fassungen der auf der Tagung gehaltenen Vorträge und ergänzt sie um eine umfassende Einleitung. Die Aufsätze basieren weitgehend auf der Rechtslage und dem Diskussionsstand im Winter 2010; einige Manuskripte sind im Frühjahr 2011 aktualisiert worden. Entsprechend der internationalen Zusammensetzung des Autorenkreises enthält der Tagungsband sowohl deutsch- als auch englischsprachige Beiträge. Ihre Reihenfolge entspricht derjenigen der mündlichen Referate. Die ersten drei Aufsätze nehmen vor allem aus ökonomischer Perspektive zu der Frage Stellung, ob es überhaupt eines speziellen Insolvenzrechts für Banken bedarf oder ob die allgemeinen insolvenzrechtlichen Regelungen auch für Kreditinstitute ausreichen. Hierbei werden aktuelle gesetzgeberische Lösungsansätze auf deutscher, europäischer und internationaler Ebene kritisch analysiert. Die beiden folgenden Beiträge widmen sich aus deutscher und aus rechtsvergleichender Perspektive der Frage, wie Auslöser für Bankinsolvenzverfahren beschaffen sein müssen, um ein geordnetes Verfahren rechtzeitig einzuleiten, ohne andererseits Gefahr zu laufen, zu früh in den Geschäftsbetrieb einer Bank und die Eigentumsrechte ihrer Gesellschafter einzugreifen. Die zwei anschließenden Aufsätze behandeln, wiederum aus deutscher und aus rechtsvergleichender Perspektive, die kritische Frage, ob in Abweichung vom allgemeinen Insolvenzrecht besondere Instrumente erforderlich sind, um ein Bankeninsolvenzverfahren erfolgreich durchführen zu können. Die beiden abschließenden Beiträge gehen auf das zentrale Thema des Gläubigerschutzes in einem Sonderinsolvenzrecht für Banken ein und analysieren die aktuellen Entwicklungen im deutschen und US-amerikanischen Recht.

Andreas Cahn

Inhaltsverzeichnis

Vorwort V
Die Autoren IX

Einleitung/Introduction

Between Bankruptcy and Bailout –
the need for a Special Resolution Regime for Financial Institutions
Patrick S. Kenadjian 3

Sind Banken anders – brauchen wir ein Sonderinsolvenzrecht für Banken/
Are Banks different – do we need Special Rules for Bank Resolution?

Are banks different – do we need special rules for bank resolution?
Andreas Dombret 27

The Problem of Bank Resolution Remains Unsolved:
A Critique of the German Bank Restructuring Law
Martin Hellwig 35

Resolution Requires Reform
Thomas F. Huertas 63

Auslöser für ein Sonderinsolvenzverfahren für Banken/
Triggers for Bank Resolution

Auslöser für ein Sonderinsolvenzverfahren für Banken
Klaus Pannen 87

Triggers for Bank Resolution
Charles Randell 105

Instrumente eines Sonderinsolvenzrechts für Banken/
Tools for Bank Resolution

Interventionsmechanismen nach dem deutschen Restrukturierungsgesetz
Dirk H. Bliesener 129

The Regulatory Responses to Bank Insolvencies in Germany and the United States
Leo Plank, Wolfgang M. Nardi, Carl Pickerill, Matthias Raphael Prause 159

Gläubigerschutz in einem Sonderinsolvenzrecht für Banken/
Creditor Protection in Bank Resolution

The Treatment of Creditors in Bank Insolvencies
John L. Douglas 199

Gläubigerschutz in einem Sonderinsolvenzrecht für Banken
Christoph Thole 219

Die Autoren

Dr. Dirk H. Bliesener

geb. 1967; Studium der Rechtswissenschaften, Geschichte und Politikwissenschaft an den Universitäten Tübingen und Bonn sowie Université de Paris – Panthéon-Sorbonne, Institut d'Etudes Politiques de Paris (Sciences Po) und Yale Law School, New Haven, Connecticut, U.S.A. (1986–1993). Maîtrise en Droit (Panthéon-Sorbonne, Paris, 1990). Certificat d'Etudes Politiques (Sciences Po, Paris, 1990), LL.M., Yale Law School (1993). Ambrose Gherini Prize der Yale Law School (1993). Wiss. Assistent am Max-Planck-Institut für ausländisches und internationales Privatrecht, Hamburg (1994–1997). Promotion an der Universität Hamburg (bei Prof. Hopt, 1998) über Aufsichtsrechtliche Verhaltenspflichten beim Wertpapierhandel. Otto-Hahn-Medaille der Max-Planck-Gesellschaft zur Förderung der Wissenschaften (1998). Attorney-at-Law (New York), Rechtsanwalt und Partner, Hengeler Mueller Partnerschaft von Rechtsanwälten, Frankfurt am Main. Herr Dr. Bliesener war Rechtsberater der Hypo Real Estate-Gruppe und der WestLB bei deren Restrukturierung.

Prof. Dr. Andreas Dombret

Dr. Andreas Dombret was born on 16 January 1960 in the USA to German parents. After completing his "Abitur" (senior school-leaving certificate) at the Neusprachliches Gymnasium in Ahlen, North Rhine-Westphalia, he trained as a bank clerk with Dresdner Bank before studying business management at the Westfälische Wilhelms University in Münster. He was awarded his PhD by the Friedrich-Alexander University in Erlangen-Nuremberg. From 1987 to 1991, he worked at Deutsche Bank's Head Office in Frankfurt as a manager with the power of procuration. From 1992 to 2002, he worked at JP Morgan in Frankfurt and London, from 1999 as a Managing Director. From 2002 to 2005, he was the Co-Head of Rothschild Germany located in Frankfurt and London, before serving Bank of America as Vice Chairman for Europe and Head for Germany, Austria and Switzerland between 2005 and 2009. He was awarded an honorary professorship from the European Business School in Oestrich-Winkel in 2009. Since May 2010, he has been a member of the Executive Board of the Deutsche Bundesbank with responsibility for Financial Stability, Statistics and Risk Control.

Dr. Andreas Dombret holds several other positions outside the Deutsche Bundesbank. He sits on the Board of Trustees of the Center for Financial Studies (CFS) in Frankfurt, the Österreichische Bankwissenschaftliche Gesellschaft (Austrian Society for Bank Research) in Vienna, the Westfälische Wilhelms University in Münster, the Schirn Kunsthalle art exhibition centre and the Städel Museum in Frankfurt, and the Museum Wiesbaden. In addition, he is a member of the Board of the International Center for Monetary and Banking Studies (ICMB) in Geneva and the Exchange Experts Commission (BSK), as well as the treasurer of the Verein für Socialpolitik and the Atlantik-Brücke. He is also a co-editor of the "Zeitschrift für das gesamte Kreditwesen" economics journal in Frankfurt.

John L. Douglas

Mr. Douglas is a partner in Davis Polk's Financial Institutions Group, heading the firm's bank regulatory practice and focusing on bank restructuring and resolutions and other issues arising from the current banking and financial crisis. He has been involved in some of the most difficult and sensitive matters during the crisis, including advising the boards of directors of Indymac and Bank United, counseling Citigroup with respect to FDIC matters, advising various parties on the fallout from the failure of Washington Mutual and advising various private equity firms on proposed investments in troubled or failed banks.

Mr. Douglas was appointed General Counsel of the Federal Deposit Insurance Corporation in 1987 and continued in that capacity through 1989. This was a period of unprecedented stress on the financial system, and he was involved in the major bank failures and restructurings of the late 1980s, participated in the landmark Financial Institutions Regulatory Reform and Restructuring Act of 1989 and assisted in the organization of the Resolution Trust Corporation.Mr. Douglas is regarded as one of the leading bank insolvency lawyers in the nation. He serves as a director and member of the executive committee of the Financial Services Volunteer Corp., a non-profit organization assisting countries as the work to develop strong banking and capital markets systems; in that capacity, he has advised the governments of Russia, Indonesia and Egypt, among others. He is a member of Financial Markets Tribunal of the Dubai Financial Services Authority. He is also a member of the executive committee of Rising Star Outreach, a non-profit organization assisting those affected by leprosy in India, and of the University of North Carolina Law School's Banking Law Institute.

He is the author of various articles and treatises dealing with financial institutions, including "Resolution of Banks and Other Financial Institutions," with Randall Guynn, in DEBT RESTRUCTURING, Oxford University Press, 2011, Restructuring and Liquidating US Financial Institutions (with Randall Guynn), in GLOBAL FINANCIAL CRISIS, Globe Business Publishing 2010; and Nation Building and Banks, 60 MAINE LAW REVIEW 2008.

Prof. Dr. Martin Hellwig

Martin Hellwig is a Director at the Max Planck Institute for Research on Collective Goods and Professor of Economics of the University of Bonn, Germany. He holds a doctorate in economics from the Massachusetts Institute of Technology. He has held university positions at Stanford, Princeton, Bonn, Basel, Harvard, and Mannheim. His research interests involve public economics, financial institutions, and competition policy. He is a fellow of the Econometric Society, a Foreign Honorary Member of the American Economic Association and the American Academy of Arts and Sciences and a Past President of the European Economic Association and the Verein für Socialpolitik (German Ecnomic Association). He is also a Member of the Academic Advisory Committee of the German Ministry of the Economy and Technology and of the European Commission's Economic Advisory Group on Competition Policy, a Past Chairman of the German Monopolies Commission and of the German Government's Advisory Committee of Wirtschaftsfonds Deutschland. From May 1, 2011, he is also Chairman of the Advisory Scientific Committee of the European Systemic Risk Board.

Thomas Huertas

Thomas Huertas is a Member of the Executive Committee at the Financial Services Authority (UK) and Alternate Chair of the European Banking Authority (EBA). Mr. Huertas joined the FSA as Director of Wholesale Firms supervision in 2004. In 2008 he assumed responsibility for the Banking Sector, where he focused on troubleshooting at weak banks as well as on policy initiatives to improve the resolution of failed banks. He was also responsible for developing and implementing the UK's approach to remuneration within banks. He is currently responsible for the FSA's international activities as well as for the development and implementation of the FSA's policy on recovery and resolution for banks.

Internationally, Thomas Huertas represents the FSA on a number of key committees. He is Alternate Chair of the EBA, Chair of the EBA's Review Panel, a member of the Basel Committee on Banking Supervision and a member of the Financial Stability Board's Steering Group on Resolution. Previously, he was Vice Chair in the EBA's predecessor organisation, the Committee of European Banking Supervisors (CEBS) as well as Chair of its Expert Group on Prudential Requirements. Thomas Huertas gained extensive practical experience in banking and finance during a long career in Citigroup, joining in 1975 and holding a number of senior positions, including Chairman and CEO of Citibank AG (Germany) and Country Corporate Officer Switzerland. He worked on regulatory issues and corporate strategy in both the United States and Europe as the Chief of Staff for the Vice Chairman. From 2001 to 2003, Thomas Huertas was Chief Executive of Orbian, an internet-based trade finance and settlement company. Mr. Huertas holds a PhD in Economics from the University of Chicago and has written extensively on financial regulation, including the book Crisis: Cause, Containment and Cure which was published by Palgrave Macmillan in 2010. The second edition will be published in 2011. He speaks frequently on finance and regulation matters, and is a guest lecturer in finance at the Johann Wolfgang von Goethe University in Frankfurt, Germany.

Patrick S. Kenadjian

Patrick S. Kenadjian is currently an Adjunct Professor at the Goethe University in Frankfurt am Main, Germany, where he teaches courses on the financial crisis and financial reform and comparative public mergers and acquisitions at the Institute for Law and Finance. He speaks frequently on topics related to financial reform, including too big to fail, the architecture of financial supervision and the new regulatory environment in the US and the EU.

Mr. Kenadjian is also Senior Counsel at Davis Polk & Wardwell, LLP in their London office. He was a partner of the firm from 1994 to 2010, during which time he opened the firm's Tokyo and Frankfurt offices in 1987 and 1991, respectively and spent over 25 years in their European and Asian offices. His practice includes cross-border securities offerings, especially for financial institutions, mergers and acquisitions, privatizations and international investments and joint ventures, as well as general corporate advice, with an emphasis on representing European clients. He has been active in securities transactions for issuers in Asia and Europe, particularly on initial public offerings and privatizations in Germany, Austria, Italy and Switzerland. He has represented bidders and targets in cross-border acquisitions throughout Europe, in particular in France, Germany, Italy, Switzerland, the United Kingdom and the United States. Mr. Kenadjian has also represented European and Asian issuers in U.S. debt private placements. He speaks French, German and Italian.

He has been listed as a leading lawyer in several industry publications, including Chambers Global: The World's Leading Lawyers for Business and Legal Media Group's Expert Guide to the World's Leading Banking Lawyers, Expert Guide to the World's Leading Capital Markets Lawyers and Expert Guide to the World's Leading Lawyers Best of the Best.

Wolfgang Nardi

Wolfgang Nardi, M.A., LL.M. (EUI) ist Rechtsanwalt und Partner in der Finance Gruppe des Münchner Büros von Kirkland & Ellis International LLP. Er berät zu allen Aspekten von Finanzierungen im Bereich von Private Equity Transaktionen und Corporate Finance, mit einem besonderen Schwerpunkt auf internationale Akquisitionsfinanzierungen und deren Restrukturierung. Daneben verfügt er über besondere Erfahrungen bei der Beratung von nachrangigen Gläubigern.

Neben seiner Anwaltszulassung in Deutschland ist Wolfgang Nardi als Solicitor in England und Wales zugelassen.

Dr. Klaus Pannen

Herr Dr. iur. Klaus Pannen führt die Rechtsanwaltskanzlei DR. PANNEN RECHTSANWÄLTE, eine der führenden Insolvenzverwalterpraxen in Deutschland. Dr. Pannen ist als Insolvenzverwalter standortübergreifend tätig und wird regelmäßig von verschiedenen Amtsgerichten bestellt. In seiner bisher 29-jährigen Praxis als Rechtsanwalt hat er u. a. zahlreiche Insolvenz-, Konkurs-, Gesamtvollstreckungs- und Vergleichsverfahren als Verwalter bearbeitet. Herr Dr. Pannen hat an vielen Sanierungen im In- und Ausland mitgewirkt. Soweit möglich, führt er die von ihm betreuten Unternehmen fort und restrukturiert sie. Über besondere Expertise verfügt Dr. Pannen bei der Insolvenz von Kreditinstituten. Herr Dr. Pannen hält seit geraumer Zeit insolvenzrechtliche Vorträge und beschäftigt sich als Mitglied einiger Gremien mit rechtspolitischen Fragestellungen. Im Jahr 2005 ist Dr. Pannen als erster deutscher Insolvenzverwalter als Mitglied des hoch angesehenen American College of Bankruptcy in Washington D.C. aufgenommen worden. Durch zahlreiche Veröffentlichungen zum Insolvenz-, Bank- und Gesellschaftsrecht ist Herr Dr. Pannen zudem wissenschaftlich ausgewiesen. Seit 2008 ist Dr. Pannen Lehrbeauftragter an der Christian-Albrechts-Universität zu Kiel. 2010 ernannte die Europäische Kommission ihn zum Mitglied der Insolvency Law Expert Group (ILEG).

Carl Pickerill

Carl Pickerill is an associate in the Corporate and Corporate Restructuring Departments of Kirkland & Ellis LLP's Chicago and Munich offices. Mr. Pickerill focuses his practice on a variety of areas including representation of chapter 11 debtors in U.S. restructuring proceedings, creditors and buy-side clients in distressed acquisition and transactional and litigation related aspects of debtor-creditor relationships, as well as corporate clients in various private equity transactions. He received his legal education from the University of Notre Dame Law School in Notre Dame, Indiana and holds a Bachelor of Arts in Sociology from the University of Chicago.

Dr. Leo Plank

Dr. iur. Leo Plank, LL.M., ist Rechtsanwalt und Partner im Praxisteam Restrukturierung und Insolvenz des Münchener Büros von Kirkland & Ellis International LLP. Er berät bei Finanzrestrukturierungen und Insolvenzen, mit besonderem Schwerpunkt auf der Vertretung von institutionellen Investoren in den Bereichen High Yield und Distressed Debt sowie von Unternehmen bei grenzüberschreitenden und multinationalen Restrukturierungen. Er verfügt über besondere Erfahrungen bei der Restrukturierung von LBO Finanzierungen und komplexen grenzüberschreitenden Sachverhalten. Neben seiner Anwaltszulassung in Deutschland ist Dr. Plank als Attorney-at-law in New York sowie als Solicitor in England und Wales zugelassen. Dr. Plank ist Autor verschiedener Fachbeiträge, insbesondere zu den Themen Restrukturierung, Sanierungsfinanzierung und Insolvenzrecht.

Matthias Raphael Prause

Matthias Raphael Prause, LL.M. (Harvard), teaches and researches at the Institute of International Law at Ludwig Maximilians University of Munich School of Law. His research focuses on Civil Procedure and Insolvency Law as well as on Alternative Dispute Resolution and particularly Mediation. He completed his legal education in Berlin and Leuven and holds an LL.M. degree from Harvard Law School where he conducted post-graduate studies as ERP Scholar (Fellow of the German Scholarship Foundation). During his two years stay he taught European Politics as a teaching fellow at Harvard Government Department and served as training director for the Harvard Negotiators. He did research on issues relating to ADR and Mediation and served as a court mediator on behalf of the Harvard Mediation Program at Quincy District Court. Since 2009 he serves as member of the board of directors of the International Academy of Dispute Resolution in Chicago.

Charles Randell

Charles Randell joined Slaughter and May in 1980 and has been a partner since 1989. In the field of restructuring of financial institutions, he advised the UK Treasury on a range of assignments arising from the financial crisis, including the resolutions of Northern Rock, Bradford & Bingley and the UK operations of Landsbanki and Kaupthing; the recapitalisation of the UK banking sector, including the Government investment of up to £45 billion in shares of RBS and £23 billion in shares of the merger Lloyds/HBOS; and the £280 billion Asset Protection Scheme. His public sector practice has included other major insolvencies and restructurings and he is also involved in a variety of mergers and acquisitions work. He is included in the highest ranking for Corporate/M&A in Chambers Global, 2011. Charles graduated from Oxford University and holds an MA in jurisprudence. He speaks French and German.

Prof. Dr. Christoph Thole

Prof. Dr. Christoph Thole, Dipl.-Kfm., ist Inhaber des Lehrstuhls für Bürgerliches Recht, Zivilprozessrecht, Europäisches und Internationales Privat- und Verfahrensrecht an der Eberhard Karls Universität Tübingen. Er wurde 1978 in Oldenburg geboren. Nach dem Studium in Bayreuth und Münster folgte 2001 das Erste Juristische Staatsexamen. Die Promotion erfolgte 2003 an der Rheinischen Friedrich-Wilhelms-Universität Bonn mit einer Arbeit zur Haftung von gerichtlichen Sachverständigen. 2005 legte Thole nach dem Referendariat in Bonn das Zweite Juristische Staatsexamen ab und erwarb den Titel eines Diplom-Kaufmanns. Seit 2005 war er Wissenschaftlicher Mitarbeiter an der Universität Bonn bei Prof. Dr. Gerhard Wagner, unter dessen Betreuung er sich 2009 mit einer Schrift zum „Gläubigerschutz durch Insolvenzrecht – Anfechtung und verwandte Regelungsinstrumente in der Unternehmensinsolvenz“ habilitierte. Nach einer Lehrstuhlvertretung an der LMU München folgte zum Sommersemester 2010 die Ernennung zum ordentlichen Professor an der Universität Tübingen. Die Forschungsschwerpunkte von Thole liegen im deutschen und europäischen Insolvenz- und Gesellschaftsrecht, im Zivilprozessrecht und im Haftungsrecht.

Einleitung

Introduction

Between Bankruptcy and Bailout – the Need for a Special Resolution Regime for Financial Institutions

Patrick Kenadjian

Table of Contents

Introduction: Why we need Special Resolution Regimes
1. SRRs: the consensus view
2. The German approach
3. The limitations of the FDIC precedent
4. The necessary elements of an SRR
5. The international dimension
6. CoCos and bail-ins
7. "Too many to fail" as well as "too big to fail"?
Conclusion
References

Introduction: Why we need Special Resolution Regimes

In his testimony before the US Financial Crisis Inquiry Commission in 2010, Federal Reserve Chairman *Ben Bernanke* concluded that "if the crisis has a single lesson, it is that the too big to fail problem must be solved."[1] While some observers prefer too important, or too interconnected, rather than "too big", it is clear that the problem remains central and unsolved. Whatever expectations big, important and/or interconnected financial institutions, their creditors and the markets may have had coming into the crisis, the rescues of AIG, Dexia, Fortis, Hypo Real Estate ("HRE"), Royal Bank of Scotland and UBS, to name but a few, have left the markets with the expectation that, despite public statements to the contrary, public officials will not be able to stand by and watch a repeat of what happened after Lehman Brothers failed in September 2008, but will intervene to prevent such consequences and thus that the government safety net has *de facto* been extended to any financial institution large or interconnected enough that its failure could cause a financial panic.

This occurs in a context where the degree of concentration in the financial services industry has increased significantly. In the United States, for example, the five largest institutions are 20% larger than they were before the crisis, controlling, according to the Federal Reserve Bank of Kansas City, $8.6 trillion of assets, equivalent to nearly 60% of

---

1 *Bernanke* (2010).

US GDP or 52% of banking industry assets. Bank of America alone has assets of $2.3 trillion, equal to the combined assets of the five largest US banks in 1999, the year of the final repeal of the Glass-Steagall Act. These are astonishingly large amounts, given the US's traditional resistance to concentration in the banking industry. Of course, the concentration in many European countries is a multiple of this figure. According to Bank for International Settlements statistics, at the end of 2009 the combined assets of the top five banks represented 466% of GDP in the UK, 464% in the Netherlands, 409% in Sweden and 344% in France.[2] The US and European examples are not in any way outliers. *Goldstein and Véron* (2011) cite statistics showing this trend is global, with the share of the 10 largest global banks (as a percentage of the assets of the largest 1000) growing from 14% in 1999, to 19% pre-crisis in 2007 to 26% in 2009. Finally, *Andrew Haldane* (2010) reports that 90% of government support worldwide since the beginning of the crisis has gone to just 145 institutions with assets of more than $100 billion each. The recent sovereign debt crisis in Ireland has shown that attempts to bail out a concentrated banking industry can risk breaking the state in an effort to avoid breaking the banks. But the problem remains unresolved because the issues involved are far from simple.

The size and concentration of the sector are important because of the fragility of the modern financial sector, amply demonstrated by the recent crisis, in which it was the largest and most interconnected of the institutions which failed or threatened to fail the most spectacularly with the greatest knock-on consequences for the system. It is a common place to say that the financial sector is "fragile", not in the sense, as *Gordon and Muller* (2010) note, that there is a high probability of bank failure, but in the sense that relatively small shocks can have highly disruptive effects, due to the liquidity mismatches between bank liabilities and assets, due to their essential functions of providing maturity transformation to the general economy, compounded by the effects of failure of one financial institution on its competitors.

If an industrial or other commercial company fails, its competitors are usually strengthened because their market share increases to include some of the customers of the failed company and competition is diminished. In contrast, if a financial institution fails, other financial institutions are more likely to be negatively than positively affected, directly because they are creditors or counterparties of the failed institution whose claims against that institution become less valuable, and indirectly because their asset values diminish as a consequence of the fire sales which either precede or follow the failure of the other financial institution. The first effect is the traditional contagion of falling dominoes that we are familiar with from prior financial crises. The second effect is one that was particularly in evidence in the 2007/2008 crisis, a form of contagion through correlation of similar one-way bets on similar assets, sometimes referred to as "similarity" or "common mode failure".[3] The indirect effect is particularly large when the financial institutions use mark to market accounting for a large portion of their assets, since such accounting will tend to accelerate the contagion effect by requiring the institutions to recognize the decline in value of their assets as losses on a current basis, thus reducing their capital cushions, but even in the absence of such accounting, the

2 BIS (2010).

3 See *Gordon and Muller* (2010).

fact is that financial institutions hold fewer unique assets, such as factories or patents or long term supply contracts which tend to hold their value and more assets such as loans and financial instruments whose value fluctuates rapidly with market developments.

Additionally, on the liability side of their balance sheets financial institutions have a very large proportion of short term liabilities, which can be withdrawn or simply not rolled over at very short notice, so that they are particularly vulnerable to panics, so-called "runs on the bank". These "panics" are often viewed as irrational events, but in fact they are rational rather than irrational occurrences, given how quickly bank assets can decline in value and how opaque bank balance sheets are to most outside investors and depositors, so that creditors cannot be sure of the value of their institution's assets, but they can be pretty sure that the last depositors or creditors in line – unless they are insured or secured – run a high risk of receiving less than 100 cents on the Euro or the dollar back. As *Gordon and Muller* note, these runs exhibit the dynamics of a prisoner's dilemma. Regardless of whether a depositor thinks a bank will fail, it is rational to try to be first in line. The natural consequence of panics, rational or irrational, is contagion that, especially in the case of large, interconnected institutions or institutions which perform a crucial, non-substitutable, role in the financial system, can have systemic consequences, meaning ultimately a negative effect on the economy at large, for example through the curtailment of credit or even possibly of payment services. Thus the need to devise a system which deals with the potential failure of such institutions in a way which minimizes the systemic consequences of their failure.

The 2007/2008 crisis demonstrated, especially in the aftermath of the failure of Lehman Brothers, that the conventional bankruptcy/insolvency system applicable to commercial enterprises generally is suboptimal for financial institutions, for a number of reasons. First, because it is too slow and financial institutions' value evaporates too quickly. Second, because central to a bankruptcy proceeding is a general stay of claims against the bankrupt, and this stay interferes with what *Tom Huertas* identifies in his paper in this volume as "the very essence of banking," "the ability to make commitments to pay." Two other problems are that a bankruptcy court is not charged with taking into consideration the need to maintain depositor confidence and financial stability and because the bankruptcy regime does not build in pre-insolvency intervention. With respect to the US bankruptcy system one should probably make two exceptions. The bankruptcy code allows sales of assets out of the bankrupt estate before the estate is settled and Lehman's US operations were sold quite quickly (within 10 days), but creditors can seek to block such sales. The US system also allows a pre-insolvency accord in the form of a "pre-packaged" bankruptcy, but these are actions taken by the institution and its creditors voluntarily and not mandated by a prudential supervisor.

A further lesson from the crisis, perhaps best exemplified by the rescue of AIG, is that in the absence of an adequate regime to deal with the failure of financial institutions, where the alternatives are a messy bankruptcy or a bail-out, the taxpayer can end up socializing enormous losses generated by the private sector, and this is politically and socially undesirable. It is also systemically undesirable for the financial system itself, as it tends to create moral hazard to the benefit of the managers, shareholders and creditors of the institutions involved, to the detriment of taxpayers and of more responsible private market actors. With respect to the socialized losses, it is important to note that these include not just the direct cost of public support to financial institutions and markets during the crisis, which were large enough (3% of GDP according to International Monetary Fund ("IMF") estimates), but also to take into account the macroeconomic costs produced by the crisis, including unemployment, slower growth, increases in public debt and the like.

Thus a consensus has built internationally that there is a need to find a middle way for the resolution of financial institutions between "disorderly failure with unpredictable consequences on one side and an open-ended injection of public funds on the other."[4] This middle way is generally referred to as a special resolution regime ("SRR"). It must be credible to the markets – meaning that the markets will believe it may be used – orderly and not too expensive for the taxpayer, so that the bulk of the losses caused by the failure of a financial institution will be internalized by the institution's stakeholders rather than spilling over to the market in the event of a bankruptcy or being borne by the taxpayer in the case of a bail-out.

On November 5, 2010, the Institute for Law and Finance at the Goethe University in Frankfurt am Main held a day long conference to consider the issues raised by this need in the context of the new German insolvency law for banks, the Credit Institution Reorganization Act of 2010 (the "German Act"). Participants included central bankers, regulators, economists, academics and practitioners from the three countries which have moved the most quickly to implement statutory solutions to this problem, Germany, the United Kingdom and the United States. This volume contains the papers published by the participants as a result of that Conference.

The remainder of this Introduction is structured as follows. Section 1 describes the emerging consensus on the need for special resolution regimes for financial institutions, based largely on the experience of the US FDIC. Section 2 briefly outlines the approach taken by the German Act. Section 3 notes certain limitations on the applicability of the FDIC's experience in resolving domestic US banks to the resolution of internationally active SIFIs. Section 4 outlines the necessary elements of a SRR. Section 5 notes the complications brought by the international dimension of SIFIs. Section 6 suggests that CoCos and bail-ins may provide a solution to the international dimension discussed in Section 5. Section 7 raises the question of whether the proposed SRRs are able to deal with the "too many to fail" problem as the "too big to fail" problem.

1. SRRs: the consensus view

The solutions chosen by Germany, the United Kingdom and the United States differ somewhat, especially in the German case, but all three contain recognizable elements of the resolution regime which the US Federal Deposit Insurance Corporation ("FDIC") has been operating for decades, primarily in the context of smaller, relatively simple organizations, such as community banks, whose liabilities consist overwhelmingly of retail deposits insured by the FDIC. *John Douglas*' paper for the Conference provides an

---

4 *Carmassi, Luchetti and Micossi* (2010).

excellent overview of how this system has functioned and how different the challenges it faced are from those which we now face in dealing with SIFIs. It is important to understand that legislators and supervisors are in effect attempting to create something which has never actually been done before, a novel system for the orderly resolution of complex internationally active financial institutions. The challenge is to see if the FDIC's tried and trusted method of dealing with smaller banks can be expanded to function in the context of much larger institutions active internationally and whose assets and liabilities contain derivatives and other complex financial instruments involving counterparties in different countries and who finance themselves to a significant extent in the international capital markets and from short term extensions of credit by other financial institutions rather than from traditional retail deposits.

The organizers of the Conference made the conscious decision to focus on the solution in one country, Germany, although we recognized that the international dimension of the problem is a key issue, because we felt that the solution has to start by putting appropriate tools into the hands of national authorities before we can move to the next level, of how those authorities will work together. That next step is complex, involving both the need for recognition of home country procedures in host countries and some acceptable form of burden sharing among the jurisdictions involved. It has been the subject of recommendations from the IMF[5] and European Commission communications (on "Bank Resolution Funds" and "An EU Framework for Crisis Management in the Financial Sector") in 2010 and a consultation paper ("Technical Details of a Possible EU Framework for Bank Recovery and Resolution") in 2011. Perhaps the best overall treatment of the subject is to be found in *Carmassi, Luchetti and Micossi* (2010). It would be an appropriate topic for a future conference, at the ILF or elsewhere, but our Conference focused on the first step, the need for a resolution regime, the key elements of such a regime and an evaluation of the extent to which the current German and US legislative solutions meet the needs for such a regime.

Another question the Conference was not asked to address is the vexed question of how to define the institutions which would be subject to the special resolution regime. While the general assumption of course is that **any** "too big to fail" institution, but also **only** "too big to fail" institutions would be subject to it, that is not necessarily the case. Under the Dodd-Frank Wall Street Reform and Consumer Protection Act ("Dodd-Frank"), for example, certain institutions are designated as systemically important, but a separate decision is required to subject an institution to the Orderly Liquidation Authority ("OLA") and having been designated a systemically important financial institution ("SIFI") is not a pre-requisite for becoming subject to the OLA.

Dodd-Frank is a bit clearer on the qualifications for being designated a SIFI, at least as they relate to classical financial institutions (for example, any bank holding company with $50 billion or more in assets), but gives the Financial Stability Oversight Council ("FSOC") considerable latitude to designate companies and groups outside the traditional circle of regulated financial institutions as SIFIs. The proposed rules put out for comment by the Federal Reserve Board (the "Fed") in early February 2011 indicate that the Fed intends to make full use of this flexibility. The point of this flexibility is of

5 *Fonteyne, Bossu et al.* (2010).

course to allow the FSOC to expand the regulatory perimeter to include "shadow banks" within the scope of the Federal Reserve Board's regulation by designating them as SIFIs. On the other hand, the experience of the crisis showed that the time point of a potential failure had a significant impact on the spill-over effects of the failure, so that institutions which, *ex ante*, might not have been viewed as SIFIs – Northern Rock in the UK and Bear Steans and Lehman Brothers in the US are often cited in this connection – may need to be resolved if they fail at a time the financial system is particularly fragile.

The consensus of the Conference participants was that conventional bankruptcy or insolvency proceedings are not well suited to banks and other financial institutions, for the reasons set forth in *Andreas Dombret's* and *Tom Huertas'* contributions to this volume, that an alternative between bailout and bankruptcy is necessary and that this alternative should take the shape of a resolution or orderly liquidation authority, modeled on that of the FDIC.

A key feature of a resolution regime is that it is an administrative as opposed to a judicial proceeding in which a resolution authority plays the central role. How different such a proceeding can be from the traditional bankruptcy regime can be seen from *Christoph Thole's* paper in this volume which, in the German tradition, places creditor protection as the central point of bankruptcy law and sees the central goal of a bankruptcy proceeding as a collective measure to enforce the debtor's obligations. That this is not the only goal of bankruptcy is of course demonstrated by Chapter 11 of the US Bankruptcy Code which, while not neglecting creditor rights and priorities, focuses more on debtor rehabilitation, as noted by *Leo Plank* and his colleagues in their contribution to this volume.

But in fact resolution for financial institutions focuses neither on the rights of creditors nor on the prospects for rehabilitation of the debtor, but rather on the protection of the financial system in which both creditors and debtors participate. As a result, a resolution system may give its resolution authority the power to ride roughshod over both debtors' and creditors' rights as normally understood in bankruptcy, as noted by *Leo Plank* and his colleagues in their contribution to this volume. As *Christoph Thole* notes, the most basic of these powers is to decide which liabilities of a debtor may be transferred together with assets to a new obligor or a bridge bank and thus increase their chances of being paid 100 cents on the dollar or Euro, and which ostensibly *pari passu* liabilities stay behind to be liquidated out of the debtor's remaining assets, thus receiving less on their claims. In fact, in most FDIC resolutions, general creditors left behind have received nothing.

In the US the resolution agency has been the FDIC and the interests it has defended have been those of the insured depositors and the deposit insurance fund. As, traditionally, the claims of insured depositors have represented on average 85% of the creditor claims of the banks the FDIC has resolved, the question of the rights of general unsecured creditors have weighed less in the balance. Dodd-Frank has extended the resolution regime to a broader number of institutions whose creditor profile is likely to be very different.

The U.S. has from the beginning exempted banks from the application of general Federal bankruptcy laws. Instead, banks' charters were revoked and a receiver appointed to liquidate assets. Since 1933 this receiver for national banks has been the FDIC, with the decision to appoint the FDIC made by the national banks' primary regulator, the Comptroller of the Currency (the "Comptroller"). The FDIC may be appointed as a receiver or, if the Comptroller thought the bank could be rehabilitated, as a conservator and, since 1987 the FDIC has had the authority to charter a "bridge bank" as an alternative to liquidation. Since 1991 the FDIC and the Federal Reserve Board have had the authority to close state chartered banks and appoint the FDIC as their receiver or conservator.[6]

A key element of the U.S. system is that the decision to close a bank is made by the bank's direct regulator (which, more often than not, is not the FDIC) and the liquidation or other resolution is administered by another entity, the FDIC. The UK Banking Act 2009, discussed by *Charles Randell* in this volume, also adopts a separation between the authority which decides on resolution (initially the FSA, now the PRA) and the resolution authority (the Bank of England). Over the years the grounds on which US regulators could close a bank have been broadened so that a refusal or inability to pay debts was no longer required, but operating in an unsafe and unsound matter or the simple need to conserve assets for the benefit of depositors and other creditors sufficed. Still, concerns about possible "regulatory forbearance," whereby the primary regulator would fail to use its power to close the bank on a timely basis have persisted. These were dealt with in 1991 in the FDIC Improvement Act ("FDICIA") by including a requirement that the appropriate regulator was required (as opposed to merely permitted) to appoint a receiver or conservator for a bank within a specified time period of finding that a bank's tangible capital ratio has fallen below the "critically undercapitalized" ratio of 2%.

The FDIC's goal is to achieve the resolution which "is least costly to the deposit insurance fund of all possible methods" and to "maximize the net present value return from the sale", of the bank's assets. However, under FDICIA, the FDIC is allowed to disregard this "least cost" method where it "would have serious adverse effects on economic conditions and financial stability."[7] The problem revealed by the 2007/2008 crisis was that this system did not apply to financial institutions other than deposit taking banks, for example investment banks, although, as demonstrated by the collapse of Lehman Brothers, they shared many of the vulnerabilities discussed above in the introductory section of this paper. In consequence, a major feature of the Dodd-Frank Act was to expand the categories of institutions that could be subject to a bank style resolution.

2. The German approach

Whereas Dodd-Frank and the U.K. Banking Act 2009 described in *Charles Randell's* contribution to this volume follow the traditional FDIC administrative model quite closely, the German Act takes a somewhat different approach or, perhaps better stated, takes two approaches to the issue. These two approaches are outlined in the papers by *Dirk Bliesener* and *Leo Plank* and his colleagues in this volume. Looked at carefully, the Act

6 *Bliss and Kaufman* (2006).
7 *Bliss and Kaufman* (2006).

seems to be in fact two acts, one which boosts the powers of the Bundesanstalt für Finanzdienstleistungsaufsicht ("BaFin"), the German Federal Financial Supervisory Authority in both the early intervention ("Section 45 powers") and resolution stages ("Section 48a procedures") and another which privileges an entirely different approach, one which presents a cross between Chapter 11 under the US Bankruptcy Code and the reorganization plan provisions of the German insolvency law.

Much attention has been focused on the latter provisions under which the financial institution itself would initiate a restructuring of its operations in a proceeding which would be entirely consensual for all its stakeholders, to be followed, if needed, by a reorganization proceeding also to be initiated by the institution itself or a restructuring consultant or the BaFin. Under the German Act, BaFin can also step into the picture directly using its Section 48a powers, for example to transfer assets to a third party or a bridge bank, at any time it believes a systemic risk exists, regardless of whether a rehabilitation or reorganization proceeding has been commenced, but how this would work in practice is unclear. The restructuring procedure does allow debt for equity swaps and haircutting of creditor claims, but requires shareholder and creditor votes to accomplish these changes. The time lines envisioned, coupled with the informational requirements of the restructuring plan, are much closer to the timeline and requirements of a US Chapter 11 proceeding or to a normal German insolvency proceeding than to an FDIC-style administrative proceeding described in more detail below and in *John Douglas'* contribution to this volume. The practical consequences of this are likely to be negative in terms of costs. A recent IMF working paper on bank recoveries in bankruptcy proceedings in the US, UK and Germany notes that even for non-financial institutions overall recovery shrinks substantially as the duration of the work-out process increases and estimates that German insolvency proceedings would have to be shortened by about one half in order for German banks to recover the same amount as UK banks do in domestic insolvency procedures.[8]

In addition to this consensual, debtor initiated reorganization and restructuring alternative, the German Act also strengthens BaFin's power to intervene in the case of systemically relevant institutions by transferring assets without needing shareholder consent. Unfortunately, the powers granted BaFin do not include the power to force conversion of debt into equity or to haircut creditor claims so that the kind of bail-in mechanism described by *Tom Huertas* in his contribution to this volume, discussed in more detail below, would not seem possible in Germany. Those powers are only possible in the context of the consensual reorganization process. The reason for this distinction appears to have been the concern among certain of the drafters of the German Act that granting such powers to an administrative body such as the BaFin might constitute an impermissible expropriation of private property.

As a US lawyer, I am not in a position to evaluate whether this is the case, but I understand that the position is not universally held in German legal circles, with certain commentators putting more weight on the public interest in avoiding financial crises as well as on the curative powers of *ex post* judicial review of the administrative decisions taken in the resolution process. That is certainly where the US and the UK have come

---

8 *Schmieder* (2011).

out on the subject. At the time the German Act was drafted, bail-ins were not a central concern on the reform agenda, so that it may not have been clear to all participants that not giving BaFin these powers risked putting Germany out of step with other jurisdictions in terms of the available tools for bank resolution. This is always a danger for first movers or early adopters. In retrospect, it is an omission to be regretted, as it was clearly the initial intention to equip BaFin with a full panoply of resolution tools, starting with early intervention powers under Section 45 of the *Kreditwesengesetz* ("KWG") and following through to the right under Section 48a KWG to transfer assets and liabilities of financial institutions to a bridge bank or a third party in the event of a danger to the financial system, and thus to put Germany in the lead group among European countries in terms of resolution powers.

However, as *John Douglas*' paper on the FDIC's procedures makes clear, a power to take actions which in effect hair cut creditor claims is an inherent part of those procedures. They are certainly central to the bail-in alternative described by *Tom Huertas*, which seems to be gaining increasing attention, as the difficulties of international resolutions are focused on more closely. The Seoul G-20 declaration and the related Financial Stability Board Report ("Reducing the Moral Hazard posed by Systematically Important Financial Institutions") as well as officials of the Bank of England (*Paul Haldane*) and the European Banking Agency (*Tom Huertas*) are all focusing on the bail-in alternative. The EU's consultation document on a possible EU framework for bank recovery and resolution also sees the value of a debt write-down tool as in practice being potentially the most useful in case of SIFIs deemed "too big to fail".

It should also be noted that the BaFin's enhanced powers under Section 48a KWG only apply to systemically important institutions, and not to any other financial institutions, so that the BaFin can only truly resolve SIFIs and not other, smaller banks.

Dirk Bliesener also notes in his contribution to this volume another potentially unfortunate omission in the German Act, which is the failure to give BaFin explicit authority to require financial institutions to prepare the kind of "living wills" discussed in Section 4 below. BaFin has extensive powers under Section 45 KWG to require information from banks already in trouble, but living wills are directed towards SIFIs not yet in trouble. Here again, the early mover may have missed an important point. Although BaFin's normal powers no doubt allow them to collect extensive information on all financial institutions under their jurisdiction, as discussed in Section 4 below, living wills require a level of information which goes far beyond what has traditionally been required and are also to be understood as a significant new regulatory tool, so much so that Dodd-Frank allows US bank regulators to levy serious sanctions on US banks which do not produce plans acceptable to their regulators. While it is likely that BaFin will be able to require German financial institutions to produce similarly elaborate – and hopefully useful – plans, more direct authority would have been desirable.

Finally, *Leo Plank* and his colleagues note in their contribution to this volume one particularly German twist to the transfer of assets by BaFin under Section 48a KWG, which is that, as in the case of normal carve-outs and spin-offs under German law, there is an element of joint liability of the new owners of the transferred assets with the old owners for liabilities left behind with the failed institution, albeit limited to the amount the left behind creditors would have been entitled to had their been no carve-out or transfer. It is hard to say whether this liability will have a significant effect on BaFin's ability to find buyers for these assets, but it is clearly a complication which purchasers from the FDIC would not have. And, given that an effect of such carve-outs can be expected to be similar to that of the FDIC's "purchase and assumption" transactions, *i.e.* a significant diminution of the recovery on the left behind liabilities, this could be a significant drawback.

3. The limitations of the FDIC precedent

The US and UK approaches are clearly modeled after the traditional FDIC approach for depository institutions. The problem there, the Conference participants noted, is that the FDIC experience may be of more limited relevance than has been generally recognized in the legislative discussion in the US and Germany, due to the nature of most of the institutions the FDIC has resolved to date, and the actual nature of the process followed by the FDIC. As described in *John Douglas'* contribution to this volume, most of the institutions the FDIC has resolved, even the very large ones such as Washington Mutual and IndyMac Bancorp, have held relatively little in the way of complex derivatives and their liabilities were largely made up of insured deposits, while their scope of activities was geographically limited to the United States. For a more complete discussion of FDIC resolutions, see *Douglas and Guynn* (2011). The process followed by the FDIC has consisted largely of transferring swiftly, usually over a weekend, as many assets and liabilities as possible to a single new owner and liquidating the remaining assets for the benefit of the remaining creditors and to pay its own expenses. Of course, while the actual transfer of assets and liabilities takes place over a weekend, the FDIC has usually been involved with the failing institution for a period of several weeks or even months (the FDIC's Resolution Handbook, available on its excellent website, presents a timeline of 90 to 100 days) before the transfer, during which it has conducted its own evaluation of the institution, set up an electronic data room for potential bidders and conducted a confidential auction before settling on a solution.

In contrast, the new paradigm contemplated by the German Act and, to some extent Dodd-Frank, in which much more complex and inevitably internationally active SIFIs are to be resolved, will confront the agencies charged with the resolution with a new set of tasks and challenges, in that SIFIs are unlikely to be resolvable over a weekend or their assets sold to a single bidder. It is also likely that the resolution agency will not have the luxury of 90 to 100 days of quiet time with the failing institution to get to know it and conduct a confidential auction before the public is aware of the institution's crisis, so that the agency may have to step in and take over the failing institution before it has found a solution and will have to actually run the "good bank" (or bridge bank) extracted from the failing institution for a period of time before finding a buyer or buyers.

Of course, the FDIC has also had to come in and operate a bank for a period of time, in cases where the bank has collapsed suddenly, and the FDIC Act provides the FDIC with the express power to act as a conservator in such cases, but 85% of the resolutions the FDIC has conducted have historically been purchase and assumption transactions in which as many assets as possible are pushed out the door as fast as possible, preferably to a single purchaser. Put another way, 85% of the FDIC's experience to date, including its largest ever bank resolution, that of Washington Mutual, which was a "whole bank" sale to JP Morgan Chase with the FDIC acting as receiver rather than conservator, will be largely inapplicable to the resolution of a SIFI.

The most prominent case of conservatorship by the FDIC involved the sudden collapse of IndyMac Bancorp, a California based savings bank specializing in Alt A mortgages, after the publication of a letter to the FDIC and the Office of Thrift Supervision ("OTS") by a US Senator from New York questioning its soundness caused a $1.3 billion run on its deposits. The OTS had to close the bank two weeks later, on July 11, 2008, so the FDIC did not have its usual 90 to 100 days to arrange an orderly receivership and so opted for a conservatorship involving creation of a bridge bank instead. It took the FDIC five months to find and agree a deal with a buyer and the transaction closed three months later.

So we are talking about a substantially longer process than the 90 to 100 days typically needed for a receivership. The FDIC also found itself confronted with unusual problems, for which it did not have established procedures, to ensure the stability of the bridge bank, from reassuring depositors and proving their authority to conduct the business to counterparties, to putting in place corporate governance structures and employee retention programs and ensuring that current lending was being conducted in compliance with all applicable laws. The sale ended up being to a private equity group at a price which was severely criticized, although not entirely fairly. Still, the loss to the FDIC's deposit insurance fund was substantial, $10.7 billion on $30 billion of assets, which, as a percentage of assets, is at the high end of the range of losses the FDIC has sustained. Uninsured depositors received a pay out equal to 50% and general creditors received nothing. It was the largest loss the FDIC had sustained in its history. The size of the loss was due in part to the make-up of IndyMac's liabilities, which included very little unsecured debt other than insured deposits, which would have been available to absorb the losses. This is in contrast to the situation of Washington Mutual, where the FDIC bore no losses on the transfer of $300 billion in assets, due in part to the presence of $15 billion in unsecured senior and subordinated notes to absorb the losses there. So it is unclear how much of the increased costs of the Indy Mac resolution were attributable to the decline in value of the assets during the conservatorship, although it is clear there was substantial deterioration, reflected in both the purchase price and the degree of loss sharing the FDIC had to agree to with the purchasers, and how much was idiosyncratic to the balance sheet structure of the institution. The *Schmieders'* work would tend to suggest the longer time frame had a negative influence.

Given that a single buyer is rather unlikely in view of competition considerations (although the UK experience has shown competition concerns can be waived in a crisis, albeit not always with happy consequences), the agency may have to divide up the "good bank" into pieces small enough to find a buyer, yet self sufficient enough to be a good value proposition for a buyer. What will happen to the value of the good assets during this time period is anyone's guess. The FDIC's experience is that bank assets decline rapidly in value and that even in the best of cases bank resolutions involve substantial losses to the insurance fund. Since the 2008 crisis these losses have been estimated at between 25 and 35% of the assets of the banks involved. Total losses to the deposit insurance fund since the summer of 2008 have totaled $75 billion as a result of 320 bank resolutions.

Who will have the expertise to run these bridge institutions is also an open question. Existing management, unless it has just been brought in (the example of *Vikram Pandit* brought in to turn around Citigroup is one example, but not many others come to mind) may not be the best candidate to do so, the agencies themselves are unlikely to have the resources internally to manage a complex, internationally active, institution and bringing new management into a crisis situation on what is likely to be only an interim basis may be equally problematic.

Because the Conference was concentrating on the German Act rather than Dodd-Frank, it did not focus on one intriguing issue raised by Dodd-Frank, which is how the FDIC would go about resolving SIFI financial groups which include a depository institution. While Section 210 of Dodd-Frank gives the FDIC the right to appoint itself receiver of any failing subsidiary of a covered holding company and thus suggests that SIFI holding companies and their non-banking subsidiaries can be resolved as a group, the Act is silent on whether the FDIC would be able to resolve a depository institution subsidiary separately from the group under its FDICIA powers. However, given that under FDICIA the FDIC operates under a depositor preference system which is distinct from the principles of Title II of Dodd-Frank for the resolution of non-banks, the FDIC might find it more expeditious to resolve the bank separately from the rest of the group and there are indications that this is the path the FDIC currently expects to choose. In a sense this is only logical, since in a bank resolution the FDIC's main priority is to protect the position of the bank's insured depositors and of its deposit insurance fund, which dictates the procedures it usually follows. In a resolution of a non-depository institution there will be by definition no insured depositors to protect directly, and the FDIC's priorities will be different: to provide for the orderly liquidation of a company or group whose failure has been determined to pose a risk to systemic stability. While the two resolutions would of course be coordinated to the extent possible, European Union expectations of consolidated group resolutions of SIFIs in the US may well be disappointed.

4. The necessary elements of an SRR

Tom Huertas' contribution to this volume contains an excellent summary of SRRs. For purposes of this discussion, I would like to focus on two elements essential to their proper functioning: (i) the right of the resolution authority to intervene early enough so that the firm involved can still be rescued by imposing a form of recovery program which the firm can implement before its situation deteriorates to the point where it must be resolved (referred to as "Prompt Corrective Action" powers under the FDICIA) and (ii) a resolution plan or "living will" to provide the resolution authority and interim management with sufficient knowledge of how the institution has been put together, where assets and liabilities are booked, where central services are performed and what systems (IT, risk, cash and liquidity management, legal etc.) are necessary to support the various parts of the business. Any sale of a part of the business will have to consider the needs of the remaining parts for assets and systems being sold. When Lehman's US activities were sold to Barclays Capital their global risk management system went with them, leaving Lehman's UK receiver, PwC and the purchaser of the UK operations, Nomura, with the need to negotiate access to those systems *ex post* with an unrelated third party, Barclays Capital.

The concept of the "living will" has been the source of not inconsiderable confusion. This has included whose document the will is and what its contents and purposes are. The will is obviously a document initially prepared by the financial institution itself, but which must be found satisfactory by its regulator(s). Dodd-Frank makes this clear and allows the regulators to impose sanctions on institutions which do not prepare acceptable plans. The will should have two primary purposes, first setting forth an action plan for recovery in case the institution's financial situation weakens (essentially how much cash can be raised through sales of assets and the issuance of securities and what discretionary uses of cash, such as distributions to shareholders and employees can be curtailed) and, second, providing a road map in case the institution must be resolved. Both purposes are important, but the greatest focus has been placed on the resolution phase in light of the difficulties encountered in the Lehman insolvency, some of which have just been mentioned.

Richard Herring (2010) has set out the main elements of a "wind-down' plan", focusing on the resolution function of such plans. They include:

- mapping lines of business into the corporate entities and justifying each separate entity;
- describing the resolution procedures required for each entity, including an estimate of the amount of time required;
- identifying key interconnections across affiliates, such as cross-guarantees, lines of credit, intra-group loans, along with operational interdependencies, such as IT systems and risk management procedures;
- maintaining an up to date virtual data room containing all relevant information;
- identifying key IT systems, where they are located and the essential personnel to operate them and planning to make them available throughout a resolution process;
- identifying systemically relevant activities and demonstrating how they can continue to operate during a resolution;
- considering how the institution could disconnect from exchanges, clearing houses, custodians and other systemically important elements of the financial infrastructure without creating serious knock-on effects; and
- updating the plan annually or more frequently as warranted by changes in the corporate structure.

It is of course clear that, in order to be useful, certain parts of the plan will have to be updated more frequently. In particular, this includes information relating to credit and other counterparty exposures, as well as funding and liquidity information, available lines of credit and other information which can change daily. This updating can best be done not by including detailed data in the plan, but by reference to the institution's internal data bases where the data is regularly updated.[9]

Simplification of corporate structures appears to be something most large financial institutions could benefit from. Lehman Brothers had 433 subsidiaries in 20 countries. Citigroup has nearly 2,500 of them. And eight of 16 large complex financial institutions identified by the Bank of England in 2007 have more than 1,000 subsidiaries each.[10] It is not clear how many of these subsidiaries perform a useful purpose and how many are left over from the structures of acquired groups or prior tax driven reorganizations, but my suspicion is that much that is confusing in corporate structures could be cleared away without requiring the institutions involved to restructure their way of doing business.

5. The international dimension

The other component of the *terra incognita* the resolution authorities will face is the theme we initially decided to put off to another day, the international dimension. As noted above, this is not an area the FDIC has had to deal with to any significant extent in its resolution activities. In fact, the FDIC points to only one situation in which it resolved a bank which had two foreign branches, both in the Far East. However its importance is so great that it became an important feature of the debate at the Conference. SIFIs are, almost by definition, internationally active and there is currently no framework for the international recognition of the actions of a resolution authority. The experience of the 2007/2008 crisis shows how difficult establishing such a system will be.

Claessens, Herring and Schoenmaker (2010) in their review of cross border bank failures during the crisis, set forth in Geneva Report 12 and covering Lehman, AIG, Dexia, Fortis and the Icelandic banks, shows that even among the Benelux countries, in the case of Fortis, what started off as a cooperative effort to recapitalize Fortis within what was viewed as a well understood framework, ended up in strife and an attempt to preserve the national interests of each of the countries involved. Only in the case of Dexia do the authors see an example of successful international cooperation, while in the case of the Icelandic banks, the UK resorted to the use of anti-terrorist legislation to protect the interests of its depositors, and that against a member of the European Economic Area. The Basel Committee on Banking Regulation came to largely the same conclusion in its March 2010 *Report and Recommendations of the Cross-border Bank Resolution Group*.

Also, as noted above, the US operations of Lehman were sold to Barclays without arrangements being made for the provision of continued essential services, such as risk management, to the rest of the group. While the Lehman example may simply be the result of lack of advance planning and extreme time pressure, the other cases reflect the inherent difficulty of the issues involved. The national authorities faced with interna-

9 See Davis Polk and McKinsey (2011).
10 See *Herring and Carmassi* (2010).

tional bank failures of SIFIs, whose assets can represent a multiple of the host or home country's GDP, are dealing with potentially huge sums and the stability of their own financial system. In such circumstances it is easy to see the situation as a zero sum game where what one country's taxpayers can be made to pay is that much less for the other country's taxpayers to pay. There are indications that some of the bail-outs during the 2008 phase of the crisis were due to uncertainty among home country authorities as to whether, should they attempt to resolve a local SIFI, their actions would be recognized by host country authorities.

The fundamental elements of an international framework are relatively clear. There will need to be non discrimination against creditors outside the home country and all concerned countries' authorities will have to have comparable resolution tools. But these two principles, on which all agree, are only a first step and in the absence of pre-existing commitments on burden sharing it is hard to see how cooperation in a crisis, even if it starts well, as in the case of Fortis, will not almost inevitably degenerate into an attempt to beggar the neighbor.

My personal view is that the best chance to establish such an international system has to be within the European Union, which already includes two of the early adopters of the resolution regime model, Germany and the UK, as well as a European authority which has recognized the need for an international system. *Carmassi, Luchetti and Micossi* (2010) provide an excellent overview of how close, as well as how far, the EU is from having a functioning cross-border system. In particular, they note that, under the EU's Winding-Up Directive (Directive 2001/24/EC), EU law already requires host countries to recognize the actions taken by home country authorities with respect to local branches but not for local subsidiaries. They make a very convincing argument that it should not be a great leap to extend that rule to subsidiaries which do not enjoy managerial autonomy and cannot effectively stand alone in case of a parent default. If this principle were recognized, not only would this be a triumph of substance over form, but it would eliminate the advantage host country authorities hope to gain by requiring the subsidiarization of branches, thus potentially taking another contentious issue off the table.

In addition, as noted above, the European Commission and the IMF have both made proposals in this area. The IMF's is the more radical, in that it proposes a uniform EU-wide resolution system for three kinds of institutions, (i) those systemically important in an EU country other than the home country, (ii) those whose size and international operations make it systemically important for the EU regardless of whether it is systemic in any individual country and (iii) those systemically important in an EU home country, combined with cross-border activities of a size large enough to affect the institution's soundness. The third category is meant to catch the case of the Icelandic banks.[11]

The European Commission's proposal is more modest and, at first glance, more practically achievable. In essence it suggests turning the existing international colleges of supervisors established for the largest cross-border financial groups in the EU into resolution colleges and tasking them with agreeing on a coordinated resolution of the

11 *Fonteyne, Bossu et al.* (2010).

institutions involved.[12] That first step can surely be taken, but, as DG Internal Market and Services notes, their proposal will require the involvement of national ministries of finance "if designated as the national authority responsible for taking decisions on resolution." What this means is that the involvement of the national government will be indispensible to commit their country's assumption of the potential fiscal burden of participating in the resolution process, which will involve at least the need for some funds to be advanced and could end up costing taxpayers substantial amounts, despite all efforts to the contrary, as demonstrated by the FDIC's experience discussed above. And that is where the real difficulties can be expected to arise. Still, both the Commission and the IMF are right in thinking that the EU has to be the best place to start, as demonstrated by *Carmassi, Luchetti and Micossi's* (2010) analysis. Should it be possible to agree a European Union system, expanding it to Switzerland and the United States could be the next logical step, but these are issues for another day and we are still a long way off from an accord, even within the EU. In the meantime, the FDIC's current strategy seems to be to seek bilateral agreements with authorities in jurisdictions where US banks have their principal operations abroad to recognize the FDIC's actions as resolution authority in exchange for the FDIC's agreement to provide funding for the foreign operations involved.

6. CoCos and bail-ins

Conference participants also touched on one much discussed alternative to the resolution authority's intervention. In this connection, it is important to note that Dodd-Frank sees resolution of SIFIs as very much an exceptional event, a "nuclear option" which, like the real thing, in the US and UK versions, requires the assent of multiple key holders. DG Internal Market and Services also agrees resolution should be a last rather than a first resort. But since we know that a normal bankruptcy or insolvency proceeding is likely to be disruptive and expensive, that leaves the need for another alternative. The alternative which has been hit upon by academics and regulators alike is some variation of a contractually agreed upon "bail-in" whereby the various classes of investors in a SIFI – principally subordinated debt and preference stock holders, but also potentially senior debt holders depending on the capital structure of the institution – would agree in advance to the recapitalization of the firm in the case that certain trigger events occur. This could take the form of contingent convertible capital ("CoCo"), as advocated by *Claessens, Herring and Schoenmaker* and others or another form, and the trigger could be regulatory or market orientated.

This would be a contractually agreed process, not a statutory bail-in, which involves the application of the kind of statutory powers to force a conversion of debt into equity which is at the core of the resolution powers granted to resolution authorities in the UK and US laws which the Conference discussed. As noted above, the German Act does not grant BaFin "strong arm" powers sufficient to effect a bail-in, but reserves them for the consensual reorganization on process. *Tom Huertas'* contribution to this volume in-

12 DG Internal Markets and Services (2011).

cludes a very clear illustration of how a bail-in would work. As with CoCos, the idea of a bail-in is to operate on the capital of the top group company in the home country, thus avoiding many of the complications which a cross-border resolution can entail in terms of host country recognition of home country resolution actions. The principal difference is that a bail-in is a regulatory tool to allow prompt intervention in the issuer's capital structure, whereas CoCos would be purely contractual in nature, agreed to between the issuer and its creditors at the time the creditors make their investment. The second difference is the point at which they would be used. Bail-ins are intended as crisis management tools, to be used, as *Tom Huertas* points out, at the point of non-viability of the institution, *i.e.* very much at what might otherwise be the resolution phase. CoCos can be implemented much earlier on the going concern/recovery/resolution spectrum, in the recovery phase. Assuming the trigger and conversion ratio would be contractually agreed, there would be no need for regulatory intervention and, because the conversion takes place within the top company's capital, there should also be no difficulty with cross-border recognition of the procedure.

Of course the devil in such solutions is, as always, in the details and there are many to work out. It is unclear how large the market for such instruments may be (although the success of recent issuances is a cause for some optimism, in all cases these have involved exchanges for existing hybrid instruments, rather than new capital), their credit ratings may be problematical if the trigger for conversion or recapitalization is regulatory (which I think would be a mistake) rather than market or rule based, they may turn out to be very expensive for the issuers and their effect on the market, especially in a crisis, is largely untested. For example, could their triggering have a negative signaling effect to the markets, leading to withdrawals by depositors and by other short term creditors? Will the market believe the recapitalization will be sufficient or indeed even that it involves a new investment? On the technical side, *Pazarbasioglu, Zhou, Le Leslé and Moore* (2011) do a very good job of cataloguing the issues involved for CoCos. How high or low you set the triggers depends on whether you are using the instrument to recapitalize the institution (in which case you want a high one so that it kicks in early enough in the process – *i.e.* in the recovery phase of the spectrum – that a rescue is still possible) or resolve it (in which case a low one, which simply insures the holders – rather than the taxpayers – will absorb part of the loss attributable to the institution's failure, is fine). Should the triggers be market based or capital based? The former are more subject to external manipulation by "speculators" and there is relatively little the issuer can do to steer against the market, while the latter tend to be lagging indicators and subject to manipulation by insiders through the creative use of accounting rules, such as Lehman's famous Repo 105s. Should the triggers be systemic, based on the condition of the whole financial system which the individual bank cannot do anything about, or bank specific? Should the conversion ratio be set at the time of investment or of conversion?

These are all legitimate and complex issues. In particular, as noted above, a difficult question will be the size of the market for such securities. It will be crucial that they not end up in the hands of other financial institutions, since conversion would then simply transmit the losses from one financial institution to other financial institutions, providing another source of contagion. A recent paper by *Adair Turner* of the Financial Services Authority estimates that 25% of the current investor base for UK bank senior debt is other banks and 12% insurance companies.[13] The desirability of excluding these investors may well indicate an upper limit on the use of such instruments. On the other hand, given that current bank equity capital is well below 10% of total bank capitalization, this upper bound may not be a serious constraint. It is also quite possible that simply exchanging the current stock of hybrid instruments financial institutions have issued (and which under Basel III will no longer count towards their capital adequacy ratios) for CoCos would suffice to provide adequate underpinning of core capital by instruments with better loss absorbing characteristics. Of course this raises the question of the conditions under which CoCos would be recognized as capital under Basel III. The Basel Committee is still considering the issue, and until they decide CoCos may be largely confined to Swiss banks whose national regulator has outlined the conditions to be met for them to count towards the supplemental capital buffers required for SIFIs under the "Swiss Finish" rules.

Also, converting existing hybrids to CoCos will not necessarily put the right amount of additional equity in the right place. However, I was recently given the following interesting analysis of Lehman Brothers. At the time it failed its capital was made up in equal amounts ($25 billion each) of common equity (including retained earnings) and of preferred stock and subordinated debt, plus $120 billion of senior debt. Thus if one assumed the hole in its balance sheet was on the order of $25 billion (which Bank of America said to have reported was the case, based on its preliminary due diligence), had the preferred stock and subordinated debt been CoCos, they would have allowed Lehman to wipe out its entire common equity to absorb that loss and still have $25 billion in capital, so maintaining its capital ratio of between 11 and 12%. This still might not have saved Lehman. In fact, the point of the presentation was to promote bail-ins, by emphasizing that a mere 15% "bail-inable" portion of senior debt, added to the preferred stock and subordinated debt would have sufficed to give Lehman a capital ratio in excess of 20%. Still, Lehman would clearly have stood a better chance of surviving and avoiding the estimated $150 billion in losses the same presentation assumed would ultimately be incurred by its liquidation. In any event, given that we really do not know how the traditional resolution tools will work on SIFIs, and that in a number of countries, including Germany, bail-in powers may not be available, it seems to me that it would be in the best interests of all potential members of the SIFI class to put their considerable creative powers in the field of new product development to work testing and perfecting instruments which could contractually effect a recapitalization before the new orderly liquidation regime could be made applicable to one of them. In this context, US SIFIs need to bear in mind that Title II of Dodd-Frank provides only for an orderly liquidation of SIFIs. The institution as such will not survive, but be liquidated. Coupled with the elimination of the Federal Reserve's powers under Section 13(3) of the Federal Reserve Act to provide targeted assistance to non-bank institutions which are in danger of failing, Dodd-Frank may thus end up tipping failing non-bank SIFIs who cannot recapitalize themselves towards liquidation.

It also strikes me that such a security would also be in the best interests of a SIFI's longer term creditors, who really face two choices. The first is to recognize that they are vulnerable to losses they may not be able to control in a resolution (or a bail-in) and to decide in advance when they make their investment decision, in an *ex ante* negotiation between

13 *Turner* (2011).

themselves and their prospective debtor, based on their own evaluation of the SIFI's assets, management and business plan, on an appropriate risk premium for the potential downside over the life of their investment. The other is to deny the danger exists and take the risk that a resolution authority will decide *ex post* on a haircut for their claims on which they may or may not – my guess is the latter – have received appropriate compensation. While I do not underestimate the complexities inherent in CoCos, I do not think denial is the superior strategy.

7. "Too many to fail" as well as "too big to fail"?

The final issue raised during the Conference was that resolution systems which focus only on SIFIs leave the vast majority of financial institutions untouched. In the US, all deposit taking banks are already covered by the existing FDIC resolution powers, but that is not necessarily the case elsewhere, including Germany. The last crisis was fueled by the fear of the larger institutions collapsing, but it is not clear to me that a system which allows intervention only in the case of the top ten or twenty institutions (or maybe even just one or three) will be sufficient next time to preserve a national financial system from contagion. The prior crisis in the US, the savings and loan ("S&L") crisis of the 1990's, did not involve any institution which alone would qualify as a SIFI, but wrought extensive damage nonetheless, and that was in an era when the avenues of contagion did not include mark to market accounting and large scale wholesale short term funding by financial institutions. The contagion then was through correlation, *i.e.* a large number of institutions all having made the same wrong way bets on local real estate, principally in the US Southeast. Using the currently fashionable nomenclature we might designate them as constituting a "too many to fail" problem and thus as "jointly systemic".[14]

Here the question will largely be whether the normal supervisory procedures available to bank regulators will suffice to deal with this multitude. In the US we tend to think that the prompt corrective action provisions added by the FDICIA in 1991 went a long way towards curing the too many to fail problem revealed by the S&L crisis. Looking at the number of small bank failures since August 2008 and the $75 billion in losses the deposit insurance fund has suffered, it is not clear to me this faith is entirely well placed. In Germany, the augmented powers granted to BaFin under Section 48a KWG apply only if there is a danger to the financial system, as well as a danger to the financial institution. At what point there would be a sufficient flood of non SIFI failures that BaFin could call a systemic danger to use those powers is an open question. Of course one can argue that the danger of a multitude of failures in Germany is smaller because of the structure of German banking where, in contrast to the community banks in the US and, say the cajas in Spain, the local savings banks are viewed as more solid than other parts of the banking sector, in particular the Landesbanken, so that a true cascade of failures at the bottom of the pyramid seems less likely. This assumes, of course, that potential losses incurred by savings banks which are shareholders of Landesbanken would not be severe enough to imperil the savings banks.

---

14 See *Thomson* (2009).

Conclusion

The steps taken so far in the direction of establishing national resolution regimes are encouraging, but they are only first steps which leave many practical questions unresolved. The German Act in particular suffers from a central ambiguity as to whether it means to promote a consensual Chapter 11 style procedure or an FDIC-style administrative procedure. Further, should bail-ins become the internationally preferred tool for international bank resolutions, it will also suffer from the failure explicitly to give BaFin the requisite powers to effect bail-ins. But in the absence of effective international cooperation, even laws which are clearer in their desire to establish an administrative SRR are likely to prove insufficient to solve the too big to fail problem. Hence the suggestion that we focus on alternatives such as bail-ins and CoCos which can be executed within a single jurisdiction to recapitalize international groups. In the last crisis we appear to have been somewhat lucky that the rescues which had to be undertaken due to the absence of an appropriate resolution regime have, with the exception of Iceland and Ireland, by and large cost us less than was once feared. Next time we may not be so lucky. And we know that a next time is coming.

References

Bernanke, Benjamin 2010. Testimony before the US Financial Crisis Inquiry Commission, Washington

BIS (Bank for International Settlements), 80th Annual Report, 2010

Claessens, Stijn, Richard J. Herring and Dirk Schoenmaker A Safer World Financial System: Improving the Resolution of Systemic Institutions, Geneva Reports on the World Economy 12, International Center for Monetary and Banking Studies, 2010

Bliss, Robert R. and George G. Kaufman A comparison of U.S. corporate and bank insolvency resolution, Federal Reserve Bank of Chicago, 2006

Carmassi, Jacopo, Elisabetta Luchetti and Stefano Micossi Overcoming Too-Big-To-Fail, Report of the CEPS-Assonime Task Force on Bank Crisis Resolution, Brussels, 2010

Davis Polk & Wardwell LLP and McKinsey & Company, Credible Living Wills: The First Generation, 2011

DG Internal Markets and Services Working Document, Technical details of a possible EU framework for bank recovery and resolution, January 2011

Douglas, John L. and Randall D. Guynn Resolution of U. S. Banks and Other Financial Institutions, in DEBT RESTRUCTURING, Look Chan Ho & Nick Segal Consultant eds., Oxford Univ. Press, 2011

Fonteyne, Wim, Wouter Bossu, Luis Cortavarria-Checkley, Alessandro Giustiniani, Alessandro Gullo, Daniel Hardy and Sean Kerr Crisis Management and Resolution for a European Banking System, International Monetary Fund Working Paper 10/70, 2010

Goldstein, Morris and Nicolas Véron Too Big to Fail: The Transatlantic Debate, WP11–2, The Peterson Institute for International Economics, January 2011

Gordon, Jeffrey N. and Christopher Muller Avoiding Eight-Alarm Fires in the Political Economy of Systemic Risk Management, Colombia Law School, 2010

Haldane, Andrew The $100 Billion Question, Speech to the Institute of Regulation and Risk, Hong Kong, March 2010

Herring, Richard J. Wind-Down Plans as an Alternative to Bailouts, Briefing Paper, Pew Financial Reform Project, Pew Charitable Trusts, 2010

Herring, Richard J. and Jacopo Carmassi The Corporate Structure of International Financial Conglomerates: Complexity and its Implications for Safety and Soundness, in the Oxford Handbook of Banking, Alan Berger, Philip Molyneux and John Wilson, eds. Oxford University Press, 2010

Pazarbasioglu, Ceyla, Jianping Zhou, Vanessa Le Leslé and Michael Moore Contingent Capital: Economic Rationale and Design Featuring, IMF Staff Discussion Note, 2011

Schmieder, Christian and Philipp Schmieder The Impact of Legislation on Credit Risk – Comparative Evidence from the United States, the United Kingdom and Germany, International Monetary Fund, 2011

Thomson, James On Systemically Important Financial Institutions and Progressive Systemic Risk Migration, Policy Discussion Paper No. 27, Federal Reserve Bank of Cleveland, 2009

Turner, Adair Reforming Finance: are we being radical enough? 2011 Clare Distinguished Lecture in Economics and Public Policy, 2011

Sind Banken anders – brauchen wir ein Sonderinsolvenzrecht für Banken?

Are Banks different – do we need Special Rules for Bank Resolution?

Are banks different – do we need special rules for bank resolution?*

Andreas Dombret

Table of Contents

1 Are banks different from other business enterprises?
2 Special rules for bank resolution
 2.1 In Europe
 2.2 In Germany
3 Reform project
 3.1 At the global level
 3.2 At the European level
 3.3 In Germany
4 Conclusion

1 Are banks different from other business enterprises?[1]

Banks are business enterprises that fulfil a wide variety of macroeconomic tasks. They are involved in virtually all economic and social processes. This creates possibilities to influence economic developments, but also a high degree of economic and social responsibility – nowhere more so than in the German system of universal banks. Banks not only settle payments, they also take deposits made by individuals, enterprises and the public sector. These funds are, in turn, lent to enterprises, households and general government in the form of credit. If banks failed to fulfil all these functions or carried them out unreliably, this would jeopardise the stability as well as the growth and development of a modern economy. The smooth functioning of the banking system is therefore valuable in its own right – in both macroeconomic and societal terms.

Banks maintain very close business ties to one another. The insolvency of one bank therefore risks bringing down other banks and triggering a chain reaction. Banks' aforementioned pivotal role means that any disruption to the services they provide may severely impair the smooth functioning of the economy. It is this key role that distinguishes the banking sector from other sectors. With this in mind, all western industrial countries have in place highly regulated banking supervision regimes. Another advantage of banking supervision for central banks is that they can implement monetary policy more efficiently, the more stable the banking sector is as a means of monetary policy transmission.

---

* Editorial status of the following contribution: September 2010.

1 I thank Andreas Meissner for his assistance.

These are just some of the reasons why banks are subjected to special prudential supervision under the German Banking Act (*Kreditwesengesetz*). In Germany, banking regulators have the legal mandate to act to resolve problems in the banking and financial services sector that could jeopardise the safety of the assets entrusted to institutions, impair the orderly conduct of banking business or the proper provision of financial services or bring about considerable disadvantages for the economy as a whole. The intensity of supervision to which the institutions are subjected depends on the nature and scale of the banking transactions and financial services they offer and the associated risks. This prudential oversight is exercised solely in the public interest and with due consideration for market principles, however. In other words, depositors cannot generally demand that banking supervisors carry out particular measures or provide compensation for any losses they may incur as a result of the collapse of a credit or financial services institution. It also means that, as a general rule, responsibility for business policy and its implementation rests with bank managers.

2 Special rules for bank resolution

As outlined above, banks – unlike other business enterprises – have a special role to play in respect of the stability as well as the growth and development of modern economies and are therefore subject to dedicated supervision. Nonetheless, the question arises as to whether this peculiar role justifies special rules for bank resolution. In a nutshell: I believe the answer to this question is a clear "yes". The current legal toolkit has proved inadequate for winding up banks above a certain size and degree of interconnectedness, as it disregards "systemic issues". Systemic risk is specific to the financial sector. The main aim of "normal" insolvency proceedings is to satisfy creditors' claims as far as possible based on the principle of fair and equal treatment. The macroeconomic impact of the insolvency does not need to be considered. In the event of a bank insolvency, however, minimising potential systemic risk is another issue to consider besides ensuring that shareholders bear their fair share of the burden in order to ensure that creditors' claims are satisfied as fully as possible. The supervisory instruments for restructuring ailing banks and insolvency legislation for winding up failed banks in their present form have proved inadequate to ensure the stability of the banking sector. Consequently, especially after the insolvency of Lehman Brothers, government intervention to rescue insolvent banks was generally the only way to safeguard the stability of the financial sector, albeit at high economic cost. The consequences of an insolvency would have been unpredictable. Initially, rescues were decided on an *ad hoc* basis at hectic weekend meetings, later under the broader shield of government rescue programmes. The German rescue programme that was established by the Financial Market Stabilisation Act (*Finanzmarktstabilisierungsgesetz*) alone had €480 billion at its disposal. Shareholders and creditors were the beneficiaries, which naturally raises the issue of moral hazard.

In the past, crises were a decisive catalyst for amending or improving the relevant legislation – and we are working to ensure that this is again the case this time round. We are not alone in this. Other countries such as the UK and the United States have taken somewhat different approaches, although I will not elaborate on this here.[2] But efforts to overcome the banking crisis through the vehicle of prudential legislation invariably focus on preventing insolvency and safeguarding the stability of the financial system. Higher liquidity and capital requirements, a narrower definition of capital and a more precise measurement of banking risks in relation to capital requirements should all help to increase banks' resilience going forward. Yet this still leaves the problem of how supervisors should deal with a bank that experiences financial stress despite tighter regulatory rules. Additional issues are how to restructure or resolve a bank without jeopardising the system as a whole and how to bail in shareholders and creditors in order to limit risk propensity. In the following, I will concentrate on the most recent initiatives towards bank restructuring and resolution. First I would like to outline the *status quo* and then go on to discuss the ideas being considered within the Financial Stability Board and the European Union, and give some details of the German government's draft legislation for restructuring ailing banks.

2.1 In Europe

The current European rules are based on the idea that a legal framework for dealing with cross-border insolvencies is a necessary feature of a functioning single European market. After all, if international market entry is to be facilitated and promoted, an orderly market exit cannot be left entirely to the competent national authorities. While the European Insolvency Directive from the year 2000 applies at the European level, it expressly excludes credit institutions. Instead, separate legislation was adopted for the banking sector in the form of the Directive on the reorganisation and winding-up of credit institutions from 2001.[3] The objective of this directive is to ensure that, where a credit institution with branches in other member states defaults, only one winding-up procedure is initiated in the interests of all creditors and investors.

Under this liquidation procedure, credit institutions are wound up in, and in accordance with the laws applicable in, the member state in which the credit institution is domiciled (home member state). The procedure is thus governed by just one set of resolution rules. This approach is consistent with the principle of home country control, on which the Banking Directive is based. If the administrative or judicial authorities in the home member state decide to initiate resolution proceedings, they are obliged without delay to inform, by any available means, the competent authorities of the member state in which the branch is located. Creditors must be treated equally throughout Europe, and the arrangements on who bears the costs and expenses incurred must be harmonised. The other member states must recognise these proceedings without having the possibility of verifying the competence of the country in which the proceedings are opened. The reorganisation directive was transposed into national law with effect from

---

2 The Anglo-Saxon countries, in particular, chose a different route. Thus the UK has implemented a procedure under the Special Resolution Regime in the Banking Act of 2009, while the corresponding legislation in the United States gives a major role to the Federal Deposit Insurance corporation.

3 Directive 2001/24/EC.

1 January 2004.[4] The Directive on the reorganisation and winding-up of credit institutions does not, however, cover banks active in other countries via subsidiaries.

2.2 In Germany

In Germany, the supervisory instruments for responding when a bank experiences stress is detailed in the third division of the Banking Act under the heading "Measures in special cases". The reorganisation directive was also transposed in this part of the Banking Act. The objective of sections 45 to 45a of the Banking Act is, where possible, to prevent an insolvency situation through timely action. Sections 46b to 46f of the Banking Act also deal directly with banks' insolvency.

In the latter case, the Bonn-based Federal Financial Supervisory Authority (BaFin) has a key role to play. The petition addressed to the insolvency court for the initiation of insolvency proceedings may only be filed by BaFin, not by the banks or their creditors.[5] This is based on the idea that outside creditors should not drive an ailing bank into collapse by potentially filing insolvency proceedings prematurely. The competent supervisory authorities should first have the opportunity to initiate restructuring measures. BaFin's competence is, however, also important in that it is often the only public entity that can identify an institution's distress. This requires inside knowledge of business figures, because credit institutions can typically hide solvency problems by procuring short-term liquidity on the interbank market to meet maturing liabilities.

3 Reform project

3.1 At the global level

At the global level, the Financial Stability Board (FSB) has also been tasked by the G20 to look at the issue of cross-border resolution as part of its concept for dealing with systemically important banks. The FSB's recommendations to the forthcoming G20 summit will include detailed proposals on this issue. The main point is to invest one supervisory body with the instruments and competencies necessary for reorganising or winding up financial groups at the global level. In addition, in-depth analyses are still being conducted to determine whether a group's structure or the form in which a group conducts business impairs reorganisation or winding up, and if so how much.

In practical terms, for large global groups crisis management groups to be set up as part of the core colleges. They are to work with the banks to draw up recovery and resolution plans (RRPs). In essence, banks are to explain to supervisors what risk factors could threaten their survival and what steps the bank would take in such a crisis (recovery plans). If the bank cannot be maintained as a going concern, the plan must outline in what way the bank can be wound up wholly or partly without government support

4 Sections 46d et seq of the German Banking Act.

5 See section 46b of the Banking Act.

(resolution plans). The objective of these plans is to organise the recovery or resolution of a bank in such a way that systemically important units or functions can be maintained. This is intended to minimise market disruption without having to turn to the taxpayer for support – and is also aimed at increasing market discipline.

3.2 At the European level

In October of last year the European Commission presented a communication paper on devising an EU framework for the orderly resolution of cross-border banks as a supplement to the new financial supervisory architecture proposed by the Commission. The project is to result in a draft directive next year.

Main points of the project

As regards the legal framework for crisis management, the Commission believes that an improved deposit insurance system and a strengthened prudential supervisory infrastructure are necessary. To this end, it has to be possible to stabilise ailing cross-border financial institutions and groups and to control the systemic impact of a failure. The Commission wants to take measures in three areas which may overlap in some cases.

1) *Early intervention* This covers measures by the supervisory authorities to restore the stability and financial soundness of ailing institutions. The starting point for such measures may be Article 136 of the Banking Directive. Additional measures comprise the special powers of supervisory authorities. These include, for example, the right to require financial institutions to prepare – before a crisis occurs – a resolution plan (now referred to as a living will) or to appoint a special administrator prior to insolvency. In this connection, it may also be important to empower supervisors to order the transfer of assets of solvent units within the group. The Commission has introduced a new term, "group interest", in this context. In addition to the harmonisation of powers of intervention, the Commission believes that the involvement of the European Banking Authority (EBA) could help to coordinate early intervention in cross-border groups.

2) *Restructuring* This covers measures by the competent national authorities to manage crises at banks. These include, for instance, supervisors' power to transfer assets, liabilities and legal relationships to a third party or, if need be, to nationalise institutions wholly or partly. The declared objective is to maintain the enterprise as a going concern. Options considered in this respect are, first, another private buyer, second, a bridge bank and, third, segregation into "clean" and "toxic" assets and their apportionment to "good" and "bad" banks through a partial transfer of assets and liabilities or by nationalising the financial institution.

3) *Insolvency* Insolvency is another approach within the scope of crisis management. In the event of a bank's insolvency, the minimum solution proposed is a cooperation framework to coordinate national measures; a further-reaching proposal under consideration is an integrated approach for the insolvency of banking groups (uniform European insolvency legislation). However, many issues still have to be clarified, making it unlikely that these plans can be implemented anytime soon.

Likewise, the establishment of a resolution fund at a European level to finance crisis resolution measures is unrealistic at present. The only viable option at the moment therefore appears to be national crisis funds, and the European Commission is already giving thought to their coordination.

A further-reaching harmonisation of insolvency regimes has also been proposed.[6] However, this would be carried out in stages. Planned for the spring of 2011, the Commission's new draft directive will initially provide, among other things, that national insolvency regimes in connection with the transfer of assets between enterprises belonging to one group be amended in order to guarantee intra-group liquidity management. In a second stage, stronger harmonisation of insolvency regimes is to be achieved in the medium term to facilitate the resolution of banks under the same procedural and material insolvency rules. Finally, an integrated insolvency regime is envisaged for the longer term, with the participation of an EU authority.

3.3 In Germany

Under the aegis of the Federal Ministry of Finance and the Federal Ministry of Justice, the Federal Government has drawn up a Bank Restructuring Act.[7] This piece of legislation was adopted by the Federal Cabinet in August of this year and is to enter into effect at the end of the year. Under the Act, restructuring and reorganisation procedures, on the one hand, and prudential resolution and restructuring powers, on the other, will be introduced, as will a bank levy. In this way, systemic risks are to be averted and the banking sector will pay part of the rescue costs.

These new restructuring and resolution provisions are necessary because conventional insolvency legislation and bank supervisory instruments are designed only to freeze business operations, if need be. As a consequence of the financial market crisis, however, a possibility must be created to prevent distressed banks from failing and to open a restructuring opportunity for them. In addition, it is to be ensured that providers of debt and equity capital bear the costs of overcoming insolvency on their own as far as possible.

Under the new Bank Restructuring Act, restructuring and reorganisation procedures are to be launched at the initiative of the financial institution itself. The first stage involves a restructuring procedure, through which the economic difficulties may be overcome by taking early and decisive action, without infringing upon third-party rights at management level. The second stage, the reorganisation procedure, is based in principle on the well-known insolvency plan procedure. Not only the creditors but also the

---

6 The Commission published a new communication paper on the topic "crisis management" on 20 October.

7 Law on the restructuring and orderly resolution of credit institutions, on the establishment of a restructuring fund for credit institutions and on the extension of the limitation period of management liability under the German Stock Corporation Act (Gesetz zur Restrukturierung und geordneten Abwicklung von Kreditinstituten, zur Errichtung eines Restrukturierungsfonds für Kreditinstitute und zur Verlängerung der Verjährungsfrist der aktienrechtlichen Organhaftung).

shareholders may be involved in this stage, under strict conditions, to keep them from thwarting a promising reorganisation plan. Shareholders will not be not expropriated, however. Instead, they are to play an active part in the planning procedure as a voting group in its own right, allowing them to represent their own financial interests.

Moreover, when no other option is possible, supervisors are to be given resolution and restructuring powers in order to ward off a threat to financial market stability. If necessary, supervisors will be empowered to transfer the assets of a systemically important bank, wholly or partly, to a private bank or, temporarily, to a state bridge bank. The advantage of transferring systemically relevant business units of a bank to another legal entity is that stabilisation measures will focus on the new bank. Meanwhile, the non-systemically-relevant elements in the old bank can be resolved using standard insolvency proceedings.

I would like to mention two main points regarding the part of the draft law that concerns reorganisation.

First, it would be desirable to make the various tasks entailed in the procedures I have just described the responsibility of one authority. However, these tasks should not be given to the supervisory authorities. After all, the supervisors are supposed to monitor the banks in a competitively neutral fashion with the help of authorisations and prohibitions. The measures under consideration, by contrast, may lead to substantial competitive distortions in the banking market through the assumption of business policy competencies (i.e. the ability to take business decisions) and possible implicit pre-emptive decisions on the use of public resources from the restructuring fund. This could bring about conflicts of interest. It therefore seems more appropriate to entrust only the Financial Market Stabilisation Agency – which has to be involved in any case when public funds are used – with restructuring tasks. However, the decision to restructure ought to be taken by the supervisory authority based on the results of an examination and evaluation process.

Second, besides this institutional aspect, an economic and legal aspect would appear to be key to an orderly restructuring. I refer here to the issue of automatic terminations or the termination of master agreements, for which a consistent solution still has to be found. On the one hand, a one-day suspension of these effects or rights starting from the initiation of a reorganisation procedure is envisaged;[8] on the other, all rights of termination and reasons for automatic termination are generally to be barred by a transfer order.[9] Apart from a new and coherent provision in the draft law, one precondition for every sustainable solution ought to be an international regulation – one that includes, in particular, the United States and the United Kingdom – of the event-of-default problem. Otherwise, it must be feared that large complex German financial institutions would either subject themselves to foreign law or suffer competitive disadvantages.

Furthermore, a bank levy will be introduced under the law through which the financial sector will shoulder part of the costs of resolving the crisis. Such a bank levy is compati-

8 Section 13 of the draft Credit Institution Reorganisation Act (Kreditinstitute-Reorganisationsgesetz).

9 Section 48 g of the recast German Banking Act (Kreditwesengesetz).

ble with the aim of systemic stability provided it does not flow into the government's general budget but is instead ring-fenced for the purpose of setting up a restructuring or support fund. Germany plans to use the bank levy to finance a separate restructuring fund for credit institutions; this is in line with what the Commission has in mind, as outlined earlier.

4 Conclusion

To sum up, I would like to stress once again that banks are different from other business enterprises. They play a special role in respect of the growth and development of modern economies. What is more, systemic risk is specific to the financial sector. Special insolvency legislation already takes into account, at European and at national level, the difference between banks and other economic agents. However, these legal provisions need to be developed further because at the moment they are too highly geared to freezing business operations and buying time, without giving distressed banks a real chance to restructure. The recent financial market crisis has also shown that change is needed. Brussels and Berlin are hard at work on the necessary adjustments. This is to be welcomed, and the Bundesbank, too, is playing a part and will continue to do so. It must be noted, however, that insolvency law can only be a last resort; crisis prevention and crisis management must be the main priority so that financial distress does not lead to insolvency in the first place.

The Problem of Bank Resolution Remains Unsolved: A Critique of the German Bank Restructuring Law[1]

Martin Hellwig

Table of Contents

1. The Need for Viable Bank Resolution Procedures
2. Shortcomings of Traditional Law: The German Government's Hands-Off Approach to Banks in the Crisis
3. How to Deal with Banks in Difficulties: Procedural Issues
   3.1 The UK Banking Act of 2009
   3.2 Bank Restructuring and Bank Reorganization under the German Bank Reorganization Act of 2010
   3.3 Supervisory Intervention under the German Bank Restructuring Act of 2010
4. How to Deal with Banks in Difficulties: Substantive Issuses
   4.1 Objectives of the Intervention: System Protection versus Creditor Protection
   4.2 What Precisely is Meant by "System Protection"?
   4.3 Depositor Protection
5. The International Dimension of Bank Resolution
6. Constitutional Concerns, Problem Adequacy, and Legal Politics
   6.1 Would a More Effective Resolution Regime Violate Constitutional Property Rights?
   6.2 Procedure and Legitimacy in a Democracy

1. The Need for Viable Bank Resolution Procedures

In the days before September 15, 2008, US authorities had come to the conclusion that it would not be a bad idea to let Lehman Brothers go into insolvency proceedings.[2] A private-sector solution without public funds was unavailable. A rescue with public funds would further worsen the moral hazard that had already been fostered a few months earlier by the use of public guarantees to forestall an insolvency of Bear-Stearns. A res-

1 This paper is based on my October 6, 2010 testimony to the Finanzausschuss (Finance Committee) of the Bundestag, http://www.bundestag.de/bundestag/ausschuesse17/a07/anhoerungen/2010/029/Stellungnahmen/17_Prof__Dr__Martin_Hellwig.pdf . I am grateful to Anat Admati, Horst Eidenmüller, Peter Englund, Hans-Jürgen Hellwig, Anil Kashyap and Beatrice Weder di Mauro for helpful discussions about various aspects of the subject.

2 For an account of developments leading up to and following the Lehman Brothers insolvency, see *A. R. Sorkin* Too Big to Fail: Inside the Battle to Save Wall Street, Allen Lane: Penguin, London 2009.

cue with public funds would also be politically explosive in an environment where people on all sides of the political spectrum were outraged by state intervention in the financial crisis, some because state intervention *per se* went against their principle and some because the state intervention went to bail out a bank that had been taking enormous risks. By contrast, the risks of a potential Lehman insolvency were downplayed. After all, market participants had had weeks, if not months, to prepare for such an event and had presumably hedged their bets. Perhaps then, the contagion effects of insolvency would be contained.

A few days later, it had become clear that letting Lehman Brothers go into insolvency proceedings had been a very bad idea indeed. All the effects that economists could think of under the heading of "systemic risk" had been turned loose: There were immediate domino effects on Lehman counterparties, money market funds holding Lehman debt (Reserve Primary Fund "breaking the buck"), as well as AIG being involved in credit default swaps with Lehman. Markets where Lehman had acted as market maker were disrupted by Lehman's no longer serving this function. Repo lenders to Lehman had difficulties in disposing of, or refinancing, collaterals. Through information contagion, this effect spread across repo markets, causing these markets to shut down completely or to work only with very large haircuts. Through information contagion, the lesson that a large bank might not be bailed out with public money also affected confidence in other banks. Without confidence of banks in each other, interbank markets came to a virtual standstill. Asset markets, in particular stock exchanges, were subject to a selling wave, partly because financial institutions that had problems raising money sold assets as a measure of self-defense, partly because the overall loss of confidence made investors apprehensive about the future.

All these developments had strong repercussions on the real economy. Until then, in Europe the real economy had hung on fairly well despite the financial crisis which had been progressing since the summer of 2007. The fourth quarter of 2008 saw a sharp decline in economic activity. A significant factor in this decline was the contraction of world trade by about one quarter. Part of this contraction could be directly traced to the breakdown of interbank relations as payment modes based on letters of credit ceased to function when confidence between banks disappeared; such payment modes rely on confidence between banks as a substitute for confidence between buyers and sellers in different countries.

The implosion of the global financial system only came to a stop when the most important countries' taxpayers were made to stand in for their banks. Since then, it seems axiomatic that many banks are too big to fail, too complicated to fail, too interconnected to fail, or simply too political to fail.

However, we must not let things stand there. For one thing, we must expect that this is a lesson that bankers, too, have taken away from the crisis: There never will be another Lehman Brothers; if ever they get into trouble in the future, they will be able to count on the taxpayer providing support.[3] For another, there comes a point where banks may not

---

3 There is substantial evidence indicating that this thinking had already shaped bank behaviour before the crisis. Already in 1994, *J. Boyd, M. Gertler* The Role of Large Banks in the Recent US Banking Crisis, Federal Reserve Bank of Minneapolis Quarterly Review, 18, 2–21, argues that

only be too big to fail but also too big to be rescued.[4] The amounts involved have strained the fiscal and political capacities of countries to the utmost. In some countries, like Iceland and Ireland, fiscal capacities have actually been insufficient. In others, fiscal capacity may yet prove to be insufficient. Moreover, in all countries, the capacities of political systems are likely to be insufficient for yet another large-scale bailout.

Given these concerns, it is of paramount importance to develop viable procedures for bank resolution, i.e., procedures that will make it possible to deal with a bank in difficulties without violating the principles of private responsibility and liability on which a market economy is built and without putting the rest of the financial system and the overall economy at risk. In Germany, such procedures have been called for by many, most notable the Council of Economic Experts and the Academic Advisory Board of the Federal Ministry for Economics and Technology.[5]

Unfortunately, progress in this direction has been sorely deficient. Most countries have not done anything. Germany and the United States have made some changes in the rules for bank resolution but, for reasons that will be explained below, I consider these changes to be insufficient.[6] The most radical, and in many ways exemplary, reform has been enacted by the United Kingdom. However, I suspect that even the United King-

---

"too big to fail" expectations were a reason for risky lending strategies of large banks. *E. Brewer III, J. Jagtiani* How much did Big Banks Pay to Become too Big to Fail?, Working Paper, Research Department, Federal Reserve Bank of Philadelphia, December 2009, http://www.philadelphiafed.org/research-and-data/publications/working-papers/2009/wp09-34.pdf, shows that significant premia were paid in mergers that were deemed to bring banks above the threshold where they would be "too big to fail". *P. Gandhi, H. Lustig* Size Anomalies in US Bank Stock Returns: Your Tax Dollars at Work, National Bureau of Economic Research Working Paper No. 16553, November 2010, http://www.nber.org/papers/w16553.pdf, shows that, in relation to earnings, stock market valuations of large banks are too high and that more than three quarters of the overvaluation can be attributed to the implicit subsidy inherent in too-big-to-fail policies.

4 I first used this expression in 1998, following the SBC/UBS merger in Switzerland; see *M. Hellwig* Zur "Volkswirtschaftlichen Verantwortung" der Banken, in: F. Jaeger, W. Stier (eds.), Die volkswirtschaftliche Verantwortung der Banken, Verlag Rüegger, Chur, Zürich 1999, 9–57.

5 Sachverständigenrat zur Begutachtung der gesamtwirtschaftlichen Entwicklung, Die Zukunft nicht aufs Spiel setzen, Jahresgutachten 2009/10, Wiesbaden 2009, 146–154, Wissenschaftlicher Beirat beim Bundesministerium für Wirtschaft und Technologie, Reform von Bankenregulierung und Bankenaufsicht nach der Finanzkrise, http://www.bmwi.de/BMWi/Redaktion/PDF/Publikationen/Studien/reform-von-bankenregulierung-und-bankenaufsicht-wissenschaftlicher-beirat,property=pdf,bereich=bmwi,sprache=de,rwb=true.pdf, 32–35. See also *J. P. Krahnen, H. Siekmann* Rescue Strategies without Moral Hazard: An Attempt to Provide a Master Plan for Avoiding Banking Crises, House of Finance Policy Platform, Frankfurt, 2010, http://www.hof.uni-frankfurt.de/index.php?option=com_docman&Itemid=299&lang=de&limitstart=25; *M. Hellwig* Finanzkrise und Reformbedarf, Gutachten E zum 68, Deutschen Juristentag, Verlag C. H. Beck, München 2010, E 53 ff.

6 This paper focuses on the German reform. For a similarly critical assessment of resolution under the Dodd-Frank Act in the United States, see *V. V. Acharya, B. Adler, M. Richardson, N. Roubini* Resolution Authority, in: V.V. Acharya, T.F. Cooley, M. Richardson, I. Walter (eds.), Regulating Wall Street: The Dodd-Frank Act and the New Architecture of Global Finance, Wiley, New York 2010, 213–240. A general overview of issues and of legal treatments in different countries is provided by *M. Marinc, R. Vlahu* The Economic Perspective of Bank Bankruptcy Law, FED Cleveland Conference on Resolving Insolvent Large and Complex Financial Institutions (2011), http://ssrn.com/abstract=1822682.

dom would prefer to provide Barclays with a bail-out rather than subject them to their Special Resolution Regime for Banks. For Barclays as an internationally operating bank, the cross-border issues involved in bank resolution would just be too vexing. On this matter, the international dimension of bank resolution, literally no progress has been made at all. If a case like Lehman Brothers or Hypo Real Estate were to arise tomorrow or a year from now, we would be in the same situation as we were in the fall of 2008. Taking the lesson of the days following September 2008 to heart, we should deem these institutions to be too big to fail and intervene to save the financial system, thus putting our fiscal and political systems at risk.

A fair amount of effort has gone into reforms that go under the heading of crisis prevention. Basel III requires banks to limit their leverage. Additional limits are being discussed for systemically important financial institutions. In the United States, the Dodd-Frank Act imposes constraints on the activities that banks can engage in, most notably the Volcker Rule, which prohibits certain kinds of proprietary trading by banks. In the United Kingdom, the Independent Commission on Banking is considering a structural separation of retail banking and international activities, with higher equity requirements and ring-fencing for retail.[7]

These efforts at crisis prevention should not be treated as a substitute for reform in bank resolution, let alone a sufficient substitute. First, the increases in equity capital requirements do not go very far. They look large only by comparison to the minuscule requirements that had been in place before. Moreover, the scope for manipulating these requirements through the use of the bank's own risk models to determine the applicable risk weights has hardly been reduced.[8]

Second, attempts to deal with the problem by a mixture of structural measures and behavior rules will only work if there is no too-big-to-fail problem with institutions outside the circumscribed sector, i.e., if institutions that engage in proprietary trading and speculation will not appear to be of systemic importance when push comes to shove. In this context, it is useful to recall the fate of Long Term Capital Management (LTCM). LTCM was a small hedge fund, far from any regulatory overview or any bailout regime. However, LTCM was highly leveraged, and LTCM had engaged in a complex network of contracting relations with multiple counterparties in multiple jurisdictions. When, in the summer of 1998, following the Russian default, the sharp rise in risk premia in international bond markets, saddled LTCM with substantial losses, in a situation where

---

7 Independent Commission on Banking, Interim Report: Consultation on Reform Options, London 2011, http://s3-eu-west-1.amazonaws.com/htcdn/Interim-Report-110411.pdf. See also *J. Kay* Narrow Banking, http://www.johnkay.com/2009/09/15/narrow-banking with its proposal for a strict separation between "utility banking" and the rest.

8 For an account of the role of equity insufficiency and regulation in the crisis, see *M.F. Hellwig* Systemic Risk in the Financial Sector: An Analysis of the Subprime-Mortgage Financial Crisis, De Economist 157 (2009), 129–208; for a critique of the Basel III approach, *M.F. Hellwig* Capital Regulation after the Crisis: Business as Usual?, CESifo DICE Report 8/2 (2010), 40–46.
A. Admati et al. Fallacies, Irrelevant Facts, and Myths in the Discussion of Capital Regulation: Why Bank Equity is *Not* Expensive, Stanford Graduate School of Business and Max Planck Institute for Research on Collective Goods, Bonn 2010, http://papers.ssrn.com/sol3/papers.cfm?ab stract_id=1669704, show that most of the arguments against higher capital requirements involve fallacious reasoning or a confusion of private and social costs.

markets were extremely nervous, the Federal Reserve Bank in the United States preferred to engineer a temporary rescue by LTCM's major creditors rather than to do experimental research on insolvency proceedings for such an institution.[9] In terms of the structural distinctions made in the Dodd-Frank Act or in the approach of the United Kingdom's Independent Commission on Banking, LTCM would have been clearly outside the protected domain. If LTCM was too complicated to fail, how can anybody believe that the too-big-to-fail problem will be solved by distinguishing beforehand which parts of the banking system are systemic and which are not, with a proviso that those which are not systemic will not be bailed out. Without a viable regime for bank resolution, any such approach is not credible.[10]

2. Shortcomings of Traditional Law: The German Government's Hands-Off Approach to Banks in the Crisis

Before discussing the reforms that have been undertaken and the reforms that we need, it will be useful to review the experience with existing law in the crisis. One of the absurdities of this experience involved the German government paying money to acquire the shares in Hypo Real Estate (HRE) that would have been worthless if it hadn't been for the government providing guarantees for HRE debt in October 2008, when HRE had trouble refinancing itself. Following the initial bailout by guarantees in October 2008, the government put in additional funds and acquired 50% of the equity in January 2009. Even then, it found it difficult to take control. To overcome shareholder resistance, in spring 2009, the "Lex HRE" was passed giving the government the power to impose a squeeze out. When the squeeze out occurred in the summer of 2009, outside shareholders still got EUR 1.30 per share. If HRE had gone under in October 2009, they would have got nothing. Why then did the shareholders of this bankrupt bank get anything at all?

The German government's handling of HRE in this crisis stands in marked contrast to the Swedish government's behavior in the crisis of 1992.[11] When that crisis broke out, the Swedish government almost immediately declared that it was guaranteeing all debt. At the same time, it took control of the banks, shoving aside incumbent management and owners. The Swedish government did not acquire shares. Shareholder retained the rights to their shares in any surplus that might eventually be available. The government used its power of control to put in new management, professional bankers, who would see this as an opportunity to get ahead in their careers. From the beginning, there was full transparency about losses. Government-installed management separated out the banks' good assets and used them to create *good banks* that would soon be privatized

9 Ten years later, the experimental research was instead done with Lehman Brothers.

10 As an investment bank, Lehman Brothers had in fact been outside the existing protection system, as had been Bear Stearns.

11 This account is based on *P. Englund* The Swedish Banking Crisis: Roots and Consequences, Oxford Review of Economic Policy 15 (1999), 80–97, and on a lecture by *Peter Englund* at a conference of the Austrian National Bank and the Max Planck Institute for Research on Collective Goods on Bank Resolution in Vienna in September 2010.

again; the proceeds went to the old, *bad banks.* Contrary to a myth that was circulated in Germany in the fall of 2008, the proceeds of the privatization were not sufficient to cover the losses of the *bad banks.* Losses turned out to be smaller than had been feared in 1992, but the cost of the bank rescue for the Swedish taxpayer still amounted to some 2% of GDP.

In early October 2008, the Academic Advisory Board of the German Ministry of Economics and Technology recommended that the Federal Government should follow the Swedish example, namely, it should maintain shareholder liability and take control of the banks at the same time as it was using taxpayer money to keep them from going under.[12] The Federal Government chose not to follow this advice, but proceeded to provide help in the form of guarantees and (mostly) [13] silent participations, without holding shareholders liable for the catastrophic situation their banks were in and without taking control. The government's choice of this mode of intervention is one reason why the cost of supporting banks in the crisis has been higher, in absolute and relative terms, for Germany than for other countries with comparable exposures.[14]

Perhaps more importantly, the hands-off approach chosen by the government has allowed the industry to avoid some necessary restructuring. There is thus a substantial risk of another crisis in the not so far future. After all, the ventures of German banks into risky investments abroad had a lot to do with excess capacity and intense competition in German banking, in particular in wholesale banking and real-estate finance. Without significant structural adjustment, i.e., without the exit of major players (in addition to Dresdner Bank), these mechanisms remain in place and can be counted on to work their mischief again in the future.[15]

The government's reluctance to take a hands-on approach is sometimes justified by legal concerns. Existing law did not permit the government to take control of banks in a way that would allow them to keep going in order to minimize fallout on the rest of the system.[16] Section 45 of the German Banking Act (Kreditwesengesetz, KWG) did allow the supervisor to intervene in the management of the bank, but, as of October 2008,

---

12 Wissenschaftlicher Beirat beim Bundesministerium für Wirtschaft und Technologie, Zur Finanzkrise, Brief an den Bundesminister für Wirtschaft und Technologie vom 10. Oktober 2008, http://www.bmwi.de/BMWi/Navigation/Service/publikationen,did=279016.html.

13 The exception was an acquisition of 25% of the common stock of Commerzbank at a cost of 1.8 bn. EUR. The purpose of this investment, however, was not to take control, but to protect the 16.4 bn. EUR that had also been provided in the form of a silent participation.

14 For an overview and cross-country comparisons, see Strategien für den Ausstieg des Bundes aus krisenbedingten Beteiligungen an Banken, Gutachten des von der Bundesregierung eingesetzten Expertenrats, January 2011, http://www.bundesfinanzministerium.de/nn_1776/DE/Wirtschaft__und__Verwaltung/Geld__und__Kredit/Kapitalmarktpolitik/15022011-Gutachten-Bankenbeteiligung-Anlage,templateId=raw,property=publicationFile.pdf. See also Eurostat Supplementary Table for the Financial Crisis, April 2011, http://epp.eurostat.ec.europa.eu/portal/page/portal/government_finance_statistics/documents/Background%20note_fin%20crisis_Apr%202011_final.pdf. At this point, all numbers must be taken with a grain of salt. Numbers for losses are largely based on write-offs. When the final accounts are done, some ten years from now, these write-offs may turn out to have been too large or too small.

15 For a more extensive discussion of these concerns, see Strategien für den Ausstieg des Bundes aus krisenbedingten Beteiligungen an Banken (fn. 14).

16 Sachverständigenrat zur Begutachtung der gesamtwirtschaftlichen Entwicklung (fn. 5), 147 ff.

such intervention was conditioned on the bank's violating statutory capital or liquidity requirements.[17] More importantly, according to Section 46 of the Banking Act, the objective of such an intervention must be the protection of the bank's creditors. In practice, this has been interpreted as a mandate to safeguard the bank's assets by freezing its activities, without considering the effects on the rest of the financial system. The model for this procedure is provided by insolvency law, which is also dominated by the objective of creditor protection.

As an outsider to the legal profession, I have been wondering about these legal concerns. *De lege lata*, there also should have been legal concerns about the use of taxpayer money for bailout operations. If such concerns could be overridden by pushing through a new law at record speed, it should also have been possible to legislate new rules that would permit the government to take control as it was providing the banks with taxpayer money.

I also have difficulties with the argument that the government's taking control of the banks would have violated the shareholders' constitutional rights to protection of property. Given that the control would have been the counterpart of the government's supporting the banks with taxpayer money and given that the support was offered without any obligation for the banks to take it, I do not see why this mode of intervention should have raised the specter of expropriation.[18]

Ostensibly, the legal concerns that had impeded the government in 2008 and 2009 were to be resolved by the Bank Restructuring Act of 2010. According to the government, this law should ensure that, in a future crisis, the taxpayer would not again have to go through something like the HRE experience. In the following, I will explain, however, that this new law is unsuited for its purpose. When the next crisis comes, the authorities will be just as ill-prepared as they were for this one. If the systemic concerns are sufficiently large, it will again be necessary to legislate a bailout with taxpayer money by a shotgun procedure.

In the following, I will substantiate my pessimistic assessments. In Section 3, I will consider procedural issues, in Section 4, substantive issues. On both sets of issues, I find the new German law to be unsuited for its purpose. It is indeed quite inferior to the UK Banking Act of 2009. Subsequently, Section 5 will address the international issues, which are unresolved even for the UK. Section 6 concludes with a discussion of constitutional concerns that have been raised in Germany.

---

17 An amendment that was enacted in July 2009 has introduced the possibility that the supervisor might intervene when current developments provide substantial reasons to believe that the bank will not be able to satisfy statutory capital or liquidity requirements in the future.

18 Given these considerations, I believe that the main reasons for the government's choice of a hands-off approach to dealing with banks in the crisis were actually political rather than legal. By providing support in the form of guarantees rather than capital injections, the government minimized the budgetary impact of the support; after all, guarantees do not cost anything. By not taking control, the government avoided the constitutional conflict that would have been associated with federal intervention in the Landesbanken; more importantly, the Federal Chancellor as President of the Christian Democratic Union avoided a conflict with the Ministerpräsidenten, leading politicians of her own party whose support would be essential for the 2009 federal election.

3. How to Deal with Banks in Difficulties: Procedural Issues

A key question is who decides what and when. In the context of bank resolution this question is particularly important because in a crisis situation speed may be essential. It is also particularly vexing because one can hardly legislate in advance what matters are to be decided and what criteria should be used to decide them.

The following issues arise:

- When to subject the bank to a resolution regime? In principle, this should be done at a time when dangers are recognized. Recognition of dangers, however, may be a matter of judgment. Attempts to constrain such judgment by formal criteria, e.g., with respect to the bank's equity capital or its liquidity position, bear a risk of undue delay which can greatly magnify the dangers.

- How to decide which parts of the bank's operations can be maintained and which parts should be closed down, shortly or over a longer time span? At the time when dangers are recognized and the bank is subjected to a resolution regime, it is usually not clear what will be the best way to proceed.

- What will be the best mode for disposing of the bank's assets? To some extent, this is a matter of which operations of the bank should be maintained and which operations should be closed down. To some extent, the question is whether the resolution authority should manage certain assets itself or whether it should sell them to a third party. For assets such as bad or dubious loans, this question involves difficult tradeoffs.

3.1 The UK Banking Act of 2009

In the United Kingdom, the Banking Act of 2009 addresses these issues on the basis of two principles:[19]

- The authorities must have great flexibility.

- There must be a clear assignment of responsibility.

Thus, the Financial Services Authority (FSA) is given authority to subject a bank to the special resolution regime created by the law if it is satisfied that the following conditions are met:

- The bank is not satisfying, or likely not to satisfy, regulatory requirements.

- It is not reasonably likely that corrective action will be taken that will enable the bank to satisfy regulatory requirements in due course.

If the bank satisfies regulatory conditions only because of assistance from the Bank of England or the Treasury, these conditions for intervention are also deemed to be met.

---

19 For a summary account of this law, see *P. Brierley* The UK Special Resolution Regime for Failing Banks in an International Context, Bank of England, Financial Stability Paper No. 5, July 2009, http://www.bankofengland.co.uk/publications/fsr/fs_paper05.pdf.

On the second condition, the FSA must consult with the Bank of England and the Treasury, but, otherwise, it is autonomous in its decision.

Following the invocation of the special resolution regime by the FSA, the law provides five alternatives:

- Sale of all or part of the bank's business to a third party
- Transfer of all or part of the bank's business to a bridge bank that is wholly owned by the Bank of England
- Temporary public ownership
- Bank insolvency procedure
- Bank administration procedure

If no public funds are used to support the bank, the Bank of England acts as a resolution authority. If public funds are used, the Treasury can decide whether to take the bank under temporary public ownership or to leave the bank with the Bank of England as the resolution authority. As a resolution authority, the Bank of England is free to sell all or part of the bank's business to a third party or to transfer all or part of the bank's business to a bridge bank. If it sells some of the bank's business to a third party, it can also ask the court to install an administrator with the task of keeping the rest of the bank going in order to supply services that are needed to operate the business that has been sold (bank administration procedure). In all these decisions, the law mandates consultation between the three institutions, FSA, Bank of England, Treasury, but the assignment of responsibility is always clear. Moreover, subject to the general objectives of the law, there is a great deal of flexibility as to what decision to take. As time goes on, decisions can also be changed and adapted to new circumstances and new information.

This is particularly true of the Bank of England in its role as a resolution authority. Not only does the Bank of England have great discretion in its choice between the different alternatives listed above. It also has great discretion over the assets and operations that it assigns to a private purchaser or to a bridge bank. Such discretion is limited only by restrictions protecting certain contracts and markets, e.g., collateral conditions or conditions on netting in derivatives markets. The Bank of England can also interfere with the bank's management, asking directors to step down and restricting shareholders' control rights.

So far, the UK Banking Act of 2009 has been used once. In the case of Bradford & Bingley, the procedures worked smoothly. One cannot tell whether they would also work smoothly in the case of a larger bank, but already the difference between the handling of Bradford & Bingley and the handling of Northern Rock, in the late summer of 2008, is notable: In the case of Northern Rock, government intervention was delayed, partly, because there was no legal basis for interfering with the bank's management prior to insolvency.[20]

20 See *Brierley* (fn. 19). The difference between Bradford & Bingley and Northern Rock was highlighted by *Peter Brierley* at the September 2010 Conference on Bank Resolution in Vienna (fn. 11).

At this point, the UK special resolution regime for banks provides a benchmark for procedural precision and clarity. In many respects, it mimics the US regime for depository institutions in the domain of the Federal Deposit Insurance Corporation (FDIC). At least relative to the post-Dodd-Frank FDIC, however, it has the advantage that it is also clear about the procedures that are to be followed if public funds are needed to support a bank in difficulties.

3.2 Bank Restructuring and Bank Reorganization under the German Bank Reorganization Act of 2010

By contrast, the German Bank Restructuring Act of 2010 does not provide a clear and workable set of procedures for dealing with banks in difficulties. On these grounds it falls far short of bank resolution regimes in both the United Kingdom and the United States. Of the two major parts of the law, the first part is procedurally clear, but practically irrelevant. The second part is procedurally unclear and therefore likely to be unworkable.

The first part, Article 1 of the Bank Restructuring Act, the so-called Bank Reorganization Act, introduces two new procedures for dealing with a bank in difficulties, a restructuring procedure and a reorganization procedure. Both procedures are intended to make room for measures to improve the bank's viability before the bank is in violation of statutory capital or liquidity requirements let alone a condition that would call for the initiation of insolvency proceedings. However, both procedures rely on the bank's management to take the initiative. Management incentives to do so are minimal. The well known problem that managers of companies in difficulties have strong incentives to delay insolvency proceedings will arise in this context as well as in the context of standard insolvency law.

Under the restructuring procedure, management indicates to the supervisory authority that the bank needs restructuring. At the same time, it submits a restructuring plan and nominates a potential restructuring agent. The supervisory authority considers the application and passes it on to the court with its own comments and recommendations. It may propose another person as restructuring agent if it considers the person proposed by the bank to be unsuitable. The court then appoints a restructuring agent and orders the restructuring plan to be carried out. The restructuring agent has wide powers to interfere with the bank's management. Going further, the supervisory authority can propose and the court can impose even stronger measures, including the temporary dismissal of incumbent management and appointment of the restructuring agent as a member of the bank's executive board.

By initiating the restructuring procedure the bank's management submits itself to significant interference by the court-appointed restructuring agent, the supervisory authority and the court. Why should it do so? The *only* advantage that the restructuring procedure provides to the bank's owners and managers comes from a provision that, under a restructuring plan, new loans can be accorded priority over incoming in subsequent insolvency proceedings – up to a maximum of ten percent of the bank's equity. I cannot imagine a bank management considering that this advantage outweighs the risks for themselves in submitting to the powers of the court-appointed restructuring agent, the supervisory authority and the court itself in a restructuring procedure. They might choose to do so in order to preempt an even stronger intervention by the supervisory authority under the Banking Act. But then the restructuring procedure is more a tool for bureaucratic plea bargaining at a late stage than a tool for implementing corrective measures at an early stage.

The reorganization procedure is hardly better. From the bank's perspective, it has the advantage that the reorganization plan can lead to haircuts for creditors or to debt-for-equity swaps, thus reducing the bank's overall indebtedness. This procedure resembles an insolvency proceeding, *except* that it is not conditioned on the bank's being unable to fulfill its current payment obligations or on the bank's being insolvent in the sense of having liabilities exceeding its assets. Indeed, procedural rules are very much like procedural rules under insolvency law, with detailed provisions as to what votes of the different classes of creditors are needed to approve the reorganization plan and under what conditions such votes can be overridden; to take account of the fact that, when the bank is still solvent, shareholders still have a say, there also is a rule on voting by shareholders on the scope for overriding their vote.

The above arguments as to why management is unlikely to initiate the restructuring procedure apply also to the reorganization procedure. From the practice of insolvency law, we know that the ability to reduce overall indebtedness through such proceedings is not sufficient to overcome the natural tendency of management to delay the initiation of any procedure that might threaten their incumbency. Given the similarity of the reorganization procedure to insolvency proceedings, I see no reason why this experience should not also be relevant for the reorganization procedure for banks.

These considerations suggest that the Bank Reorganization Act is likely to be irrelevant in practice. This may even be a good thing. If the experience with decision making processes under insolvency law is any guide, these voting procedures are likely to be difficult and lengthy. In the meantime, the bank's refinancing is likely to have evaporated. To be sure, deposits are to some extent guaranteed, but wholesale money market refinancing is not. The experience of Bear Stearns and Lehman Brothers has shown that even repo refinancing may suddenly dry up when lenders believe that they are severely at risk even though, legally, they are actually the owners of the collateral. Given the importance of wholesale short-term refinancing for certain large banks, the sudden evaporation of this refinancing can destroy the viability of the bank from one day to the next, with disastrous implications for the rest of the system. Luckily, anticipation of this risk may be yet another reason for why a bank's management will not be likely to willingly initiate the reorganization (or even the restructuring) procedure.

The authors of this law must be congratulated on the legal precision with which they have transferred key procedural elements from insolvency law to bank reorganization law. However, they either did not see or did not care that these procedures are fully unsuited to dealing with banks in difficulties.

3.3 Supervisory Intervention under the German Bank Restructuring Act of 2010

The German Bank Restructuring Act of 2010 also provides for changes in the rules for supervisory intervention according to the Banking Act. The following changes are noteworthy:

- Whereas the 2009 amendment to Section 45 of the Banking Act introduced the possibility of supervisory intervention even when capital or liquidity requirements are not yet violated and there is only a danger of such violations in the future, a further amendment now specifies certain adverse developments in the bank's capital and liquidity positions that would warrant the presumption of such a prospect. When it intervenes, the supervisory authority can ask the bank to present a three-year business plan and to explain possible measures to reduce its risks, to improve its equity and liquidity position, and to avert the danger of insolvency. If the bank is actually in violation of capital or liquidity requirements or if the measures proposed and taken by the bank's management itself seem insufficient to avert the prospect of such a violation, the supervisory authority can prohibit payments to owners and payments of variable parts of remuneration to managers; it can also ask the bank to restrict lending, and to present a restructuring plan. These interventions, however, presuppose that the supervisor has given the bank a certain delay for improvements and that this delay has not been used satisfactorily.
- Under a new Section 45c of the Banking Act, the supervisory authority can install a restructuring agent in order to perform certain specified tasks in the bank. This restructuring agent is entitled to participate in all meetings and to obtain any information he requests. As examples of tasks to be assigned the law mentions management tasks replacing the bank's own directors if there are grounds for mistrusting them or if there are no longer sufficiently many of them, imposition of measures to curb risks if the bank has substantially violated prevailing regulations, supervision of management execution of mandates from the supervisor, design of a restructuring plan and implementation of measures to avert dangers when the bank's management has not done so to the supervisor's satisfaction.
- The new Sections 48a–48s of the Banking Act create the possibility that the supervisory authority can order the transfer of all or part of the assets and liabilities of the bank to a third party, typically a bridge bank. According to Section 48a (2), this can be done *only* if the bank's existence is in danger and this danger poses a threat for the stability of the financial system, which cannot be averted by any other means. According to Section 48b (1), the bank's existence is in danger if insolvency is imminent; the law specifies values of capital and liquidity indicators that would justify such a presumption. According to Section 48b (2), the danger to the bank's existence poses a threat to the system there could be serious negative effects on other financial institutions, financial markets, or general confidence of market participants in the system. Here, too, the law names different indicators that are to be considered. The assessment whether the bank's existence is in danger and whether this poses a threat to the system is in the hands of the financial supervisor, following a consultation with the Deutsche Bundesbank.

- Article 3 of the Bank Restructuring Act, the so-called Restructuring Fund Act, creates a new fund, financed by a levy on the banking industry, which is to provide support in cases where a bank's problems pose a threat to the stability of the financial system. Thus, the bridge bank to which the bank's assets and liabilities are to be transferred under Section 48a of the Banking Act might itself be a subsidiary of this fund, more precisely, the agency running it. Alternatively, if the bridge bank is a private institution, the restructuring fund might guarantee that institution's obligations or it might contribute to recapitalizing that institution. Whenever the transfer under Section 48a of the Banking Act involves a recourse to the resources of the restructuring fund, the transfer order must first be approved by that institution's governing body.

These changes go in the right direction. However, they do not go far enough. The following shortcomings should be noted:

- Procedures for intervention prior to insolvency are unwieldy. The addition to Section 45 of the Banking Act giving examples of conditions creating a presumption that such an intervention is justified are not very helpful. These examples refer to adverse developments in quarterly reports about capital and liquidity positions. In a crisis, however, events are likely to move much faster. HRE provides an example.
- The procedure is also unwieldy in that the authority has to give the bank time to correct matters. This involves further delays. If, during the delay, information about the supervisor's prospective intervention were to leak out, an immediate breakdown of market refinancing would have to be expected. The legislator has failed to take account of the possibility that procedural delays that are normal for German administrative law might not be suited to dealing with institutions in fast-moving markets.
- The division of responsibilities between the bank's management, the restructuring agent, and the supervisory authority is unclear. Whereas under UK law, the FSA's triggering the intervention implies that the Bank of England takes control of the bank, the German Banking Act fails to distinguish clearly between a situation where the bank is still in the hands of its management, under orders from the supervisor, without a restructuring agent, a situation where the bank is in the hands of its management, with a restructuring agent ensuring that management follows the supervisor's orders, a situation where the restructuring agent is part of the bank's management, and a situation where the restructuring agent is fully in charge. It would have been preferable to have a clearcut definition of the event when the supervisor and its restructuring agent take over.
- The conditions under which the supervisor can order the restructuring agent to take over some or all responsibility are somewhat "iffy": They involve a judgment, substantiated by material facts, that incumbent management is untrustworthy. It is not clear how this condition relates to the notion that, regardless of how one judges the character of incumbent managers, protection of the financial system may require a change of strategy, which is best implemented by a change of personnel, with new people, who do not have a stake in whatever caused the bank's difficulties in the first place.
- In the case of a transfer of assets and liabilities under the new Section 48a , the division of responsibilities between the supervisory authority, the third party that ac-

quires all or part of the bank's assets and liabilities, and the Restructuring Fund Authority is also unclear. No distinction is made between the case where the third party is an independent private institution, the case where the third party is a private institution that relies on support from the Restructuring Fund, and the case where the third party is a wholly owned subsidiary of the Restructuring Fund. When only a part of the bank's assets and liabilities is transferred to a third party, responsibilities for the parts that are transferred and for the parts that are not transferred are split between the acquirer and the combination of incumbent management, restructuring agent and supervisor that is in charge of the original bank. Section 48k of the law stipulates that in this case, the original bank must provide the acquirer with whatever services it may need "at an appropriate price" but is unclear about the governance of the relation.

- Transfers of assets and liabilities to a third party under the new Section 48a appear as one-time, piecemeal measures, without any account of their relation to the rest of the intervention. The law does not even distinguish between transfers of "toxic" assets to a "bad bank", which is presumably to be wound down, leaving the original bank in a better position, and transfers of assets and liabilities to a "good bank", leaving the original bank to be wound down, with shares in the "good bank" as part of the bank's assets. According to the new Section 48d of the Banking Act, the counterpart to the transfer is to be provided in terms of shares of the acquirer if the net value of the transfer is assessed to be positive and in terms of a payment obligation of the original bank if the net value of the transfer is assessed to be negative.[21] Presumably, a transfer of assets and liabilities under Section 48a must be based on some prior acquisition of information about the bank's position, prospects and risks and some notion of what the transfer implies for the future, especially if it results in a splitting off of part of the bank's operation. Such information might be acquired by the restructuring agent that the supervisory authority could have sent into the bank under Section 45 c; but then the procedural issues surrounding the authority's intervention under Sections 45 and 45c have repercussions for the application of Section 48a.

Underlying these shortcomings, there is a deeper conceptual problem. The UK Banking Act of 2009 is founded on the assessment that, under certain circumstances, the public interest requires control of the bank to be taken over by a government institution even though the bank is not insolvent and even though it is not even in violation of any regulation. In contrast, the German Bank Restructuring Act is based on the presumption that, as long as the supervisor has not closed it down, "the bank" maintains its own corporate autonomy. Given this presumption, the German law avoids the UK approach of saying that, under certain conditions, the authorities simply take control. Instead, it names conditions under which the supervisor can impose certain obligations on the bank, under which the supervisor can have a restructuring agent supervising the bank, sharing in the bank's management, taking over the bank's management altogether. This procedure seems like an attempt to have one's cake and eat it too, namely to maintain the fiction that corporate autonomy is only eliminated when the bank is insolvent and at the same time find ways of intervening prior to insolvency so as to reduce sys-

21 The question of what the prospect of such a payment obligation does to the solvency of the original bank is not addressed, however.

temic fallout from the bank's difficulties. However, the resulting lack of clarity in the assignment of responsibilities will give rise to significant legal uncertainty. When push comes to shove, in a crisis that involves a systemically important bank, I would expect the authorities to handle this legal uncertainty by first delaying intervention – contrary to the professed objective of the lawgiver – and then, if some intervention is needed after all, to improvise new rules as they did in the fall of 2008.

4. How to Deal with Banks in Difficulties: Substantive Issues

4.1 Objectives of the Intervention: System Protection versus Creditor Protection

The difference in conceptual approaches in the United Kingdom and Germany is also apparent in the objectives of public interventions that are given in their respective laws. The UK Banking Act of 2009 introduces the special resolution regime for banks as a means of pursuing the following objectives:

- To protect and enhance the stability of the financial systems of the

United Kingdom.

- To protect and enhance public confidence in the stability of the

banking systems of the United Kingdom.

- To protect depositors.
- To protect public funds.
- To avoid interfering with property rights in contravention of a

Convention right (within the meaning of the Human Rights Act 1998).

Whereas the Banking Act itself does not provide any further details, the Treasury has provided a Code of Practice,[22] which does, explaining, e.g., the term "stability of the financial systems of the UK" with reference to "the stable functioning of the systems and institutions (including trading, payment and settlement infrastructure) supporting the efficient operation of financial services and markets for purposes including capital-raising, risk-transfer, and the facilitation of domestic and international commerce in addition to day-to-day banking operations." According to the Code of Practice, the different objectives are not ranked, but "are to be balanced as appropriate in each case." Even so, the prominence of concerns about the stability of financial systems and about public confidence in the stability of the banking systems is noteworthy.

In contrast, the German law is again based on the assumption that you can have your cake and eat it too, namely that you introduce systemic concerns without deducting

22 HM Treasury, Banking Act 2009 – Special Resolution Regime: Code of Practice, http://www.hm-treasury.gov.uk/d/bankingact2009_code_of_practice.pdf.

anything from the traditional creditor protection objective of insolvency law. The key formulation in Section 46 of the German Banking Act has not been changed. This section names creditor protection as *the* objective of supervisory intervention under Section 45. As mentioned above, in the past, this has been interpreted as implying that supervisory intervention under Section 45 must to some extent replicate intervention under insolvency law, freezing the bank's activities in order to safeguard its assets, without considering the fallout on the rest of the financial system. *Systemic* concerns enter only in the new Section 48 a of the Banking Act, which introduces the possibility of transferring assets and liabilities of the bank to a third party. As stated in this section, such transfers are admissible *only* if they are needed to avert an insolvency which in turn might threaten the entire financial system and *only* if there is no other way to avert the danger to the financial system.

I read this formulation as saying that, although Section 46 only refers to creditor protection, yet, system protection is also an objective of supervisory intervention. However, the law gives no account of the relation of this objective to the objective of creditor protection. On the one hand, Section 46 of the Banking Act names creditor protection as the only goal of supervisory intervention. On the other hand, Section 48 a of the Act allows for system protection to take precedence under certain circumstances. I read the "only" in Section 48 a as saying that the circumstances are taken to be exceptional and that, in a legal dispute, the burden of proof for showing that they are satisfied would lie with the supervisory authority.

Given the legal uncertainty that is thereby created, I would expect the authority to be very cautious in applying Section 48 a. Such caution of the supervisory authority is welcome in normal times but involves a risk of undue delay in a time of crisis. Therefore I am not convinced that the changes to the Banking Act that have occurred will in fact liberate us from the straightjacket of the analogy to insolvency law that has in the past been deduced from the creditor protection objective of Section 46 of the Banking Act.

4.2 What Precisely is Meant by "System Protection"?

A comparison of UK and German law also reveals a difference in the substantive content of the objectives, in particular, the notion of what is meant by "system" protection. The Treasury's Code of Practice for the UK Banking Act of 2009 specifies this objective in terms of the functioning of the different elements of the system. The new Section 48 b of the German Bank Law instead relates systemic concerns to the threat of significant negative effects on other financial institutions, financial markets, or the general confidence of market participants.

One way to think about "system protection" concerns the functioning of the different mechanisms that make the financial system work, payment and settlement systems, collateralization, the organization of markets. When Lehman Brothers was declared insolvent, they were no longer available as a market maker in certain repo markets; as a result those markets broke down. When, following the Lehman insolvency, confidence between banks evaporated, international payment systems on the basis of letters of credit were severely impaired. In earlier times, in the banking crises of 1931 and 1933, bank "holidays" caused breakdowns of national payment systems. The Treasury's Code of Practice for the UK Banking Act of 2009 seems to embrace this notion of "system" protection.

Another way to think about "system protection" concerns the avoidance of domino effects of one institution's problems on other institutions. This notion of "system protection" focuses on counterparties rather than the functioning of the different mechanisms that make up the financial system. Section 48b of the German Banking Act seems to embrace this second notion of "system protection". Even the reference to "negative effects on … financial markets" seems to express a concern about market prices rather than the functioning of these markets.

The distinction between the two notions of "system protection" is not a purely academic one. To be sure, in certain circumstances, protection of the functioning of the different mechanisms that make up the financial system may require the protection of certain counterparties. In the United Kingdom, therefore, the Bank of England in its role of a resolution authority may decide that the purpose of the law is best served by bailing out the problem institution's creditors. However, such concern about domino effects is not written into the legal norm as such. Whether systemic concerns mandate a creditor bail-out is for the resolution authority to decide.

In contrast, the German law mentions domino effects on counterparties directly as a systemic concern, without distinguishing between domino effects that severely damage the functioning of the system and domino effects that hurt the immediate counterparties but otherwise do not have much of an effect. In this context, it is useful to take another look at the German government's interventions in the fall of 2008. These interventions have effectively bailed out *all* creditors of the banks in question, including the holders of hybrid securities, i.e., debt securities that are treated as non-common-stock equity (Tier 1 and Tier 2) for regulatory purposes.

Hypo Real Estate was a case in point. According to Mr. Rehm, the Chairman of Soffin, government protection of Hypo Real Estate was needed in order to protect the holders of covered bonds ("Pfandbriefe") and thereby the instrument of the covered bond itself and to protect holders of unsecured loans amounting to some 100 bn. EUR; as Mr. Rehm put it, these holders included social insurance systems, pension funds, and churches.[23] In the years prior to the crisis, low rates of return on long-term securities had induced many private and institutional investors to accept risk from unsecured and subordinated debt in order to obtain a return that would be somewhat closer to the rates of return that they had been used to in the past. The Rehm interview suggests that protection of these investors was a major concern of the government. In Mr. Rehm's words, "Systemic risk" was a matter of social policy as well as finance.

The formulation of the new German law suggests that such indiscriminate bail-outs of creditors will be on the agenda in the future as well as the fall of 2008. Such a prospect of indiscriminate counterparty protection will enhance rather than reduce moral hazard

23 Frankfurter Allgemeine Zeitung, March 15, 2009. Other media reports named the Bundesbank, Allianz, several municipalities, and the public radio and television institutions as investors in HRE securities.

in the financial system. Why should the large insurance company Allianz pay much attention to the default risks of a bank if they can count on the restructuring fund to bail the bank out if the bank's going under threatens Allianz?

The Basel Committee on Banking Supervision has strongly criticized that, in the crisis, government support was provided without imposing appropriate liability on the holders of instruments that were there to absorb losses, in particular instruments that were treated as capital for regulatory purposes.[24] According to the Basel Committee, the insulation of such instruments from the consequences of the crisis undermines the functioning of the system as it reduces or eliminates incentives for acquirers of such instruments to pressure the bank into reducing risks. The Basel Committee is therefore proposing to introduce a mechanism whereby the holders of non-common-stock Tier 1 and of Tier 2 securities will automatically be subjected to a haircut or a debt-equity swap if the bank has recourse to public support. The German law's indiscriminate reference to domino effects on counterparties is incompatible with such an approach.

The same concerns hold for the German law's reference to negative effects of a bank's failure on financial markets. The law does not discriminate between negative effects on prices in these markets and negative effects on the functioning of these markets. The two are not necessarily the same. A price decline, even a severe price decline, may be called for as the bank's failure provides new information – not just about the bank, but possibly also about the prospects and the viability of the activities that the bank has been involved in. Such a reaction is painful to investors holding those assets but may be fully appropriate as a way of processing the new information. A malfunctioning of markets involves more than just a price decline. Market malfunctioning involves markets becoming very illiquid or even disappearing altogether because in situations of great uncertainty or information asymmetry, counterparties are afraid of being taken advantage of and behave very defensively. Here again, I find the UK interpretation of "system protection" more appropriate because it makes the proper distinction. Under the UK interpretation of the term, a price fall in an otherwise well functioning market would not be a systemic concern; under the German definition, it must at least be considered. I am worried that this may lead to the use of public funds to support banks in order to prevent price declines that are no more than a necessary adjustment to new information.

4.3 Depositor Protection

The UK Banking Act of 2009 names protection of depositors as an objective of government intervention, the German Banking Act does not. Both laws make reference to depositor protection systems and their role in bank resolution. However, beyond that, the German law gives no special status to depositors. I consider this to be problematic.

In the United States, depositor protection was introduced after the Great Depression. In the event of a bank failure, the Federal Deposit Insurance Corporation (FDIC) takes over

24 Basel Committee on Banking Supervision, Proposal to ensure the loss absorbency of regulatory capital at the point of non-viability – Consultative Document, Basel 2010, http://www.bis.org/publ/bcbs174.pdf.

the bank and sees to it that depositors are reimbursed with a minimal delay. From a normative perspective, depositor protection is justified by the notion that deposits form the basis of the payment system, which is an essential part of the economy's infrastructure. Moreover, because the multitude of small depositors are not in a position to do any serious monitoring of what their bank is doing, the moral hazard effects of protection on investors are relatively smaller for depositors than, say for institutional investors buying bank bonds.[25]

Perhaps more importantly, from a political economy perspective, when a bank is in difficulties, calls for a government bail-out are likely to be irresistible when they involve the mass of depositors. The FDIC regime in the US provides a proper procedure for such protection without regard for other creditors. The UK Banking Act's privileged mention of depositor protection as an objective of the special resolution regime also provides a basis for separating depositor protection from the protection of other creditors. In contrast, under German law, depositors have the same standing as any other unsecured creditors. There is therefore a risk that any intervention in favor of depositors will have to be extended to all other unsecured creditors. This can be very expensive and, as explained in the preceding subsection, is likely to be a source of significant moral hazard.

In this context, it is important to appreciate that, unlike the United States and the United Kingdom, Germany does not have a regime of government guarantees for deposits. Depositor protection is handled as a matter of self-regulation, where each of the three parts of the banking system (private banks, public banks, co-operative banks) have their institutions providing guarantees for deposits. These guarantees are just as good as the guarantors. More seriously, in a crisis, these guarantees themselves can be source of systemic risks. If HRE and Commerzbank had not been bailed out by the government, the private-bankers' association's guarantee fund would have been in line to fulfill its guarantees. This would have imposed a large burden on Deutsche Bank as the largest contributor to the fund. The government's intervention in favor of HRE and Commerzbank thus was also a way of forestalling the systemic risk that was implicit in the self-regulation approach to deposit insurance.

This source of systemic risk has not been eliminated. There is thus a prospect that, in a future crisis, public support will be needed to forestall this systemic risk. Because depositor protection as such is not adequately handled, intervention that is needed to protect depositors will then again provide for an indiscriminate protection of all unsecured creditors of banks.

4.4 The Role of Government Funding

In the preceding discussion, I have used the term "public support" without going into details about the institutional framework and, in particular, the sources of the support. On this matter, the UK Banking Act of 2009 simply refers to "public funds" and calls for

---

25 However, accounts of the US Savings and Loans crisis of the eighties put a lot of weight on deposit insurance having enabled savings institutions to attract additional deposits and use the additional funds to "gamble for resurrection", on the principle: "Heads – we win and survive, tails – the FDIC loses".

Treasury involvement whenever public funds are to be used; temporary public ownership is named as the stabilization option to be used in this event. In contrast, the German Bank Restructuring Act of 2010 is based on the principle that never again shall taxpayer money be used to bail out banks. The industry itself must pay for its rescue if the need arises. For this purpose, the law creates a restructuring fund. This fund is financed by a levy on the different institutions in the industry. In normal times, an annual fee is imposed to build the fund up. If the fund intervenes, e.g., to support a bridge bank receiving a transfer of assets and liabilities from a bank in difficulties under the new Section 48a of the Banking Act, and if the available funds are insufficient, it can either impose an extra levy on the industry right then, or it can borrow up to 20 bn. EUR against the credit of the Federal Government and then use an additional levy on the industry to service this debt over time.

The German approach here is similar in spirit to the US approach under the Dodd-Frank Act. Under the Dodd-Frank Act, the FDIC providing an Orderly Liquidation Authority for large complex financial institutions covers its financing needs by drawing on the so-called Orderly Liquidation Fund, which is housed with the US Treasury. For this purpose, the FDIC will issue debt securities to the Treasury. To service these securities, it will rely on clawbacks from creditors who receive higher payouts under FDIC proceedings and, if necessary, on an *ex post* levy on participating institutions. Thus, as in Germany, temporary peaks in funding needs are covered by borrowing from the US Treasury but, ultimately, the norm is that the industry itself should pay for the costs of FDIC interventions, including of course the costs of depositor protection.[26]

The approach that Germany and the United States are taking rests on an illusion and is not credible. In a severe crisis, the Restructuring Fund or the FDIC will not have enough funds at their disposal. If the crisis poses a threat that financial systems may implode as in the wake of the Lehman insolvency, governments will see the need to step in anyway. Moreover, they will do so regardless of whether there is a prospect that the industry will reimburse the taxpayer.

To understand this assessment, consider the relevant numbers for the German Restructuring Fund. Aggregate annual contributions will be in the single-digit billion euro bracket. Thus it will take some time to reach a sizeable level. The target level for the fund is about 70 bn. EUR. With the resources at its disposal, at this point, the Restructuring Fund is empowered to provide guarantees for up to 100 bn. EUR and recapitalization contributions of up to 20 bn. EUR. These numbers fall far short of the more than 170 bn. EUR in guarantees and more than 30 bn. EUR in recapitalization contributions that SoFFin, the Restructuring Fund's predecessor has provided in the recent crisis.[27]

---

26 For a critique of the US approach, see *Acharya, Adler, Richardson, Roubini* Resolution Authority (fn. 6).

27 According to the chief administrator of both funds, both positions together reached a peak 204 bn. EUR in mid 2010; see *H. Rehm* Vom Sanieren zum Restrukturieren, Frankfurter Allgemeine Zeitung, May 13, 2011. In this article, *Rehm* also writes that the stock of outstanding contributions to recapitalizations will go down to 18 bn. EUR if Commerzbank repays 14.3 bn. EUR of the Federal Government's silent participation, as announced. See also Strategien für den Ausstieg des Bundes aus krisenbedingten Beteiligungen an Banken (fn. 14).

Nor can we be sanguine about the prospect of making up the shortfall by a special levy on the industry. In a crisis situation when all banks are in difficulties, a special levy on the industry to cover the shortfall is likely to push some banks over the brink that otherwise might cope on their own. Allowing the industry to defer the payments by having the Restructuring Fund borrow and asking the industry to provide for the debt service does not avoid this problem. The obligation to provide for this debt service imposes a burden on the banks. This burden may threaten their solvency. The threat is hidden if they are not obliged to put the present value of the special levy on their books, but it is nonetheless there, a legal obligation to provide a certain payment stream over the course of the next few years. For an institution that is barely coping on its own, the imposition of such a burden may ring in the end as its financiers develop doubts about the institution's future.

In this context, it is also of interest to reflect on the fact that the assets that West LB and HRE have put into "bad banks" administered by SoFFin amount to some 250 bn. EUR or on the fact that, even after the shrinkage that has occurred, the liabilities of West LB are still close to 200 bn. EUR and those of HRE well above 300 bn. EUR. The order of magnitude of these numbers raises questions about the viability of a bridge bank that the Restructuring Fund might create as a vehicle to receive assets and liabilities from a problem bank in application of Section 48a of the Banking Act. If a bank with assets and liabilities of hundreds of billions of euros has problems and, in application of Section 48a of the Banking Act, the supervisory authority orders the transfer of the bank's assets and liabilities to a bridge bank, the question arises how this bridge bank is going to be financed. Legal and factual limits on the Restructuring Fund being what they are, the Restructuring Fund is unable to provide a full guarantee for the bridge bank. But then, the debt holders, first of the problem bank and then of the bridge bank, must have doubts about the safety of the claims that they have. Such doubts may induce them to withdraw funding as soon as they can, especially, since the transfer itself provides them with a signal, if any is needed, that there are problems. Given the importance of short-term funding in bank finance, such withdrawals may very quickly destroy the viability of the bridge bank, as they would destroy the viability of the original bank.[28]

To avert this danger, the Restructuring Fund would have to provide guarantees to the creditors of the bridge bank. To provide such guarantees on a sufficiently large scale, however, the law would have to be changed.

Politically, the principle that the industry will pay for itself and that taxpayers will never again have to bail out banks is very popular. To base the legislation on this principle, however, involves an element of deception, perhaps of self-deception. When push comes to shove, in a crisis, the law will be changed again in order to make room for the intervention that is considered necessary. Given that this can be foreseen, it would be

28 This risk puts into question the recommendation of the Committee to Design Exit Strategies for the Federal Government's Participations in Banks in the Crisis that the government should examine the possibility of "exiting" from HRE by slowly winding the bank down (and the analogous recommendation for West LB, where, however, the Federal Government is not the sole owner); see: Strategien für den Ausstieg des Bundes aus krisenbedingten Beteiligungen an Banken (fn. 14). The problem, however, is not so much with the recommendation as with the Bank Restructuring Act of 2010.

more honest to make room for this eventuality right away – and to have proper procedures for it as of now. Of the three countries that have even addressed the issue, only the UK meets this standard.

5. The International Dimension of Bank Resolution

Even the United Kingdom, however, would not wish to submit Barclays to the special resolution regime for banks. For a bank whose business is mainly domestic, the special resolution regime would seem to offer the most workable arrangement that one can imagine. For an internationally active bank, however, even this regime is likely not to be workable. Indeed, some of the very mechanisms that turned the Lehman insolvency into a nightmare would still be operative today.

As yet, literally nothing has been done to improve the handling of cross-border issues in bank resolution. The following issues are relevant.

- Under the home country principle, national law applies to banks with headquarters in the country and to the foreign branches of these banks. It does not apply to foreign subsidiaries of these banks; as formally independent legal entities, these subsidiaries are subject to the law of the country in which they are incorporated. Resolution and/or insolvency proceedings will therefore be split between the authorities of the different countries in which the bank and its subsidiaries are located. In these proceedings, therefore, unified group management is eliminated. Complementarities between the different units are likely to be destroyed.

- Different countries apply different legal principles. Apart from the United States, the United Kingdom, and Germany, most countries deal with banks in difficulties under general insolvency law, without consideration of systemic concerns. In terms of procedure as well as substance, national insolvency law differs from country to country. Even the three countries with special provisions for banks that allow for systemic concerns have very different procedural and substantive rules. The differences in legal rules exacerbate the frictions from having different resolution regimes for a bank and its foreign subsidiaries.

- The problem of fragmentation of intervention is exacerbated when a bank has several home countries, as was the case with Fortis. In the case of Fortis, the lack of a prior agreement between Belgium and the Netherlands on how to share the burden of intervening to save the bank was a major cause of frictions, inducing delay and, ultimately, causing the bank to be broken up along national boundaries.

- Some countries, most importantly the United States, do not recognize the home country principle but apply a territoriality principle. Thus the authorities in the United States might decide to intervene by ring-fencing the assets of the US branch of a foreign bank in order to pay off the depositors of that branch. Such interference with a branch of a foreign bank would contribute to destroying the bank as a business unit and would further complicate the task of the home country's resolution authority.

- The home country principle itself is problematic if the bank's home country authorities discriminate against depositors at foreign branches of the bank. The treatment of the depositors of branches of Icelandic banks in the United Kingdom and the Netherlands provides an example. Ostensibly, this problem would not arise if Iceland was part of the European Union. One may suppose, however, that, even within the European Union, through implicit rather than explicit modes of discrimination, a bank's home country authorities might find ways to provide less protection to the bank's depositors at branches in other member states than to its depositors at home. One may also suppose that a bank's home country authorities will be less concerned about systemic fallout in other countries, e.g., the fallout from having depositors at branches in other countries lose the ability to receive and make payments without any ado.
- Within the European Economic Area, application of the territoriality principle would seem to be excluded by the Credit Institutions Reorganization and Winding-Up Directive of 2001.[29] However, as formulated, the Directive concerns proceedings that are intended to provide for the reorganization and continued existence or for the winding-up of the bank, both standard procedures under insolvency law. Whether its impact extends to an intervention under the new UK and German laws is an open question. After all, these interventions are intended to take place well ahead of a possible insolvency; moreover, the transfer of the bank's assets and liabilities to a bridge bank under UK or German rules cannot automatically be subsumed under either one of the interventions named in the Directive, reorganization or winding-up.[30]
- Many financial contracts, in particular derivative contracts, contain covenants that are triggered by certain events such as a change of control or a default on some other contractual obligation. If public intervention under UK or German law was deemed to provide a trigger for change-of-control clauses, cross-default clauses, closeout netting and the like, the objective of continued maintenance of the bank's operations for the purpose of system protection would be voided from the start. To prevent this from happening, these countries' laws stipulate that such intervention should not trigger these covenants. One must have doubts, however, whether these provisions would be respected by a US court of justice.

As mentioned in the introduction, the problem of cross-border resolution was fully recognized at the time of the LTCM crisis, in 1998. At the time, there was a clear understanding that something needed to be done. But nothing was done. Ten years later, when the financial crisis struck, the seriousness of the omission became obvious. Now, more than two years further along, we must say that, still, effectively nothing has been done on the problem of cross-border resolution.

---

29 Directive 2001/24/EC of the European Parliament and of the Council of 4 April 2001 on the reorganisation and winding up of credit institutions, Official Journal of the European Communities L125/15–23, 5. 5. 2001.

30 I am grateful to *Horst Eidenmüller* for alerting me to this issue.

6. Constitutional Concerns, Problem Adequacy, and Legal Politics

Members of the German legal community with whom I have discussed the substantive weaknesses of the German Bank Restructuring Act of 2010, academics, members of the ministerial bureaucracy, administrators, have usually responded that legislation was constrained by constitutional concerns and that these constitutional concerns precluded any more effective treatment of the problems that I was pointing out. In particular, such concerns would preclude anything like the UK special resolution regime for banks.

Two constitutional concerns are usually mentioned:

- Constitutional protection of private property precludes any stronger intervention of public authorities in a bank at a time when it is not insolvent and not even in violation of any regulatory requirement. The UK regime, where the FSA triggers the imposition of the special resolution regime on the grounds that the bank is not satisfying or likely not to satisfy regulatory requirements would be deemed to be an infringement of private property.
- Under the German constitution, any decision and any action of a public authority must be legitimized by the democratic process. Any decision or action taken by the authority should therefore be interpretable as the mere application of an act of parliament to the facts of the case at hand. This condition is not satisfied if the authority has a great deal of freedom to exert its own judgment as to what decision or action is appropriate. In particular, the freedom of action given the Bank of England as a resolution authority under the UK Banking Act of 2009 would not be compatible with constitutional principles in Germany.

As formulated, I find neither of these concerns convincing. I appreciate that, as an economist, I have no competence in this area. Nevertheless I will express and explain my misgivings.

6.1 Would a More Effective Resolution Regime Violate Constitutional Property Rights?

Concerns about property rights – of shareholders and debt holders – were clearly articulated by representatives of the German Federal Ministry of Justice at the *Deutscher Juristentag*, the annual congress of the German legal community, which took place in Berlin in September 2010. The very detailed procedural provisions of the Bank Reorganization Act[31] reflect the desire to avoid any violation of such rights in a situation where the bank is not yet insolvent and not yet in violation of any regulation. I take it that the procedural provisions in Sections 45 and 45c of the Banking Act are motivated by a similar desire.

---

31 See Section 3.2 above.

With due respect for the constitutional protection of private property, I fail to see why the constitution would mandate that the problem of bank resolution be handled under principles and procedures derived from insolvency law. Insolvency law is a system of legal rules that are intended to put some order into relations between a debtor and his creditors – and into relations between the different creditors – when the debtor is unable to fulfill his obligations to all creditors and the different creditors' claims are in conflict with each other. Relations between a debtor and his creditors are a matter of private contracting. The state comes in because private contracting relies on its protection under the law. Insolvency law contributes to this protection as it provides for (hopefully) clear rules on how to resolve the conflicts that arise when a debtor is unable to fulfill his obligations. As such, insolvency law must be guided by the question of what *ordre public* must be imposed on insolvency proceedings so as to perform this function of protection for private contracting and best contribute to the peace keeping function of the law.

In contrast, the problem of bank resolution is not just a matter of private contracts and their protection. Banking gives rise to systemic concerns that transcend private contracting between the bank and its financiers. These concerns are a reason why we have a Banking Act in the first place. When the Banking Act was first introduced, in 1934, the motivation was not just to make the banks subservient to Nazi financing wishes, but also to have a supervisory regime that would forestall a repetition of the 1931 experience when the disastrous banking crisis plunged the German economy even more deeply into depression. Nowadays, Section 6 of the Banking Act mandates the supervisory authority to counteract any abuses in banking that might put the bank's financiers at risk, endanger the orderly execution of bank business, or harm the economy as a whole. The latter concern, in particular, shows that we are dealing with a matter of public interest that transcends the protection of private contracting between the bank and its financiers.

Suppose that a fire is seen to develop in a house and there is a danger that, unless the fire is contained, the house will burn down and, in the process, the fire will extend to the neighboring houses. Does the constitutional protection of private property prevent the police or the fire brigade from entering the house? Or is the community's interest in having the fire contained sufficient justification to break into the house and put out the fire even against the wishes of the owner? When I raised this question at the *Juristentag* in Berlin, Wolfram Höfling, as a specialist in constitutional law, drew attention to the fact that the German constitution's protection of private property is not absolute. According to Article 14 of Germany's Basic Law, the content and limits of the rights attached to private property are determined by general legislation. In Höfling's view, protection against systemic risk would be a sufficient condition for interference.[32]

At this point, it may be useful to take a step back and ask what rights of private property we are actually concerned about. The government's written arguments for the Bank Reorganization Act mentioned shareholders and debt holders. Shares and debt instru-

---

32 See also his written report to the Juristentag; *W. Höfling* Finanzmarktregulierung – Welche Regelungen empfehlen sich für den deutschen und europäischen Finanzsektor? Gutachten F zum 68. Deutschen Juristentag, Verlag C.H. Beck, München 2010, F 57 ff.

ments are securities. The rights that are attached to these securities depend on the legal environment. In the country of co-determination, students of corporate law learn early on that, in contrast to some[33] Anglo-American notions, the shareholders are not the owners of the corporation, but the owners of the corporation's shares. Owning the corporation's shares entitles them to the rights that are attached to the shares, but these rights are determined by the law and by the charter of the corporation. No shareholder has a right to the corporation's assets the way an owner of the assets would.

Indeed, historically, in the United States, the publicly traded joint-stock corporation was developed as a tool to limit the power of shareholders to be paid off or even to dispose of the firm's assets. This development was designed to eliminate abuses of such rights of shareholders in partnerships, thus giving the firm some permanence and, therefore, credibility with prospective creditors and employees, as well as reducing holdup problems between partners.[34] Limitations of shareholder rights have thus been built into this institution from the very beginning. How to specify these limitations, is part of the problem of corporate governance. In continental Europe, the legal framework for corporate governance, including the rights of shareholders and the limitation of these rights, is routinely treated as part of the *ordre public*, to be regulated by legislation.[35]

Given this tradition of corporate law, I fail to see why precisely the constitutional protection of private property is deemed to preclude a stronger intervention of the authorities prior to any violation of capital or liquidity requirements, along the lines of the UK Banking Act of 2009. Protection of the financial system and the community as a whole from negative systemic effects to me seems a legitimate public concern. Moreover, experiences with Lehman Brothers and Hypo Real Estate suggest, that the imposition of something like the special resolution regime would not be incommensurate to the problem on hand.[36]

6.2 Procedure and Legitimacy in a Democracy

The principle that a public authority must not have too much room for exercising its own judgment without being constrained by the will of the legislature reflects a standard concern in German constitutional law. In many contexts, however, choices of appropriate decisions hinge on subtle tradeoffs the outcome of which cannot be legislated in advance. In such contexts, there is a conflict between the principle that the

---

33 Even in the United States, these notions are not universally accepted. See for instance *M. Blair, L. Stout* Specific Investment and Corporate Law, European Business Organization Law Review 7 (2006), 473–500.

34 *M. Blair* Locking in Capital: What Corporate Law Achieved for Business Organizers in the 19th Century, UCLA Law Review 51 (2003), 387–455; *M. Blair* Reforming Corporate Governance: What History Can Teach Us, Berkeley Business Law Review 1 (2004), 1–44.

35 *M. Hellwig* Zur Problematik staatlicher Beschränkungen der Beteiligung und der Einflussnahme von Investoren bei großen Unternehmen, Zeitschrift für das gesamte Handelsrecht und Wirtschaftsrecht 172 (2008), 768–787, especially 763 ff.

36 In this context, it should be noted that, under the UK special resolution regime, financial claims of shareholders to residual returns, if there are any, are preserved.

decision powers of public authorities must be restricted and the principle that the decisions taken should be adequate for the case at issue.

This conflict has also arisen in other areas of economic relation, for instance, in the regulation of network industries. Thus, for the telecommunications sector in Germany, the Telecommunications Act of 1996 provided a fairly rigid framework for regulatory decisions. This law tied, e.g., the regulation of consumer prices to findings of market dominance, which could be assessed by procedures that were firmly grounded in statutory law and case law. Decisions to take some telecommunications markets out of the purview of regulation altogether were reserved to the legislature. Subsequently, the Telecommunications Act of 2004 provided the regulatory authority with extensive powers to assess whether a market should be regulated at all and, if it was to be regulated, which regulatory tools were to be used. In providing the regulatory authority with these powers to exercise its own judgment, the legislature was implementing the European Telecommunication Directives of 2002. Given these Directives, and given the Schröder government's political agenda for the network industries, constitutional concerns about the decision powers of public authorities all of a sudden were moved backstage.[37]

In the context of the Bank Restructuring Act of 2010, I find it difficult to match the procedural provisions of the changes to the Banking Act with the constitutional principle concerning the powers of public authorities. In Section 3.3 above, I noted that, in an intervention under Sections 45 and 45c, the division of responsibilities between the bank's management, the restructuring agent and the supervisory authority is unclear. I also noted that, in the case of a transfer of assets and liabilities under the new Section 48a, the division or responsibilities between the supervisory authority, the third party that is acquiring the assets and liabilities and the Restructuring Fund Authority is unclear. Such unclear divisions of responsibility do not go well with the notion that any public authority should have a clearly defined task so that its decisions in any case are easily derived from the mandate given by the law.

I am even more bothered by the prospect that, if a case like HRE is going to come up again, the insufficiency of the present law will induce the government to push through some emergency legislation again by a shotgun procedure. In 2008, the emergency law was introduced into the Bundestag on October 13 and passed into law on October 18. Such a procedure makes a mockery of any notion of democratic legitimacy based on parliamentary deliberation and decision making. No doubt, the emergency law was needed. However, neither chamber of the legislature had any time for serious consideration of what they were deciding. For the population at large, this was a matter of government and parliament committing taxpayer money to rescue gambling bankers without even thinking about the matter. This impression has hardly enhanced the political legitimacy of the law or of the underlying constitutional order. If the procedure

37 On the discussion about regulatory discretion in the Telecommunications Act of 2004, see Monopolkommission, Zur Reform des Telekommunikationsgesetzes, Sondergutachten 40, Nomos, Baden-Baden 2004. On the need for regulatory discretion in the governance of network industries, see *M.F. Hellwig* Competition Policy and Sector-Specific Regulation for Network Industries, in: X. Vives (ed.), Competition Policy in the EU: Fifty Years on from the Treaty of Rome, Oxford University Press, Oxford 2009, 203–235.

were to be repeated, the impact on our democracy would be even more disastrous. At that point, we will not have the excuse that the possibility of such an emergency could not have been foreseen. By now, the government and the legislature know about this possibility. However, fearful for the principle that an arrangement like that of UK Banking Act of 2009 would give the resolution authority too much power, they have willfully accepted the risk that, in another emergency, the prevailing legal regime would again be inadequate and another piece of legislation at gunpoint would be needed to avoid an immediate catastrophe, with serious consequences for the legitimacy of the constitutional order itself.

Given the importance that constitutional law assigns to the principle that decisions taken by a public authority must reflect the will of the democratically elected legislature, one might have supposed that the issues considered here would have been a subject of parliamentary debate. In fact, there was hardly any room for such a debate. The Executive Branch took over a year and a half before it introduced the draft of the Bank Restructuring Law into the legislative procedure.[38] The legislature was then given less than four months to pass the law. According to one deputy, the time pressure under which the legislature was working prevented any serious discussion of substantive issues, let alone any substantive changes. The time pressure was due to the concern that, without the new Restructuring Fund Act, the Financial Markets Stabilization Authority, which had been created by the emergency legislation in October 2008, would go out of existence on December 31, 2010.

The Executive Branch took as long as it did because the different ministries that were involved found it difficult to adjudicate the differences in their views about the tradeoff between constitutional concerns and problem adequacy. By taking as long as they did, they effectively precluded the legislature from discussing the issue on its own. It is somewhat incongruous to see the Executive Branch making sure to keep a dispute about the proper legislative treatment of the administration of bank resolution in its own ranks. If they really cared about the will of the democratically elected legislature, they would have respected the fact that decisions about a piece of legislation should be left to the legislature.

---

38 Work on the law began in early 2009. In March 2009, I was shown a draft of a reorganization law and raised the objections in Section 3.2 above. The Federal Ministries of Finance and Justice presented a draft in late June 2010, the Federal Cabinet decided about the matter in late August 2010.

Resolution Requires Reform

*Thomas F. Huertas**

Table of Contents

Bankruptcy doesn't work for banks
Bail-outs are not the solution
What we need now
Better regulation and better supervision
Robust infrastructures
Banks require a special resolution regime
Who pulls the trigger?
What is the trigger?
Who is the resolution authority?
What governs the choice of resolution method?
Resolution methods
Insured deposit pay-off/liquidation.
Deposit transfer
Bridge bank
Temporary public ownership: bail-out or bail-in?
Bail-in via stay on investor capital
Bail-in via conversion
Conclusion: the route to better resolution
References

Resolution requires reform. In particular, banks need a special resolution regime, and this special resolution regime must put an end to too big to fail. Why should this be the case? Briefly put, the answer is twofold – bankruptcy doesn't work for banks, and too big to fail is too costly to continue.

Better resolution should complement other measures that are necessary to cure crises – better macroeconomic policy, better deposit guarantee schemes, better regulation and better supervision.[1] Much progress is being made in these areas, but must more remains to be done, especially with respect to resolution of systemically important firms (SIFIs).

---

* The author is Alternate Chair, European Banking Authority; Member Basel Committee on Banking Supervision and Director, Banking Sector, Financial Services Authority (UK). The opinions expressed here are those of the author and do not necessarily represent the views of the EBA, BCBS or the FSA.

1 *Huertas* 2010 a.

Bankruptcy doesn't work for banks

The very essence of banking is the ability to make commitments to pay – depositors at maturity, sellers of securities due to settle, borrowers who wish to draw on lending commitments, derivative counterparties who contracted with the bank for protection from interest rate, exchange rate or credit risks. Putting a stay on payments to creditors is equivalent to stopping the bank's operating business. Unlike airlines, retailers or automobile companies, banks cannot readily operate in bankruptcy. So bankruptcy for a bank is tantamount to liquidation.

That is not a good result, either for the creditors of the bank or for society at large. Liquidation imposes very significant incremental losses relative to the losses that would be realised if the entity can continue to operate whilst its capital is being restructured. That is true for banks as well.[2]

Indeed, it is especially true for banks, for banks are interconnected to a far greater degree than would generally be the case for non-financial firms in the same industry. It is in the nature of the financial system that banks incur extensive exposures to other banks. Although these exposures have increasingly been controlled directly through limits on large exposures and indirectly via measures to make payments, clearing and settlement systems more robust as well as measures to channel derivative transactions through central counterparties, the failure of one bank may have significant knock-on effects on other banks and on society at large.

Bail-outs are not the solution

Following the failure of Lehmans governments intervened massively to stabilise the financial system. They prevented systemic firms from failing by providing solvency and liquidity support in unprecedented amounts as well as initiating asset protection schemes. Total support amounted to over $13 trillion.[3] Together with massive monetary and fiscal stimulus, this support for the financial system turned what might have become the Great(er) Depression into what economists are now calling the Great Recession.

But bail outs are not a sustainable solution. Indeed, too big to fail is too costly to continue. Too big to fail distorts competition, creates moral hazard and threatens the public finances. Just as we need an exit strategy from monetary and fiscal stimulus, we need an exit strategy from too big to fail.

A simple example illustrates why. Take the case where there are two banks, "Likely to be rescued" and "Likely to be abandoned". For each bank the probability that intervention will be required is 20% and the loss given intervention (assuming no bail out) is 25%. If a bail out occurs, the loss to the creditor given bail out is zero. The only difference between the two banks is the market's estimate of the probability that the authorities will

2 *Huertas* 2011.

3 *Huertas* 2010a: 2.

bail out the institution, if intervention is required.[4] For "Likely to be rescued" the probability of bail out is 95%. For "Likely to be abandoned" the probability of bail out is 5%. For the former the expected loss is 25 basis points; for the latter, the expected loss is 475 basis points.

Table 1
Probability of bail out determines risk

	Likely to be rescued	Likely to be abandoned
Probability of intervention	20%	20%
Loss with bail out	0%	0%
Loss without bail out, or Loss given default	25%	25%
Probability of bail out	95%	5%
Expected loss to private creditor	25 bp	475 bp

This dramatic difference in expected loss will lead to significant differences in the risk premiums that the two borrowers would have to pay. 'Likely to be rescued' can fund itself at significantly cheaper rates, and likely to be rescued pays little more if anything at all for raising the risk of its asset portfolio. In other words, the market exercises little or no discipline on 'likely to be rescued'. The only discipline on banks will come from management, shareholders and possibly from supervisors. Management and shareholders have the incentive to maximise returns; to the extent that shareholders influence banks, it is as much or more to ensure that banks are taking risk so as to maximise returns. Supervisors may discipline banks, but they are usually behind the curve and their power to intervene is limited until the risks actually crystallise into losses and result in the bank's failing to meet capital and/or liquidity requirements. The net result is a greater market share for likely to be rescued and a greater probability that rescue will be required.

That is not a good result for the public finances. Bank balance sheets can amount to 100% or more of the home country's GDP. So rescuing a failing bank can cause public debt to skyrocket. Indeed, the bank rescues of 2008 have stretched the public finances in many countries to the limit – and in some cases possibly beyond (as the case of Ireland demonstrates).

Nor is it a good result for competition. Big banks will grow at the expense of small banks, and some of these big banks may succeed in building a dominant position. Big banks in big countries may have a particular advantage, for big countries are more able to bail out big banks. Within the EU that undermines the basis for the single market. Although the Commission has reviewed the rescue packages and assured that they

4 Note that this market estimate may differ from the probability that the authorities themselves would assign to the possibility that they would bail out the institution, should intervention be required.

formally complied with state aid rules, the fact remains that a large Member State is more able to provide the aid in the first place than a small Member State. So in a too-big-to-fail world where the home country pays for the rescue, it pays for a bank to have its headquarters in a big Member State.

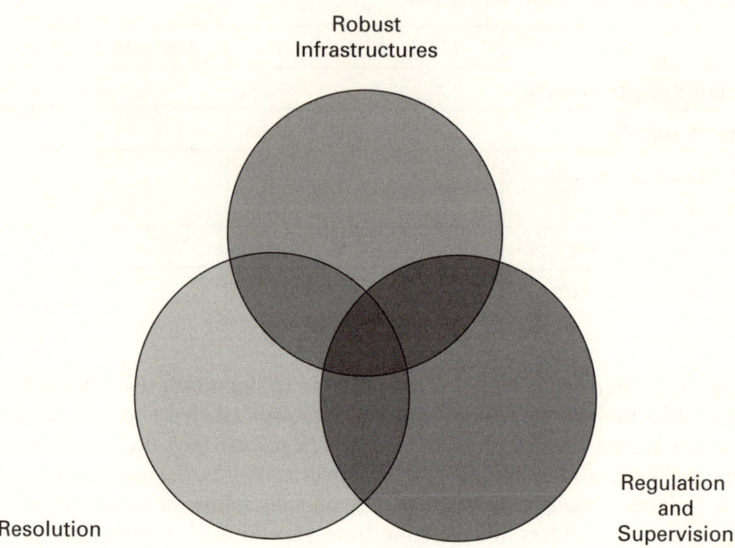

What we need now

So how do we move away from too big to fail? Three steps are necessary:

- *better regulation and supervision*. This will reduce the probability that the bank will fail.
- *robust infrastructures*. This is vital to avoid the risk that the failure of one bank will result in others toppling over as well.
- *A special resolution regime for banks*. This will allow the authorities to resolve banks promptly at no cost to the taxpayer and at minimal social cost.

Better regulation and better supervision

Significant improvements have already been made to regulation and supervision, and further initiatives are underway, particularly with respect to systemically important firms (SIFIs).

The Basel Capital Reform Programme

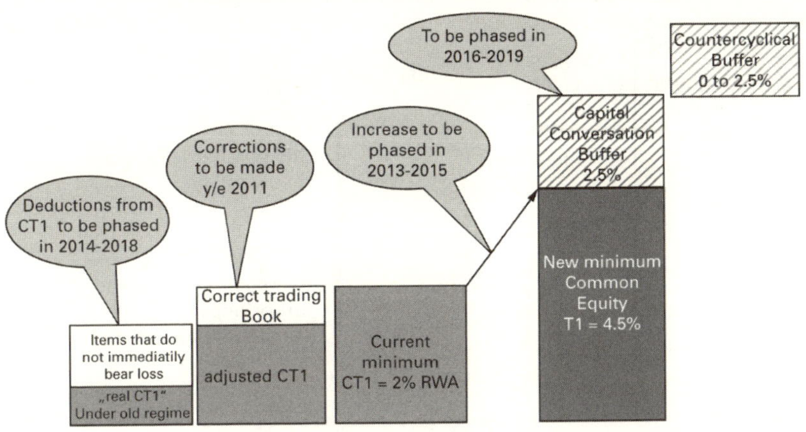

The Basel Committee on Banking Supervision has materially revamped capital regulation.[5] It has strengthened the definition of capital, raised the minimum amount of common equity Tier 1 capital that banks must hold, increased requirements for trading book assets, introduced a capital conservation buffer and a countercyclical capital buffer and imposed a leverage ratio as a backstop to the risk-based capital regime. In addition, the Committee has strengthened the quality of non-core Tier 1 and Tier 2 capital so that such capital bears loss (either through write down or conversion to equity) at the point at which the bank becomes non-viable in private markets. This amounts to a very significant increase in capital requirements and should lead to a material reduction in the probability that a bank could fail.

The Basel Committee has introduced for the first time a global liquidity standard for banks.[6] This includes a requirement that banks measure and report their liquidity risk as well as a requirement that they maintain a buffer of liquid assets sufficient to offset a liquidity shock that would persist for a month. Finally, the new liquidity regime imposes a net stable funding ratio on banks. This is designed to assure that longer term illiquid assets are funded either with longer term liabilities or with deposits that will reliably 'stick' to the bank even if the bank comes under pressure. Over time, as the new liquidity regime is introduced, banks vulnerability to liquidity risk should diminish and this too should reduce the probability that the bank will fail.

5 BCBS 2010a.
6 BCBS 2010b.

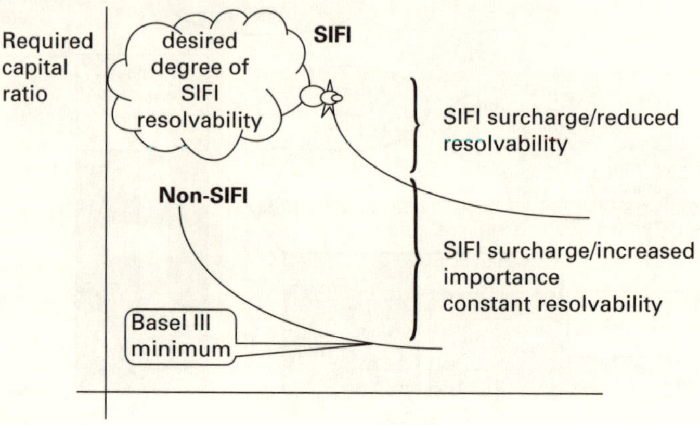

For SIFIs something extra may be needed. The G-20 agreed that SIFIs should have a greater degree of loss absorbency than other banks.[7] This should be related to the bank's degree of systemic importance as well as the "resolvability" of the bank, where "resolvability" means the ability to resolve a bank at no cost to the taxpayer (in terms of solvency support) and with minimal social cost. Banks that are less resolvable will require higher amounts of capital so as to reduce the likelihood that intervention will be required.

Tougher supervision will complement tighter regulation. In particular, supervisors are demanding that systemically important financial institutions submit so-called living wills, or recovery and resolution plans[8]. The recovery plan is for the institution to develop and own and for the authorities to review. The recovery plan documents what the institution could do to rebuild its capital and/or liquidity in the event that the firm comes under extreme stress. Ideally, the firm would have a number of options that would allow it to restore capital and/or access liquidity and ward off intervention. These options might include selling assets and/or businesses, accessing contingent sources of funding, running down trading books, closing particular lines of business or selling the entire firm. The important criterion from a supervisory point of view is that the options be substantial in size and readily executable, so that they can make a significant difference to the condition of the institution within a short period of time.

7 FSB 2010.

8 *Huertas* 2010 b.

Recovery and resolution plans ('living wills')

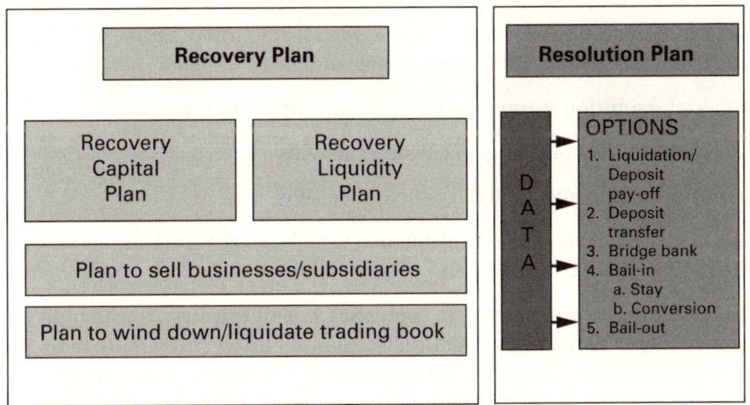

In contrast, the resolution plan is for the authorities to develop and own. What the living will asks the bank to do is provide the authorities with the data that would be required for the authorities to make a determination of whether or not the bank is resolvable and to give some consideration in advance of the actual intervention to the method or methods that the authorities would use to resolve the bank, should intervention be required.

Robust infrastructures

Banks will only be resolvable, if infrastructures are robust. If the failure of a bank causes a major payments, clearing and/or settlement infrastructure to fail as well, the initial bank's failure will quickly spread throughout the financial system. This can cause other banks to fail and lead to declines in output and employment.

Moreover, the potential risk to infrastructures is highly correlated. Most major payments, clearing and settlement infrastructures have a high proportion of members in common. Hence, the failure of a SIFI potentially threatens not just one infrastructure but many, in many different countries.

For this reason, each of the major payments, clearing and settlement infrastructures must be made robust, able to withstand the simultaneous failure of two or more of its largest participants. This may be done by capitalising the infrastructure, limiting the exposure of the infrastructure to each of its participants and requiring that each of the participants post collateral with the infrastructure that may that may be liquidated in the event one of the participants fails.

Banks require a special resolution regime

If banks are to be resolvable, they require a special resolution regime. For the reasons outlined above, bankruptcy for banks will not work.

Such a special resolution regime should meet the following criteria:

- It should ensure the continuity of customer activity.
- It should work for banks of all sizes, including SIFIs.
- It should be capable of being implemented rapidly, so that resolution can be accomplished overnight or over a weekend.

A special resolution regime for banks comprises several features: (i) who pulls the trigger, (ii) a rule that determines when the trigger is pulled, (iii) who is the resolution authority, and what are its powers, (iv) what rules the resolution authority should use to choose among resolution methods and (v) the establishment of permissible resolution methods.

Who pulls the trigger?

The answer to the question of who pulls the trigger is simple. It is the bank's supervisor who pulls the trigger. Either the bank's formal supervisor is the entity that is empowered to determine that the bank no longer meets threshold conditions, or the entity that is empowered to make that decision is in fact the bank's supervisor. There is no more significant or difficult decision for a supervisor to make than the decision to pull the trigger and send the bank into the special resolution regime. So the entity empowered to pull the trigger is in fact the supervisor at least for prudential purposes.

What is the trigger?

The trigger for putting a bank into the special resolution regime should be the point at which the bank fails to fulfil the requirements for maintaining its banking license. In UK terminology, this is the point at which the bank fails to meet threshold conditions and is unlikely to return quickly to the point where it can again meet threshold conditions. In plainer English, that is the point at which the bank no longer has adequate resources, in terms of capital, liquidity or management, and no hope of getting adequate resources any time soon. In effect, the trigger into the special resolution regime is the point at which the bank is no longer viable in private markets.[9]

9 Note that this point may be at a point where the bank still has positive net worth. Technically, the bank need not be balance-sheet insolvent. It can still have positive net worth. Indeed, one of the purposes of setting a minimum capital requirement is to assure that intervention can occur

There should be no doubt that the trigger will be pulled at the point where the bank no longer meets threshold conditions. Neither banks nor their creditors should reckon that the authorities will ride to the rescue by providing solvency support, such as an early equity injection as was done in October 2008. There should be certainty that failure to maintain the bank in good condition as required under the terms of its license will result in intervention by the authorities. The institution will be put into resolution, and investors will be exposed to loss.

Who is the resolution authority?

The special resolution regime must clearly designate a resolution authority and empower it to resolve a bank promptly, as soon as the trigger is pulled. There are many possible candidates who could act as the resolution authority including the deposit guarantee scheme (such as in the United States) or the central bank (such as in the United Kingdom).

However, the identity of the authority is secondary to its powers. It has to have the ability to take control of the bank as soon as the trigger is pulled, and it has to have the authority to choose the resolution method (see below) and execute that method, including the authority to sell assets or lines of business, transfer deposits, etc. Finally, it has to have the authority to do this promptly, whilst there may still be significant value to the bank's franchise.

Given the need for speed, it is extremely difficult, if not impossible, for a special resolution regime for banks to function well, if prior court or creditor approval is required for adoption of the resolution method. Instead, the resolution authority must be given the power to act. Shareholders and creditors should have the power to seek compensation, if they can make a case that they received less than they would have received had the bank been liquidated.

If, however, the resolution method requires the use of public funds and/or exposes the public finances to significant risk, it is logical to require that the resolution authority seek the prior approval from the finance ministry for the expenditure of such funds. And, if the resolution method requires the provision of liquidity support from the central bank, the central bank will need to be drawn into the process (if the central bank is not the resolution authority).

The special resolution regime should make clear the need for close coordination between the resolution authority and the entity that pulls the trigger. If the trigger is pulled, the "gun" (resolution authority) has to operate without a hitch. That argues for providing the resolution authority with the right to provide advice to the entity empowered to pull the trigger on the point at which the trigger should be pulled. Indeed, it would be counterproductive to pull the trigger, if the gun cannot fire. For this reason, the UK Banking Act 2009 provides the resolution authority (Bank of England) and the

---

at a point where the bank still has positive net worth. This will reduce loss given intervention to depositors and other creditors.

finance ministry the right to provide advice to the supervisor on when the trigger should be pulled.

What governs the choice of resolution method?

The special resolution regime should also set out the criteria that the resolution authority should use when it chooses a resolution method. Ideally, the regime would set a standard that would force the resolution authority to choose the method that resulted in no cost to the taxpayer and the least cost to society at large.

No cost to the taxpayer, rather than least cost to the taxpayer, is an important distinction. "No cost to the taxpayer" seeks to constrain governments from bailing out banks, on the grounds that the long run costs of doing so (lack of market discipline on banks, leading to greater risk-taking and higher probability of failure) far outweigh on a properly discounted basis the short run costs that may result from allowing the bank to fail and imposing losses on investors and uninsured creditors. This is the approach that the United States has adopted in the Dodd Frank Act. The FDIC as resolution authority is prohibited from selecting a resolution method that would result in taxpayer support for investor capital.

If the possibility of taxpayer support is contemplated at all in the special resolution regime, it should not simply be at the option of the resolution authority. At a minimum, it should require the prior approval of the finance ministry (as is required under the UK Banking Act 2009), and it may make sense to require the resolution authority to meet a tougher test before making application to the finance ministry for the use of public funds to facilitate resolution of a failing financial institution. This is envisaged for example in the United States under the Dodd Frank Act, prior to an entity's being declared a "covered financial corporation" that would be resolved under the Orderly Liquidation Authority and eligible for assistance from the Orderly Liquidation Fund.[10]

"Least cost to society at large," also requires some explanation. Costs to investors in the failed bank's capital should not be taken into account. These instruments bear risk of loss, if the bank requires intervention. Investors are effectively compensated up front. They receive a risk premium. If that risk materialises, they do not need and should not receive additional compensation.

The word "society" also deserves some comment. "Society" is the right perspective, for the failure of a bank can have far broader implications than causing cost to the deposit insurance fund or even to depositors generally. The failure of a bank can interrupt access of clients to their assets, cut off lending capacity to consumers and small business, disrupt markets and pose threats to infrastructures such as payment, clearing and settlement systems. These broader effects need to be taken into account.

So too do international dimensions, particularly for large, complex, cross-border banks. This is a difficult perspective for national legislation to require national regulators to

---

10 *Acharya, Adler, Richardson and Roubini* 2010: 221–222.

take, particularly if the use of the funds from the nation's taxpayers may be required to facilitate resolution. However, the ramifications of resolution for global markets have to be considered, and arriving at special resolution regimes for banks that are internationally consistent and mutually reinforcing is needed to assure financial stability globally.

Resolution methods

Finally, the special resolution regime needs to lay out the methods that the resolution authority could use in order to resolve a bank. These include (i) insured deposit pay-off/liquidation, (ii) deposit transfer, (iii) bridge bank and (iv) share transfer/temporary public ownership. Table 2 provides an overview of the methods from various perspectives, including whether they require taxpayer and/or liquidity support, the degree to which they cause immediate and/or long term social cost and whether the method can practically be used to resolve a systemically important financial institution (SIFI).

Table 2
Overview of Resolution Methods

Resolution method	Taxpayer (solvency) and liquidity support	Immediate social impact/cost	Long-term social impact/cost (moral hazard)	Practical for a SIFI?
Deposit pay-off liquidation	None	Very high	Eliminates moral hazard	No
Deposit transfer	Limited to none	High	Improves market discipline and reduces cost	No
Bridge bank	No solvency or liquidity support to failed bank; possible solvency and/or liquidity support to bridge bank	Medium high	Improves market discipline and reduces cost	Perhaps
Share transfer/ TPO	TBD	TBD	TBD	Perhaps, if executed via bail-in

Insured deposit pay-off/liquidation.

Under this method the failed bank is liquidated much the way an insolvent non-bank financial corporation would be liquidated. Receivers would be appointed and they would liquidate the assets of the bank, paying out proceeds to the liability holders in strict order of seniority. The deposit guarantee scheme would promptly pay out insured deposits to eligible depositors and step into their claim for recoveries over time against the estate of the failed bank. As a result, insured depositors suffer no loss. In contrast, all other liability holders of the bank are at risk, including depositors who are not eligible for coverage. Deposits held by eligible depositors that are above the ceiling on the deposit guarantee scheme are also at risk.

For this method to be feasible, the deposit guarantee scheme must be able to pay out the claims of eligible depositors promptly. Failure to do so would undermine the credibility of the deposit guarantee scheme and provoke the very panic that deposit guarantees are intended to prevent.

Deposit pay-off/liquidation is unlikely to work for a large bank with extensive retail operations. It would certainly stretch even the most proficient deposit guarantee scheme to the limit of its operational and financial capacity. Even if the deposit guarantee scheme were up to the task of paying out tens of millions of personal accounts within a very short time period and had access to the tens of billions of euros, dollars or pounds that might be required in order to do so, additional costs would loom large. These would include the possible interruption in credit provision to very large numbers of businesses, including hundreds of thousands even millions of small to medium sized enterprises (SMEs) as well as the possible loss of access by clients to their non-deposit assets (such as securities positions) held in custody or trading accounts at the failed bank and/or its investment affiliates. So deposit pay-off for a SIFI with large retail operations is likely to result in unacceptably large social costs.

Deposit transfer

This method of resolution reduces the operational/logistical problems associated with deposit pay-off, but otherwise has similar effects to bank liquidation. The only difference to deposit pay-off is that the insured deposits are transferred to a third party rather than having the deposit guarantee scheme pay off the insured deposits. All other liability holders are exposed to loss. Depositor preference facilitates the execution of this resolution method, for it allows the resolution authority to effectively cherry pick the best of the bank's unencumbered assets to go along with the deposits to be transferred to the third party.

Following the transfer of the deposits to a third party, the remainder of the bank is placed into receivership and liquidated, with all the costs that liquidation implies, including without limitation, the interruption of credit facilities and the possible loss of access by clients to the assets that they may have held at the failed bank pending the reconciliation of the failed bank's client money accounts and the transfer of client money to a third party.

Deposit transfer is really only practical if there is another bank into which the deposits of the failed bank might be quickly transferred. Absent such a bank, deposit transfer will not work. For the very largest banks, there is simply no larger bank available to which the deposits of the failed bank might be transferred. Even if there were, such a transfer could give rise to antitrust or competition issues. So it is unlikely that deposit transfer will prove to be an acceptable method of resolution for a SIFI.

Bridge bank

This method allows for a greater continuity of customer business, limits the immediate social cost, but preserves market discipline. Under a bridge bank, the resolution authority transfers to a new bridge bank B such assets and liabilities of the failed bank A as are required to have the bridge bank be capable of independent and ongoing operation.

This transfer would work roughly as depicted below. Upon a finding that Bank A required intervention (failed to meet threshold conditions), the resolution authority would transfer selected assets to a completely new bank (Bank B), a bridge bank. Assets transferred to the bridge bank would be good assets, in the sense that they would either have a readily ascertainable market value (such as cash and marketable securities) or be very conservatively valued. The liabilities transferred would include deposits and other selected liabilities. Depending on the value of the assets, some of the liabilities transferred into Bank B might have to be transferred at a haircut value.

Resolution via bridge bank

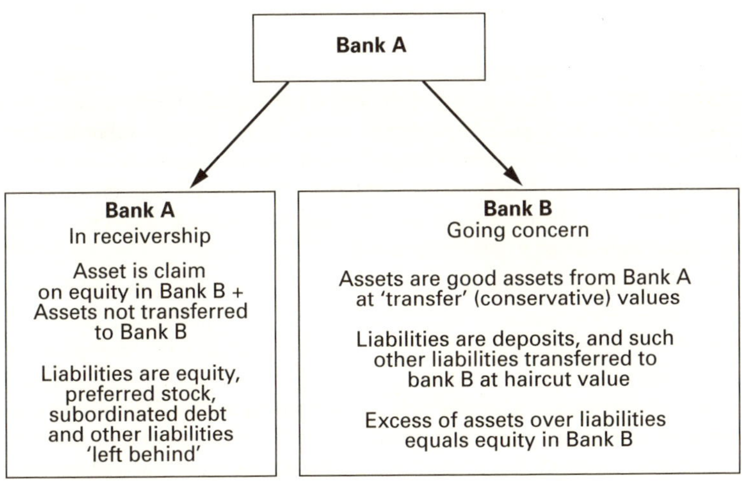

Following the transfer of selected assets and liabilities into the bridge bank, Bank A goes into receivership. Left behind in Bank A on the asset side of the balance sheet are two things: (i) any assets not transferred to bank B and (ii) a claim on the equity of Bank B. The liability side of bank A (in receivership) is the capital instruments of Bank A (its common equity, preferred stock and subordinated debt) plus any senior debt/other liabilities not transferred to Bank B (if some portion of these liabilities were transferred to Bank B at a haircut value the difference between the haircut value and the par value of the liability would remain in Bank A (in receivership) as a liability and would rank senior to the capital instruments.

To the extent that Bank A receives cash from realisation of the bad assets left in Bank A and/or from its equity claim on Bank B, this cash will be distributed to the liability holders in Bank A (in receivership) in strict order of seniority. In other words, any senior debt not transferred to Bank B will be repaid first, then subordinated debt, then preferred stock, then common stock.

Essentially, the resolution authority makes a determination at the point of resolution on the assets and liabilities of the failed bank that should be transferred into a new bank (bridge bank). For the activities transferred into the bridge bank, operations continue. The bridge bank should simply be the successor to the failed bank. The bridge bank would take over the failed bank's obligations to clients and rights vis-à-vis clients, and clients would have the same rights and obligations vis-à-vis the bridge bank that they had had vis-à-vis the failed bank prior to its being put into resolution.

The key question, therefore, is what goes into the bridge bank and what doesn't. Liabilities of the failed bank that get transferred to the bridge bank will retain some liquidity and have the risk of the bridge bank, not the risk of the failed bank. Liabilities that do not get transferred essentially remain in receivership, will have no liquidity and will almost certainly experience loss of principal.

So much rides on what the resolution authority decides to put into the bridge bank. Liabilities transferred into the bridge bank will effectively have seniority over liabilities that are not transferred and remain in the original bank. For two classes of liabilities the answer is clear: insured deposits should always go into the bridge bank; and the failed bank's capital instruments should always stay out. Indeed, the US Dodd Frank Act prohibits the FDIC from putting any of the failed bank's capital instruments (common equity Tier 1, other Tier 1 [such as preferred stock], Tier 2 [such as subordinated debt]) into the bridge bank. The failed bank's capital instruments effectively stay in the receivership, and they have the right to receive (in strict order of seniority) any proceeds from the receivership upon their realisation, including the proceeds that might be realised from the sale or liquidation of the bridge bank.

However, beyond these two precepts the answer is unclear. Does the resolution authority have to respect the seniority of the liabilities in the failed bank? And, does the resolution authority have to indicate in advance what it would do with respect to classes of liabilities, or should it determine this on a case-by-case basis? In a situation where the failed bank had an immense capital shortfall, a requirement that all liabilities pari passu or senior to deposits would have to be transferred to the bridge bank may not be feasible without taxpayer capitalisation of the bridge bank. So the most practical approach is to allow the resolution authority the flexibility of a case-by-base determination of the liabilities of the failed bank to transfer to the bridge bank with the safeguard that the liability holder would fare no worse as a result of the transfer to the bridge bank than it would have fared under liquidation. This in fact is the approach taken in the UK Banking Act 2009.

In theory, a bridge bank can be applied to even the largest bank or financial institution, and this is the approach taken in the United States under the Dodd Frank Act.[11] But such a method requires a rapid valuation of the bank's entire balance sheet so that an estimate can be made of the haircut that will need to be imposed on the bank's uninsured liabilities. The largest bank for which a bridge bank has ever been executed is Washington Mutual, and despite its size this was a relatively simple bank with limited trading operations and limited activity in payments, clearing and settlement systems.

It would be considerably more difficult to execute a bridge bank solution for a large, complex, internationally active financial institution with significant capital markets and derivative activities and/or international subsidiaries and affiliates. Key questions are:

- How would the bridge bank solution treat derivative transactions – would they be transferred in their entirety to the bridge bank?
- How would derivatives contracts and derivatives counterparties treat the initiation of a bridge bank – would this trigger close out?
- How would the bridge bank solution be applied to the parent bank's foreign branches, subsidiaries and affiliates?
- Would employees and service providers transfer smoothly to the bridge bank, particularly if these providers were third parties or affiliates located in foreign countries?

Lack of certainty as to how derivatives would be treated under a bridge bank solution could lead to "runs" by derivative counterparties as the situation of a bank deteriorates, for the resolution regime could potentially override the super-priority that derivatives currently enjoy, at least under US bankruptcy law.[12] Even if the derivatives are transferred to the bridge bank, the bridge bank solution is likely to be successful if and only if the transfer does not trigger close out. If the transfer triggers close out, this is likely to lead to very significant capital losses as well as a drain on the liquidity of the bridge bank itself.[13] Similar questions apply to secured borrowings such as repos.

A further question is whether the bridge bank solution a global solution, applicable to the group as a whole, or a solution that applies only the to home country jurisdiction? If the intent is to apply such a solution globally, does this necessitate harmonisation of resolution regimes, at least among the major jurisdictions (US, EU, Japan, Hong Kong, Singapore, Switzerland) in which SIFIs are headquartered and/or active? Presumably it does, but much remains to be done on this score. If the bridge bank solution is restricted to the home country and/or focuses solely on assuring financial stability in the home country, the bridge bank solution may cause financial distress/instability elsewhere in the world, just as the resolution of Lehmans did.

---

11 *Acharya, Adler, Richardson and Roubini* 2010.

12 *Roe* 2010.

13 *Duffie* 2010:23–29.

Finally, will employees and service providers simply transfer to the bridge bank so that it can smoothly initiate operations and conduct banking operations? Will the bridge bank instantly acquire the counterparty limits that it would need in order to trade with other institutions? Can the bridge bank simply succeed to the failed bank's membership in payments, clearing and settlement infrastructures? Even if this can be accomplished via legislation or regulation in the bank's home country can it be done in jurisdictions where the failed bank had branches or subsidiaries?

Temporary public ownership: bail-out or bail-in?

A fourth resolution method is temporary public ownership. This can be done via the mandatory transfer of the bank's common equity to the state. This effectively transfers control of the bank to the state and allows the state to take rapid decisions with respect to the sale of some or all of the bank's business.

Temporary public ownership may imply a bail out of investor capital or it can be used to implement a bail-in of such capital. A simple nationalisation of the equity of the failing bank could signal to the market that the government has undertaken to guarantee, explicitly or implicitly, all the liabilities of the bank (in the sense that a government would not readily put a wholly owned institution into bankruptcy). That would amount to a bail out, particularly if the process resulted in protection for some components of "investor capital," such as subordinated debt or preferred stock.

However, bail out is not the only possible route that TPO can take. TPO can also be used to bail-in investor capital. Bail-in offers perhaps the most effective means to resolve a SIFI at no cost to the taxpayer and at minimum social cost. Effectively, bail-in allows the authorities to expand greatly the immediate loss bearing capacity of the bank from common equity alone to all elements of investor capital without having to put the bank into liquidation. Resolution can potentially be accomplished at no cost to the taxpayer and at a minimum social cost, for the bank itself would remain a going concern. And, in contrast to the bridge bank solution, bail-in does not involve the creation of a new corporate entity, the necessity for rapid transfer of assets and liabilities and the requirement for an immediate valuation of the entire balance sheet.

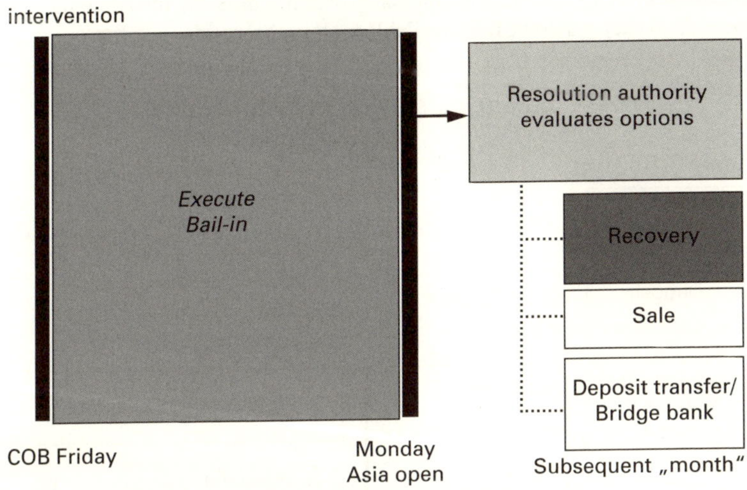

In concept, bail-in would work as follows. Upon a determination by the supervisor that the bank no longer met threshold conditions, the resolution authority would implement the bail-in of investor capital. This would occur immediately, prior to placing the bank into administration or liquidation and would effectively amount to a pre-pack recapitalisation of the bank. This would allow the bank to reopen on the "Monday" morning as a going concern. The entity would remain under the control of the authorities, who would determine over the next "month" whether the institution could recover or how it might be gradually wound-down. This approach should allow the bank to continue in operation and avoid the reduction in asset values and other costs that liquidation might impose. It would also preserve the continuity of customer activity.

Bail-in can potentially be implemented with respect to a SIFI. Two variants hold promise: bail-in via a stay on investor capital and bail-in via conversion. Each would avoid the need for transfers of assets and liabilities to a bridge bank and possibly provide greater assurance of continuity of operations. It would allow the bank to remain a going concern, but avoid the need for taxpayer support of the bank's solvency. Each might be more readily implemented on a global scale, for bail-in is essentially an exercise to be conducted in the bank's headquarters/home country at the top of its capital structure.

Bail-in via stay on investor capital

The bail-in via a stay on investor capital would work as follows. Upon a determination by the supervisor that the bank no longer met threshold conditions, the resolution authority would take control of the bank. Under the share transfer/temporary public ownership authority, the resolution authority would acquire at zero up front cost the entire share capital of the bank, all the preferred stock, the subordinated debt and any senior debt subject to bail-in. Contractual payments on such instruments would be suspended, and they would be fully available for loss absorption.

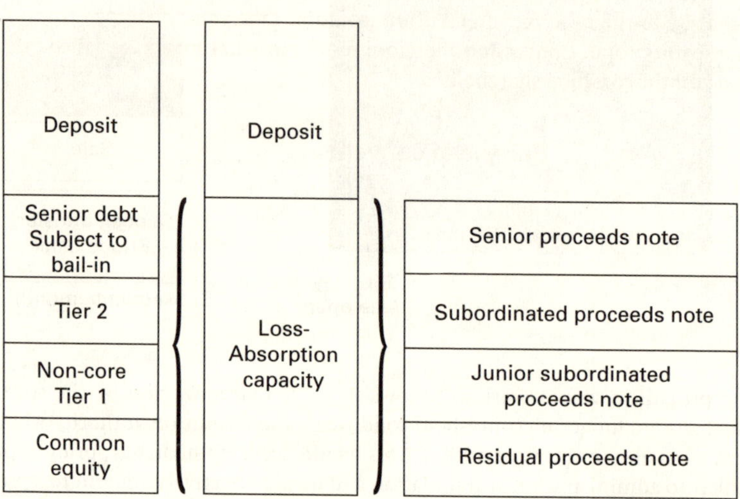

The resolution authority would continue to operate the bank as a going concern. Customer liabilities would continue to be paid, and close-out of derivative contracts should not be triggered (although the ISDA master contracts may need to be amended to give effect to this). Holders of instruments subject to bail-in would receive certificates entitling them to proceeds from the wind-down/liquidation of the institution. These proceeds would be distributed according to strict seniority, with senior debt being paid first, then subordinated debt, then preferred stock and, if any proceeds remained, common stock. In economic terms, this result is roughly equivalent to what would be achieved under a successfully implemented bridge bank approach and should be superior to what would be achieved under liquidation, since the bank remains a going concern.

Bail-in via conversion

It would also be possible to conduct a bail-in via conversion, and this approach may provide the best chance for the failed institution to recover. Under this approach, the resolution authority would also take control of the bank upon a finding by the supervisor that the bank no longer met threshold conditions, and the resolution authority would also acquire at zero up front cost all the failed bank's investor capital (common equity, non core Tier 1 capital [e.g. preferred stock], Tier 2 capital [e.g. subordinated debt] and any senior debt subject to bail-in). The resolution authority would then convert the non-equity elements of this investor capital into common equity, such that a euro of preferred stock (par value) received significantly fewer shares of common stock than a euro of subordinated debt (par value) and a euro of subordinated debt received significantly fewer shares of common stock than a euro of senior debt. Following the conversion of the back-up capital into common equity, the immediately apparent losses that gave rise to the need for intervention would be taken and deducted from the new common equity total. Conversion therefore results in what might be called "death by dilution" for the common shareholder.

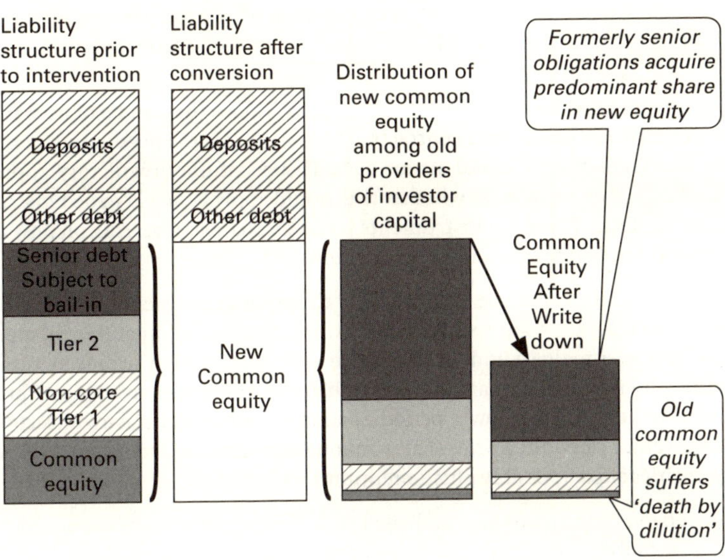

There remain the questions of who should establish the conversion ratios and when they should be established. There are two candidates for who should decide the conversion ratios: the resolution authority or the bank itself. And there are two points at which the conversion ratios could be established: prior to intervention or after the point of intervention. This yields the 2 x 2 possibility matrix shown in Table 3.

Table 3
Bail-in via conversion
Timing and decision-maker for conversion ratios

		Point at which conversion ratio is determined	
		Prior to intervention	After intervention
Decision maker for conversion ratios	Resolution authority	Possible via statute or regulation but could not be institution-specific and may not be comprehensive	Possible, but would be subject to review/revision
	Bank itself	Possible via contract as part of new issues and/or amendment of old	Not feasible immediately, but could potentially be negotiated subsequent to intervention

If the conversion ratio is established prior to intervention, this can be done either on a statutory/regulatory basis or on a contractual basis as part of the negotiation of the bank with the providers of capital and senior debt. If the statutory/regulatory approach is adopted, there is a question as to whether this would apply to newly issued instruments only, or to the stock of existing instruments – a factor that has a bearing on how quickly a transition to a bail-in regime might be accomplished.

If the conversion ratios are to be established at the point of intervention, it is really only feasible for the resolution authority to do this, and the resolution authority must have the requisite power to do so under the relevant special resolution regime(s). If the resolution authority is given the mandate to establish the conversion ratios, some provision would need to be made to allow a period of time for the junior classes of securities to buy out the senior classes at a price that would be equivalent to redeeming their unconverted securities at par (possibly plus a premium).

If the conversion ratios are to be established after the intervention has occurred, but the resolution authority doesn't have the power to set them unilaterally, the bank (under the control of the resolution authority) will have to negotiate with the holders of the back-up capital regarding the appropriate ratios for conversion as well as determine whether to attempt to convert all of the back-up capital at once or to convert only so much back up capital as may be required (after taking any immediately appropriate write-downs) to restore the common equity of the institution to its minimum required level. It is unlikely that such a negotiation could successfully take place over a "resolution weekend".

If conversion ratios are not predetermined, and the regulator has no power to set them, then bail-in by conversion would have to be implemented in stages. The first stage would be bail-in by stay of investor capital; the second would be an offer by the bank (under the control of the resolution authority) to convert one or more classes of non-equity investor capital into common equity – a process very similar to a debt for equity conversion that might be employed in a bankruptcy proceeding.

Finally, there is the question of how the bank should operate post-conversion. The conversion will bring about a change in the ownership of the bank, and the new owners should be able to assume control rights over the bank, if the bank post conversion has adequate resources (including adequate capital and liquidity). These control rights include the right (subject to regulatory approval) to nominate a new Board of Directors and new management. The resolution authority should work with the supervisor to accomplish this handover to the new owners as quickly as possible.

Conclusion: the route to better resolution

The above discussion underlines the importance of implementing a special resolution regime for banks. But to assure that banks are in fact resolvable, two additional steps are required:

1. **Create a class of instruments subject to bail-in.** The recent Basel decision[14] points in this direction. It mandates that non-core Tier 1 capital and Tier 2 capital be written down or converted into equity at the point at which the bank becomes non-viable in private markets. This write-down or conversion feature can be imposed by statute and/or embedded in contracts.[15]
2. **Require banks to have a minimum amount of back-up capital outstanding.** This should be enough to completely recapitalise the bank, in the event that intervention is required. This suggests that banks should hold a minimum amount of back-up capital equal to 7% of risk weighted assets. This would allow the bank to fully recapitalise itself and meet the minimum requirement (4.5% of risk weighted assets) as well as the capital conservation buffer (2.5% of risk weighted assets).[16]

Provided the special resolution regime grants the resolution authority the power to bail-in the back-up capital at the point of non-viability (i.e. at the point at which the bank fails to meet threshold conditions but prior to a declaration of formal insolvency or liquidation of the bank), these two steps should assure that a bank (even a SIFI) would be resolvable. Investors in back-up capital would bear loss, not taxpayers, and the bail-in would give the bank at a minimum a stay of execution and possibly a way toward recovery. This will minimise, if not totally eliminate, the social costs that the failure of bank could cause.

---

14 BCBS 2011.

15 Consideration might also be given to allowing senior debt to be subject to bail-in. However, this would involve creating a clear distinction between senior debt subject to bail-in and other senior obligations. This would be accomplished most effectively (i) by making such debt explicitly subordinate to deposits (but still senior to subordinated debt/Tier 2 capital) and (ii) doing so by means of contract so that investors in senior debt subject to bail-in knew in advance that they would be subject to such a risk as well as the terms and conditions of nay write down or conversion.

16 If senior debt is subject to bail in, then consideration should be given toward allowing such debt to count toward the minimum requirement for back-up capital.

References

Acharya, Viral V., Barry Adler, Matthew Richardson and Nouriel Roubini 2010 “Resolution Authority,” in Viral V. Acharya, Thomas F. Cooley, Matthew P. Richardson and Ingo Walter, eds., Regulating Wall Street: The Dodd Frank Act and the New Architecture of Global Finance, (Hoboken, NJ: John Wiley & Sons): 213–240.

Basel Committee on Banking Supervision (BCBS) 2010a. ‘Basel III: A global regulatory framework for more resilient banks and banking systems’ available at http://www.bis.org/publ/bcbs189.pdf.

Basel Committee on Banking Supervision (BCBS) 2010b. ‘Basel III: International framework for liquidity risk measurement, standards and monitoring’ available at http://www.bis.org/publ/bcbs188.pdf.

Basel Committee on Banking Supervision (BCBS) 2011. ‘Basel Committee issues final elements of the reforms to raise the quality of regulatory capital’ available at http://www.bis.org/press/p110113.pdf.

Duffie, Darrell 2010. How Big Banks Fail and What to Do about It (Princeton: Princeton University Press).

Financial Stability Board (FSB) 2010. ‘Reducing the moral hazard posed by systemically important financial institutions: FSB Recommendations and Time Lines’ available at http://www.financialstabilityboard.org/publications/r_101111a.pdf.

Huertas, Thomas F. 2010a. Crisis: Cause, Containment and Cure (London: Palgrave Macmillan).

Huertas, Thomas F. 2010b. “Living Wills: How Can the Concept be Implemented?” Remarks before the Conference Cross-Border Issues in Resolving Systemically Important Financial Institutions, Wharton School of Management, University of Pennsylvania, Philadelphia, 12 February. available at http://www.fsa.gov.uk/pages/Library/Communication/Speeches/2010/0212_th.shtml.

Huertas, Thomas F. 2011. ‘Barriers to Resolution’ available from author upon request.

Roe, Mark J. 2010. “The Derivatives Market’s Payment Priorities as Financial Crisis Accelerator,” Stanford Law Review, forthcoming. Available at http://ssrn.com/abstract=1567075.

Auslöser für ein Sonderinsolvenzverfahren für Banken

Triggers for Bank Resolution

Auslöser für ein Sonderinsolvenzverfahren für Banken

Klaus Pannen

Gliederung

1. Einleitung
2. Die Aufsichtsmaßnahmen nach §§ 45 ff. KWG
   2.1 Bisherige Rechtslage
      2.1.1 § 45 KWG
      2.1.2 § 46 KWG
      2.1.3 Maßnahmen nach § 46 a KWG – Moratorium
   2.2 Änderungen durch das Restrukturierungsgesetz
      2.2.1 Änderung des § 45 KWG
      2.2.2 § 45 c KWG: Bestellung eines Sonderbeauftragten
      2.2.3 Änderung der §§ 46 und 46 a KWG
      2.2.4 Änderung des § 46 b KWG
3. Sanierungs- und Reorganisationsverfahren
   3.1 Sanierungsverfahren
   3.2 Reorganisationsverfahren
4. Die Ausgliederung nach §§ 48 a ff. KWG
   4.1 Grundsatz
   4.2 Voraussetzungen
5. Fazit

1. Einleitung

Im Rahmen der Finanzkrise hat die Aufarbeitung der möglichen Auslöser eines Sonderinsolvenzverfahrens für Banken an Bedeutung gewonnen. Dabei fällt es nicht leicht, rein juristisch auf die möglichen Auslöser einer Bankeninsolvenz einzugehen, da in der Praxis die konkreten Auslöser einer Bankeninsolvenz betriebs- bzw. volkswirtschaftlicher Natur sind. So wurde etwa der Zusammenbruch der Herstatt Bank KGaA im Jahre 1974 im Wesentlichen durch den Verfall des Dollarkurses verursacht.[1] Die nachfolgenden Ausführungen konzentrieren sich deshalb auf die juristischen Maßnahmen, die unmittelbar vor Eröffnung eines Insolvenzverfahrens ergriffen werden können, und die nicht zum gängigen wirtschaftlichen Instrumentarium gehören.

Aufgrund der aktuellen Finanzkrise wurde eine Neuregelung des Bankkrisenrechts in Betracht gezogen. Der erste Entwurf eines Gesetzes zur Ergänzung des Kreditwesengesetzes wurde durch das Bundeswirtschaftsministerium Anfang August 2009 vorgelegt.

---

1 Hierzu z. B. *Zimmermann* BKR 2005, 208.

Ihm folgte am 26. 8. 2009 ein gemeinsamer Diskussionsentwurf für ein Kreditinstitute-Reorganisationsgesetz des Bundesjustizministeriums und des Bundesministeriums der Finanzen.[2] Am 25. 8. 2010 hat das Bundeskabinett den Entwurf eines Gesetzes zur Restrukturierung und geordneten Abwicklung von Kreditinstituten, zur Errichtung eines Restrukturierungsfonds für Kreditinstitute und zur Verlängerung der Verjährungsfrist der aktienrechtlichen Organhaftung (kurz: Restrukturierungsgesetz) beschlossen.[3] Das Restrukturierungsgesetz vom 9. 12. 2010[4] ist im Wesentlichen am 1. 1. 2011[5] in Kraft getreten.[6] Bei dem Restrukturierungsgesetz handelt es sich um ein sogenanntes Artikelgesetz, das aus siebzehn Artikeln besteht. Von besonderer Bedeutung sind insbesondere folgende drei Artikel:

- Artikel 1: Gesetz zur Reorganisation von Kreditinstituten (Kreditinstitute-Reorganisationsgesetz – KredReorgG);
- Artikel 2: Änderung des Kreditwesengesetzes;
- Artikel 3: Gesetz zur Errichtung eines Restrukturierungsfonds für Kreditinstitute (Restrukturierungsfondsgesetz- RStruktFG).

Die übrigen Artikel enthalten unter Anderem Änderungen des FMStFG, des FMStBG, des AktG, des EStG, des GKG, des PfandBG sowie des EAEG.

Der Gesetzgeber geht davon aus, dass die bisherigen Bestimmungen des KWG und der InsO den Anforderungen der derzeitigen Krisensituation im Finanzsektor nicht gerecht werden.[7] Die Eröffnung eines Insolvenzverfahrens über das Vermögen eines Kreditinstitutes geht regelmäßig mit einem Vertrauensverlust der Kunden einher. Schon die Anordnung eines Moratoriums kann als Vorbereitungsmaßnahme für die Abwicklung des Institutes betrachtet werden. So zeigt die Erfahrung vieler Jahre, dass die Sanierungen von Bankhäusern im Rahmen eines Moratoriums in der Regel nicht gelungen sind.[8] Das Finanzmarktstabilisierungsgesetz ermöglichte zwar eine finanzielle Stärkung von Unternehmen des Finanzsektors,[9] doch handelte es sich hierbei nur um eine vorübergehende Lösung.[10]

---

2 http://www.bmj.bund.de/files/-/3891/DiskE%20KredReorgG.pdf.

3 http://www.bundesfinanzministerium.de/nn_82/DE/BMF__Startseite/Aktuelles/Aktuelle__Gesetze/Gesetzentwuerfe__Arbeitsfassungen/20100825-Gesetzentwurf-Restrukturierungsgesetz__anl,templateId=raw,property=publicationFile.pdf.

4 BGBl. I 2010, S. 1900.

5 Art. 3 und 4 sind am 31. 12. 2010 und Art. 2 Nr. 16a sowie Art. 5 bis 7 am Tag nach der Verkündung in Kraft getreten.

6 Wichtige Etappen des Gesetzgebungsverfahrens sind: Gesetzentwurf der Bundesregierung vom 27. 9. 2010, BT-Drucks. 17/3024, Beschlussempfehlung des Finanzausschusses vom 26. 10. 2010, BT-Drucks. 17/3407, Bericht des Finanzausschusses vom 28. 10. 2010, BT-Drucks. 17/3547, Gesetzesbeschluss vom 5. 11. 2010, BR-Drucks. 681/10.

7 Zum bisherigen Bankeninsolvenzrecht siehe *Pannen* Krise und Insolvenz bei Kreditinstituten, 3. Aufl.; Grieser/Heemann-*Pannen* Bankaufsichtsrecht, S. 73 ff.; *Pannen* ZInsO 2009, S. 596 ff. (Sonderheft für Manfred Obermüller); *Obermüller/Obermüller* Maßnahmen der Bankaufsicht bei Vorliegen einer Bankkrise, in: Kölner Schrift zur InsO, 3. Aufl. (2009).

8 Siehe *Pannen* Krise und Insolvenz bei Kreditinstituten, Einleitung.

9 Hierzu *Jaletzke/Veranneman* (Hrsg.) FMStG Kommentar (2009); *Becker/Mock* FMStG Kommentar (2009).

10 Vgl. Gesetzentwurf der Bundesregierung, BT-Drucks. 17/3024, S. 65. Die Stabilisierungsmaßnahmen konnten nur bis zum 31. 1. 2010 ergriffen werden.

Um diese Regelungslücke zu füllen, ist im Restrukturierungsgesetz ein neues zweistufiges Verfahren vorgesehen, das aus einem Sanierungs- und einem Reorganisationsverfahren besteht. Das Sanierungs- bzw. Reorganisationsverfahren dient gemäß § 1 Abs. 1 KredReorgG der Stabilisierung des Finanzmarktes durch die Restrukturierung von Kreditinstituten. Parallel hierzu sind sowohl ein administratives Verfahren zur Krisenbewältigung (sog. Ausgliederung) als auch ein Restrukturierungsfonds für Kreditinstitute vorgesehen, die vor dem Hintergrund der derzeitigen Planungen der EU-Kommission zum EU-Rahmenwerk für das grenzüberschreitende Krisenmanagement zu sehen sind.[11] Der Restrukturierungsfonds soll durch die sog. „Bankenabgabe" finanziert werden.

Mit Inkrafttreten des Restrukturierungsgesetzes gibt es drei verschiedene Wege des Bankkrisenrechts:

- Erstens bleiben nach wie vor, allerdings mit zahlreichen Modifizierungen, die §§ 45 ff. KWG für alle Kreditinstitute anwendbar. Diese stellen den „normalen" Weg zur Eröffnung eines Bankinsolvenzverfahrens dar.
- Zweitens kann ein Sanierungs- bzw. Reorganisationsverfahren zum Zwecke der Restrukturierung eines Kreditinstitutes eingeleitet werden.
- Drittens kann die BaFin die Ausgliederung eines systemrelevanten Kreditinstitutes auf eine „Brückenbank" anordnen.

2. Die Aufsichtsmaßnahmen nach §§ 45 ff. KWG

2.1 Bisherige Rechtslage

2.1.1 § 45 KWG

§ 45 KWG stellt die erste Stufe des Sanierungssystems für Banken dar. Bei den in § 45 KWG normierten Maßnahmen handelt es sich um rein prophylaktische Maßnahmen, die schon dann getroffen werden können, wenn noch keine konkrete Gefahr vorliegt.[12] Das Anliegen besteht darin, eine eventuelle Gefährdung der Erfüllung der Verpflichtungen eines Instituts zu vermeiden, um die Wiederherstellung der Solvabilität und Liquidität des angeschlagenen Kreditinstitutes zu erreichen. Die BaFin darf allerdings die Maßnahmen nach § 45 KWG erst dann ergreifen, wenn eine Frist zur Beseitigung des jeweiligen Mangels erfolglos verstrichen ist.[13] In der Praxis stellt die Fristsetzung eine große Bedrohung bzw. Androhung für das jeweilige Insitut dar, das sich in aller

11 Die EU-Kommission plant die Schaffung von Bankenrettungsfonds in jedem Mitgliedstaat, die durch eine Bankenabgabe finanziert werden sollen. Siehe hierzu die Kommunikation der EU-Kommission zum Bankenrettungsfonds vom 26. 5. 2010, http://ec.europa.eu/internal_market/bank/docs/crisis-management/funds/com2010_254_de.pdf.

12 *Samm* in: Beck/Samm/Kokemoor, § 45 KWG Rn. 5; *Pannen* Krise und Insolvenz bei Kreditinstituten, Kap. 1 Rn. 6.

13 *Fischer* in: Schimansky/Bunte/Lwowski, Bankrecht-Handbuch, § 133 Rn. 3; *Reischauer/Kleinhans* § 45 KWG Anm. 1; *Samm* in: Beck/Samm/Kokemoor, § 45 KWG Rn. 64.

Regel dann bemühen wird, den gerügten Mangel zu beheben.[14] Sollte jedoch Gefahr im Verzug bestehen, könnte die Erforderlichkeit einer Fristsetzung ein schnelles Eingreifen der BaFin verhindern. Aus diesem Grund sieht § 45 Abs. 4 Satz 2 KWG in der durch das Gesetz zur Stärkung der Finanzmarktaufsicht (kurz: FMVAStärkG) vom 29. 7. 2009[15] eingeführten Fassung nunmehr vor, dass – soweit dies zur Verhinderung einer kurzfristig zu erwartenden Verschlechterung der Eigenmittelausstattung oder der Liquidität des Instituts erforderlich ist, die Maßnahmen nach § 45 KWG auch ohne vorherige Fristsetzung zulässig sind.[16]

Voraussetzung für die Anordnung von Maßnahmen gemäß § 45 KWG ist entweder:

1. dass das Institut nicht über eine angemessene Eigenmittel verfügt (§ 10 Abs. 1 KWG)

oder

2. dass es nicht über hinreichende Liquidität verfügt (§ 11 Abs. 1 KWG).

Die Eigenmittelausstattung ist in § 10 KWG normiert. Im Interesse der Gläubiger müssen hiernach Kreditinstitute angemessene Eigenmittel vorhalten, um so ihre Verpflichtungen gegenüber Gläubigern jederzeit erfüllen zu können.[17] Die Liquidität eines Kreditinstitutes wird in § 11 KWG geregelt. Nach dem subjektbezogenen Liquiditätsbegriff setzt sie sich aus der Fähigkeit, sämtliche fälligen Zahlungsverpflichtungen vollständig und termingerecht erfüllen zu können, und der erforderlichen Zahlungsbereitschaft zusammen.[18] Detaillierte Anordnungen sind seit dem 1. 1. 2007 in der Liquiditätsverordnung (LiqV) geregelt, die überwiegend quantitative Vorgaben enthält.[19]

Um eine präventive Finanzaufsicht der BaFin zu erlauben, wurde durch das FMVAStärkG in § 45 Abs. 1 KWG die Möglichkeit eingefügt, bereits bei einer nur drohenden Verschlechterung der Lage des Institutes Aufsichtsmaßnahmen zu ergreifen. Dies hat zur Folge, dass die Anforderungen der §§ 10 und 11 KWG nur noch eine indikative Wirkung haben.[20] Das bloße Einhalten dieser Kennziffern reicht für sich nicht mehr aus. Wenn eine schnelle Verschlechterung der Vermögenssituation droht, beispielsweise durch absehbare erforderliche Abschreibungen oder Mittelabflüsse, kann bereits das Unterschreiten eines höheren Puffers oberhalb der mindestens einzuhaltenden Kennziffern ein Einschreiten der BaFin erforderlich machen.[21]

2.1.2 § 46 KWG

Die zweite Stufe der Maßnahmen im Vorfeld des Insolvenzverfahrens ist in § 46 KWG vorgesehen. Während § 45 KWG schon dann eingreifen kann, wenn noch keine konkre-

---

14 *Pannen* Krise und Insolvenz bei Kreditinstituten, Kap. 1 Rn. 8.

15 BGBl. I, S. 2305.

16 Siehe hierzu *Pannen* Die Erweiterung der Finanzaufsichtsbefugnisse der BaFin durch das FMVAStärkG, in: Berger/Kayser/Pannen (Hrsg.), FS Ganter (2010).

17 *Reischauer/Kleinhans* § 10 KWG Anm. 11.

18 *Reischauer/Kleinhans* § 11 KWG Anm. 2.

19 *Reischauer/Kleinhans* § 11 KWG Anm. 5.

20 *Pannen* Die Erweiterung der Finanzaufsichtsbefugnisse der BaFin durch das FMVAStärkG, in Berger/Kayser/Pannen (Hrsg.), FS Ganter, S. 26.

21 Gesetzentwurf der Bundesregierung, BT-Drucks. 16/12783, S. 17.

te Gefahr für die Gläubiger der Bank besteht, setzt § 46 KWG eine eingetretene Gefährdung der Gläubigerinteressen voraus. Das Ergreifen von Maßnahmen nach § 45 KWG ist keine Voraussetzung für die Anwendung des § 46 KWG.[22]

Die BaFin kann die Maßnahmen nach § 46 KWG anordnen, wenn eine „konkrete Gefahr"[23] für die Sicherheit der dem Kreditinstitut anvertrauten Vermögenswerte oder für die Erfüllung sonstiger Verpflichtungen gegenüber den Gläubigern besteht. § 46 KWG präzisiert nicht, wann eine Gefahr für die Erfüllung der Verpflichtungen einer Bank besteht. Die Formulierung entspricht jedoch weitgehend derjenigen des § 35 Abs. 2 Nr. 4 KWG, wonach eine solche Gefahr bei einem Verlust in Höhe der Hälfte des maßgebenden, haftenden Eigenkapitals vorliegt oder bei einem Verlust in Höhe von jeweils mehr als 10% des maßgebenden, haftenden Eigenkapitals in mindestens drei aufeinanderfolgenden Geschäftsjahren. Diese Grundsätze können auch im Rahmen des § 46 KWG herangezogen werden.[24] Sind die Voraussetzungen des § 35 Abs. 2 Nr. 4 KWG erfüllt, so stellt dies eine widerlegbare Vermutung dar, dass die Voraussetzungen des § 46 Abs. 1 Satz 1 1. Alt KWG erfüllt sind.[25]

Eine weitere Fallgruppe für die konkrete Gefahr gemäß § 46 KWG liegt dann vor, wenn Tatsachen vorhanden sind, die nach der Lebenserfahrung die Besorgnis erheblicher wirtschaftlicher Schwierigkeiten begründen.[26] Dies ist insbesondere bei Liquiditätsschwierigkeiten der Fall. Die Zahlungsunfähigkeit sowie die drohende Zahlungsunfähigkeit der Bank rechtfertigen auch das Ergreifen von Maßnahmen gemäß § 46 KWG.

Die zweite Konstellation, in der Maßnahmen nach § 46 KWG ergriffen werden können, ist der Verdacht, dass eine wirksame Aufsicht über die Bank nicht möglich ist. Anders als bei der ersten Alternative reicht hier das Vorhandensein einer abstrakten Gefahr aus.[27] In diesem Fall sind die Maßnahmen gerechtfertigt, weil die BaFin ihre Kontrolle

---

22 *Pannen* Krise und Insolvenz bei Kreditinstituten, Kap. 1 Rn. 29.

23 So schon zum ursprünglichen § 45 KWG die Begründung des Regierungsentwurfs zum Kreditwesengesetz (BT-Drucks. 3/1114), Abschn. B. zu § 45, abgedruckt in: *Reischauer/Kleinhans* Kza. 575 (dort S. 45); KG Berlin, Beschluss vom 26. 10. 1984 – AR (B) 109/84 – 5 Ws (B) 251/84 – 330 OWi 404/83 – abgedruckt in: *Beckmann/Bauer* Nr. 9 zu § 46; *Schork* § 46 Rn. 1; *Reischauer/Kleinhans* § 46 KWG Anm. 1, 2; *Samm* in: Beck/Samm/Kokemoor, § 46 KWG Rn. 24; *Lindemann* in: Boos/Fischer/Schulte-Mattler, § 46 Rn. 2; *Nirk* KWG S. 51 f.; für „einfache Gefahr" nur VG Berlin, Beschluss vom 13. 10. 1995, Az. VG 25 A 234.94 – nicht veröffentlicht; dagegen aber die Rechtsmittelentscheidung des OVG Berlin vom 22. 5. 1995, Az. OVG 1 S 27.95 – nicht veröffentlicht.

24 OVG Nordrhein-Westfalen, WM 2002, 847 und Vorinstanz VG Köln, WM 2001, 1612, sowie dazu Anm. *Zietsch/Sterzenbach* WuB I L 1. § 46a KWG 1.01, 1281, 1283; *Neeff* Einlagensicherung S. 134; *Schork* § 46 Rn. 3; *Bähre/Schneider* § 46 Anm. 2; *Szagunn/Haug/Ergenzinger* § 46 Rn. 4; *Samm* in: Beck/Samm/Kokemoor (Hrsg.), § 46 KWG Rn. 35 f.; *Lindemann* in: Boos/Fischer/Schulte-Mattler (Hrsg.), § 46 Rn. 9; *Fischer* in: Schimansky/Bunte/Lwowski (Hrsg.), Bankrecht-Handbuch, § 133 Rn. 9.

25 VG Köln, WM 2001, 1612, 1613; *Szagunn/Haug/Ergenzinger* § 46 Rn. 4; *Pannen* Krise und Insolvenz bei Kreditinstituten, Kap. 1 Rn. 35 f.

26 *Bähre/Schneider* § 46 Anm. 2; *Samm* in: Beck/Samm/Kokemoor (Hrsg.), § 46 KWG Rn. 32; *Lindemann* in: Boos/Fischer/Schulte-Mattler (Hrsg.), § 46 Rn. 8.

27 Vgl. Begründung des Regierungsentwurfs zum 6. Änderungsgesetz zum KWG (BT-Drucks. 13/7142), Abschn. B. I. zu Nr. 66 (§ 46), abgedruckt in *Reischauer/Kleinhans* Kza. 599 (dort S. 78): Die BaFin kann „bereits im Vorfeld eingreifen, bevor [sie] eine konkrete Gefahr […] feststellt." So auch *Samm* in: Beck/Samm/Kokemoor (Hrsg.), § 46 KWG Rn. 39.

nicht mehr ausüben kann. Alle aufsichtsrechtlichen Befugnisse der BaFin würden ins Leere laufen, so dass eine erfolgreiche Sanierung des Institutes schon von vornherein ausgeschlossen ist.[28]

§ 46 Abs. 1 KWG verweist ferner auf § 33 Abs. 3 KWG. Hiernach kann die BaFin insbesondere dann Maßnahmen anordnen,

- wenn das Institut in ein Beteiligungsgeflecht eingebunden ist, das durch seine Struktur oder mangelhafte wirtschaftliche Transparenz eine wirksame Aufsicht beeinträchtigt,
- wenn sich eine Aufsichtsbeeinträchtigung aus den für die an einem solchen Unternehmensverbund beteiligten Personen oder Unternehmen geltenden Rechts- oder Verwaltungsvorschriften eines Drittstaates ergibt (§ 33 Abs. 3 Satz 2 Nr. 2 KWG) und
- wenn es sich um ein Tochterunternehmen eines ausländischen Instituts handelt, welches im Staat seines Sitzes nicht wirksam beaufsichtigt wird oder dessen Aufsichtsstelle nicht zu einer befriedigenden Zusammenarbeit mit der Bundesanstalt bereit ist (§ 33 Abs. 3 Satz 2 Nr. 3 KWG).

2.1.3 Maßnahmen nach § 46a KWG – Moratorium

Nach den beiden Stufen in §§ 45 und 46 KWG stellte § 46a KWG bis zum RestrukturierungsG gleichsam die nächste und zugleich letzte Stufe des Sanierungsinstrumentariums, das der BaFin zur Verfügung steht, dar. Bei § 46a KWG handelte es sich um ein Maßnahmenbündel, das allgemein in der Praxis als Moratorium bezeichnet wurde, obwohl diese Bezeichnung nicht im Gesetz zu finden war. Nach Verhängung des Moratoriums gelang es nur in Ausnahmefällen, das Insolvenzverfahren abzuwenden. Die Anordnung hatte daher vor allem die Funktion, den Marktaustritt des Kreditinstituts einzuleiten und dabei die Interessen der Gläubiger bis zur Verfahrenseröffnung zu sichern.[29] Für die Voraussetzungen verwies § 46a KWG weitgehend auf die Voraussetzungen des § 46 Abs. 1 Satz 1 KWG, die bereits oben dargestellt wurden.

Nach dem Wortlaut des § 46a KWG waren ferner Maßnahmen gemäß § 46a KWG „zur Vermeidung des Insolvenzverfahrens“ zu treffen. Die Natur dieses Passus war im Schrifttum umstritten. Es stellte sich insbesondere die Frage, ob es sich um ein Tatbestandsmerkmal oder um eine Ermessensbeschränkung handelte. Nach überwiegender Auffassung handelte es sich hierbei um ein Tatbestandsmerkmal,[30] was zur Folge hatte, dass neben den Voraussetzungen des § 46 Abs. 1 Satz 1 KWG auch eine „Insolvenznä-

28 *Pannen* Krise und Insolvenz bei Kreditinstituten, Kap. 1 Rn. 40.

29 So auch *Uhlenbruck* InsO § 14 Rn. 110.

30 BGH ZIP 1986, 1537, 1538 f.; so auch bereits der Bericht und Antrag des Finanzausschusses über den Regierungsentwurf eines 2. Änderungsgesetzes zum KWG (BT-Drucks. 7/4631), Abschn. A. II. Nr. 17a § 46a, abgedruckt in *Reischauer/Kleinhans* Kza. 583 (dort S. 13); ferner *Schork* § 46a Rn. 3; *Reischauer/Kleinhans* § 46a KWG Anm. 3; *Szagunn/Haug/Ergenzinger* § 46a Rn. 2; *Kokemoor* in: Beck/Samm/Kokemoor (Hrsg.), § 46a KWG Rn. 14; *Waschbusch* Bankenaufsicht S. 539; *Zietsch* WM 1997, 954; offengelassen in VG Köln, WM 2001, 1612, 1616.

he" oder „Insolvenzgefahr" vorliegen muss.[31] Richtigerweise stellte die Insolvenzgefahr zugleich ein Tatbestandsmerkmal und eine Ermessensbeschränkung dar.[32]

Problematisch war ferner die Auslegung des Begriffs der Insolvenzgefahr, da dieser nicht legal definiert war. Unumstritten lag eine Insolvenzgefahr dann dar, wenn ein Insolvenzgrund vorlag, das heißt bei Zahlungsunfähigkeit oder Überschuldung.

Eine Insolvenzgefahr lag auch dann vor, wenn bei einem Unterlassen des Einschreitens ein Insolvenzverfahren droht,[33] das heißt bei drohender Überschuldung oder drohender Zahlungsunfähigkeit.[34] Zur Konkretisierung der im Gesetz nicht geregelten Überschuldung wurde die Regelung des § 35 KWG herangezogen. Danach besteht eine Gefahr für die Erfüllung der Verpflichtungen des Institutes gegenüber seinen Gläubigern, wenn mehr als die Hälfte seines haftenden Eigenkapitals aufgezehrt ist. Als zweite Alternative nennt § 35 Abs. 2 Nr. 4b KWG einen Verlust in Höhe von jeweils mehr als 10% des maßgebenden, haftenden Eigenkapitals in mindestens drei aufeinander folgenden Geschäftsjahren. Eine solche Entwicklung lässt die Überschuldung in naher Zukunft befürchten. Das Vorliegen dieser Eröffnungsgründe verpflichtete die BaFin nicht, sofort einen Insolvenzantrag zu stellen. Vielmehr lag die Antragstellung in ihrem Ermessen.[35]

2.2 Änderungen durch das Restrukturierungsgesetz

Durch das Restrukturierungsgesetz haben die §§ 45 ff. KWG erhebliche Änderungen erfahren.

2.2.1 Änderung des § 45 KWG

§ 45 KWG wurde sowohl hinsichtlich der Voraussetzungen als auch der möglichen Maßnahmen modifiziert. Durch die Änderungen sollte der präventive Charakter dieser Norm betont werden.[36] Im Unterschied zu der bisherigen Fassung ist die drohende Verschlechterung der Hauptanwendungsfall des § 45 KWG geworden. So kann die BaFin nunmehr nach § 45 Abs. 1 Satz 1 KWG Maßnahmen zur Verbesserung der Eigenmittelausstattung und Liquidität ergreifen, wenn die Vermögens-, Finanz- oder

---

31 So ausdrücklich der BGH ZIP 1986, 1537, 1538 f.: „Die [...] angeordneten Maßnahmen durften gem. §§ 46, 46a KWG nur erlassen werden, wenn Konkursgefahr und Gefahr für die Erfüllung der Verpflichtungen eines Kreditinstituts gegenüber seinen Gläubigern [...] bestand."

32 *Pannen* Krise und Insolvenz bei Kreditinstituten, Kap. 1 Rn. 97.

33 Bericht und Antrag des Finanzausschusses über den Regierungsentwurf eines 2. Änderungsgesetzes zum KWG (BT-Drucks. 7/4631), Abschn. A. II. Nr. 17a § 46a, abgedruckt in *Reischauer/Kleinhans* Kza. 583 (dort S. 13); *Bähre/Schneider* §§ 46a–c Anm. 2; *Reischauer/Kleinhans* § 46a KWG Anm. 3; *Szagunn/Haug/Ergenzinger* § 46a Rn. 2.

34 *Pannen* Krise und Insolvenz bei Kreditinstituten, Kap. 1 Rn. 98.

35 OVG Berlin, Beschluss vom 25. 8. 1980 – OVG I S 100/80 – abgedruckt in *Beckmann/Bauer* Nr. 2 zu § 46b; VG Berlin, WM 1996, 295, dazu *Gramlich* VG Berlin EWiR § 46b KWG 1/96, 133, 134; VG Köln WM 2001, 1612, 1617; *Szagunn/Haug/Ergenzinger* § 46b Rn. 4; *Lindemann* in: Boos/Fischer/Schulte-Mattler (Hrsg.), § 46b Rn. 12; *Kokemoor* in: Beck/Samm/Kokemoor (Hrsg.), § 46b KWG Rn. 17; *Uhlenbruck* InsO § 14 Rn. 109.

36 Gesetzentwurf der Bundesregierung, BT- Drucks. 17/3024, S. 59.

Ertragsentwicklung eines Instituts die Annahme rechtfertigt, dass es die Anforderungen des § 10 oder des § 11 KWG nicht dauerhaft erfüllen können wird. Hierdurch soll ein möglichst frühzeitiges Einschreiten der BaFin zur Verhinderung einer finanziellen Schieflage der Bank ermöglicht werden.[37]

Um die Feststellung dieser Annahme zu vereinfachen, enthält § 45 Abs. 1 Satz 2 KWG eine Vermutung, wonach die Annahme der Nichterfüllung regelmäßig gerechtfertigt ist, wenn sich

1. die Gesamtkennziffer über das prozentuale Verhältnis der anrechenbaren Eigenmittel und der mit 12,5 multiplizierten Summe aus dem Gesamtanrechnungsbetrag für Adressrisiken, dem Anrechnungsbetrag für das operationelle Risiko und der Summe der Anrechnungsbeträge für Marktrisikopositionen einschließlich der Optionsgeschäfte nach der Solvabilitätsverordnung (SolvV) von einem Meldestichtag zum nächsten um mindestens 10 Prozent oder die nach der Liquiditätsverordnung (LiqV) zu ermittelnde Liquiditätskennziffer von einem Meldestichtag zum nächsten um mindestens 25 Prozent verringert hat und aufgrund dieser Entwicklung mit einem Unterschreiten der Mindestanforderungen innerhalb der nächsten zwölf Monate zu rechnen ist oder

2. die Gesamtkennziffer über das prozentuale Verhältnis der anrechenbaren Eigenmittel und der mit 12,5 multiplizierten Summe aus dem Gesamtanrechnungsbetrag für Adressrisiken, dem Anrechnungsbetrag für das operationelle Risiko und der Summe der Anrechnungsbeträge für Marktrisikopositionen einschließlich der Optionsgeschäfte nach der SolvV an mindestens drei aufeinander folgenden Meldestichtagen um jeweils mehr als 3 Prozent oder die nach der LiqV zu ermittelnde Liquiditätskennziffer an mindestens drei aufeinander folgenden Meldestichtagen um jeweils mehr als 10 Prozent verringert hat und aufgrund dieser Entwicklung mit einem Unterschreiten der Mindestanforderungen innerhalb der nächsten 18 Monate zu rechnen ist

und keine Tatsachen offensichtlich sind, die die Annahme rechtfertigen, dass die Mindestanforderungen mit überwiegender Wahrscheinlichkeit nicht unterschritten werden. Ob und wann diese Annahme gerechtfertigt ist, bleibt jedoch weiterhin eine Entscheidung, die die Bundesanstalt im Einzelfall unter Berücksichtigung der Nachhaltigkeit der Entwicklung, der konkreten Eigenmittelausstattung bzw. der Liquiditätslage des Instituts sowie einer Gesamtwürdigung der Umstände des Instituts zu treffen hat.[38]

Zusätzlich zu den bisherigen Befugnissen der BaFin wird ferner in § 45 Abs. Nr. 7 KWG die Möglichkeit vorgesehen, die Vorlage eines Restrukturierungsplans zu verlangen. In diesem Plan muss das Institut darlegen, wie und in welchem Zeitraum seine Eigenmittelausstattung oder Liquidität nachhaltig wiederhergestellt werden soll. Die BaFin kann zudem anordnen, dass das Institut ihr sowie der Deutschen Bundesbank regelmäßig über den Fortschritt dieser Maßnahmen zu berichten hat.[39]

---

37 Gesetzentwurf der Bundesregierung, BT- Drucks. 17/3024, S. 59.
38 Gesetzentwurf der Bundesregierung, BT- Drucks. 17/3024, S. 59.
39 Gesetzentwurf der Bundesregierung, BT- Drucks. 17/3024, S. 59.

2.2.2 § 45 c KWG: Bestellung eines Sonderbeauftragten

Durch den neuen § 45 c KWG sollte die Befugnis der BaFin, einen Sonderbeauftragten einzusetzen, als eigenständiges Aufsichtsinstrument mit überwiegend präventivem Charakter etabliert werden.[40] Die bisherige knappe Regelung in § 36 Abs. 1 a KWG wird somit durch eine umfassende Norm ersetzt, die sowohl die vom Sonderbeauftragten zu erfüllenden Voraussetzungen als auch die übertragbaren Befugnisse sowie die Haftung und die Vergütung des Sonderbeauftragten detailliert regelt.

Nach § 45 c Abs. 1 KWG kann die BaFin einen Sonderbeauftragten bestellen, diesen mit der Wahrnehmung von Aufgaben bei einem Institut betrauen und ihm die hierfür erforderlichen Befugnisse übertragen. Der Sonderbeauftragte muss unabhängig,[41] zuverlässig und zur ordnungsgemäßen Wahrnehmung der Aufgaben geeignet sein. Er soll nicht notwendigerweise die Aufgaben und Befugnisse eines Organs oder Organmitglieds insgesamt übernehmen, sondern auch für spezielle, eingegrenzte Aufgaben, wie etwa die Verbesserung der mangelhaften Geschäftsorganisation in einem bestimmten Geschäftsbereich, eingesetzt werden.

In § 45 c Abs. 2 KWG werden beispielhaft Befugnisse aufgelistet, die die BaFin dem Sonderbeauftragen übertragen kann, wie insbesondere:

1. die Aufgaben und Befugnisse eines oder mehrerer Geschäftsleiter wahrzunehmen, wenn Tatsachen vorliegen, aus denen sich ergibt, dass der oder die Geschäftsleiter des Instituts nicht zuverlässig sind oder nicht die zur Leitung des Instituts erforderliche fachliche Eignung haben;

2. die Aufgaben und Befugnisse eines oder mehrerer Geschäftsleiter wahrzunehmen, wenn das Institut nicht mehr über die erforderliche Anzahl von Geschäftsleitern verfügt, insbesondere weil die Bundesanstalt die Abberufung eines Geschäftsleiters verlangt oder ihm die Ausübung seiner Tätigkeit untersagt hat;

3. die Aufgaben und Befugnisse von Organen des Instituts insgesamt oder teilweise wahrzunehmen, wenn die Voraussetzungen des § 36 Absatz 3 Satz 3 oder Satz 4 vorliegen;

4. die Aufgaben und Befugnisse von Organen des Instituts insgesamt oder teilweise wahrzunehmen, wenn die Aufsicht über das Institut aufgrund von Tatsachen im Sinne des § 33 Absatz 3 beeinträchtigt ist;

5. geeignete Maßnahmen zur Herstellung und Sicherung einer ordnungsgemäßen Geschäftsorganisation einschließlich eines angemessenen Risikomanagements zu ergreifen, wenn das Institut nachhaltig gegen Bestimmungen dieses Gesetzes, des Gesetzes über Bausparkassen, des Depotgesetzes, des Geldwäschegesetzes, des In-

---

40 Gesetzentwurf der Bundesregierung, BT- Drucks. 17/3024, S. 60.

41 Dass der Sonderbeauftragte selbständig sein muss, wurde erst im Bericht des Finanzausschusses hinzugefügt, siehe BT-Drucks. 17/3547, S. 10. Dies bedeutet, dass der Sonderbeauftragte unter Berücksichtigung seiner sonstigen Tätigkeit und seiner professionellen Eignung und Stellung in der Lage sein muss, frei von diesen potentiellen Sonderinteressen seine Aufgaben allein an den Interessen des Unternehmens unter dem Blickwinkel der Wahrung der Folgen der Geschäftspolitik des Instituts für die Finanzmarktstabilität auszuüben.

vestmentgesetzes, des Pfandbriefgesetzes, des Zahlungsdiensteaufsichtsgesetzes oder des Wertpapierhandelsgesetzes, gegen die zur Durchführung dieser Gesetze erlassenen Verordnungen oder gegen Anordnungen der Bundesanstalt verstoßen hat;

6. zu überwachen, dass Anordnungen der Bundesanstalt gegenüber dem Institut beachtet werden;
7. einen Restrukturierungsplan für das Institut zu erstellen, wenn die Voraussetzungen des § 45 Absatz 1 Satz 3 oder Absatz 2 vorliegen, die Ausführung eines Restrukturierungsplans zu begleiten und die Befugnisse nach § 45 Absatz 2 Satz 4 und 5 wahrzunehmen;
8. Maßnahmen des Instituts zur Abwendung einer Gefahr im Sinne des § 35 Absatz 2 Nummer 4 oder der § 46 Absatz 1 Satz 1 zu überwachen, selbst Maßnahmen zur Abwendung einer Gefahr zu ergreifen oder die Einhaltung von Maßnahmen der Bundesanstalt nach § 46 zu überwachen;
9. eine Übertragungsanordnung nach § 48 a vorzubereiten;
10. Schadenersatzansprüche gegen Organmitglieder oder ehemalige Organmitglieder zu prüfen, wenn Anhaltspunkte für einen Schaden des Instituts durch eine Pflichtverletzung von Organmitgliedern vorliegen.

Im Unterschied zur bisherigen Regelung in § 36 Absatz 1 a KWG enthält somit § 45 c Abs. 2 KWG eine umfangreiche Liste mit typischen Anwendungsfällen für das Instrument des Sonderbeauftragten.[42] Diese Auflistung ist jedoch nicht abschließend, wie es sich aus der Formulierung ergibt.

Auch die Vergütung des Sonderbeauftragten wurde in § 45 c Abs. 6 KWG geregelt. Hiernach fallen die durch die Bestellung des Sonderbeauftragten entstehenden Kosten (Vergütung und Auslagen) dem betroffenen Institut zur Last. Bei der Höhe der Vergütung sollte der Umfang, die Komplexität und Schwierigkeit der übertragenen Aufgabe, die Größe und Komplexität des Instituts und die feste Vergütung, d.h. ohne ggf. vereinbarte variable Vergütungsanteile des zu ersetzenden Organs in Betracht gezogen werden.[43]

Die Haftung des Sonderbeauftragten ist in § 45 c Abs. 7 KWG geregelt. Bis zur Finanzkrise im Jahre 2008 war diese Haftung unbegrenzt, was es jedoch in der Praxis immer schwieriger machte, geeignete Sonderbeauftragte zu finden.[44] Daher wurde im Rahmen des Finanzmarktstabilisierungsgesetzes die Haftung der Sonderbeauftragten für fahrlässiges Handeln der Höhe nach beschränkt. Nach Art. 3 FMStG beschränkt sich die Ersatzpflicht bei fahrlässigem Handeln auf eine Million Euro für die Tätigkeit bei einem Institut.[45] Diese Haftungsbeschränkung wurde in § 45 c Abs. 7 KWG übernommen.[46] Handelt es sich um eine Aktiengesellschaft, deren Aktien zum Handel im regu-

42 Gesetzentwurf der Bundesregierung, BT- Drucks. 17/3024, S. 60.
43 Gesetzentwurf der Bundesregierung, BT- Drucks. 17/3024, S. 60.
44 Gesetzentwurf der Fraktionen, BT-Drucks. 16/10600, S. 20.
45 Jaletzke/Veranneman-*Horbach/Diehl* FMStG Kommentar, Art. 3 FMStG Rn. 6 f.
46 Gesetzentwurf der Bundesregierung, BT- Drucks. 17/3024, S. 60.

lierten Markt zugelassen sind, so beschränkt sich die Ersatzpflicht auf 50 Millionen Euro (statt bisher 4 Millionen Euro). Diese zweite Alternative betrifft den Fall der börsennotierten Gesellschaften nach § 3 Abs. 2 AktG.

Die Aussagen in der Gesetzesbegründung, wonach durch diese Übernahme der Regelung in § 45c Abs. 7 die im Rahmen des FMStG nur vorübergehende Regelung dauerhaft gemacht wurde,[47] ist unzutreffend. Im Rahmen des Gesetzes zur Stärkung der Finanzmarkt- und der Versicherungsaufsicht vom 29. 7. 2009 (FMVAStärkG)[48] hatte der Gesetzgeber bereits von der nur vorübergehenden Beschränkung der Haftung von Sonderbeauftragten Abstand genommen und die Änderungen des KWG dauerhaft gemacht. Zu diesem Zweck wurden die Absätze 1 und 2 von Art. 6 FMStG mit Wirkung zum 1. 1. 2009 aufgehoben, was zur Folge hatte, dass die Änderung der bisherigen Regelung des Sonderbeauftragten in § 36 Abs. 1a KWG permanent würde.[49]

2.2.3 Änderung der §§ 46 und 46a KWG

Neben dieser umfassenden Änderung des § 45 KWG sind auch die zweite und die dritte Stufe des bisherigen Bankkrisenrechts, namentlich §§ 46 und 46a KWG, tiefgreifend geändert worden. Die Regelung des Moratoriums in § 46a KWG wurde aufgehoben und – mit Veränderungen – in § 46 KWG überführt. Diese Veränderungen betreffen sowohl die Voraussetzungen des Moratoriums als auch die Ausnahmen vom Veräußerungsverbot.[50]

Regelungstechnisch wurde § 46 Abs. 1 Satz 2 Nr. 4 KWG a. F. durch § 46a Abs. 1 Satz 1 KWG a. F. ersetzt. Dies hat zur Folge, dass die Kernmaßnahmen des Moratoriums, namentlich das Veräußerungs- und Zahlungsverbot, die Schließung des Institutes sowie das Entgegennahmeverbot bereits bei Vorhandensein der Voraussetzungen von § 46 KWG angeordnet werden können. Es ist somit nicht mehr erforderlich, dass die Maßnahmen „zur Vermeidung des Insolvenzverfahrens“ ergriffen werden. Vielmehr reicht bereits eine konkrete Gefahr aus.[51] Das Moratorium stellt keine dritte Etappe in einem abgestuften Krisenabwehrsystem mehr dar, sondern lediglich eine weitere Modalität der Maßnahmen bei Gefahr, und kann somit früher angeordnet werden.

Parallel zur dieser Änderung wurden auch die Ausnahmen vom Veräußerungsverbot modifiziert. Während § 46a Abs. 1 Satz 1 Nr. 3 KWG a. F. von der Entgegennahme von Zahlungen, die nicht zur Tilgung von Schulden gegenüber dem Institut bestimmt sind, sprach, erwähnt nunmehr § 46 Abs. 1 Satz 2 Nr. 6 KWG die „Entgegennahme von Zahlungen, die nicht zur Erfüllung von Verbindlichkeiten gegenüber dem Institut bestimmt sind“. Hierdurch wurde der Anwendungsbereich der Ausnahmen zum Entgegennahmeverbot eindeutig erweitert.

47 So Gesetzentwurf der Bundesregierung, BT- Drucks. 17/3024, S. 60.

48 Gesetz vom 29. 7. 2009, BGBl I S. 2305; Geltung ab dem 1. 8. 2009.

49 Dies gilt auch für Versicherungsunternehmen. Nach § 83a VAG ist die Haftung des Sonderbeauftragten ebenfalls beschränkt, wobei diese Beschränkung im Rahmen des FMVAStärkG dauerhaft gemacht wurde.

50 Gesetzentwurf der Bundesregierung, BT-Drucks. 17/3024, S. 60.

51 Hierzu siehe oben Gliederungspunkt 2.1.2.

2.2.4 Änderung des § 46b KWG

Eine weitere Änderung betrifft § 46b KWG, der eine spezielle Regelung des Insolvenzantrags für Kreditinstitute enthält. Geändert wurde der Fall der drohenden Zahlungsunfähigkeit. Nach § 46b Abs. 1 Satz 5 KWG darf die BaFin im Falle der drohenden Zahlungsunfähigkeit den Insolvenzantrag nur mit Zustimmung des Instituts und im Falle einer nach § 10a Abs. 3 Satz 6 oder Satz 7 KWG als übergeordnetes Unternehmen geltenden Finanzholding-Gesellschaft mit deren Zustimmung stellen. Durch diese Änderung sollte klargestellt werden, dass einem Insolvenzantrag wegen drohender Zahlungsunfähigkeit immer das jeweilige Kreditinstitut zustimmen muss und eine Finanzholding-Gesellschaft nur dem Insolvenzantrag über ihr eigenes Vermögen nicht aber dem Insolvenzantrag über mit ihm verbundene Institute zustimmen muss.[52]

Im Vergleich zur bisherigen Rechtslage ist es bei drohender Zahlungsunfähigkeit ferner nicht mehr erforderlich, dass Maßnahmen nach § 46 oder § 46a KWG nicht erfolgversprechend erscheinen.[53]

3. Sanierungs- und Reorganisationsverfahren

Artikel 1 des Restrukturierungsgesetzes enthält das Gesetz zur Reorganisation von Kreditinstituten (kurz: KredReorgG), das 23 Paragraphen umfasst. Das KredReorgG sieht ein zweistufiges Verfahren für Kreditinstitute vor, das die Sanierung eines systemrelevanten Institutes ohne Insolvenzverfahren ermöglichen soll.[54] In einer ersten Etappe kann ein Sanierungsverfahren eröffnet werden, das sodann, wenn der Sanierungsplan ohne Erfolg bleibt, in ein Reorganisationsverfahren übergehen kann. Im Sanierungsverfahren steht eine breite Palette von Handlungsoptionen zur Verfügung, wobei jedoch Eingriffe in Drittrechte nicht zulässig sind. Möglich ist auch die Eröffnung eines Reorganisationsverfahrens ohne vorheriges Sanierungsverfahren, wenn dieses von vornherein aussichtslos wäre, § 7 Abs. 1 KredReorgG. Das Reorganisationsverfahren orientiert sich an dem Insolvenzplanverfahren nach §§ 217 ff. InsO, weist aber einige Besonderheiten auf.[55]

Diese beiden Stufen basieren auf der Mitwirkung des betroffenen Kreditinstitutes. Ist diese nicht vorhanden, können ohne vorheriges Sanierungs- bzw. Reorganisationsverfahren aufsichtsrechtliche Maßnahmen, insbesondere eine Ausgliederung nach §§ 48a ff. KWG, ergriffen werden.

---

52 Gesetzentwurf der Bundesregierung, BT-Drucks. 17/3024, S. 60 f.

53 Zur bisherigen Rechtslage: *Pannen* Krise und Insolvenz bei Kreditinstituten, Kap. 3 Rn. 21.

54 Gesetzentwurf der Bundesregierung, BT- Drucks. 17/3024, S. 40.

55 Gesetzentwurf der Bundesregierung, BT- Drucks. 17/3024, S. 40.

3.1 Sanierungsverfahren

Die betroffene Bank leitet das Sanierungsverfahren durch Anzeige der Sanierungsbedürftigkeit bei der BaFin ein, § 2 Abs. 1 Satz 1 KredReorgG. Zusammen mit der Anzeige ist ein Sanierungsplan vorzulegen und ein Sanierungsberater vorzuschlagen, Abs. 2. Nach § 2 Abs. 1 Satz 2 KredReogG liegt die Sanierungsbedürftigkeit vor, wenn die Voraussetzungen des § 45 Abs. 1 Satz 1 und 2 KWG erfüllt sind.[56] Durch diesen Rückgriff auf § 45 KWG soll ein Einschreiten des Sanierungsverfahrens bereits zu einem sehr frühen Zeitpunkt, in dem lediglich eine drohende Fehlentwicklung vorliegt, ermöglicht werden.[57] Mit dieser Anzeige bei der BaFin genügt ferner das Institut seiner Pflicht nach § 46b Abs. 1 KWG. Nach dieser Vorschrift muss ein Kreditinstitut seine Zahlungsunfähigkeit oder Überschuldung unverzüglich der BaFin anzeigen. Im Falle der Anzeige der Sanierungsbedürftigkeit nach § 2 Abs. 1 KredReorgG erübrigt sich ohnehin die Anzeige nach § 46b Abs. 1 KWG, da die BaFin bereits hinreichend darüber informiert wird, dass das Institut einer besonders intensiven Beaufsichtigung bedarf.[58]

Die BaFin hat anschließend die Anzeige zu prüfen. Sie nimmt Stellung dazu, ob Sanierungsaussichten bestehen und ob der vorgeschlagene Sanierungsberater geeignet ist. Die BaFin stellt dann den Antrag auf Eröffnung des Verfahrens bei dem Oberlandesgericht, das für Klagen gegen die BaFin zuständig ist, und fügt ihre Stellungnahme hinzu, § 2 Abs. 3 KredReorgG. Nach Anhörung des Kreditinstitutes kann die BaFin einen anderen Sanierungsberater vorschlagen, wenn sie den von dem Kreditinstitut vorgeschlagenen Sanierungsberater für ungeeignet hält.

Entscheidet das OLG, das Verfahren zu eröffnen, so wird nach § 3 KredReorgG ein Sanierungsberater bestellt, dessen zentrale Funktion in Anlehnung an den Sonderbeauftragten nach § 36 Abs. 1a KWG und an den vorläufigen Insolvenzverwalter normiert wurde.[59] Seine Hauptaufgabe besteht nach § 6 Abs. 1 Satz 1 KredReorgG in der Umsetzung des Sanierungsplans. Dabei hat er die Möglichkeit, diesen im Einvernehmen mit der BaFin und dem OLG zu ändern.[60]

Nach § 4 Abs. 1 KredReorgG ist der Sanierungsberater berechtigt,

- die Geschäftsräume des Kreditinstituts zu betreten und dort Nachforschungen anzustellen,
- Einsicht in Bücher und Geschäftspapiere des Kreditinstituts zu nehmen und die Vorlage von Unterlagen sowie die Erteilung aller erforderlichen Auskünfte zu verlangen,
- an allen Sitzungen und Versammlungen sämtlicher Organe und sonstiger Gremien des Kreditinstituts in beratender Funktion teilzunehmen,
- Anweisungen für die Geschäftsführung des Kreditinstituts zu erteilen,

---

56 Siehe hierzu oben Gliederungspunkt 2.1.1. Der Regierungsentwurf enthielt hingegen keine Legaldefinition der Sanierungsbedürftigkeit, siehe BT-Drucks. 17/3024, S. 10.

57 Bericht des Finanzausschusses, BT-Drucks. 17/3547, S. 8.

58 Bericht des Finanzausschusses, BT-Drucks. 17/3547, S. 8.

59 Gesetzentwurf der Bundesregierung, BT- Drucks. 17/3024, S. 40.

60 Gesetzentwurf der Bundesregierung, BT- Drucks. 17/3024, S. 48.

- eigenständige Prüfungen zur Feststellung von Schadensersatzansprüchen gegen Organe oder ehemalige Organe des Kreditinstituts durchzuführen oder Sonderprüfungen zu veranlassen,
- die Einhaltung bereits getroffener Auflagen nach dem Finanzmarktstabilisierungsfondsgesetz zu überwachen.

Ferner kann das Oberlandesgericht nach § 5 Abs. 1 KredReorgG auf Vorschlag der BaFin weitere Maßnahmen anordnen, wie zum Beispiel:

1. den Mitgliedern der Geschäftsleitung und den Inhabern die Ausübung ihrer Tätigkeit untersagen oder diese beschränken,
2. anordnen, den Sanierungsberater in die Geschäftsleitung aufzunehmen,
3. Entnahmen durch die Inhaber oder Gesellschafter sowie die Ausschüttung von Gewinnen untersagen oder beschränken,
4. die bestehenden Vergütungs- und Bonusregelungen der Geschäftsleitung auf ihre Anreizwirkung und ihre Angemessenheit hin überprüfen und gegebenenfalls eine Anpassung für die Zukunft vornehmen sowie Zahlungsverbote bezüglich nicht geschuldeter Leistungen aussprechen und
5. die Zustimmung des Aufsichtsorgans ersetzen.

Der ursprüngliche Regierungsentwurf sah vor, dass das Gericht als weitere Maßnahme auch die Abberufung der Geschäftsleitung verlangen können sollte. Dies wurde im weiteren Verlauf des Gesetzgebungsverfahrens mit der Begründung gestrichen, dass die bloße Möglichkeit einer solchen Abberufung geeignet sei, Geschäftsleiter von der Einleitung eines Sanierungsverfahrens abzuhalten.[61]

3.2 Reorganisationsverfahren

Wenn eine Sanierung der Bank im Rahmen des Sanierungsverfahrens nicht möglich oder aussichtslos ist, kann die zweite Stufe – das Reorganisationsverfahren – gemäß §§ 7 ff. ReorgG eingeleitet werden. Diese zweite Stufe ist stark inspiriert durch das Insolvenzplanverfahren nach §§ 217 ff. InsO.[62] Der maßgebliche Unterschied zwischen Sanierungs- und Reorganisationsverfahren besteht darin, dass beim Reorganisationsverfahren Eingriffe in Drittrechte vorgesehen werden können.[63]

Auch bei dem Reorganisationsverfahren ist zwischen Anzeige- und Antragsbefugnis zu unterscheiden. Antragsbefugt ist lediglich die BaFin, wie es sich aus § 7 Abs. 2 KredReorgG ergibt. Der Antrag erfolgt jedoch nach einer Anzeige, die entweder durch den Sanierungsberater nach Scheitern eines Sanierungsverfahrens oder durch das Institut, wenn es das Sanierungsverfahren von vornherein für aussichtslos hält, eingereicht werden kann, § 7 Abs. 1 KredReorgG. Die Formulierung des § 7 Abs. 2 Satz 1 KredRe-

---

61 Bericht des Finanzausschusses, BT-Drucks. 17/3547, S. 9.
62 Gesetzentwurf der Bundesregierung, BT- Drucks. 17/3024, S. 40.
63 Gesetzentwurf der Bundesregierung, BT- Drucks. 17/3024, S. 41.

orgG „Nach der Anzeige durch das Kreditinstitut kann die Bundesanstalt [...]" ist insoweit irreführend, als dadurch der Eindruck erweckt wird, dass nur das Kreditinstitut die Anzeige betätigen kann, was in direktem Widerspruch zu § 7 Abs. 1 Satz 2 KredReorgG steht. Durch diese Formulierung sollte dem Missverständnis entgegengewirkt werden, dass nach § 7 Abs. 2 KredReorgG die BaFin befugt sei, von sich aus ein Reorganisationsverfahren zu beantragen, ohne dass eine Anzeige seitens des betroffenen Kreditinstitutes vorliegt.[64] Diese Formulierung, die klarstellen sollte, dass eine Anzeige stets erforderlich ist, ist somit dahingehend zu verstehen, dass die Anzeige sowohl vom Kreditinstitut als auch vom Sanierungsberater herkommen kann.

Ein Antrag auf Eröffnung eines Reorganisationsverfahrens setzt eine Bestandsgefährdung voraus, die zu einer Systemgefährdung beitragen kann (Reorganisationsbedürftigkeit). Dieses Erfordernis war jedoch in dem Regierungsentwurf nur aus einem Rückschluss aus § 7 Abs. 2 KredReorgG zu schließen. Der jeweilige Anwendungsbereich des Sanierungs- und des Reorganisationsverfahrens war infolgedessen nicht einfach festzustellen.[65] Mit der Klarstellung in § 1 Abs. 1 Satz 2 KredReorgG erschließt sich auf dem ersten Blick, dass während das Sanierungsverfahren allen Kreditinstituten offen steht, das Reorganisationsverfahren nur dann zulässig ist, wenn eine Gefährdung der Stabilität des Finanzsystems zu besorgen ist.[66] Die Bestandsgefährdung wird in § 7 Abs. 2 KredReorgG in Verbindung mit § 48b Abs. 1 KWG als die Gefahr eines insolvenzbedingten Zusammenbruchs des Instituts für den Fall des Unterbleibens korrigierender Maßnahmen definiert.

Zusammen mit der Anzeige ist auch ein Reorganisationsplan vorzulegen, der gemäß § 8 ReorgG aus einem darstellenden Teil und einem gestaltenden Teil besteht. Die Abstimmung über den Plan erfolgt in Anlehnung an das Insolvenzplanverfahren in verschiedenen, durch den Reorganisationsplan festgelegten Gläubigergruppen, wobei zur Annahme des Plans grundsätzlich die Zustimmung aller Gruppen erforderlich ist.[67] Daraufhin erfolgt eine gerichtliche Bestätigung des Reorganisationsplans durch das OLG.

4. Die Ausgliederung nach §§ 48a ff. KWG

4.1 Grundsatz

Das zweite Instrument, das durch das Restrukturierungsgesetz eingeführt wurde, ist die Möglichkeit einer Ausgliederung durch die BaFin, die gegebenenfalls auch gegen den Willen der Betroffenen angeordnet werden kann. Diese Ausgliederung ist in den neu eingeführten §§ 48a ff. KWG geregelt. Hiermit wurde sichergestellt, dass die BaFin

---

64 Bericht des Finanzausschusses, BT-Drucks. 17/3547, S. 8.

65 Siehe hierzu Stellungnahme DAV 36/10, S. 4; *Pannen* Festschrift Uhlenbruck, ZInsO 2010, 2026, 2027.

66 Bericht des Finanzausschusses, BT-Drucks. 17/3547, S. 8.

67 Gesetzentwurf der Bundesregierung, BT- Drucks. 17/3024, S. 41.

jederzeit eingreifen kann, wenn eine Bank in Schwierigkeiten gerät.[68] Dass diese Maßnahmen aufgezwungen werden kann, steht in einem Spannungsfeld mit dem Grundrecht auf Eigentum im Sinne von Art. 14 GG, wird aber durch folgende Abwägung gerechtfertigt: Im Fall einer Bestandsgefährdung haben zwar die Anteilsinhaber eine umfassende Entscheidungsmacht, die wirtschaftlichen Folgen der zu treffenden Entscheidungen werden aber auch von der Allgemeinheit zu tragen sein.[69] Hieraus resultiert der Anreiz für die Anteilsinhaber, als Trittbrettfahrer von dem Umstand zu profitieren, dass der Staat im öffentlichen Interesse an der Bewahrung der Stabilität des Finanzmarktes sich gezwungen sieht, das Institut zu stützen.[70] Nach Ansicht des Gesetzgebers stellt die Ausgliederung nach §§ 48a ff. KWG keine Enteignung dar, sondern eine intensiv eingreifende Inhaltsbestimmung: Die Ausgliederung soll zur Abwendung einer Gefahr, deren Bewältigung den Anteilseignern nicht mehr zuzutrauen ist, das in seinem Bestand gefährdete und deshalb zugleich für das Finanzsystem gefährliche Unternehmen der Bestimmungsgewalt seiner Eigentümer entzogen werden.[71]

Nach § 48a KWG kann die BaFin anordnen, dass das Vermögen eines Kreditinstitutes einschließlich seiner Verbindlichkeiten auf einen bestehenden Rechtsträger im Wege der Ausgliederung übertragen wird. Diese Anordnung wird als Übertragungsanordnung legaldefiniert. Der Rechtsträger gibt im Gegenzug seine Anteile an das übertragende Institut aus. Diejenigen Vermögensteile, die nicht systemrelevant sind, bleiben jedoch beim alten Rechtsträger. Dieser kann anschließend, ohne Risiko für die Finanzmärkte, im Rahmen eines Liquidationsverfahrens liquidiert werden. Für dieses Insolvenzverfahren gelten dann die „normalen Regeln“ des Bankkrisenrechts, die sich aus der kumulierten Anwendung der InsO und des KWG ergeben. Insbesondere ist ein Insolvenzantrag von Seiten der BaFin erforderlich. Durch die Geltung der Insolvenzordnung für das „Rumpfkreditinstitut“ wird der faktische Zwang beseitigt, bei systemrelevanten Kreditinstituten auf das Insolvenzverfahren zu verzichten und stattdessen Stabilisierungsmaßnahmen – wie zum Beispiel im Rahmen des FMStG – gewähren zu müssen.

4.2 Voraussetzungen

In § 48a KWG werden die Voraussetzungen geregelt, unter denen die BaFin eine Übertragungsanordnung zur Abwendung von Gefahren für die Stabilität des Finanzsystems erlassen kann. Die Ausgliederung setzt nach § 48a Abs. 2 KWG die Bestandsgefährdung der Bank und eine Gefährdung des Finanzsystems (Systemgefährdung) voraus. Zudem darf sich die Bestandsgefährdung der Bank nicht auf anderem Wege als durch die Übertragungsanordnung in gleich sicherer Weise beseitigen lassen. Ferner wird in § 48a Abs. 2 Satz 3 KWG klargestellt, dass die für die BaFin zum Zeitpunkt ihres Handelns erkennbare Verhältnisse für die Beurteilung der Rechtsmäßigkeit des Vorgehens maßgeblich sind. Darf die BaFin annehmen, dass die Voraussetzungen für die Übertragungsanordnung gegeben sind, ist ihr Handeln deshalb auch dann rechtsmäßig, wenn

68 Gesetzentwurf der Bundesregierung, BT-Drucks. 17/3024, S. 42.
69 Gesetzentwurf der Bundesregierung, BT-Drucks. 17/3024, S. 61.
70 Gesetzentwurf der Bundesregierung, BT-Drucks. 17/3024, S. 62.
71 Gesetzentwurf der Bundesregierung, BT-Drucks. 17/3024, S. 62.

sich im Nachhinein herausstellt, dass die Voraussetzungen tatsächlich nicht erfüllt waren.[72]

Die Bestandsgefährdung ist gemäß § 48b Abs. 1 Satz 1 KWG die Gefahr des insolvenzbedingten Zusammenbruches eines Kreditinstitutes für den Fall des Unterbleibens korrigierender Maßnahmen. Eine Bestandsgefährdung wird nach § 48b Abs. 1 Satz 2 KWG vermutet, wenn

1. das verfügbare Kernkapital das nach § 10 Abs. 1 KWG erforderliche Kernkapital zu weniger als 90% deckt;
2. das modifizierte verfügbare Eigenkapital die nach § 10 Abs. 1 KWG erforderlichen Eigenmittel zu weniger als 90% deckt;
3. die Zahlungsmittel, die dem Institut in einem durch die LiqV definierten Laufzeitband zur Verfügung stehen, die in demselben Laufzeitband abrufbaren Zahlungsverpflichtungen zu weniger als 90% decken oder
4. Tatsachen die Annahme rechtfertigen, dass eine Unterdeckung nach den Nummern 1, 2 oder 3 eintreten wird, wenn keine korrigierenden Maßnahmen ergriffen werden; dies ist insbesondere der Fall, wenn nach der Ertragslage des Instituts mit einem Verlust zu rechnen ist, infolgedessen die Voraussetzungen der Nummern 1, 2 oder 3 eintreten würden.

Eine Systemgefährdung liegt gemäß § 48b Abs. 2 KWG vor, wenn zu besorgen ist, dass sich die Bestandsgefährdung der Bank in erheblicher Weise negativ auf andere Unternehmen des Finanzsektors, auf die Finanzmärkte oder auf das allgemeine Vertrauen in die Funktionsfähigkeit des Finanzsystems auswirkt. Dabei sind nach § 48b Abs. 2 Satz 2 KWG insbesondere zu berücksichtigen:

1. Art und Umfang der Verbindlichkeiten des Kreditinstituts gegenüber anderen Instituten und sonstigen Unternehmen des Finanzsektors,
2. der Umfang der von dem Institut aufgenommenen Einlagen,
3. die Art, der Umfang und die Zusammensetzung der von dem Institut im Rahmen von außerbilanziellen Geschäften eingegangenen Risiken sowie die Verhältnisse auf den Märkten, auf denen entsprechende Positionen gehandelt werden,
4. die Vernetzung mit anderen Finanzmarktteilnehmern,
5. die Verhältnisse auf den Finanzmärkten, insbesondere die von den Marktteilnehmern erwarteten Folgen eines Zusammenbruchs des Instituts auf andere Unternehmen des Finanzsektors, auf den Finanzmarkt und das Vertrauen der Einleger und Marktteilnehmer in die Funktionsfähigkeit des Finanzmarktes.

Vor der Anordnung der Ausgliederung kann die BaFin der Bank eine Frist zur Vorlage und Ausführung eines Wiederherstellungsplans setzen und damit die Möglichkeit verschaffen, die Bestandsgefährdung selbst abzuwenden.[73] In dem Wiederherstellungsplan sind die Maßnahmen anzugeben, aufgrund derer die Bestandsgefährdung

72 Gesetzentwurf der Bundesregierung, BT-Drucks. 17/3024, S. 63.
73 Gesetzentwurf der Bundesregierung, BT-Drucks. 17/3024, S. 64.

innerhalb von sechs Wochen nach Vorlage des Plans abgewendet und die Angemessenheit der Eigenmittel und die ausreichende Liquidität langfristig sichergestellt werden soll, § 48 c Abs. 1 KWG.

5. Fazit

Durch das Restrukturierungsgesetz hat das „Bankkrisenrecht" eine tiefgreifende Änderung erfahren. Statt des bisherigen einheitlichen Wegs über § 45 ff. KWG und Eröffnung des Insolvenzverfahrens stehen nunmehr differenzierte Instrumente zur Verfügung, wodurch eine größere Sanierungsquote erreicht werden soll. Ob das Sanierungs- bzw. Reorganisationsverfahren und die Ausgliederung sich in der Praxis als Alternative zum Insolvenzverfahren etablieren werden, bleibt jedoch abzuwarten.

Triggers for Bank Resolution

Charles Randell

Table of Contents

I. Introduction
II. The need for intervention powers
  A. The United Kingdom experience
  B. Global consensus
III. Public law background
  A. European Convention on Human Rights
  B. Other administrative law constraints
  C. State aid
IV. Key issues relating to triggers
  A. Objectives and guidance
  B. Preparation and implementation of recovery measures
  C. Resolution triggers: quantitative or qualitative?
  D. Resolution triggers: mandatory or discretionary?
  E. Who exercises the triggers?
  F. Role of the affected institution
  G. The role of creditors
  H. How public support is treated
  I. Judicial review
  J. The cross-border aspect
V. Conclusion

I. Introduction

The financial crisis which first manifested itself in 2007 and which continues to reverberate around the world exposed the need for a range of intervention powers to address bank failure. These powers include the requirement for contingency planning before the onset of difficulties and, following their onset, enhanced supervision, recovery measures and resolution measures.

This paper describes how the UK experience of the financial crisis illustrates the need for intervention powers, before discussing a number of issues that arise in relation to how such powers should be triggered.[1]

---

1 This paper was finalised in February 2011 and does not reflect legal or policy developments since then.

II. The need for intervention powers

A. The United Kingdom experience

As the United Kingdom entered 2007, the year in which the financial crisis first manifested itself, the UK had, in terms of its gross domestic product, one of the most significant and concentrated banking sectors in the world. This remains the case: as of the end of 2009, each of RBS, Barclays and HSBC had consolidated assets exceeding the UK's gross domestic product and exceeding one fifth of all UK banking sector assets. The total consolidated assets of the top ten UK institutions at the end of 2009 represented over 450 per cent of the UK's gross domestic product.[2]

Whilst there had been a number of bank failures in the course of the 20th century, broadly speaking these had been resolved by the use of private law measures, sometimes involving the participation of other industry players and often with the participation or encouragement of the Bank of England. The last classic retail deposit run on UK banks had occurred in the 19th century.[3]

As is now well known and documented,[4] Northern Rock was a former building society based in the north east of England which grew rapidly to become the fifth largest provider of mortgages in the United Kingdom. It did so by increasing its use of the wholesale financial markets, including by securitisation and the issue of covered bonds, to raise the necessary funding to grow its mortgage book. When wholesale funding markets dried up in the second half of 2007, Northern Rock had to turn to the Bank of England for an emergency liquidity facility. In September 2007, liquidity support facilities were made available to Northern Rock by the Bank of England, authorised by the Chancellor of the Exchequer. The UK authorities judged that the situation affecting Northern Rock posed a genuine threat to the stability of the financial system and that action was necessary to avoid a serious disturbance to the UK economy. In short, if Northern Rock had been allowed to fail, there was a serious risk of a loss of confidence in the UK banking system as a whole.

However, when these facilities became publicly known, customers nevertheless withdrew their deposits and closed their accounts, creating a run on the bank. This behaviour may in part have been due to the fact that at that time the UK deposit guarantee scheme, the Financial Services Compensation Scheme ("FSCS"), did not provide full protection to even the smaller depositors; it may also have been due to customer concerns that even if their savings were guaranteed, it was not clear how long they would have to wait to receive payment of them from the FSCS. In order to stop a run on the

---

2 See *Mervyn King* (Governor of the Bank of England) Banking: From Bagehot to Basel, and Back Again, 2010, Table 1, www.bankofengland.co.uk/publications/speeches/2010/speech455.pdf (accessed 14 February 2011).

3 The run on British banks triggered by the failure of Overend, Gurney & Co. in 1866 was widely cited in the aftermath of the run on Northern Rock. A run on a number of British banks also occurred in 1878 in the aftermath of the failure of the City of Glasgow Bank.

4 House of Commons Treasury Committee (2007–08), The Run on the Rock (HC 56-I, 2008), www.publications.parliament.uk/pa/cm200708/cmselect/cmtreasy/56/56i.pdf (accessed 14 February 2011).

bank, it was necessary for the Chancellor of the Exchequer to announce that, if necessary, arrangements would be put in place by the Government to guarantee all existing deposits of Northern Rock.

These measures stabilised the position of Northern Rock sufficiently to enable a process to be undertaken to seek to restructure the bank in the private sector with capital from existing or new shareholders. All of the private sector proposals would, however, have required continued Government support in the medium term and, in the event, the Government judged that the proposals received were inadequate; the risk that the Government would have to run under those proposals, and the subsidy that it would have to provide, would be too great relative to the return, if any, that the taxpayer would receive for underwriting that risk.

The Government therefore introduced into Parliament what became the Banking (Special Provisions) Act 2008, legislation of general application to UK banks which was passed in a few days, and which among other things enabled the Government to take Northern Rock into temporary public ownership by the transfer of its shares to the Government. Since then, using powers under the legislation, Northern Rock has been restructured, with its deposit-taking business and branches held by one company that is intended to be returned to the private sector, and many of its historic assets being held by another company that will seek to optimise the recoveries from these assets for the benefit of the taxpayer and other creditors.

The extended process that was required before the position of Northern Rock could be stabilised in the public sector contrasts with the speed of the process subsequently used by the UK authorities to resolve the position of another UK mortgage bank, Bradford & Bingley. Using the new powers available to them, the UK authorities were able over the course of a weekend to conduct an accelerated auction for the deposit business of Bradford & Bingley, transfer its deposit liabilities to Santander, the winning bidder, and take the residue of the bank into public ownership.

Notwithstanding the existence of the new legal powers to resolve failing banks that were enacted in 2008, the more extreme circumstances that prevailed in the autumn of 2008 and the much larger size and complexity of the banks affected by them meant that the positions of the Royal Bank of Scotland, Lloyds and HBOS could not be resolved using these powers. Instead, the UK Government recapitalised these banks with substantial amounts of taxpayer funds and introduced a number of other measures, including additional credit and liquidity support measures, that were made available to the banking sector generally.

The legislation passed in 2008 was time-limited in its application and was therefore replaced in due course by the Banking Act 2009.[5] The 2009 Act sets out a Special Resolution Regime for banks, which includes three stabilisation options:[6]

---

5 For an overview of the Special Resolution Regime, see *Peter Brierley* The UK Special Resolution Regime for failing banks in an international context, Bank of England Financial Stability Paper no. 5, 2009, www.bankofengland.co.uk/publications/fsr/fs_paper05.pdf (accessed 14 February 2011).

6 Banking Act 2009, Pt1.

- a transfer of property or securities to a **private sector purchaser;**
- a transfer of property to a **bridge bank**; and
- a transfer of securities to **temporary public ownership.**

The Special Resolution Regime also includes a bank insolvency procedure and a bank administration procedure.[7]

In addition, as part of the effort to address the problem of "Too Important To Fail", the Government introduced further powers through the Financial Services Act 2010[8] to require firms to prepare recovery plans and resolution plans – so-called "living wills". The process of evaluating the recovery and resolution plans that were part of the initial pilot study conducted by the Financial Services Authority ("FSA") is still under way, but it is to be hoped that these plans will make a significant contribution to addressing the Too Important To Fail problem.

B. Global consensus

The experience of the United Kingdom has been shared by many other jurisdictions. Few jurisdictions entered the financial crisis with a set of resolution powers that were adequate: even in the United States, with its many decades of experience of resolution action by the Federal Deposit Insurance Corporation ("FDIC"), the available powers were not adequate to deal with systemically important groups and taxpayer recapitalisation and other taxpayer backed solutions were required.

Since the start of the financial crisis, a general consensus has emerged from discussions among national and supra-national authorities on many points relating to intervention powers. This consensus is evident in the large volume of publications that have been issued by supra-national bodies: the IMF/World Bank study of April 2009;[9] the Basel Committee Report and Recommendations of the Cross-Border Bank Resolution Group of March 2010;[10] the Financial Stability Board's interim report to G20 leaders in June 2010;[11] and the EU Commission's Communication on Crisis Management in the Financial Sector of October 2010,[12] as further elaborated in a Working Document issued in January 2011 by DG Internal Market and Services (the "Working

7 Banking Act 2009, Pts2 and 3.

8 Financial Services Act 2010, s7 (inserting new ss139B to 139F into the Financial Services and Markets Act 2000).

9 IMF/World Bank, An overview of the legal, institutional, and regulatory framework for bank insolvency, 2009, www.imf.org/external/np/pp/eng/2009/041709.pdf (accessed 14 February 2011).

10 Bank for International Settlements, Report and Recommendations of the Cross-Border Bank Resolution Group, 2010, www.bis.org/publ/bcbs169.pdf (accessed 14 February 2011).

11 Financial Stability Board, Reducing the moral hazard posed by systemically important financial institutions, interim report to G20 Leaders, 2010, www.financialstabilityboard.org/publications/r_100627b.pdf (accessed 14 February 2011).

12 Commission Communication, An EU Framework for Crisis Management in the Financial Sector (COM (2010) 579 final), ec.europa.eu/internal_market/bank/docs/crisis-management/framework/com2010_579_en.pdf (accessed 14 February 2011).

Document").[13] This Working Document draws heavily on the approach adopted in the UK Banking Act 2009.

The general consensus emerging from this work is that a graduated scale of intervention powers is required, starting with recovery and resolution planning before the onset of any difficulties and, as issues emerge, escalating through enhanced supervision to implementation of recovery measures (corrective action) and finally resolution measures.

III. Public law background

The exercise of intervention powers may lead to significant intrusions into the domain of private rights. The way in which the exercise of these powers is triggered raises, therefore, difficult questions relating to the balance between the rights of private firms and their private investors and other stakeholders on the one hand and the interests of the state on the other. The triggers for intervention powers must therefore be considered against the background of the public law restrictions on their use.

In the United Kingdom, in addition to the many European directives and regulations in the area of financial institutions, the key public law restrictions arise from the Human Rights Act 1998, which has given effect to the European Convention on Human Rights in UK law; other requirements of domestic administrative law relating to the exercise of administrative powers; and European state aid rules.

Public law restrictions on incurrence of expenditure and other financial commitments, which are significant in a number of other jurisdictions, have relatively little impact in the United Kingdom. It is notable, for example, that the more than £1 trillion of interventions by the UK Government in the banking sector in the period from 2007 to 2009 took place without any specific prior authorisation by Parliament of the scale of this commitment. This is a topic which perhaps deserves greater attention, but it is beyond the scope of this paper.[14]

A. European Convention on Human Rights

The key Convention rights which have a major impact on when and how the authorities utilise intervention powers are the right to property, contained in Article 1 of the First Protocol to the Convention ("A1P1") and the right to a fair trial, contained in Article 6. Article 14 (prohibition of discrimination) may also be relevant.

---

13 DG Internal Market and Services Working Document, Technical Details of a Possible EU Framework for Bank Recovery and Resolution, 2011, ec.europa.eu/internal_market/consultations/docs/2011/crisis_management/consultation_paper_en.pdf (accessed 14 February 2011).

14 *Julia Black* Managing the Financial Crisis – The Constitutional Dimension, LSE Law, Society and Economy Working Papers, 12/2010.

A1P1 provides that:

"Every natural or legal person is entitled to the peaceful enjoyment of his possessions. No one shall be deprived of his possessions except in the public interest and subject to the conditions provided for by law and by the general principles of international law.

The preceding provisions shall not, however, in any way impair the right of a State to enforce such laws as it deems necessary to control the use of property in accordance with the general interest or to secure the payment of taxes or other contributions or penalties."

The principles that emerge from the jurisprudence of the European Court of Human Rights are that a fair balance must be struck between the public interest and the private rights to which A1P1 applies; that actions of the State affecting such private rights should be proportionate; and that the authorities of a State enjoy a margin of appreciation in making these assessments.[15]

The compulsory acquisition by the Government of the shares of Northern Rock under the legislative powers granted by Parliament in the Banking (Special Provisions) Act 2008 was the subject of a claim for judicial review founded on A1P1 brought by hedge fund shareholders who had acquired shares in Northern Rock after its troubles emerged, and certain other shareholders.[16] The claimants did not challenge the taking of Northern Rock into public ownership but instead complained about the legislative provisions for compensation. The 2008 Act provided, as the Banking Act 2009 now provides, that compensation in such a case should be assessed on the assumption that public support (other than ordinary assistance by the Bank of England) was withdrawn and no further such support made available. The principal claim by the former shareholders was in essence that since Northern Rock was not insolvent (because such public support was not in fact withdrawn), assessing compensation on a (fictional) basis that in all likelihood amounted to insolvency was manifestly disproportionate. The answer given by the Government to this point was that the shareholders of a bank should not in principle be compensated for value attributable to public financial support to which the institution was not entitled as of right and which was given not for the benefit of the shareholders but in the public interest. Both the Divisional Court and the Court of Appeal dismissed the former shareholders' claim, and their further appeal is now pending in Strasbourg.

Article 6 of the Convention provides that:

"In the determination of his civil rights and obligations ... everyone is entitled to a fair and public hearing within a reasonable time by an independent and impartial tribunal established by law ..."

This is supported by Article 13, which provides that:

"Everyone whose rights and freedoms as set forth in this Convention are violated shall have an effective remedy before a national authority notwithstanding that the violation has been committed by persons acting in an official capacity."

---

15 *Eva H. G. Hüpkes* Special bank resolution and shareholders' rights: balancing competing interests, Journal of Financial Regulation and Compliance, 2009, p. 277. See also the judgment of the English Court of Appeal in SRM Global Master Fund, n16 below.

16 SRM Global Master Fund and others v. the Commissioners of HM Treasury [2009] EWCA Civ 788, on appeal from the judgment of the Divisional Court [2009] EWCA Admin 227.

The key decisions of the House of Lords (now the Supreme Court) in the United Kingdom establish that, in the normal case, the availability of *ex post* judicial review will provide the necessary "full jurisdiction" that has been required by the Strasbourg court in cases concerning Article 6.[17] The standard of judicial review applied by the courts in the United Kingdom in administrative law cases, i.e. review limited to cases of illegality, procedural impropriety or irrationality rather than full re-examination of the facts and the decision, is normally sufficient to satisfy the requirement of "full jurisdiction".[18]

B. Other administrative law constraints

In addition to the constraints on triggering intervention powers that derive from the European Convention on Human Rights, judicial review of the exercise of intervention powers by the UK authorities may lie under long-standing principles of domestic English law where powers are exercised unlawfully, either in the sense that the action taken goes beyond the legal limits of the powers or amounts to an abuse of power; where action is taken without duly following procedure; or where the action taken is irrational (an action that no reasonable authority would have taken). Judicial review may also lie where the actions of the authority are unfair or contrary to the legitimate expectations created by the authority.

C. State aid

Finally, where the exercise of intervention powers by the authorities involves the provision of any state aid, the EU state aid rules must be complied with.

Prior to the financial crisis, aid was normally assessed under what is now Article 107(3)(c) of the Treaty on the Functioning of the European Union and the Rescue and Restructuring Guidelines.[19] As the financial crisis worsened, the Commission accepted that aid could where appropriate be assessed under Article 107(3)(b) as aid which was necessary to remedy a serious disturbance in the economy of a member state. However, the Commission emphasised that as regards the financial sector, invoking Article 107(3)(b) is possible only in genuinely exceptional circumstances where the entire functioning of financial markets is jeopardised.[20] The Commission has since extended the applicability

---

17 R (Alconbury Developments Limited) v Secretary of State for the Environment [2001] UKHL 23; Runa Begum v Tower Hamlets London Borough Council [2003] UKHL 5.

18 IKSCON v United Kingdom, No. 20490/92, decision of the European Human Rights Commission (8 March 1994): "It is not the role of Article 6 of the Convention to give access to a level of jurisdiction which can substitute its opinion for that of the administrative authorities on questions of expediency and where the courts do not refuse to examine any of the points raised …."

19 Commission Communication, Community guidelines on state aid for rescuing and restructuring firms in difficulty (2004/C 244/2), http://eur-lex.europa.eu/LexUriServ/LexUriServ.do?uri=OJ:C:2004:244:0002:0017:EN:PDF (accessed 20 February 2011).

20 Commission Communication, The application of state aid rules to measures taken in relation to financial institutions in the context of the current global financial crisis (2008/C270/02), para 11, eur-lex.europa.eu/LexUriServ/LexUriServ.do?uri=OJ:C:2008:270:0008:0014:EN:PDF (accessed 20 February 2011).

of Article 107(3)(b) until 31 December 2011 in the context of a gradual transition to a more permanent regime of state aid guidelines which should, market conditions permitting, apply as of 1 January 2012.[21]

IV. Key issues relating to triggers

A. Objectives and guidance

Bank resolution powers are necessarily broad and involve a measure of supervisory discretion. As a result, they raise issues of legal certainty and the rule of law. In order to address these issues, and to reduce the risk of administrative law challenge to the exercise of the powers, it may be helpful for the powers to be accompanied by a clear statement of the objectives for which they will be exercised and, where possible, by further guidance on the way in which they will be exercised.

This is the approach taken in the United Kingdom. The Banking Act 2009 sets out clearly the objectives to which the authorities are to have regard in using the stabilisation powers conferred by that Act or the bank insolvency or bank administration procedures. The Act[22] defines five objectives:

- to protect and enhance the stability of UK financial systems (including continuity of banking services);
- to protect and enhance public confidence in the stability of UK banking systems;
- to protect depositors;
- to protect public funds; and
- to avoid interfering with property rights in contravention of the Convention.

This approach of explicitly setting out in the legislation the context in which the intervention powers may be triggered is, it is suggested, a helpful contribution to the task of defining the scope of the public interest in resolving failing financial institutions. By defining this public interest more closely, greater transparency is afforded to the process; it can be hoped that a clear focus on the objectives of the process will make it more likely that resolution options will be chosen which strike the correct balance between the public interest and the rights of shareholders, creditors and other affected parties.

The Working Document suggests a similar approach.[23] The objectives set out in the document are similar but not identical to the first four objectives set out in the Banking Act 2009, namely:

---

21 Commission Communication, The application, from 1 January 2011, of state aid rules to support measures in favour of banks in the context of the financial crisis (2010/C329/07), para 17, http://eur-lex.europa.eu/LexUriServ/LexUriServ.do?uri=OJ:C:2010:329:0007:0010:EN:PDF (accessed 20 February 2011).

22 Banking Act 2009, s4.

23 Working Document, pp48–89.

- to ensure the continuity of essential financial services;
- to avoid adverse effects on financial stability, including by preventing contagion;
- to protect public funds; and
- to protect insured depositors.

The fifth objective set out in the Banking Act 2009, that of avoiding interfering with property rights in contravention of the Convention, is not included. It is submitted that this omission is correct: non-contravention of the Convention should be a condition of the use of the intervention powers, not an objective of their use. The Working Document states that where the use of resolution tools or powers is not necessary having regard to the resolution objectives, the services of DG Internal Market and Services consider that a credit institution that is failing or is likely to fail should be liquidated under the applicable insolvency proceedings.

The objective of protecting the deposit guarantee scheme is not included in either the list of objectives in the Banking Act 2009 or the list in the Working Document. As the UK system currently operates, with an FSCS that is not adequately pre-funded to deal with the failure of a significant financial institutions, such a failure is likely to require the Government to provide funding to the FSCS pending its recovery of funds from contributing institutions through the levy. As a result, protection of the deposit guarantee scheme and protection of public funds are currently likely to lead to similar results in the United Kingdom. However, if the FSCS were to become substantially pre-funded, the case for an explicit objective of protecting the FSCS might need to be re-examined.

The Banking Act 2009 seeks to address further the issues of legal certainty and the rule of law by requiring the Treasury to issue a Code of Practice about the use of the stabilisation powers, the bank insolvency procedure and the bank administration procedure, to which the authorities must have regard.[24] The Code of Practice currently in effect contains a requirement that, following actions taken under the Special Resolution Regime, the authorities shall make a public statement explaining: (a) how they have acted with regard to the special resolution objectives; and (b) how they have balanced the objectives against each other.[25]

B. Preparation and implementation of recovery measures

It has long been contended that early intervention minimises the negative externalities resulting from bank failure.[26] Early use of powers to require that recovery measures are

---

24 Banking Act 2009, ss5 and 6.

25 HM Treasury, Banking Act 2009 Special Resolution Regime: Code of Practice, 2010, www.hm-treasury.gov.uk/d/bankingact2009_code_of_practice.pdf (accessed 20 February 2011). Guidance from the FSA on the way in which it will assess whether the condition in the Banking Act 2009, section 7(3) is fulfilled is contained in FINMAR 3 in the FSA Handbook.

26 *Stephen A. Buser, Andrew H. Chen and Edward J. Kane* Federal Deposit Insurance, Regulatory Policy, and Optimal Bank Capital, Journal of Finance, vol. 36 (March 1981), pp51–60; *George J. Benston and George G. Kaufman* Risk and Solvency Regulation of Depository Institutions: Past Policies and Current Options, Staff Memorandum 88-1 (1988), Federal Reserve Bank of Chicago.

taken can be important in minimising the exposure of the deposit guarantee scheme or the taxpayer and in preventing disruption to the economy.

Under a graduated system of intervention, appropriate recovery plans and resolution plans should be prepared in respect of relevant institutions before difficulties emerge. As the institution encounters difficulties, powers of enhanced supervision should be available to the authorities when they consider that the circumstances of the institution require such supervision. Enhanced supervision does not represent a significant incursion into private rights and it is submitted that it is not necessary from that viewpoint alone to have carefully defined triggers or safeguards at this stage.[27] Beyond that point, however, recovery measures (such as asset disposals) will have an increasing potential for conflict with the interests of the firm's shareholders and creditors, and greater definition of triggers and safeguards may be appropriate.[28]

As regards the requirement for recovery plans and resolution plans, a key "trigger" question is to which firms these requirements should apply. Clearly, recovery and resolution plans should be prepared in respect of systemically important financial institutions. However, the financial crisis demonstrated that in times of extreme financial stress firms that have not previously been considered systemic may become so. The requirement for recovery and resolution plans should, therefore, be imposed applying the precautionary principle and extended to firms which have the potential to be systemically important. Indeed it can be argued that in some cases until the plans have been prepared it will not be clear what the consequences of an unplanned failure of the firm would be. In addition, in the interest of minimising losses to the deposit guarantee scheme, there is an argument for extending the requirement to firms which have no potential to become systemically important.

The new provisions inserted into the Financial Services and Markets Act 2000 by the Financial Services Act 2010[29] adopt this last argument and require recovery plans and resolution plans to be made for any institution in respect of which Special Resolution Regime powers under Part 1 of the Banking Act 2009 are exercisable, i.e. any bank. In addition, rules may be made for other authorised firms or for specified categories of authorised firms.

This new regime of recovery and resolution planning is still under development in the United Kingdom. A pilot study involving major UK banks is continuing and a consultation paper from the FSA is expected shortly. The provisions set out in the Financial Services Act 2010 do not address in any detail the powers of the authorities to require the plans, once prepared, to be implemented. It is possible that the Financial Services Bill which is to be published later in 2011 may contain expanded provisions dealing with these plans and confirming that the necessary rule-making powers are conferred

---

27 However, greater definition of triggers at each stage of intervention may be important in limiting forbearance: see Section III.D below.

28 One such recovery measure would include triggering the conversion of contingent capital instruments, which is worthy of a separate paper: see *Rinke Bax and Phoebus Athanassiou* Contingent debt instruments and their challenges: some insights, Journal of International Banking and Financial Law, Vol. 1, 2011, p20.

29 Financial Services and Markets Act 2000, ss139B to 139F, inserted by Financial Services Act 2010, s7.

on the Prudential Regulation Authority ("PRA") to facilitate implementation of the plans.[30]

The Working Document follows a similar approach to that taken by the UK legislative provisions on recovery and resolution plans in proposing that all credit institutions should draw up and maintain recovery plans[31] and that the relevant resolution authorities for those credit institutions should draw up resolution plans.[32] The Working Document raises the question of how to define the investment firms to which the recovery and resolution regime would also apply, and puts forward for comment alternative suggestions: investment firms which pass a size criterion; and investment firms which are part of a banking group.[33] Although the former suggestion will pose difficult questions of definition, the latter will not necessarily catch investment firms of systemic importance. The Working Document also correctly raises the question of bringing bank holding companies within thc scope of the regime.

As regards the point at which early intervention powers, including the power to require implementation of measures in the institution's recovery plan, should be exercisable, the Working Document suggests that these should arise in the event of a *likely breach* of the requirements of the Capital Requirements Directive. Particularly when compared with the Prompt Corrective Action provisions of the Federal Deposit Insurance Act of 1950 ("FDIA"), mentioned further in Section III.D, this point appears to be too late: an institution whose capital resources are close to breaching the requirements of the Capital Requirements Directive but where likelihood of breach cannot be established should surely not be permitted, for example, to make significant acquisitions.[34] It is submitted that the early intervention powers should arise, at the latest, when the authorities determine that there is a *serious risk of a breach* of the requirements of the Capital Requirements Directive.

---

30 A requirement to implement a recovery plan could be imposed by way of an Own Initiative Variation of Permission ("OIVOP") but it may be preferable to make specific provision for such a requirement.

31 Working Document, pp19 to 22.

32 Working Document, pp31 to 38. Note that the relevant UK provisions (see nn8 and 29 above) currently impose the duty to prepare resolution plans on the firm, not the authorities. Neither approach is wholly satisfactory: the firm will lack incentives to prepare for its own resolution; the authorities will suffer from asymmetry of information. Perhaps the best compromise would be to provide for a resolution plan to be prepared by the firm and revised and "owned" by the authority, whilst at the same time imposing a duty on the firm and its senior management to ensure that the authority is promptly informed of any changes to the plan which become necessary in the light of changes in the firm's circumstances. There may be some benefit in imposing this duty on one or more nominated senior officers of the firm in order to ensure the appropriate level of personal responsibility.

33 Working Document, pp 12 and 13.

34 The capital buffer conservation measures in Basel III would, when implemented, prevent dividends and other distributions once a bank's capital had been eroded beyond a certain point.

C. Resolution triggers: quantitative or qualitative?

Under the Banking Act 2009 the two general conditions for exercise of a stabilisation power are:

- that the FSA is satisfied that the bank is failing, or is likely to fail, the threshold conditions for its authorisation; and
- that, having regard to timing and other relevant circumstances, it is not reasonably likely that (ignoring the stabilisation powers) action will be taken by or in respect of the bank that will enable it to satisfy those threshold conditions.[35]

The threshold conditions are those set out in COND2 in the FSA's Handbook. They address, in general terms, such matters as capital resources, liquidity, infrastructure and suitability of management. To that extent, it may be said by some that the first critical decision that the UK authorities take on the path to resolution of a bank – particularly given the "likely to fail" formulation which introduces a second tier of judgment – involves some quite subjective or qualitative, rather than objective or quantitative, criteria, and that this is unsatisfactory having regard in particular to the fundamental implications of the exercise of resolution powers for the property rights of shareholders and other third parties. Given the public interest in ensuring that the authorities are able to intervene sufficiently early, it is submitted that this is not a valid criticism.

These general conditions are of course not the only conditions which must be satisfied before a stabilisation power may be exercised under the 2009 Act. The Bank of England, when exercising its powers, must generally be satisfied that the exercise of the power is necessary, having regard to the public interest in the stability of the financial systems of the United Kingdom, the maintenance of public confidence in the stability of the banking systems of the United Kingdom or the protection of depositors.[36] The Treasury, when exercising its powers, must generally be satisfied that the exercise of the power is necessary to resolve or reduce a serious threat to the financial systems of the United Kingdom.[37] The application of these conditions is somewhat modified where public support has been provided.

The approach taken by the Banking Act 2009 contrasts with the regime put forward by DG Internal Market and Services in their Working Document. This document proposes that the triggers for resolution action should be financial in their focus and largely quantitative.[38] The Working Document suggests three possible trigger conditions for resolution, which might be adopted singly or in combination:

Option 1: one or more of the following circumstances applies to the credit institution:

- it has incurred or is likely to incur losses that will deplete its equity;
- the assets of the credit institution are or are likely to be less than its obligations; or
- it is or is likely to be unable to pay its obligations in the normal course of business.

---

35 Banking Act 2009, s7.

36 Banking Act 2009, s8.

37 Banking Act 2009, s9.

38 Working Document, pp46–48.

Option 2: the credit institution no longer fulfils, or is likely to fail to fulfil, the financial conditions for authorisation.

Option 3: the credit institution no longer possesses, or is likely to fail to possess, sufficient Tier 1 instruments, as required under Chapter 2 of Title V of the Capital Requirements Directive to meet the requirements of Article 75 of the Capital Requirements Directive.

Thus Options 1 and 2 in the Working Document include both capital and liquidity triggers, supporting the view that banks, even if well capitalised, are not entitled to liquidity assistance from the authorities as of right. Option 3 does not address the question of liquidity and is not, therefore, sufficient.

The Working Document suggests that in addition to one or more of the financial conditions specified above, two other conditions would need to be satisfied:

- no other measures are likely to avert failure and restore the condition of the institution in a reasonable timeframe. The Working Document states that this should ensure that resolution is a last resort; and
- the application of the resolution tools is necessary in the public interest.

It may be questioned whether the Working Document is right to focus exclusively on financial measures.[39] Intervention may be required in other circumstances: for example, if a bank is involved in fraud or serious misconduct or if reliable data about the condition of the bank are not available. In practice, in the case of a financial institution with severe record-keeping problems, where it is not yet known how severe its losses are due to the poor quality of the information available to the authorities, it would be easier for the authorities to intervene under a test requiring a likelihood of failing threshold conditions for authorisation than under a test requiring a likelihood of failing financial tests, due to the problem of establishing the latter in the absence of the necessary data. It is notable that the grounds for appointment of a conservator or receiver of a federal depository institution set out in the FDIA include substantially broader criteria, such as "an unsafe or unsound condition to transact business",[40] concealment or refusal to submit books, records or papers,[41] and violations of law.[42]

D. Resolution triggers – mandatory or discretionary?

Closely related to the issue of facilitating early intervention and the question whether triggers should be formulated as quantitative or qualitative is the question whether they should be discretionary, permitting but not requiring the authorities to exercise

---

39 The Commission's October 2010 Communication (see n12 above) raised the possibility of "more qualitative options includ[ing] a supervisory assessment that the institution no longer meets, or is expected to fail to meet, the conditions of its licence to carry on banking or investment business", but this approach does not appear to have been pursued in the Working Document.

40 FDIA, s11(c)(5)(C).

41 FDIA, s11(c)(5)(E).

42 FDIA, s11(c)(5)(H).

intervention powers, or whether the use of intervention powers should be mandatory once certain trigger requirements are satisfied.

Purely discretionary triggers may not address the risk that the authorities will forbear from intervening when they should not. Since the Savings & Loan crisis in the United States in the late 1980s there has been a growing awareness that a combination of external factors (e.g. political pressure) and self-interest (e.g. reluctance to confront their own supervisory failures) gives rise to this risk.[43] This realisation led to the introduction into the FDIA of the "Prompt Corrective Action" regime by the Federal Deposit Insurance Corporation Improvement Act of 1991.[44] The Prompt Corrective Action regime requires banks to be classified according to the severity of their capital inadequacy, and graduated measures aimed at the preservation and restoration of their capital position to be imposed.

The UK Banking Act 2009 has not introduced a system mandating intervention at any particular point. For the time being, Articles, 10(1), 75 and 136 of the Capital Requirements Directive[45] provide the main boundary beyond which forbearance by the FSA may not go. However, the UK Government's most recent consultation document on the reform of financial regulation in the UK proposes a "Proactive Intervention Framework" to be applied across all sectors regulated by the PRA and which will set out clearly demarcated stages and a list of presumed actions at each of those stages, although none of these actions would be automatic.[46] This is an interesting and potentially valuable idea, although few additional details are available at this stage.

Although the Working Document proposes[47] that Article 136, and in particular the list of powers that may be exercised under that Article, should be extended, it does not envisage that intervention at any particular point should be mandated beyond the existing requirements of the Capital Requirements Directive.

In the absence of a "Prompt Corrective Action" regime *requiring* intervention by the authorities, there will continue to exist some risk of regulatory forbearance that ultimately worsens a crisis or the cost of resolution, both in the UK and the broader European context.[48] In the UK, the reorganisation of financial regulation, concentrating

---

43 *Edward J. Kane* The S&L Insurance Mess: How did it Happen?, The Urban Institute Press, Washington DC, 1989.

44 *Christopher J. Pike and James B. Thomson* FDICIA's Prompt Corrective Action Provisions, Federal Reserve Bank of Cleveland Economic Commentary, Issue 1, September 1992.

45 Directive 2006/48/EC of 14 June 2006 relating to the taking up and pursuit of the business of credit institutions (recast), http://eur-lex.europa.eu/LexUriServ/LexUriServ.do?uri=CONSLEG:2006L0048:20100330:EN:PDF (accessed 20 February 2011).

46 HM Treasury, A new approach to financial regulation: building a stronger system, 2011 (CM 8012), paras 3.33 to 3.35, www.hm-treasury.gov.uk/d/consult_newfinancial_regulation170211.pdf (accessed 20 February 2011).

47 Working Document, pp39–40.

48 In the European context, the inadequate recent approach of the European authorities to stress testing of banks during the Eurozone crisis has shown that the risk of forbearance is not a purely theoretical one. See also *David G. Mayes, María J. Nieto and Larry Wall* Multiple safety net regulators and agency problems in the EU: is Prompt Corrective Action a partial solution? Bank of Finland Research Discussion Papers, 7/2007.

both prudential supervision and intervention under the Bank of England,[49] may have implications for the extent of the forbearance risk, and it will be interesting to see how far the Proactive Intervention Framework proposals, when further articulated, address that risk. The European Commission might also benefit from exploring similar proposals.

E. Who exercises the triggers?

In most jurisdictions the parties who are directly involved in the resolution process will generally be: the authority responsible for supervising the bank; the central bank; the deposit guarantee scheme; and the finance ministry. The allocation of supervisory functions among different authorities may of course differ from one jurisdiction to another; in the United Kingdom, the current Government is in the process of transferring prudential supervision of most significant firms from the FSA to the PRA (to be established as a subsidiary of the Bank of England), while conduct of business regulation will be transferred to a newly-established Financial Conduct Authority.[50]

The prudential supervisor will generally be the authority with the best information about the financial position of the bank and, therefore, best able to judge whether intervention powers need to be exercised. It may also be the authority with the best information to make decisions about resolution methods and their implementation. However, the deposit guarantee scheme or the finance ministry may be the party which stands to lose most directly from a failure to intervene effectively in the affairs of the bank. As discussed in Section III.D, the judgment of the supervisory authority may be compromised by failures of supervision which have contributed to the possible failure of the bank; for this reason, there is a risk that the supervisor will be inclined to exercise forbearance when the right course to minimise risk to depositors and to the taxpayer would be to resolve the bank without delay.

This risk of forbearance can be addressed in a number of different ways. In the United Kingdom, the risk of forbearance is currently mitigated to some extent by having some

---

49 The Government's latest consultation (see n46 above) states that "the Government's view is that the potential for conflicts to arise is limited (for example, around the triggering of the [Special Resolution Regime]), because the roles and legal responsibilities are clear, and because … the PRA will be operationally independent of the rest of the Bank. However, the Government will consider whether it is appropriate to make specific provision in the [Special Resolution Regime] Code of Practice about managing conflicts, deal with this explicitly in the crisis management [Memorandum of Understanding] … or both: HM Treasury A new approach to financial regulation: building a stronger system, 2011, para 2.152. The fact is, however, that the new system will involve the same body that was responsible for prudential regulation of a firm, the PRA, pulling the first trigger for its resolution by its parent, the Bank of England, which is a structure which seems to present scope for conflicts and forbearance. In addition to the Proactive Intervention Framework, a possible mitigant is the power of the new Financial Conduct Authority to apply for a failing institution to be brought into the bank insolvency procedure, although the PRA would be able to prevent this on specified grounds.

50 HM Treasury, A new approach to financial regulation: judgment, focus and stability, 2010 (CM 7874), www.hm-treasury.gov.uk/d/consult_financial_regulation_condoc.pdf (accessed 20 February 2011). See also the further consultation document referred to in n46 above.

involvement of other authorities in the process. Under current UK legislation, the FSA is the lead agency in respect of a firm's recovery and resolution planning and in the enhanced supervision phase that commences as the firm encounters difficulties. Once the FSA is satisfied that the bank is failing, or is likely to fail, the threshold conditions for its authorisation and that, having regard to timing and other circumstances, it is not reasonably likely that action will be taken by or in respect of the bank that will enable it to satisfy those threshold conditions, further decisions in respect of the use of Special Resolution Regime pass to the Bank of England or (if public funds are involved) to the Treasury. Thus in one sense the FSA pulls the trigger for the onset of the Special Resolution Regime; alternatively it can be said that it passes a loaded gun to the Bank of England or the Treasury, who decide where to point it and whether and when to pull the trigger. The decision whether the bank should be resolved by use of the stabilisation options or should merely be allowed to enter bank insolvency or bank administration does not lie with the FSA.

Both the Guidance issued by the Treasury under the Banking Act 2009 and the Memorandum of Understanding that has been entered into by the Treasury, the Bank of England and the FSA make it clear that there is to be regular information exchange and co-operation between the authorities, which helps to mitigate the risk of forbearance.

Under the Government's proposed new regulatory structure, these decisions will to a greater extent be concentrated under the Bank of England. A subsidiary of the Bank of England, the PRA, will be responsible for the prudential regulation of banks and other significant investment firms. The Bank of England will be responsible for implementing the Special Resolution Regime. Although the PRA, overseen by independent non-executive directors, will have a measure of operational independence it will be more closely aligned with the Bank of England than is currently the case with the FSA; for example, senior officers of the Bank of England will sit on the PRA's board, with the Governor of the Bank of England being *ex officio* Chair of the PRA. This reorganisation, although no doubt desirable from other viewpoints, has some potential to increase the risk of conflicts and forbearance. It remains to be seen whether sufficiently robust governance measures will be put in place to address this risk adequately.[51]

Other jurisdictions approach the issue of who should exercise the triggers and the problem of forbearance in different ways. In addition to its Prompt Corrective Action provisions, the FDIA provides some independent ability of the FDIC to appoint itself as receiver of an institution where the relevant supervisory authority has failed to act and the FDIC considers it necessary to reduce the risk or losses incurred by the deposit insurance fund.[52] By contrast, in relation to systemically important institutions that are resolved under the Dodd-Frank Act,[53] that Act provides for a relatively complicated allocation of responsibilities in the exercise of triggers, in a process in which the Secretary of the Treasury, the FDIC, the financial institution concerned, the Board of Governors of the Federal Reserve System and potentially the courts become involved.[54] The penultimate step in the process is taken by the Secretary of the Treasury, following which either the

51 See also the Proactive Intervention Framework proposal mentioned in Section III.D.

52 FDIA, s11(c)(10).

53 Dodd-Frank Wall Street Reform and Consumer Protection Act of 2010.

54 Dodd-Frank Act, ss202 and 203.

board of the financial institution will acquiesce in or consent to the appointment of the FDIC as receiver or the Secretary of the Treasury will petition the District Court in Washington, DC for an order appointing the FDIC as receiver. It is questionable whether a process of this complexity would be appropriate under crisis conditions.[55]

The Working Document raises for consultation the question of whether the resolution authority should be separate from the supervisory authority but does not propose an answer to this question. The Commission's earlier Communication[56] noted that "in many jurisdictions resolution authorities are appropriately separated from supervisors and considers such separation to be important to minimise the risks of forbearance".

Although, therefore, there are differing approaches in different jurisdictions, it can perhaps be concluded that in principle:

- the decision as to whether a bank is of systemic importance should involve the central bank and fiscal authority as well as the prudential supervisor;
- a resolution regime should ensure that the central bank and the fiscal authority have some involvement in decisions about whether resolution powers should be invoked in relation to a systemically important institution;
- the risk of forbearance may be lower if the supervisory authority is not the authority, or is not the sole authority, making decisions about the use of intervention powers.

F. Role of the affected institution

The role of the affected institution in the triggering process is likely to diminish as its position worsens. In the early stage of recovery planning, the institution has the lead role of preparing the plan; as its situation worsens, but there is still time to attempt to rectify the position, the enhanced supervision and recovery measures required by the authorities are likely to involve the institution's management; however, at the point when resolution measures need to be implemented the role of the institution in the process may become an increasingly passive one.[57]

Some regimes, perhaps out of concern about state interventions of the scale and severity of resolution measures and the implications for private rights, explicitly give the management of the institution a role in the final resolution stage. The orderly liquidation authority provisions of the Dodd-Frank Act, for example, provide for the Secretary of

---

55 It should, however, be noted that the House of Commons Treasury Committee has voiced similar reservations about the complexity of the UK system: "We have some doubts about a system in which one authority decides whether or not to put an institution into resolution, another related institution decides what form that such a resolution arrangement should take and a third is responsible for the decision to use public funds". House of Commons Treasury Committee (2010–11), Financial Regulation: a preliminary consideration of the Government's proposals (HC 430-I, 2011), para 179, www.publications.parliament.uk/pa/cm201011/cmselect/cmtreasy/430/430i.pdf (accessed 21 February 2011).

56 See n12 above.

57 See, however, the suggestion in Section III.B that a duty should be imposed on nominated senior officers with respect to the resolution plan.

the Treasury to seek the consent or acquiescence of the board of an institution deemed systemic under the terms of the Act[58] and provides that the directors will not be liable to shareholders or creditors for acquiescing or consenting in good faith.[59] It is perhaps difficult to imagine that the board of a bank, faced with a determination by the Secretary of the Treasury, backed by the advice of the FDIC and the Governors of the Federal Reserve System, will at that stage be able to come up with a viable plan to rescue the bank without state intervention. This perhaps explains why the Banking Act 2009 stabilisation powers do not confer any explicit role on the bank that is to be subject to them, and no such role is envisaged by the Working Document.

G. The role of creditors

The Banking Act 2009 contains provisions giving the FSA and the Bank of England a period to react to insolvency proceedings against a bank by a third party, enabling the authorities to activate the Special Resolution Regime.[60] However, generally speaking the Special Resolution Regime only enables the authorities to interfere with the rights of creditors to a limited extent and the Banking Act 2009 and secondary legislation made under it grant significant safeguards to creditors,[61] including those required by the Settlement Finality and Financial Collateral Arrangements Directives.[62]

It is for consideration whether a more comprehensive stay on creditor action should be imposed from the point when the authorities start resolution proceedings. The Working Document proposes the temporary suspension of certain obligations and rights of close out netting, subject to appropriate safeguards. It also proposes that the resolution authority should have the right to request a stay or up to 90 days in any proceedings in which the credit institution is or becomes a party, and proposes a stay on insolvency proceedings relating to the institution.[63] The interaction between resolution regimes and the Settlement Finality and Financial Collateral Arrangements Directives (as well as netting under contract or applicable law) is a critically important topic for debate, but goes beyond the scope of this paper.

H. How public support is treated

The Northern Rock saga illustrated that, in the case of a firm judged to be systemically important, a certain circularity can develop between the need for public support and the

58 See Dodd-Frank Act, s203(b).

59 Dodd-Frank Act, s207.

60 Banking Act 2009, s120.

61 The Banking Act 2009 (Restriction of Partial Property Transfers) Order 2009 (SI 2009/322), as amended by The Banking Act 2009 (Restriction of Partial Property Transfers) (Amendment) Order 2009 (SI 2009/1826).

62 Directive 98/26/EC on settlement finality in payment and securities settlement systems and Directive 2002/47/EC on financial collateral arrangements as regards linked systems and credit claims, as amended by Directive 2009/44/EC amending the Settlement Finality Directive and the Financial Collateral Arrangements Directive.

63 Working Document, pp64 to 66.

judgment that the firm is failing its financial conditions for authorisation. In the Northern Rock case, the authorities judged that the public interest required broad assurances to be given to depositors and other creditors which would probably lead them to conclude that the firm would be given all the necessary financial support to ensure that it did not fail. How then, the hedge fund shareholders argued, could it be justifiable to assess compensation for former shareholders on the basis of a firm that had failed?

The Banking Act 2009 addresses this circularity by requiring the FSA, in its assessment of whether the conditions relating to failure to meet threshold conditions have been met, to ignore financial assistance provided by the Treasury or by the Bank of England (other than ordinary market assistance offered by the Bank of England on its usual terms).[64] The Working Document does not address this issue.

I. Judicial review

The availability of judicial review is a key aspect of the consistency of intervention powers with the European Convention on Human Rights. In the United Kingdom, this will normally be an *ex post* review.

While the inclusion of *ex ante* judicial involvement may appear to provide better protection for the rights of the institution and its shareholders and other stakeholders, in the majority of cases this protection will be illusory. By the time that the authorities have decided that resolution action is the only course available to them, it is likely that the institution's position will be quite precarious. The ability of a judge to second-guess the judgment of the authorities will be limited. Any hearing is likely to take place on an attenuated basis with limited opportunity for evidence-gathering. For this reason, it may be better not to compromise the ability of the courts to pass a final judgment on the actions of the authorities *ex post* by requiring them to become involved at this earlier stage.

The Working Document[65] states that judicial review should be limited to a review of the legality and legitimacy of the decision and its implementation by the resolution authority; the court should not have power to overturn the decision under review and remedies should be limited to compensation.

J. The cross-border aspect

Much remains to be done in the area of cross-border co-operation and mutual recognition of bank resolution regimes. In an ideal world, authorities exercising intervention powers in one country would be required to inform and consult with their counterparts in other countries where the institution or its group had substantial activities and such

64 Banking Act 2009, s7(4).
65 Working Document, p66.

information and consultation procedures would be built in to the triggers for intervention.

The Working Document takes a step forward in this direction in the European context by proposing mechanisms which encourage a single decision to be taken with respect to the recovery or resolution of a group with cross-border activities.[66] It envisages that disagreements between the supervisory college established under Article 131 a of the Capital Requirements Directive as to recovery measures will referred to a European authority, possibly the European Banking Authority, and that the supervisors should comply with its decision. In relation to resolution measures, however, the Working Document proposes that the group level resolution authority should determine whether group resolution is desirable and prepare a group resolution scheme, but accepts that a resolution authority covered by the scheme may decide not to comply and take independent measures. The prospect of a binding mechanism for co-ordination of cross-border resolution remains, therefore, some way off.[67]

In the meantime, it is submitted that the review the operation of the Reorganisation and Winding-up Directive (2001/24/EC), and in particular the definitions of reorganisation measures and winding-up proceedings (which are both unclear and unsuited to ensuring mutual recognition of the measures proposed in the Working Document), is a high priority.[68]

V. Conclusion

Following the onset of the financial crisis in 2007, a general global consensus has emerged that authorities should have available to them a graduated scale of powers to intervene in the affairs of failing banks. The United Kingdom experience well illustrates this need. These powers should start with recovery and resolution planning before the onset of any difficulties and, as issues emerge, escalate through enhanced supervision to implementation of recovery measures (corrective action) and finally resolution measures. The exercise of these intervention powers may lead to significant intrusions into the domain of private property rights and, as a result, use of the triggers should be proportionate and the principles governing their use should be as transparent as possible.

---

66 Working Document, pp43–45 and 75–82.

67 However, the Working Document (p7) states that the Commission considers that, following the adoption of a legislative proposal for a harmonised EU resolution regime and the examination of further harmonisation of domestic insolvency regimes, a third step should include the creation of an integrated resolution regime, possibly based on a single European Resolution Authority, by 2014. Given the surrender of fiscal sovereignty that would be likely to be inherent in such a regime, this is an ambitious aim.

68 See *G.H. Garcia, Rosa M. Lastra and María J. Nieto* Bankruptcy and reorganisation procedures for cross-border banks in the EU: Towards and integrated approach to the reform of the EU safety net, LSE Financial Markets Group Paper Series, May 2009, pp11–15.

The UK Banking Act 2009 and its associated Code of Practice is a coherent response to these issues and the Working Document prepared by DG Internal Market and Services draws heavily on this precedent. As regards triggers, however, there remain a number of areas where further work is needed, particularly in developing recovery plans and resolution plans, further defining the options for early intervention, addressing the issue of forbearance and making progress in the difficult area of cross-border co-operation.

Instrumente eines Sonderinsolvenzrechts für Banken

Tools for Bank Resolution

Interventionsmechanismen nach dem deutschen Restrukturierungsgesetz

*Dirk H. Bliesener**

Gliederung

I. Das Restrukturierungsgesetz – Übersicht
 1. Verfahren nach dem Kreditinstitute-Reorganisationsgesetz
  a) Sanierungsverfahren
  b) Reorganisationsverfahren
 2. Interventionsbefugnisse der BaFin und der FMSA
  a) Präventive Eingriffsrechte der BaFin
  b) Korrektive Eingriffsrechte der BaFin
  c) Hilfsmaßnahmen des Restrukturierungsfonds
II. Die Übertragungsanordnung
 1. Verfahren und Ausgestaltung im Überblick
  a) Gegenleistung
  b) Ausgliederung durch Verwaltungsakt und Zustimmung des übernehmenden Rechtsträgers
  c) Haftungsregime
  d) Rechtsschutz
 2. Materielle Voraussetzungen der Übertragungsanordnung
  a) Bestandsgefährdung
  b) Systemgefährdung
  c) Ultima ratio
 3. Gesamtübertragung vs. Teilübertragung
  a) Gesamtübertragung, partielle Übertragung, partielle Rückübertragung
  b) Auswahl der zu übertragenden Unternehmensteile
  c) Unübertragbare und unteilbare Gegenstände
 4. Anerkennung im Ausland und negative Transferfolgen
  a) Gegenstände mit Auslandsbezug
  b) Globale Wirkung der Ausgliederung nach deutschem Recht
  c) Fehlende Anerkennung in ausländischen Jurisdiktionen
  d) Negative Transferfolgen
  e) Due Diligence
 5. Brückeninstitut
  a) Rechtsform
  b) Refinanzierung
  c) Kapitalausstattung
 6. Ausblick

---

* Der Beitrag ist auf dem Stand vom 31. Januar 2011; einzelne Literaturbeiträge sind bis 31. August 2011 berücksichtigt. Der Autor dankt Herrn Rechtsreferendar Till Wansleben für seine Mitwirkung an diesem Beitrag.

Das Restrukturierungsgesetz vom 9. Dezember 2010[1] vereint ein Bündel von Maßnahmen zur Prävention und Bewältigung von Bankenkrisen in Deutschland. Ausgangspunkt für die gesetzgeberischen Maßnahmen war die akute Bankenkrise im September und Oktober 2008 im Anschluss an die Insolvenz von Lehman Brothers. In dieser Situation stand der Bankenaufsicht und der Bundesregierung außer der Stützung aus Steuermitteln kein probates Mittel zu Gebote, eine insolvenzbedingte Liquidation und die dadurch befürchteten negativen Auswirkungen auf das deutsche und globale Finanzsystem zu vermeiden.[2] Als staatliche Rettungsmaßnahme wurde der Finanzmarktstabilisierungsfonds (SoFFin) geschaffen und durch das Finanzmarktstabilisierungsgesetz[3] das Instrumentarium zur Stützung von Liquidität[4] und Eigenmitteln[5] von Unternehmen des Finanzsektors sowie später Mechanismen zur Abtrennung ganzer Geschäftsbereiche[6] eingeführt.[7] Da diese Maßnahmen von vorneherein eine vorübergehende Notlösung mit unerwünschten Fehlanreizen für Management, Eigen- und Fremdkapitalgeber darstellten[8] und in künftigen Krisen zumindest der Einsatz von Steuergeldern vermieden werden soll[9], wurde auf internationaler, europäischer und nationaler Ebene nach effektiven Steuerungsinstrumenten und optimierten Restrukturierungs- oder Abwicklungsverfahren gesucht, um die Restrukturierung oder den Marktaustritt von Banken systemschonend umzusetzen.[10]

---

1 Gesetz zur Restrukturierung und geordneten Abwicklung von Kreditinstituten, zur Errichtung eines Restrukturierungsfonds für Kreditinstitute und zur Verlängerung der Verjährungsfrist der aktienrechtlichen Organhaftung (Restrukturierungsgesetz), BGBl. I, S. 1900 vom 14. Dezember 2010. Die Änderungsvorschläge des Bundesrates (Stellungnahme des Bundesrates, BR-Drucks. 534/10 (Beschluss) vom 15. Oktober 2010) und des Finanzausschusses des Bundestages (Bericht des Finanzausschusses, BT-Drucks. 17/3547 vom 28. Oktober 2010) waren nicht sehr umfangreich ausgefallen und wurden teilweise berücksichtigt. S. auch *Obermüller*, NZI 2011, 81; *Wolfers/Voland* WM 2011, 1159.

2 S. etwa *Hopt/Fleckner/Kumpan/Steffek* WM 2009, 821 (821 f.); *Hüpkes* EBOR 10 (2009), 369 (372 f.); *Zimmer/Fuchs* ZGR 2010, 597 (600 ff.).

3 Gesetz zur Umsetzung eines Maßnahmenpakets zur Stabilisierung des Finanzmarktes vom 17. Oktober 2008, BGBl. I, S. 1982 (FMStG), mit dem insbesondere das Finanzmarktstabilisierungsfondsgesetz (FMStFG) und das Finanzmarktstabilisierungsbeschleunigungsgesetz (FMStBG) erlassen wurde. 2009 wurde das FMStG ergänzt durch das Gesetz zur weiteren Stabilisierung des Finanzmarktes vom 7. April 2009, BGBl. I, S. 725, sowie das Gesetz zur Fortentwicklung der Finanzmarktstabilisierung vom 17. Juli 2009, BGBl. I, S. 2305.

4 Bereitstellung von Garantien des SoFFin, § 6 FMStFG.

5 Rekapitalisierung durch den SoFFin, § 7 FMStFG.

6 Übertragung von Risikopositionen und nicht strategienotwendigen Geschäftsbereichen auf eine Abwicklungsanstalt nach § 8 a/§ 8 b FMStFG.

7 Zu diesen Maßnahmengesetzen beispielsweise *Becker/Mock* DB 2009, 1055; *Binder* ZBB 2009, 19 (22 f.); *Ewer/Behnsen* NJW 2008, 3457; *Horn* BKR 2008, 452; *Karpenstein* ZBB 2009, 413; *Kroll* DÖV 2009, 477; *Langenbucher* ZGR 2010, 75; *Obermüller/Obermüller* ZInsO 2010, 305; *Pannen* Krise und Insolvenz bei Kreditinstituten, 2010, Kapitel 2; *Spindler* DStR 2008, 2268; *Wieneke/Fett* NZG 2009, 8; *Wolfers/Rau* NJW 2009, 2401; *Ziemons* NZG 2009, 369.

8 S. *Binder* ZBB 2009, 19 (22).

9 Begründung RegE RestrG, BT-Drucks. 17/3024, S. 1.

10 Beschlussempfehlung des Finanzausschusses, BT-Drucks. 17/3407, S. 1. Dazu auch *Sester* ECFR 2010, 512; vgl. auch *Binder* ZBB 2009, 19 (20); zu weiteren Reformen beispielsweise *Lorenz* NZG 2010, 1046 (1047). Zu den europäischen Ansätzen s. Europäische Kommission, Mitteilung, KOM(2009) 561 sowie Europäische Kommission, Staff Working Document, SEC(2009) 1407; s. dazu beispielsweise Begründung RegE RestrG, BT-Drucks. 17/3024, S. 42 li. Sp.; *Bachmann* ZBB

I. Das Restrukturierungsgesetz – Übersicht

In Deutschland ist das Ergebnis der Überlegungen das Restrukturierungsgesetz, das mit einem Abstand von über zwei Jahren nach dem Höhepunkt der Finanzkrise und auch im Vergleich zu anderen Ländern (beispielsweise Großbritannien) erst spät kommt. Das Gesetz trat, gestuft nach unterschiedlichen Artikeln, bis zum 1. Januar 2011 vollständig in Kraft. Das Restrukturierungsgesetz baut in einzelnen Teilen auf einem Entwurf des Bundesministeriums der Justiz aus dem Jahre 2009[11] auf.[12] Der Entwurf eines Restrukturierungsverwaltungsgesetzes des Bundesministeriums für Wirtschaft und Technologie aus dem Jahre 2009 wurde nicht weiter verfolgt.[13] Die Grundsatzentscheidung der Bundesregierung war am 31. März 2010 in einem Eckpunktepapier des Bundeskabinetts veröffentlicht worden[14]. Das Restrukturierungsgesetz hat zwei primäre Stoßrichtungen: Zum einen wird mit dem Gesetz zur Reorganisation von Kreditinstituten (Kreditinstitute-Reorganisationsgesetz – KredReorgG)[15] ein eigenes, bankenspezifisches Instrument der präinsolvenzlichen Sanierung und Restrukturierung eingeführt. Zum anderen werden die aufsichtsrechtlichen Befugnisse in der Krise detaillierter geregelt und erheblich erweitert.[16]

1. Verfahren nach dem Kreditinstitute-Reorganisationsgesetz

Das KredReorgG sieht zwei freiwillige gerichtliche Verfahren vor, die unter Einbindung der Bundesanstalt für Finanzdienstleistungsaufsicht (BaFin), aber auf Initiative des Kreditinstituts selbst eingeleitet werden können.

a) Sanierungsverfahren

Zunächst ermöglicht das Restrukturierungsgesetz ein Sanierungsverfahren, das in einem frühen Stadium der wirtschaftlichen Schwierigkeiten eingeleitet werden kann. Voraussetzung ist, dass das Institut sanierungsbedürftig ist. Sanierungsbedürftigkeit liegt vor, wenn die Voraussetzungen des § 45 Abs. 1 Satz 1 und 2 KWG erfüllt sind, d. h., wenn die gesetzlichen Eigenmittel- oder Liquiditätsanforderungen nicht dauerhaft erfüllt werden können.[17] Dies ist regelmäßig der Fall, wenn der Tatbestand eines der

---

2010, 459 (461); *Höche* in: FS Hopt, 2010, S. 2001 (2008); *Kafsack* Banken sollen Krisenpläne entwickeln, F.A.Z. vom 20. Oktober 2010; *Moenninghoff/Wieandt* Revue d'Economie Financière 101 (2011), 231, 245 ff.; *Heuer/Gosejacob* ZKredW 2011, 720, 721.

11 Abdruck s. WM 2009, 770 (771).

12 S. auch *Lorenz* NZG 2010, 1046 (1048).

13 Dieses Konkurrenzmodell zum Reorganisationsverfahren sah u. a. vor, dass durch Verwaltungsakt eine Restrukturierungsverwaltung der BaFin anhand eines Restrukturierungsplanes durchgeführt werden sollte, s. dazu etwa *Lorenz* WM 2009, 770 (770 f.); *Eidenmüller* in: FS Hopt, 2010, S. 1712 (1726 ff.); *Höche* in: FS Hopt, 2010, S. 2001 (2009); *Lorenz* NZG 2010, 1046 (1048); *Pannen* Krise und Insolvenz bei Kreditinstituten, 2010, Kapitel 7 Rz. 5 ff.

14 Abrufbar unter http://www.bundesfinanzministerium.de/nn_82/DE/Wirtschaft__und__Verwaltung/Geld__und__Kredit/20100331-Eckpunkte-Finanzmarktregulierung.html.

15 Artikel 1 des Restrukturierungsgesetzes.

16 Artikel 2 (und 3) des Restrukturierungsgesetzes.

17 § 2 Abs. 1 Satz 2 KredReorgG.

Regelbeispiele des § 45 Abs. 1 Satz 2 KWG[18] eintritt. Sollte die Geschäftsleitung feststellen, dass die Voraussetzungen der Sanierungsbedürftigkeit gegeben sind, wird bei der Abwägung von Chancen und Risiken eines Sanierungsverfahrens die Öffentlichkeit dieses gerichtlichen Verfahrens und ihre Auswirkungen auf die Reputation ("Franchise") und die Liquiditätslage eine erhebliche Rolle spielen. Falls das Verfahren eingeleitet werden soll, hat das Institut einen Sanierungsplan auszuarbeiten, einen Sanierungsberater auszuwählen und eine entsprechende Anzeige an die BaFin zu erstatten. Die BaFin prüft die Zweckmäßigkeit der Durchführung eines Sanierungsverfahrens und die Eignung des vorgeschlagenen Sanierungsberaters – im Benehmen mit der Bundesanstalt für Finanzmarktstabilisierung (FMSA), falls zuvor Stabilisierungsmaßnahmen nach dem FMStFG durchgeführt wurden – und stellt ggf. einen Antrag auf Durchführung des Sanierungsverfahrens beim zuständigen Oberlandesgericht Frankfurt am Main. Mit dem Antrag hat die BaFin zum Sanierungsplan und vorgeschlagenen Sanierungsberater Stellung zu nehmen. Das Oberlandesgericht Frankfurt am Main kann das Sanierungsverfahren anordnen und den Sanierungsberater ernennen, der über eine Reihe von Teilhabe-, Informations- und Weisungsrechten verfügt (§ 4 KredReorgG).[19] Das Sanierungsverfahren stellt den Rahmen für eine vertragliche Einigung zwischen Bank, Eigentümern und Gläubigern dar und kommt ohne gerichtlich angeordnete Eingriffe in Drittrechte aus.[20] Allerdings kann der Sanierungsplan die Aufnahme von Sanierungskrediten vorsehen, die in einem innerhalb von drei Jahren nach Anordnung des Sanierungsverfahrens stattfindenden Insolvenzverfahren privilegiert sind.[21] Daneben können vom Gericht weitere Maßnahmen autorisiert und bei-

---

18 § 45 Abs. 1 Satz 2 KWG lautet: "Die Annahme, dass das Institut die Anforderungen des § 10 Absatz 1 oder Absatz 1b, des § 45b Absatz 1 Satz 2 oder des § 11 nicht dauerhaft erfüllen können wird, ist regelmäßig gerechtfertigt, wenn sich

1. die Gesamtkennziffer über das prozentuale Verhältnis der anrechenbaren Eigenmittel und der mit 12,5 multiplizierten Summe aus dem Gesamtanrechnungsbetrag für Adressrisiken, dem *Anrechungsbetrag* für das operationelle Risiko und der Summe der Anrechnungsbeträge für Marktrisikopositionen einschließlich der Optionsgeschäfte nach der Rechtsverordnung nach § 10 Absatz 1 Satz 9 von einem Meldestichtag zum nächsten um mindestens 10 Prozent oder die nach der Rechtsverordnung nach § 11 Absatz 1 zu ermittelnde Liquiditätskennziffer von einem Meldestichtag zum nächsten um mindestens 25 Prozent verringert hat und aufgrund dieser Entwicklung mit einem Unterschreiten der Mindestanforderungen innerhalb der nächsten zwölf Monate zu rechnen ist oder
2. die Gesamtkennziffer über das prozentuale Verhältnis der anrechenbaren Eigenmittel und der mit 12,5 multiplizierten Summe aus dem Gesamtanrechnungsbetrag für Adressrisiken, dem Anrechnungsbetrag für das operationelle Risiko und der Summe der Anrechnungsbeträge für Marktrisikopositionen einschließlich der Optionsgeschäfte nach der Rechtsverordnung nach § 10 Absatz 1 Satz 9 an mindestens drei aufeinanderfolgenden Meldestichtagen um jeweils mehr als 3 Prozent oder die nach der Rechtsverordnung nach § 11 Absatz 1 zu ermittelnde Liquiditätskennziffer an mindestens drei aufeinanderfolgenden Meldestichtagen um jeweils mehr als 10 Prozent verringert hat und aufgrund dieser Entwicklung mit einem Unterschreiten der Mindestanforderungen innerhalb der nächsten 18 Monate zu rechnen ist und keine Tatsachen offensichtlich sind, die die Annahme rechtfertigen, dass die Mindestanforderungen mit überwiegender Wahrscheinlichkeit nicht unterschritten werden."

19 Begründung RegE RestrG, BT-Drucks. 17/3024, S. 47 li. Sp.

20 Begründung RegE RestrG, BT-Drucks. 17/3024, S. 45 re. Sp.

21 Kritisch im Hinblick auf die Neutralität gegenüber Gläubigerrechten die Stellungnahme des Bundesrates, BR-Drucks. 534/10 (Beschluss) vom 15. Oktober 2010, S. 5; *Hirte* Stellungnahme

spielsweise die Geschäftsleitung abberufen werden (§ 5 KredReorgG). Nach der Umsetzung des Sanierungsplans wird das Sanierungsverfahren aufgehoben.[22]

b) Reorganisationsverfahren

Wenn ein Sanierungsverfahren erfolglos durchgeführt wurde oder von vorneherein vom Institut für aussichtslos gehalten wird, kann das Institut ein Reorganisationsverfahren einleiten. Voraussetzung für die Durchführung eines Reorganisationsverfahrens ist, dass eine Bestandsgefährdung des Instituts vorliegt, die zu einer Systemgefährdung führt.[23] Werden die Voraussetzungen der Bestands- und daraus folgenden Systemgefährdung bejaht, kann die Geschäftsleitung des Instituts nach Abwägung von Chancen und Risiken ein Reorganisationsverfahren durch Anzeige an die BaFin initiieren. Daneben ist ein Reorganisationsplan vorzulegen und ein Reorganisationsberater vorzuschlagen. Die BaFin prüft die Voraussetzungen des Reorganisationsverfahrens – wiederum im Benehmen mit der FMSA im Falle vorausgehender Stabilisierungsmaßnahmen nach FMStFG – und stellt ggf. einen Antrag auf Durchführung des Reorganisationsverfahrens beim Oberlandesgericht Frankfurt am Main. Dabei ist eine Stellungnahme zum Reorganisationsplan und dem vorgeschlagenen Reorganisationsberater vorzulegen. Das Gericht weist den Antrag zurück, falls die Vorschriften über den Inhalt des Reorganisationsplans nicht erfüllt sind. Nach Anhörung der BaFin, der Bundesbank und des Instituts kann das Gericht die Durchführung des Reorganisationsplans anordnen. Zentraler Bestandteil eines Reorganisationsverfahrens ist der Reorganisationsplan, der – wie ein Insolvenzplan – aus einem darstellenden und einem gestaltenden Teil besteht. Der Reorganisationsplan kann gemäß § 8 Abs. 1 Satz 4 KredReorgG auch als Liquidationsplan ausgestaltet sein. In den Reorganisationsplan werden neben den Gläubigern auch die Anteilseigner einbezogen, die als eigene Gruppe über den Plan abstimmen (§§ 8, 17 f. KredReorgG). Neben dem Eingriff in Gläubigerrechte, die nicht durch einen Sicherungsfonds geschützt sind,[24] kann insbesondere ein Debt-to-Equity Swap mit Zustimmung der betroffenen Gläubiger, aber ggf. gegen den Willen der Anteilsinhaber durchgeführt werden (§ 9 KredReorgG).[25] Im gestaltenden Teil des Reorganisationsplans kann auch vorgesehen werden, dass das Kreditinstitut sein Vermögen ganz oder in Teilen auf einen anderen Rechtsträger ausgliedert (§ 11 KredReorgG). Der Reorganisationsplan ist von den Gläubigern und Anteilsinhabern anzunehmen und anschließend vom Gericht zu bestätigen. Die Zustimmung gilt, bezogen auf einzelne Gläubigergruppen, auch ohne die erforderliche Mehrheit unter bestimmten Voraussetzungen als erteilt. Nach der Bestätigung des Reorganisationsplans wird das Reorganisationsverfahren aufgehoben. Die Verfahren nach dem KredReorgG sollen einen effektiven Rahmen für kollektive Verhandlungsmodelle liefern.[26] Ob allerdings relativ

---

Restrukturierungsgesetz, S. 4, abrufbar unter http://www.bundestag.de/bundestag/ausschuesse17/a07/anhoerungen/2010/029/Stellungnahmen/19_Hirte.pdf.

22 § 6 Abs. 3 KredReorgG.

23 § 7 Abs. 2 KredReorgG, s. auch näher unten Abschnitt II 2b.

24 § 12 KredReorgG.

25 S. auch § 225 a InsO-E des Diskussionsentwurfes für ein Gesetz zur weiteren Erleichterung der Sanierung von Unternehmen, abrufbar unter http://zip-online.de/pdf/zip/Diskussionsentwurf.pdf.

26 Begründung RegE RestrG, BT-Drucks. 17/3024, S. 2.

langwierige und öffentlichkeitswirksame Verfahren wie das Sanierungs- oder Reorganisationsverfahren im Bankensektor praxistauglich sind, erscheint zweifelhaft: Jedenfalls bei einem Reorganisationsverfahren kann eine mindestens monatelange Verfahrensdauer erwartet werden,[27] und die Nachricht über die Einleitung eines solchen Verfahrens könnte erst recht den Fortbestand des Instituts in Frage stellen und seine Liquiditätssituation schwächen ("self-fulfilling prophecy") und dadurch sogar eine Systemkrise auslösen.[28] Auch fehlen Anreize für ein Kreditinstitut, die Durchführung eines solchen Verfahrens anzustoßen.[29] Insbesondere beim Sanierungsverfahren hängt der Erfolg von der Einigung der Gläubiger und Eigentümer ab, die auch Voraussetzung einer außergerichtlichen Sanierung ist.

2. Interventionsbefugnisse der BaFin und der FMSA

Neben den Sanierungs- und Reorganisationsverfahren wird durch das Restrukturierungsgesetz das Repertoire der Befugnisse der BaFin vor und in einer insolvenznahen Gefahrensituation erweitert. Hierbei handelt es sich um neue Rechte und Aufgaben der BaFin nach dem Gesetz über das Kreditwesen (KWG), die insbesondere die Aufspaltung eines Kreditinstituts ermöglichen,[30] und neue Rechte der FSMA nach dem Gesetz über einen neu zu schaffenden Restrukturierungsfonds (RStruktFG)[31], der den ab 31. Dezember 2010 abzuwickelnden SoFFin gleichsam abgelöst hat. Die Befugnis der BaFin, aufsichtsrechtliche Maßnahmen zu ergreifen, besteht auch, wenn bereits ein Sanierungs- oder Reorganisationsverfahren nach dem KredReorgG durchgeführt wird (§ 1 Abs. 5 KredReorgG). Denn die BaFin soll frühzeitig und jederzeit Sanierungsschritte von dem betreffenden Institut fordern und durchsetzen können. Etwas anderes gilt gemäß § 48c Abs. 2 Satz 2 KWG nur dann, wenn bereits ein Reorganisationsverfahren eingeleitet wurde und kein Zweifel besteht, dass das Reorganisationsverfahren geeignet ist, die Bestandsgefährdung rechtzeitig abzuwenden, und der übermittelte Reorganisationsplan rechtzeitig angenommen, bestätigt und umgesetzt wird. In diesem Ausnahmefall kann die BaFin keine Übertragungsanordnung nach § 48a KWG erlassen. Die neuen aufsichtsrechtlichen Instrumente umfassen präventive Eingriffsrechte, die eine Schieflage von Instituten verhindern sollen, korrektive Eingriffsrechte, die einer entstandenen Krise begegnen sollen, sowie Hilfsmaßnahmen des Restrukturierungsfonds, die Maßnahmen aufgrund der korrektiven Eingriffsrechte der BaFin flankieren und

27 Selbst bei detaillierter Vorbereitung des Reorganisationsplans sind Gläubiger zur Anmeldung ihrer Forderungen innerhalb von mindestens drei Wochen aufzufordern (§ 14 KredReorgG) und bedarf der von Gläubigern und Anteilsinhabern angenommene Reorganisationsplan der Bestätigung durch das Oberlandesgericht Frankfurt am Main innerhalb einer weiteren Frist von einem Monat (§ 20 Abs. 1 Satz 3 KredReorgG).

28 *Zimmer* Was das Gesetz zur Rettung der Banken taugt, F.A.Z. vom 9. September 2010, S. 12; *ders.* Stellungnahme RestrG, S. 4, abrufbar unter http://www.bundestag.de/bundestag/ausschuesse 17/a07/anhoerungen/2010/029/Stellungnahmen/35_Prof__Dr__Daniel_Zimmer.pdf.

29 Vgl. *Bachmann* ZBB 2010, 459 (462); *Eidenmüller* in: FS Hopt, 2010, S. 1712 (1724 f.); *Krahnen/Siekmann* Stellungnahme RestrG, HoF Policy Platform, S. 4, abrufbar unter http://www.hof.uni-frankfurt.de/component/option,com_docman/Itemid,288/gid,13/task,doc_download/; *Lorenz* NZG 2010, 1046 (1049); *Schuster* Börsen-Zeitung vom 1. September 2010, S. 2.

30 Artikel 2 des Restrukturierungsgesetzes.

31 Artikel 3 des Restrukturierungsgesetzes.

dadurch eine finanzmarktschonende Abwicklung von Kreditinstituten ermöglichen sollen.

a) Präventive Eingriffsrechte der BaFin

Das Restrukturierungsgesetz hat die präventiven Eingriffsrechte der BaFin gegenüber Kreditinstituten und ihren Organen (§§ 6 und 45, 46 und 46a KWG) aktualisiert, ergänzt und in größerer Detailtiefe festgelegt. Neu geregelt wurde die Funktion eines Sonderbeauftragten, der von der BaFin eingesetzt werden kann (§ 45c KWG).[32] Die Befugnisse nach §§ 45, 45b KWG sind auf eine abstrakte Gefahrenlage zugeschnitten, während die Instrumente der §§ 45c, 46 und 48a KWG einer bereits konkretisierten Gefahrenlage begegnen sollen. Die BaFin kann gemäß § 45 Abs. 1 KWG gegenüber einem Institut Maßnahmen zur Verbesserung seiner Eigenmittelausstattung und Liquidität anordnen, wenn die Annahme gerechtfertigt ist, dass das Institut seine gesetzlichen Solvabilitäts- oder Liquiditätsanforderungen dauerhaft nicht mehr erfüllen können wird. Auch wenn ein Tatbestand der Regelbeispiele des § 45 Abs. 1 Satz 2 KWG[33] noch nicht eingetreten ist, kommt der BaFin ein erheblicher Beurteilungsspielraum hinsichtlich der Wahrscheinlichkeit einer nicht mehr dauerhaften Compliance des Instituts mit Solvabilitäts- und Liquiditätskennzahlen zu. Bejaht die BaFin die Voraussetzungen, kann sie als mögliche Maßnahmen dem Institut Informations-, Berichts- und Darlegungspflichten auferlegen.[34] Zusätzlich zu den bereits in § 45 Abs. 1 KWG a. F. enthaltenen Pflichten kann die BaFin anordnen, dass das Institut mittels eines "Restrukturierungsplans" darlegt, wie die Eigenmittelausstattung oder Liquidität des Instituts wiederhergestellt werden soll.[35] Die bisher eher stiefmütterlich geregelte Aufsichtsperson, die von der BaFin bestellt worden konnte,[36] wird als Sonderbeauftragter mit einem erweiterten Anwendungsgebiet und damit als eigenständiges Aufsichtsinstrument mit überwiegend präventivem Charakter neu etabliert.[37] Einem Sonderbeauftragten können nach Wahl der BaFin weitreichende Befugnisse übertragen werden. Erstaunlicherweise ist die Bestellung dieses Sonderbeauftragten nach dem Wortlaut des Gesetzes weder von einer abstrakten noch von einer konkreten Gefahrenlage abhängig.[38] Bei der Übertragung einzelner Befugnisse müssen zwar entsprechende Voraussetzungen erfüllt sein, die Aufzählung ist aber nicht abschließend. Es wird jedoch bei der Bestimmung seines Befugnisrahmens der Grundsatz der Verhältnismäßigkeit zu beachten sein.[39] Eine ausdrückliche Regelung zu Notfallplanungen ("Funeral Plans", "Living Wills") fehlt in dem neuen Regelwerk.[40] Darunter versteht man Pläne, in denen das Institut der Bankenaufsicht ex ante erläutert, durch welche Maß-

---

32 S. dazu schon *Amend* ZIP 2009, 589 (598).

33 S. oben Fn. 18.

34 S. auch *Lorenz* NZG 2010, 1046 (1051 f.).

35 S. auch Begründung RegE RestrG, BT-Drucks. 17/3024, S. 59 re. Sp.

36 Zur Aufsichtsperson beispielsweise *Lindemann* in: Boos/Fischer/Schulte/Mattler, KWG, 3. Aufl. 2008, § 46 Rz. 37 ff.; *Pannen* Krise und Insolvenz bei Kreditinstituten, 2010, Kapitel 1 Rz. 63 f.; *Schwennicke* in: Schwennicke/Auerbach, KWG, 2009, § 46 Rz. 27 ff.

37 *Lorenz* WM 2010, 1426.

38 Kritisch *Lorenz* NZG 2010, 1046 (1052); begrüßend dagegen *Bachmann* ZBB 2010, 459 (469).

39 Begründung RegE RestrG, BT-Drucks. 17/3024, S. 60 li. Sp.; *Bachmann* ZBB 2010, 459 (469).

40 Vgl. auch *Bachmann* ZBB 2010, 459 (470 f.).

nahmen das Institut im Krisenfall stabilisiert oder abgewickelt werden könnte.[41] Die Aufsicht dürfte sich hinsichtlich der Anforderung von Notfall- oder Abwicklungsplänen und deren Gestaltung auf die allgemeine Vorschrift des § 25a KWG über die ordnungsgemäße Geschäftsorganisation und das Risikomanagement stützen.[42] Schon bisher werden Notfallkonzepte als Bestandteil des Risikomanagement nach § 25a Abs. 1 Satz 3 Nr. 3 KWG verlangt.[43] Es erscheint allerdings nicht ganz unzweifelhaft, ob auch Eventualplanungen mit dem Ziel der Abwicklung des Bankbetriebs von der Anordnungsbefugnis nach § 25a Abs. 1 Satz 8 KWG erfasst sind, da Notfallkonzepte nach § 25a KWG als Sicherungsvorkehrung zur Abwendung von Gefahren mit dem Ziel der Rückkehr zum "Normalbetrieb" zu verstehen sind. Wenn die Voraussetzungen erfüllt sind, können Anordnungen der BaFin im Zusammenhang mit Notfallplanungen zur Verhinderung von Missständen bei einem Institut, die die Sicherheit der ihm anvertrauten Vermögenswerte gefährden können, auf § 6 Abs. 3 Satz 1 KWG gestützt werden.

b) Korrektive Eingriffsrechte der BaFin

Neben diesen präventiven Eingriffsrechten verankert das Restrukturierungsgesetz als wichtiges Novum die Befugnis der BaFin, eine sog. Übertragungsanordnung zu erlassen (§§ 48a ff. KWG). Damit kommt Deutschland einem Petitum des Financial Stability Board[44] nach und entspricht – dem Vorbild der U.S.-amerikanischen Einlagensicherung (FDIC)[45] folgend – dem Standard moderner Gesetzgebung zur Abwicklung von Banken in der Krise. Hervorzuheben sind aus jüngster Zeit der U.S.-amerikanische Dodd-Frank Wall Street Reform and Consumer Protection Act (2010)[46] und der britische Banking Act 2009[47].[48] Mit der Übertragungsanordnung kann die BaFin das gesamte Vermögen oder Unternehmensteile auf einen anderen Rechtsträger übertragen und so das Institut in

---

41 Vgl. *Zimmer* Gutachten G, Verhandlungen des 68. DJT, Berlin 2010, Band I, S. G 50; *ders./Fuchs* ZGR 2010, 597 (605 ff.).

42 Für eine entsprechende Ergänzung im KWG *Zimmer/Fuchs* ZGR 2010, 597 (606); wohl auch *Riethmüller* WM 2010, 2295 (2299 f.); vgl. dazu auch *Zimmer* Gutachten G, Verhandlungen des 68. DJT, Berlin 2010, Band I, S. G 55.

43 Insbesondere für IT-Systeme, s. MaRisk AT 7.3; dazu *Braun* in: Boos/Fischer/Schulte/Mattler (Hrsg.) KWG 3. Aufl. 2008, § 25a Rz. 14, 449 ff.

44 *Financial Stability Board*, Reducing the moral hazard posed by systemically important financial institutions, 20. Oktober 2010, S. 3 ff., abrufbar unter http://www.financialstabilityboard.org/publications/r_101111a.pdf.

45 Dazu beispielsweise *Binder* ZBB 2009, 19 (23 ff.).

46 Title II, insbesondere Sec. 210; dazu beispielsweise *Spindler* AG 2010, 601 (614 f.); *ders./Brandt/Raapke* RIW 2010, 746 (751 f.).

47 Insbesondere Sec. 11–13; dazu beispielsweise *Binder* Bankenintervention und Bankenabwicklung in Deutschland: Reformnotwendigkeiten und Grundzüge eines verbesserten Rechtsrahmens, Sachverständigenrat Arbeitspapier 05/2009, S. 43 ff., abrufbar unter: http://46.4.4.24/fileadmin/dateiablage/Arbeitspapiere/Bankenintervention_und_Bankenabwicklung_in_Deutschland.pdf; *Brierley* Financial Stability Paper No. 5, July 2009, S. 7 ff., abrufbar unter http://www.bankofengland.co.uk/publications/fsr/fs_paper05.pdf; *Kaserer/Köndgen/Möllers* ZBB 2009, 142 (146); *Spindler* AG 2010, 601 (613 f.); vgl. zu weiteren Reformen in Großbritannien auch *Binder* ZBB 2009, 19 (28 ff.); *Tricot* in: Jaletzke/Veranneman (Hrsg.) FMStG, 2009, Anhang I B. Rz. 23 ff.

48 S. dazu auch *Čihák/Nier*, IMF Working Paper WP/09/200, S. 15 ff., abrufbar unter http://www.imf.org/external/pubs/ft/wp/2009/wp09200.pdf; *Höche* WM 2011, 49, 51 f.

eine "Good Bank" und eine "Bad Bank" aufteilen.[49] Das neu geschaffene Instrument der Übertragungsanordnung sieht die Übertragung von Aktiv- und Passivermögen und Vertragsbeziehungen (*property transfer*) vor, nicht aber die Übertragung von Anteilen an dem in die Krise geratenen Kreditinstitut (*share transfer*). Ein solches Instrument kann in Krisensituationen wünschenswert sein.[50] Daher ist ein *share transfer* im Vereinigten Königreich durch Verwaltungsakt möglich[51]. Der deutsche Gesetzgeber hatte 2009 mit dem Rettungsübernahmegesetz (RettungsG)[52] lediglich eine zeitlich befristete Möglichkeit zur Enteignung geschaffen.[53] Übernimmt man eine solche Eingriffsbefugnis in das deutsche Recht, stellen sich insbesondere verfassungsrechtliche Fragen.[54] Die Klärung dieser Fragen hat der Gesetzgeber vermieden und die Übertragungsbefugnis der BaFin auf den Geschäftsbetrieb, ob ganz oder in Teilen, beschränkt.[55]

c) Hilfsmaßnahmen des Restrukturierungsfonds

Die Eingriffsbefugnis der BaFin nach § 48a KWG wird flankiert durch die Möglichkeit von Hilfsmaßnahmen eines neu zu schaffenden Restrukturierungsfonds, insbesondere zur Unterstützung der Refinanzierung und ggf. Rekapitalisierung von Unternehmen, die den Bankbetrieb oder einzelne Geschäftsbereiche von einer in Schieflage geratenen Bank übernehmen. Diese Hilfsmaßnahmen werden nunmehr – anders als beim SoFFin – nicht durch Steuergelder, sondern durch Beiträge der Marktteilnehmer selbst finanziert.[56] Allerdings werden die Mittel in dem neugeschaffenen Restrukturierungsfonds nicht von den Marktteilnehmern oder einer von ihnen getragenen Organisation wie dem Einlagensicherungsfonds des Bundesverbands deutscher Banken, sondern von der FMSA verwaltet.

---

49 S. unten Abschnitt II 3; vgl. auch *Bachmann* ZBB 2010, 459 (466).

50 Ebenso *Bachmann* ZBB 2010, 459 (470) m. w. N.; *Zimmer* Stellungnahme RestrG, S. 3, abrufbar unter http://www.bundestag.de/bundestag/ausschuesse17/a07/anhoerungen/2010/029/Stellungnahmen/35_Prof__Dr__Daniel_Zimmer.pdf.

51 In Großbritannien ist ein *share transfer* in Sec. 14 ff. Banking Act 2009 vorgesehen, dazu beispielsweise *Eidenmüller* in: FS Hopt 2010, S. 1713 (1715 ff.).

52 Gesetz zur Rettung von Unternehmen zur Stabilisierung des Finanzmarkts vom 7. April 2009, BGBl. I, S. 729.

53 Zum RettungsG etwa *Amend* ZIP 2009, 589 (592 f.); *Pannen* Krise und Insolvenz bei Kreditinstituten 2010, Kapitel 2 Rz. 89 ff.

54 Zur Verfassungsmäßigkeit des RettungsG etwa *Bauer* DÖV 2010, 20; *Hopt/Fleckner/Kumpan/Steffek* WM 2009, 821 (830 ff.); *Kaserer/Köndgen/Möllers* ZBB 2009, 142 (149 ff.); *Wolfers/Rau* NJW 2009, 1297 (1298 ff.); kritisch auch *Böckenförde* NJW 2009, 2484 (2489 ff.).

55 Die Übertragungsanordnung soll nach der in der Gesetzesbegründung ausführlich dargelegten Auffassung mangels gezielten Vorgehens zum Allgemeinwohl keine Enteignung, sondern nur eine Inhaltsbestimmung bzw. Nebenfolge sein. Begründung RegE RestrG, BT-Drucks. 17/3024, S. 62 f.; dazu auch *Schuster* ZGR 2010, 325, 354. Ob sich dies bei einer direkten Anteilsübertragung letztlich anders als bei Übertragung des gesamten Geschäftsbetriebs darstellt, ist zweifelhaft, s. auch *Bachmann* ZBB 2010, 459 (470).

56 Zu den verfassungsrechtlichen Fragen der Bankenabgabe s. *Schön/Hellgardt/Osterloh-Konrad* WM 2010, 2145.

II. Die Übertragungsanordnung

Effektive Restrukturierungsmaßnahmen müssen destabilisierende Wirkungen auf das Marktumfeld vermeiden und insbesondere vertikale oder horizontale Dominoeffekte[57] und den Zusammenbruch des Zahlungsverkehrs verhindern. Die folgenden Überlegungen beleuchten aus Sicht der Praxis einige ausgewählte Themen bei der Durchführung einer Übertragungsanordnung. § 48a Abs. 1 KWG definiert die Übertragungsanordnung als einen im Ermessen[58] der BaFin stehenden Verwaltungsakt, der auf die Übertragung des Vermögens eines Kreditinstituts einschließlich seiner Verbindlichkeiten (oder eines Teils des Vermögens, der Verbindlichkeiten und der Rechtsverhältnisse nach § 48k KWG) auf einen bestehenden Rechtsträger im Wege der Ausgliederung gerichtet ist.[59] Die Übertragungsanordnung steht nur im Hinblick auf inländische Kreditinstitute i. S. v. § 1 Abs. 1 KWG zur Verfügung.[60]

1. Verfahren und Ausgestaltung im Überblick

Sofern die BaFin feststellt, dass die materiellen Voraussetzungen[61] für den Erlass einer Übertragungsanordnung vorliegen, kann sie je nach Gefahrenlage gemäß § 48c KWG dem Kreditinstitut eine Frist für die Vorlage und Ausführung eines sog. Wiederherstellungsplanes[62] setzen und eine Übertragungsanordnung androhen. Damit wird dem Kreditinstitut die Möglichkeit eingeräumt, die Bestandsgefährdung selbst abzuwenden und einer Übertragungsanordnung zuvorzukommen. Im Anschluss steht es im Ermessen der BaFin, dem Institut noch eine (weitere) letzte Frist zu setzen, wenn innerhalb der ursprünglich gesetzten Frist kein oder kein den Anforderungen entsprechender Wiederherstellungsplan vorgelegt wird oder die Ausführung des Plans scheitert, die Gefahrenlage aber eine weitere Fristsetzung zulässt.[63] Wesentliche Voraussetzungen einer Übertragungsanordnung sind die Auswahl eines geeigneten übernehmenden Rechtsträgers, der entweder bereits ein Kreditinstitut mit Sitz im Inland ist[64] oder im Zuge der Überragungsanordnung eine entsprechende Bankerlaubnis erhält (§ 48g

57 *Mülbert* in: FS U.H. Schneider 2011, S. 855, (861 f.).

58 Kritisch dazu *Riethmüller* WM 2010, 2295 (2299).

59 Sofern Leistungen aus dem Restrukturierungsfonds gewährt werden sollen, ergeht die Übertragungsanordnung gemäß § 48a Abs. 3 Satz 1 KWG im Einvernehmen mit dem Lenkungsausschuss.

60 S. dazu auch *Riethmüller* WM 2010, 2295 (2297).

61 Hierzu sogleich unten Abschnitt II 2.

62 Das Restrukturierungsgesetz wird dominiert von “Plänen”: Der Sanierungsplan und der Reorganisationsplan nach dem KredReorgG, der Restrukturierungsplan nach § 45 Abs. 2 Nr. 7 KWG, den die BaFin verlangen kann, und der Wiederherstellungsplan nach § 48c Abs. 1 KWG. Bei dem Wiederherstellungsplan findet sich auch eine Verknüpfung mit dem Reorganisationsplan nach dem KredReorgG, welcher gemäß § 48c Abs. 2 Satz 1 KWG den Anforderungen nach § 48c Abs. 1 KWG genügt, wenn er zur rechtzeitigen Abwendung der Bestandsgefährdung geeignet ist und Aussicht hat, rechtzeitig angenommen, bestätigt und umgesetzt zu werden. Besteht daran kein Zweifel und wird das Reorganisationsverfahren bereits durchgeführt, darf die BaFin keine Übertragungsanordnung erlassen (§ 48c Abs. 2 Satz 2 KWG).

63 § 48c Abs. 1 Satz 4 KWG.

64 Kritisch unter europarechtlichen Gesichtspunkten *Schuster/Westpfahl* DB 2011, 282 (283).

Abs. 6 KWG),[65] sowie die Festlegung der Ausgliederungsgegenstände[66] und der dem Kreditinstitut geschuldeten Gegenleistung.

a) Gegenleistung

Ferner hat die BaFin in der Übertragungsanordnung die Gegenleistung für den übertragenen Geschäftsbetrieb festzusetzen, die dem Kreditinstitut gewährt wird,[67] vorausgesetzt, der Wert der übertragenen Gegenstände ist „in seiner Gesamtheit positiv" (§ 48d Abs. 1 Satz 1 KWG). Damit ist der Nettowert des übertragenen Geschäftsbetriebs gemeint. Die Gegenleistung muss in einem angemessenen Verhältnis zum Wert der übertragenen Gegenstände stehen. Die Angemessenheit der Gegenleistung ist durch einen sachverständigen Prüfer zu prüfen (§ 48d Abs. 3 KWG). Die Prüfung der Angemessenheit der Gegenleistung wird eine Bewertung der Aktiv- und Passivpositionen voraussetzen, die zum übertragenen Vermögen gehören. Gleich ob der gesamte Geschäftsbetrieb oder nur ein Teil davon als Ausschnitt des Aktiv- und Passivvermögens des Kreditinstituts übertragen wird, kann die Bewertung der übertragenen Aktivitäten einen positiven oder negativen Nettowert oder einem Wert von Null ergeben. Ist der Nettowert Null, wird trotz der Abtrennung eines Geschäftsbetriebs dem Kreditinstitut keine Gegenleistung geschuldet. Ist der Nettowert negativ, entsteht eine Ausgleichsverbindlichkeit des Kreditinstituts gegenüber dem übernehmenden Rechtsträger (§ 48d Abs. 6 KWG). Ist der Nettowert positiv, besteht die Gegenleistung nach dem gesetzlichen Leitbild der Ausgliederung grundsätzlich in Anteilen an dem übernehmenden Rechtsträger.[68] Während die Bestandsgefährdung der übertragenen Unternehmensteile in den Händen des Brückeninstituts oder sonstigen übernehmenden Rechtsträgers andauert und nicht nachhaltig abgewendet ist, sind die Anteile am übernehmenden Rechtsträger zugunsten der BaFin vinkuliert.[69] Solange die übertragenen Unternehmensteile in ihrem Bestand gefährdet sind und das Sanierungsziel beim übernehmenden Rechtsträger noch nicht erreicht wurde, kann die BaFin das Kreditinstitut anweisen, die ihm in der Anteilsinhaberversammlung zustehenden Stimmrechte in bestimmter Weise auszuüben (§ 48l Abs. 2 Satz 1 KWG). Ausnahmsweise entsteht als Gegenleistung eine Ausgleichsforderung des Kreditinstituts, sofern eine Anteilsgewäh-

65 Der übernehmende Rechtsträger darf nicht den Ausschlussgründen nach § 48c Abs. 5 KWG unterfallen, denn gemäß § 48g Abs. 6 KWG enthält die Übertragungsanordnung ggf. auch die Erlaubnis zur Fortführung der übertragenen Geschäfte. Die Ausschlussgründe sollen sicherstellen, dass der übernehmende Rechtsträger die Voraussetzungen für die Erteilung einer Bankerlaubnis erfüllt. Durch die Erteilung der Bankerlaubnis durch die Übertragungsanordnung soll eine Verzögerung der Umsetzung der Übertragungsanordnung durch ein eigenständiges Erlaubnisverfahren und Unsicherheiten bei den Marktteilnehmern vermieden werden, s. Begründung RegE RestrG, BT-Drucks. 17/3024, S. 64 re. Sp., 66 f.

66 Hierzu unten Abschnitt II 3 b.

67 § 48d Abs. 1 KWG.

68 In diesem Fall wird auch eine Sacheinlagenprüfung gemäß § 48d Abs. 5 KWG durchgeführt. Gemäß § 48e Abs. 2 KWG sind bei einer Ausgliederung mit Anteilsgewährung genauere Angaben zur Gegenleistung und Angemessenheit zu machen. Dies ist nötig, da anders als bei einer Ausgliederung nach dem UmwG kein Umwandlungsbericht vorgelegt werden muss, s. auch Begründung RegE RestrG, BT-Drucks. 17/3024, S. 65 re. Sp.

69 Nach § 48l Abs. 3 KWG darf das Kreditinstitut in diesem Fall nicht ohne vorherige schriftliche Zustimmung der BaFin über die ihm zustehenden Anteile verfügen.

rung unzumutbar ist oder den Zweck der Übertragungsanordnung zu vereiteln droht. Nach der Regierungsbegründung ist dies beispielsweise der Fall, wenn keine hinreichende Sicherheit darüber gewonnen werden kann, ob der Wert der Gegenstände den gesellschaftsrechtlich zwingenden Mindestausgabebetrag erreicht.[70] Ob die Anteilsgewährung den Zweck der Übertragungsanordnung, insbesondere die Überwindung der eingetretenen Destabilisierung der übertragenen Unternehmensteile und des Finanzsystems, zu vereiteln droht, hat die BaFin zu beurteilen. Dabei wird zunächst zu berücksichtigen sein, ob die Durchführung einer für die Anteilsgewährung erforderlichen förmlichen Kapitalerhöhung beim übernehmenden Rechtsträger auf Grund des bestehenden Zeitdrucks tunlich ist.[71] Da die Anteilsgewährung u. U. zu einer Konsolidierungspflicht des Kreditinstituts im Hinblick auf den übertragenden Rechtsträger führt, könnte damit eine etwa beim Kreditinstitut vorhandene Eigenmittellücke vergrößert werden.[72] Ferner ist zu erwägen, ob der übernehmende Rechtsträger, insbesondere ein Brückeninstitut, als Beteiligungs- oder Tochterunternehmen der Restbank deren Kontrolle unterworfen werden soll,[73] jedenfalls nachdem das Sanierungsziel erreicht ist.[74] Darüber hinaus ist es nicht unwahrscheinlich, dass die Trennung von systemrelevanten und überlebensfähigen Geschäftsbereichen und dem Restvermögen zur Abwicklung der Restbank ggf. in einem Insolvenzverfahren führt und bei Anteilsgewährung an die Restbank die Beteiligung von einem Insolvenzverwalter nach den Regeln der Insolvenzordnung und dem Willen der verbleibenden Gläubiger der Restbank zu verwerten wäre. Dabei kann nicht ausgeschlossen werden, dass im Zeitpunkt der Verwertung durch den Insolvenzverwalter die Vinkulierung der Anteile und die Kontrolle über die Stimmrechte nicht mehr greift. Dann hätte die BaFin beim Exit aus der Beteiligung kein Mitspracherecht. Auch könnte der Insolvenzverwalter oder ggf. ein Erwerber die Kontrolle über ein vom Restrukturierungsfonds zur Verfügung gestelltes "systemrelevantes" Brückeninstitut erlangen. Vorbehaltlich der einzelfallspezifischen Umstände dürften jedenfalls beim Einsatz eines Brückeninstituts insgesamt erhebliche Zweifel an der Praktikabilität der Anteilsgewährung bestehen und gute Gründe für die Gewährung einer Ausgleichsforderung anstelle von Anteilen sprechen.

---

70 Begründung RegE RestrG, BT-Drucks. 17/3024, S. 65 li. Sp.

71 Besteht die Gegenleistung für die Übertragung in Anteilen an dem übernehmenden Rechtsträger und ist dafür ein Beschluss erforderlich, darf die Übertragungsanordnung erst ergehen, wenn der Beschluss gefasst ist und nicht mehr mit der Rechtsfolge einer möglichen Rückabwicklung angefochten werden kann, s. auch *Schuster*, Börsen-Zeitung vom 1. September 2010, S. 2. So wird gewährleistet, dass der übernehmende Rechtsträger zur Ausgabe der Anteile verpflichtet werden kann, ohne dass in die durch die Kapitalrichtlinie garantierten und von § 187 Abs. 2 AktG geschützten Kompetenzen der Hauptversammlung eingegriffen wird (Zweite Richtlinie 77/91/EWG des Rates vom 13. Dezember 1976 zur Koordinierung der Schutzbestimmungen, die in den Mitgliedstaaten den Gesellschaften im Sinne des Artikels 58 Absatz 2 des Vertrages im Interesse der Gesellschafter sowie Dritter für die Gründung der Aktiengesellschaft sowie für die Erhaltung und Änderung ihres Kapitals vorgeschrieben sind, um diese Bestimmungen gleichwertig zu gestalten, Amtsblatt Nr. L 026 vom 31. 1. 1977, S. 1.), s. die Begründung RegE RestrG, BT-Drucks. 17/3024, S. 64 re.Sp. Die weiteren Maßnahmen der Kapitalerhöhung können gemäß § 48 g Abs. 3 KWG erst nach dem Erlass der Übertragungsanordnung vorgenommen werden. Eine Privilegierung entsprechend §§ 7 ff. FMStBG ist nicht vorgesehen.

72 Vgl. auch *Schuster/Westpfahl* DB 2011, 282 (284).

73 S. auch Begründung RegE RestrG, BT-Drucks. 17/3024, S. 65 li. Sp.

74 § 48 l Abs. 2 KWG.

b) Ausgliederung durch Verwaltungsakt und Zustimmung des übernehmenden Rechtsträgers

Die Ausgliederung nach §§ 48a ff. KWG setzt die Übertragungsanordnung der BaFin und die Zustimmung des übernehmenden Rechtsträgers voraus und wird durch Bekanntgabe der Übertragungsanordnung gegenüber dem in Schieflage geratenen Kreditinstitut und dem übernehmenden Rechtsträger wirksam.[75] Danach ist die Ausgliederung unverzüglich zur Eintragung im Handelsregister (§ 48f Abs. 3 bis 5 KWG) anzumelden; die Eintragung hat lediglich deklaratorische Bedeutung. Werden die Anmeldungen verzögert oder unterlassen, kann die FMSA die Eintragung gemäß § 48f Abs. 5 KWG vornehmen. Dass dies nicht – wie die übrigen Entscheidungen und Maßnahmen – in die Zuständigkeit der BaFin fällt, wird die Effizienz des Verfahrensablaufs nicht erhöhen. Die Registergerichte haben gemäß § 48f Abs. 4 KWG die Eintragung unverzüglich vorzunehmen; Klagen oder sonstige Rechtsbehelfe gegen die Übertragungsanordnung oder die Eintragung der Ausgliederung oder der Kapitalerhöhung stehen dem nicht entgegen. Die Eintragung kann nur durch gerichtliche Anordnung im einstweiligen Rechtsschutzverfahren verhindert werden.[76] Darüber hinaus ist die Übertragungsanordnung gemäß § 48c Abs. 6 Satz 3 KWG unverzüglich im elektronischen Bundesanzeiger zu veröffentlichen. Im Anschluss ist die BaFin gegenüber dem Kreditinstitut und dem übernehmenden Rechtsträger zu weiteren Maßnahmen berechtigt (§§ 48l, 48m KWG). Adressat des Verwaltungsaktes ist das sich in der Krise befindende Kreditinstitut. Die Übertragung ist sowohl dem Institut als auch dem übernehmenden Rechtsträger bekannt zu geben (§ 48c Abs. 6 Sätze 1 und 2, § 48g Abs. 1 KWG) und kann nur mit Zustimmung des übernehmenden Rechtsträgers zu der vorher im Entwurf zuzuleitenden Übertragungsanordnung (§ 48c Abs. 3 Satz 2 KWG) wirksam werden. Der Verwaltungsakt ersetzt damit nur die Erklärung bzw. Zustimmung des übertragenden Kreditinstituts bzw. seiner Organe und Anteilsinhaber zu einer Ausgliederung, die auch im übrigen geringeren formalen Anforderungen als eine gewillkürte Ausgliederung nach dem Umwandlungsgesetz unterliegt.[77] Damit wird die Möglichkeit eröffnet, die für die Stabilisierung des betroffenen Instituts und des Finanzsystems erforderlichen Maßnahmen auch gegen den Willen des Instituts oder seiner Anteilsinhaber ergreifen zu können und die systemrelevanten Teile von der Insolvenz des Instituts abzuschotten.[78] Insofern unterscheidet sich die Ausgliederung durch Übertragungsanordnung auch von den freiwilligen, mit Zustimmung der Aufsichtsbehörde erfolgenden Bestandsübertragungen nach § 14 VAG oder § 32 PfandBG. Ähnlich wie bei der Übertragung auf Abwicklungsanstalten nach § 8a Abs. 9 FMSFG i. V. m. § 16 Abs. 1 Satz 3 FMStBG[79] ist die Ausgliederung durch Übertragungsanordnung im Hinblick auf die Kündigung und Beendigung von Schuldverhältnissen privilegiert, um die Kontinu-

---

75 Der Bundesrat hatte eine förmliche Zustellung für die Übertragungsanordnung angeregt, die nicht in das Gesetz übernommen wurde, s. Stellungnahme des Bundesrates, BR-Drucks. 534/10 (Beschluss) vom 15. Oktober 2010, S. 14.

76 Begründung RegE RestrG, BT-Drucks. 17/3024, S. 66 re. Sp.

77 Ein Ausgliederungsvertrag, -bericht oder -beschluss des Kreditinstituts oder des übernehmenden Rechtsträgers sind gemäß § 48f Abs. 1 Satz 2 KWG nicht erforderlich.

78 Begründung RegE RestrG, BT-Drucks. 17/3024, S. 61 re. Sp.

79 Zu dieser Regelung, jedoch im Zusammenhang mit einer Einzelrechtsübertragung nur nach dem FMStBG, *Diem/Neuberger* BKR 2009, 177 (179).

ität des übertragenen Geschäftsbetriebs zu fördern. Daher kann ein Schuldverhältnis auf Grund der Ausgliederung nicht beendet werden, und die Übertragung ist kein Kündigungsgrund; entgegenstehende Vereinbarungen sind unwirksam (§ 48g Abs. 7 Satz 1 bis 3 KWG).[80] Diese Beschränkung ist nicht befristet.[81] Die Beschränkungen gelten aber dann nicht, wenn bei einer partiellen Übertragung die § 48k Abs. 2 Satz 1 bis 3 KWG nicht eingehalten wurden.

c) Haftungsregime

Das Kreditinstitut haftet gemäß § 48h Abs. 1 KWG, der insoweit von § 131 UmwG abweicht, im Außenverhältnis für die übertragenen Verbindlichkeiten nur subsidiär, d.h. soweit vom übertragenden Rechtsträger keine Befriedigung erlangt werden kann. Die Haftung ist zeitlich unbegrenzt, aber der Höhe nach auf den Betrag beschränkt, der bei der Abwicklung des Kreditinstituts durch Gläubiger erlöst worden wäre. In der Praxis wird man auf Liquidationswerte abstellen können,[82] aber auch deren Feststellung wird ex post schwierig sein.[83] Die Haftung des übernehmenden Rechtsträgers im Außenverhältnis ist ebenfalls beschränkt. Bei einer Gesamtübertragung mit partieller Rückübertragung haftet der übernehmende Rechtsträger gemäß § 48j Abs. 4 KWG für zurück übertragene Verbindlichkeiten nur subsidiär, soweit vom Kreditinstitut keine Befriedigung erlangt werden kann; die Haftung ist beschränkt auf den Betrag, der bei der Abwicklung des Kreditinstituts durch Gläubiger erlöst worden wäre. Bei einer partiellen Übertragung wird hinsichtlich der bei der Restbank verbleibenden Verbindlichkeiten eine unmittelbare, nicht subsidiäre Haftung angeordnet,[84] die der Höhe nach beschränkt ist auf den Betrag, der im Rahmen der Abwicklung des Kreditinstituts erlöst worden wäre (§ 48k Abs. 3 KWG). Die Haftung bei Teilübertragungen ist – anders als im Falle der umwandlungsrechtlichen Nachhaftung (§ 131 UmwG) – zeitlich unbegrenzt und setzt wiederum die praktisch schwierige Bewertung des hypothetischen Abwicklungserlöses ohne Übertragungsanordnung voraus.

---

80 Dies gilt dann nicht, wenn sich die Kündigungs- oder Beendigungsgründe nicht darin erschöpfen, dass das Schuldverhältnis übertragen wurde oder dass die Voraussetzungen für seine Übertragung vorlagen oder wenn die Kündigungs- oder Beendigungsgründe in der Person des übernehmenden Rechtsträger begründet sind. Dies kann man nahezu als Aufruf verstehen, Kündigungs- und Beendigungsgründe so zu formulieren, dass sie von dieser Ausnahme umfasst sind, in dem beispielsweise entsprechend weite Formulierungen gewählt werden, s. zu gängigen Klauseln auch *Amend* ZIP 2009, 589 (596 f.). Der praktische Nutzen des Beendigungsverbotes erscheint daher zweifelhaft, skeptisch auch *Zimmer* Stellungnahme RestrG, S. 2, abrufbar unter http://www.bundestag.de/bundestag/ausschuesse17/a07/anhoerungen/2010/029/Stellungnahmen/35_Prof__Dr__Daniel_Zimmer.pdf.

81 *Obermüller/Kuder* ZInsO 2010, 2016 (2021).

82 So ordnet etwa das britische Recht an, dass Gläubiger durch eine Übertragung nicht schlechter gestellt werden dürfen, als es bei einer Liquidation durch Insolvenz wären (sec. 60(2) Banking Act 2009), s. *Binder* Bankenintervention und Bankenabwicklung in Deutschland: Reformnotwendigkeiten und Grundzüge eines verbesserten Rechtsrahmens, Sachverständigenrat Arbeitspapier 05/2009, S. 43 f., abrufbar unter: http://46.4.4.24/fileadmin/dateiablage/Arbeitspapiere/Bankenintervention_und_Bankenabwicklung_in_Deutschland.pdf.

83 Kritisch auch *Bachmann* ZBB 2010, 459 (468); *Lorenz* NZG 2010, 1046 (1051).

84 S. auch *Riethmüller* WM 2010, 2295 (2302).

d) Rechtsschutz

Gegen die Übertragungsanordnung kann mit einer Anfechtungsklage nach § 48 r Abs. 1 KWG innerhalb von vier Wochen vor dem Hessischen Verwaltungsgerichtshof in Kassel vorgegangen werden. Soweit es um die Angemessenheit der Gegenleistung oder der Ausgleichsverbindlichkeit geht, kann die Klage gemäß § 48 r Abs. 2 KWG nur auf Anpassung gerichtet sein. § 48 r Abs. 1 KWG gilt entsprechend für Klagen gegen Weisungen der BaFin im Zusammenhang mit der Ausübung von Stimmrechten des übernehmenden Rechtsträgers (§ 48 l Abs. 2 KWG). Die Folgenbeseitigung durch Rückgängigmachung der Ausgliederung ist aus Gründen der Rechtssicherheit und Vertrauensbildung am Markt nur zulässig, wenn dies nicht unmöglich, nicht zu einer Systemgefährdung zu führen droht und keine schutzwürdigen Interessen Dritter bedrohen würde. In der Praxis dürfte die rückwirkende Aufhebung der Ausgliederung somit weitgehend ausgeschlossen sein. Dem Kreditinstitut steht nach § 48 s Abs. 2 KWG ein Entschädigungsanspruch zu, wenn die Vollzugsfolgenbeseitigung gemäß § 48 s Abs. 1 KWG ausgeschlossen ist oder die Übertragungsanordnung nicht aufgehoben wird, weil das Handeln der Bundesanstalt nach § 48 a Abs. 2 Satz 2 KWG rechtmäßig ist und das Institut die dort genannten Umstände nicht zu vertreten hat.

2. Materielle Voraussetzungen der Übertragungsanordnung

Materielle Voraussetzungen für den Erlass einer Übertragungsanordnung sind gemäß § 48 a Abs. 2 Satz 1 Nr. 1 KWG, dass

(i) eine Bestandsgefährdung des Kreditinstituts und

(ii) eine dadurch eingetretene Systemgefährdung festgestellt werden und

(iii) die von der Bestandsgefährdung ausgehende Systemgefährdung gemäß § 48 a Abs. 2 Satz 1 Nr. 2 KWG nicht auf anderem Wege als durch eine Übertragungsanordnung in gleich sicherer Weise beseitigt werden kann (*ultima ratio*).

a) Bestandsgefährdung

Bestandsgefährdung ist die Gefahr des insolvenzbedingten Zusammenbruchs für den Fall des Unterbleibens korrigierender Maßnahmen (§ 48 b Abs. 1 Satz 1 KWG). Die Bestandsgefährdung wird nach § 48 b Abs. 1 Satz 2 vermutet bei dem drohenden oder tatsächlichen qualifizierten Unterschreiten von Kernkapital- oder Eigenmittelquoten oder bei drohender oder tatsächlicher qualifizierter Verletzung von Liquiditätsanforderungen. Zum Beispiel kann eine Bestandsgefährdung nach der in § 48 b Abs. 1 Satz 2 Nr. 4 i. V. m. Nr. 3 normierten Vermutung vorliegen, sobald Tatsachen die Annahme rechtfertigen, dass künftig ohne Gegenmaßnahmen die in einem Laufzeitband verfügbaren Zahlungsmittel die in demselben Laufzeitband abrufbaren Zahlungsverpflichtungen zu weniger als 90% decken werden.[85] Eine solche Situation muss zwar nicht mit

---

85 § 48 b Abs. 1 Satz 2 Nr. 4 i. V. m. Nr. 3 KWG.

der Insolvenz des Instituts einhergehen.[86] Da eine Krise aber häufig mit Liquiditätsschwierigkeiten beginnt, dürften gerade hier Abgrenzungsfragen zur bloßen Sanierungsbedürftigkeit (§ 45 Abs. 1 KWG) und zur drohenden Zahlungsunfähigkeit (§ 46b KWG) auftreten, die einer auch weiterhin geltenden strafbewehrten Anzeigepflicht der Geschäftsleitung des Instituts unterliegt.[87]

Während die Sanierungsbedürftigkeit voraussetzt, dass die gesetzlichen Eigenmittel- oder Liquiditätsanforderungen nicht dauerhaft erfüllt werden können,[88] ist Bestandsgefährdung die Gefahr eines insolvenzbedingten Zusammenbruchs. Davon zu unterscheiden ist die drohende Zahlungsunfähigkeit, die gegeben ist, wenn das Institut voraussichtlich nicht in der Lage sein wird, die bestehenden Zahlungspflichten im Zeitpunkt der Fälligkeit zu erfüllen. Bei Feststellung der drohenden Zahlungsunfähigkeit verlässt das Institut typischerweise die Zone, in der die eigenverantwortliche Sanierung außerhalb eines Insolvenzverfahrens noch wahrscheinlich ist, wenn auch die BaFin nur mit Zustimmung des Instituts den Antrag auf Eröffnung eines Insolvenzverfahrens stellen darf.[89] Mit der Sanierungsbedürftigkeit und der Bestandsgefährdung hat das Restrukturierungsgesetz dem herkömmlichen Test der drohenden Zahlungsunfähigkeit zwei neue Tatbestände hinzugefügt, wobei von einer Überlappung aller drei Tatbestände auszugehen ist. Dies hat bereits der Gesetzgeber erkannt und bestimmt, dass jedenfalls aus Sicht des Instituts die Anzeige der Sanierungsbedürftigkeit oder die Anzeige zur Einleitung eines Reorganisationsverfahrens der Anzeigepflicht des § 46b KWG genügt (§ 2 Abs. 1 Satz 3, § 7 Abs. 5 Satz 1 KredReorgG). Diese Überlappung von Bestandgefährdung und drohender Zahlungsunfähigkeit bedeutet andererseits, dass die BaFin dann neben dem möglichen Erlass einer Übertragungsanordnung auch Maßnahmen nach §§ 45 ff. KWG, z. B. den Erlass eines Zahlungsverbots ("Moratorium" betreffend ein Institut) als ggf. passendes Eingriffsinstrument zu prüfen hat. U. U. sind beide Maßnahmen parallel zu treffen, wobei allerdings ein Moratorium betreffend den übernehmenden Rechtsträger den Zweck der Übertragungsanordnung torpedieren dürfte.

---

86 S. auch *Riethmüller* WM 2010, 2295 (2298).

87 § 46b Abs. 1 Satz 1 KWG lautet: „Wird ein Institut oder eine nach § 10a Abs. 3 Satz 6 oder Satz 7 als übergeordnetes Unternehmen geltende Finanzholding-Gesellschaft zahlungsunfähig oder tritt Überschuldung ein, so haben die Geschäftsleiter, bei einem in der Rechtsform des Einzelkaufmanns betriebenen Institut der Inhaber und die Personen, die die Geschäfte der Finanzholding-Gesellschaft tatsächlich führen, dies der Bundesanstalt unter Beifügung aussagefähiger Unterlagen unverzüglich anzuzeigen; die im ersten Halbsatz bezeichneten Personen haben eine solche Anzeige unter Beifügung entsprechender Unterlagen auch dann vorzunehmen, wenn das Institut oder die nach § 10a Abs. 3 Satz 6 oder Satz 7 als übergeordnetes Unternehmen geltende Finanzholding-Gesellschaft voraussichtlich nicht in der Lage sein wird, die bestehenden Zahlungspflichten im Zeitpunkt der Fälligkeit zu erfüllen (drohende Zahlungsunfähigkeit).“

88 § 2 Abs. 1 Satz 2 KredReorgG. Sanierungsbedürftigkeit ist regelmäßig gegeben, wenn eine der Voraussetzungen nach § 45 Abs. 1 Satz 2 Nr. 1 oder Nr. 2 KWG („Regelbeispiele") erfüllt sind.

89 § 46b Abs. 1 Satz 5 KWG.

b) Systemgefährdung

Eine Systemgefährdung tritt nach § 48b Abs. 2 KWG ein, wenn zu besorgen ist, dass sich die Bestandsgefährdung in erheblicher Weise negativ auf andere Unternehmen des Finanzsektors, auf die Finanzmärkte oder auf das allgemeine Vertrauen der Einleger und anderen Marktteilnehmer in die Funktionsfähigkeit des Finanzsystems auswirkt. Zu berücksichtigen sind dabei insbesondere die Verbindlichkeiten gegenüber anderen Marktteilnehmern, der Umfang der Einlagen bei dem Institut, die Risikostruktur und Vernetzung des Instituts sowie die Verhältnisse auf den Finanzmärkten (§§ 48b Abs. 2 Satz 1 Nrn. 1 bis 5 KWG).[90] Bezugspunkt dieser Gesichtspunkte ist stets der Finanzmarkt und nur mittelbar die Realwirtschaft.

Die Feststellung der Systemgefährdung wie auch der Bestandsgefährdung obliegt der BaFin nach Anhörung der Deutschen Bundesbank. Wie bei anderen Maßnahmen der Gefahrenabwehr im Wirtschaftsverwaltungsrecht steht der BaFin dabei ein erheblicher Beurteilungsspielraum zu. Die auf Grund der "Beurteilungsermächtigung" des § 48b Abs. 3 KWG von der Bankenaufsicht gefundene und dokumentierte Beurteilung unterliegt nur einer eingeschränkten gerichtlichen Kontrolle (Einschätzungsprärogative der Verwaltung).[91] Hinzu kommt, dass nach § 48a Abs. 2 Satz 2 KWG das Verwaltungshandeln auch dann rechtmäßig ist, wenn BaFin, FMSA oder der Lenkungsausschuss „bei verständiger Würdigung der ihr zum Zeitpunkt ihres Handelns erkennbaren Umstände annehmen dürfen, dass die gesetzlichen Voraussetzungen für ihr Handeln vorliegen".[92]

Die Eindämmung der Systemgefährdung ist das Kardinalziel des Verwaltungshandelns nach §§ 48a ff. KWG. Wegen der Unbestimmtheit und Offenheit des Begriffs wird es darauf ankommen, die im Gesetz angelegten Schutzgüter zu bestimmen.[93] Nicht erforderlich ist es aber, sog. systemrelevante Institute zu definieren.[94]

---

90 Mit Verweis auf den IMF auch *Riethmüller* WM 2010, 2295 (2298 f.).

91 Vgl. nur *Aschke* in: Bader/Ronellenfitsch (Hrsg.) BeckOK VwVfG, § 40 Rz. 26 (Stand: 1. Januar 2011); s. auch *Mülbert* in: FS U.H. Schneider 2011, S. 855 (869); *Günther* WM 2010, 825 (828 f.).

92 Damit wird eine § 93 Abs. 1 Satz 2 AktG angenäherte "business judgement rule" für die Aufsichtsbehörden eingeführt. Begründung RegE RestrG, BT-Drucks. 17/3024, S. 61 li. Sp.; *Bachmann* ZBB 2010, 459 (466); *Lorenz* NZG 2010, 1046 (1050). Davon unabhängig bleibt aber die Frage, ob überhaupt eine Haftung besteht, so Bericht des Finanzausschusses, BT-Drucks. 17/3547 vom 28. Oktober 2010, S. 8 li. Sp.

93 Dazu näher unten Abschnitt II 3 b.

94 S. zu Definitionsansätzen *Mülbert* in: FS U.H. Schneider, 2011, S. 855; *Günther* WM 2010, 825 (826 ff.); zum Begriff auch *Amend* ZIP 2009, 589 (594); *Becker/Mock* FMStG 2009, § 4 Rz. 40 ff.; *Uwe H. Schneider* ZRP 2009, 119 (119 ff.); ferner auch *Höfling* Gutachten F, Verhandlungen des 68. DJT, Berlin 2010, Band I, S. F 55 ff. Die BaFin hatte vor dem Restrukturierungsgesetz „systemrelevante Institute" als Institute definiert, „deren Bestandsgefährdung aufgrund ihrer Größe, der Intensität ihrer Interbankbeziehungen und ihrer engen Verflechtung mit dem Ausland erhebliche negative Folgeeffekte bei anderen Kreditinstituten auslösen und zu einer Instabilität des Finanzsystems führen könnte", Art. 6 Abs. 3 Satz 1 der Richtlinie der BaFin zur Durchführung und Qualitätssicherung der laufenden Überwachung der Kredit- und Finanzdienstleistungsinstitute durch die Deutsche Bundesbank vom 21. Februar 2008.

c) Ultima ratio

Die BaFin hat vor Erlass einer Übertragungsanordnung nicht nur zu prüfen, ob die Maßnahme zur wirksamen Abwehr der von der Bestandsgefährdung des Kreditinstituts ausgehenden Systemgefährdung geeignet ist, sondern darf den Eingriff nur vornehmen, wenn er erforderlich und auch verhältnismäßig ist. Das Kriterium der Erforderlichkeit hat der Gesetzgeber in § 48a Abs. 2 Satz 1 Nr. 2 besonders herausgestellt. Danach setzt eine Übertragungsanordnung voraus, dass sich die Systemgefährdung nicht auf anderem Wege in gleich sicherer Weise beseitigen lässt, z. B. durch eine freiwillige Sanierungsvereinbarung. Damit sind insbesondere Stützungsmaßnahmen angesprochen, die von den bestehenden Sicherungssystemen des privaten, öffentlichen und genossenschaftlichen Bankensektors durchgeführt werden können. Kleinere Institute sind bereits in der Vergangenheit von den Sicherungssystemen aufgefangen worden.[95] Im Fall des öffentlichen und genossenschaftlichen Sektors dürfte die Solidarität des Haftungsverbunds eine wichtige Rolle beim Rating und den damit einhergehenden Refinanzierungskonditionen der angeschlossenen Institute spielen. Um die Reputation des Haftungsverbunds beim Investorenpublikum nicht durch einen Ausfall des Sicherungssystems zu beschädigen, dürften die jeweiligen Bankensektoren ein vitales Interesse an einer sektorinternen Lösung von Stützungsfällen haben. Nur wenn eine Sanierung scheitert, kann und soll die BaFin durch eine Übertragungsanordnung eingreifen.

3. Gesamtübertragung vs. Teilübertragung

a) Gesamtübertragung, partielle Übertragung, partielle Rückübertragung

Zulässige Ausgliederungsgegenstände sind grundsätzlich alle Aktiva und Passiva sowie Vertrags- und sonstigen Rechtsverhältnisse des Kreditinstituts (arg. § 48k Abs. 1 Satz 1 KWG). Die Übertragungsanordnung muss angeben, ob die Übertragung des Vermögens einschließlich der Verbindlichkeiten des Kreditinstituts in seiner Gesamtheit (Gesamtübertragung, § 48e Abs. 1 Nr. 2 KWG) erfolgt oder eine Übertragung von bestimmten Vermögensgegenständen, Verbindlichkeiten und Rechtsverhältnissen (partielle Übertragung, § 48k Abs. 1 KWG) durchgeführt wird. Falls einzelne Gegenstände durch eine Rückübertragungsanordnung (partielle Rückübertragung, § 48j KWG) ggf. später retransferiert werden sollen, muss ein entsprechender Vorbehalt in der originären Übertragungsanordnung enthalten sein. Bei einer Gesamtübertragung ist keine genaue Bezeichnung der einzelnen zu übertragenden Gegenstände in der Übertragungsanordnung erforderlich.[96] Wird dagegen eine partielle Übertragung durchgeführt, müssen die übergehenden Gegenstände gemäß § 48k Abs. 1 Satz 2 KWG oder die beim Kreditinstitut verbleibenden Gegenstände angegeben werden.[97] Welche Anforderungen daran

95 S. etwa die Rettungsaktion des Einlagensicherungsfonds der privaten Banken im Falle der Düsseldorfer Hypothekenbank AG im Jahr 2008.

96 Begründung RegE RestrG, BT-Drucks. 17/3024, S. 65 re. Sp.

97 Vgl. auch *Schuster/Westpfahl* DB 2011, 282 (283).

zu stellen sind, ist nicht besonders geregelt.[98] Die detaillierte Bezeichnungspflicht wird zu erheblichen Schwierigkeiten führen und die Übertragung langwierig und komplex gestalten.[99] Bei einer partiellen Übertragung kann die BaFin gemäß § 48k Abs. 5 KWG innerhalb von vier Monaten nach dem Wirksamwerden einer Ausgliederung weitere Übertragungsanordnungen (auch für eine Übertragung des gesamten Restbankbetriebs) erlassen.[100] Diese Folgeanordnungen lösen die viermonatige Frist nicht erneut aus. Falls einzelne Ausgliederungsgegenstände durch eine Rückübertragungsanordnung gemäß § 48j Abs. 1 Satz 1 KWG wieder auf das Kreditinstitut zurückübertragen werden sollen, ist diese Anordnung ebenfalls innerhalb einer Frist von vier Monaten ab Wirksamwerden der Ausgliederung zu erlassen.[101] Eine Rückübertragung ist gegenüber dem Kreditinstitut und dem übernehmenden Rechtsträger bekannt zu geben und wird mit Bekanntgabe wirksam (§ 48j Abs. 2 Satz 1 KWG). Es folgt eine (deklaratorische) Eintragung in die betroffenen Handelsregister. Die BaFin hat sowohl eine Gesamtübertragung des Geschäftsbetriebs des Kreditinstituts auf ein Brückeninstitut oder einen sonstigen Übernehmer als auch eine Teilübertragung zu prüfen. In Betracht kommt auch die Übertragung des gesamten Bankbetriebs durch zwei oder mehrere partielle Übertragungsanordnungen entweder auf denselben übernehmenden Rechtsträger oder auf unterschiedliche Rechtsträger. Eine Mehrzahl von Übertragungen muss jedenfalls innerhalb von vier Monaten nach dem Wirksamwerden der ersten Ausgliederung erfolgen (§ 48k Abs. 5 KWG). Dies schließt aber die gleichzeitige partielle Übertragung auf mehrere Rechtsträger nicht aus. Ebenso möglich ist eine „Nachbefüllung" des Brückeninstituts innerhalb von vier Monaten nach der ursprünglichen Übertragung.

Die teilweise Übernahme des Geschäftsbetriebs durch ein Brückeninstitut oder einen sonstigen Rechtsträger lässt sich durch eine partielle Übertragung oder durch eine Gesamtübertragung mit anschließender partieller Rückübertragung umsetzen. Da insbesondere Verbindlichkeiten, die in einem Insolvenzverfahren der Restbank abgewickelt werden, und solche, die von einem Brückeninstitut übernommen werden, ein ganz unterschiedliches Schicksal haben, liegt bei nur teilweiser Übertragung (Ein-Schritt-Verfahren) oder der Gesamtübertragung mit anschließender partieller Rückübertragung (Zwei-Schritt-Verfahren) der Schwerpunkt der Ermessensentscheidung der BaFin in der Auswahl der Bestandteile der Passivseite, die in dem Brückeninstitut bzw. in der Restbank verbleiben.

---

98 S. zu den Bezeichnungsanforderungen nach UmwG beispielsweise *Kallmeyer/Sickinger* in: Kallmeyer, UmwG, 4. Aufl. 2010, § 126 Rz. 19 ff.; *Priester* in: Lutter/Winter, UmwG, 4. Aufl. 2009, § 126 Rz. 49 ff.; *Simon* in: Kölner Kommentar UmwG, 2009, § 126 Rz. 52 ff.

99 *Bachmann* ZBB 2010, 459 (467); *Schuster/Westpfahl* DB 2011, 282 (283 f.).

100 Begründung RegE RestrG, BT-Drucks. 17/3024, S. 68 li. Sp. Die enge zeitliche Begrenzung einer Rückübertragungsanordnung auf vier Monate nach der ursprünglichen Übertragung schränkt die Flexibilität angesichts der u. U. längeren Prüfungsdauer bei komplexen Portfolien unnötig ein.

101 § 48j Abs. 1 Satz 1 KWG. Die Beschränkung der Viermonatsfrist gilt gemäß § 48j Abs. 5 KWG jedenfalls nicht, falls ein Vertragspartner entgegen § 48g Abs. 7 KWG die Kündigung oder Beendigung eines Schuldverhältnisses erklärt oder behauptet. In diesem Fall kann unabhängig von der Viermonatsfrist das betreffende Schuldverhältnis innerhalb von zehn Tagen nach Zugang der Erklärung wieder zurück übertragen werden.

b) Auswahl der zu übertragenden Unternehmensteile

Bei einem Teiltransfer richtet sich die Auswahl der Vermögensgegenstände und Verbindlichkeiten gemäß §§ 48j Abs. 3 Satz 4 bis 6, 48k Abs. 2 Satz 4 KWG nach deren Bedeutung für eine effektive und kosteneffiziente Abwehr der Systemgefährdung und bei Gleichrangigkeit nach der im Insolvenzverfahren maßgeblichen Rangfolge (u. a. § 39 InsO).[102] Die Auswahlentscheidung wird gemäß §§ 48j Abs. 6, 48k Abs. 2 Satz 3 KWG im Einvernehmen mit der FMSA getroffen, wenn Leistungen des Restrukturierungsfonds erforderlich sind oder werden können. Hinzu kommen einige Sonderregeln. So ist etwa die Auswahl der Gegenstände für eine partielle Übertragungs- oder Rückübertragungsanordnung nach §§ 48j Abs. 3, 48k Abs. 2 KWG bestimmten Beschränkungen im Hinblick auf Schuldverhältnisse unterworfen, die in Aufrechnungsvereinbarungen einbezogen sind.[103] Ferner dürfen nach Maßgabe von § 48k Abs. 2 KWG Gegenstände, die für eine Finanzsicherheit i. S. d. § 1 Abs. 17 KWG bestellt wurden, nicht ohne diese übertragen werden und umgekehrt. Ausgliederungsgegenstände, die in ein Zahlungs-, Wertpapierliefer- oder -abrechnungssystem i. S. d. § 1 Abs. 16 KWG oder in ein System von Zentralbanken einbezogen sind, dürfen nicht ohne die für sie bestellten Sicherheiten übertragen werden und umgekehrt. Bei der Befüllung von Abwicklungsanstalten hat die Geschäftsleitung des Kreditinstituts die übergehenden Risikopositionen und nichtstrategischen Geschäftsbereiche selbst selektiert. Bei der Übertragungsanordnung hingegen hat die Selektionsentscheidung der BaFin den allgemeinen Anforderungen an eine zur Abwehr der Systemgefährdung geeignete, erforderliche und im engeren Sinne verhältnismäßige Auswahl von Gegenständen Rechnung zu tragen. Das Gesetz kennt keine „systemrelevanten" oder „überlebensfähigen" Geschäftsaktivitäten. Gleichwohl wird es darauf ankommen, vor dem Hintergrund der gesetzlichen Parameter der Systemgefährdung (§ 48b Abs. 2 KWG) Kriterien zu entwickeln, die die Auswahl angemessen leiten können. Zu diesen Parametern gehören insbesondere Art, Umfang und Zusammensetzung von Verbindlichkeiten der Kreditinstitute, insbesondere der von ihnen verwalteten Einlagen sowie sonstiger Risikopositionen gegenüber anderen Marktteilnehmern, aber auch die Funktionsfähigkeit des Finanzmarkts. In den persönlichen Schutzbereich der Maßnahmen zur Überwindung der Systemgefährdung fallen insbesondere Gläubiger und sonstige Kontrahenten des in Schieflage geratenen Kreditinstituts, die Risikopositionen – beispielsweise aus Schuldverschreibungen, Derivategeschäften oder offenen Kreditlinien – gegenüber dem Kreditinstitut halten, sowie auch andere Finanzmarktteilnehmer, die von einer abrupten Beendigung von Zahlungsverkehrs-, Finanzierungs- oder sonstigen Dienstleistungen des Kreditinstituts betroffen wären. Bei der Auswahl von Passivpositionen sind einzelne in- und ausländische Akteure innerhalb der zu definierenden Gläubigergruppen gleich zu behandeln, die entweder auf die

---

102 Vgl. hierzu *Schelo* NJW 2011, 186 (190).

103 Danach können u. a. Gegenstände, die einer nach § 206 Abs. 1 SolvV berücksichtigungsfähigen Aufrechnungsvereinbarung unterfallen (z. B. ISDA Master Agreement, Deutscher Rahmenvertrag für Finanztermingeschäfte) nur einheitlich als Gesamtheit übertragen werden (§ 48j Abs. 3 Satz 2 und Abs. 5 Satz 2 KWG). Damit soll weiterhin ein „Netting" ermöglicht werden, s. Begründung RegE RestrG, BT-Drucks. 17/3024, S. 67 li. Sp.; zum Netting auch *Paech*, WM 2010, 1965 (1969 f.). Bei einer partiellen Übertragung oder Rückübertragung nach § 48j Abs. 5 Satz 1, § 48k Abs. 2 Satz 3 KWG gehen die in die Aufrechnungsvereinbarung einbezogenen Schuldverhältnisse mit über bzw. dürfen nur gemeinsam übertragen werden.

Brückenbank übertragen werden oder bei der Restbank bleiben sollen. Bei der Auswahl, die letztlich auch zu einer Negativauswahl der nicht schutzwürdigen Gruppen von Gläubigern und Finanzmarktteilnehmern führt, werden die Rückwirkungen und Anreizeffekte zu berücksichtigen sein, die die Begünstigung einzelner Gruppen von Gläubigern und Finanzmarktteilnehmern im Vorgriff auf künftige Schieflagen und Krisen auf die Refinanzierungskonditionen von Kreditinstituten und auf die Liquiditätsentwicklung einer in Schwierigkeiten geratenen Bank haben kann.[104] Wenn bestimmte Gläubigergruppen, etwa Privateinleger und Kapitalsammelstellen wie Pensionskassen, Versicherungen und Einlagenkreditinstitute, mit einer Verlagerung auf ein Brückeninstitut rechnen könnten, würden sie als Anleger in Bankverbindlichkeiten voraussichtlich für das Institut günstigere Konditionen verlangen und in Krisensituationen weniger Neigung zum Abzug ihrer Gelder verspüren als etwa Akteure aus Gläubigergruppen, die als nicht systemrelevant eingestuft würden und daher damit rechnen müssten, in einer Restbank zurückgelassen zu werden.

c) Unübertragbare und unteilbare Gegenstände

Die Übertragung im Rahmen der Ausgliederung durch Übertragungsanordnung erfolgt durch Sonderrechtsnachfolge nach § 48g Abs. 2 Nr. 1 KWG, die der (partiellen) Gesamtrechtsnachfolge gemäß § 131 Abs. 1 Nr. 1 UmwG entspricht. Insgesamt gelten bei der Übertragungsanordnung auch die gleichen Einschränkungen im Hinblick auf die Übertragbarkeit einzelner Gegenstände wie nach dem UmwG.[105] Zwar haben Übertragungshindernisse keine Geltung, so dass eine Zustimmung des Vertragspartners nicht erforderlich ist.[106] Von der Übertragung ausgenommen sind aber bestimmte höchstpersönliche Rechte und Pflichten.[107] Dazu gehört etwa die Gesellschafterstellung in einer Personengesellschaft.[108] Soweit verschiedene Rechtspositionen durch Gesetz untrennbar miteinander verknüpft sind, können sie ebenfalls nicht getrennt übertragen werden.[109] Die Sonderrechtsnachfolge erfasst auch Verbindlichkeiten außer Pfandbriefen.[110] Die Zustimmung von Gläubigern ist – anders als bei der Einzelrechtsnachfolge – nicht erforderlich.[111] Mit Blick auf die Möglichkeit einer Selektion der Verbindlichkeiten nach Gläubigergruppen ist davon auszugehen, dass Verbindlichkei-

---

104 Zu Anreizeffekten vgl. auch *Krahnen/Siekmann* Stellungnahme RestrG, HoF Policy Platform, S. 5, abrufbar unter http://www.hof.uni-frankfurt.de/component/option,com_docman/Itemid,288/gid,13/task,doc_download/.

105 Begründung RegE RestrG, BT-Drucks. 17/3024, S. 65 f.

106 *Kallmeyer/Sickinger* in: Kallmeyer, UmwG, 4. Aufl. 2010, § 131 Rz. 2; *Schröer* in: Semler/Stengel, UmwG, 2. Aufl. 2007, § 131 Rz. 34 ff.

107 *Hörtnagl* in: Schmitt/Hörtnagl/Stratz (Hrsg.) UmwG, 5. Aufl. 2009, § 131 Rz. 92 und 13 ff.; *Kallmeyer/Sickinger*, in: Kallmeyer UmwG 4. Aufl. 2010, § 131 Rz. 2; *Simon* in: Kölner Kommentar UmwG 2009, § 131 Rz. 16.

108 *Hörtnagl* in: Schmitt/Hörtnagl/Stratz (Hrsg.) UmwG, 5. Aufl. 2009, § 131 Rz. 38; *Schröer* in: Semler/Stengel, UmwG, 2. Aufl. 2007, § 131, Rz. 25.

109 *Simon* in: Kölner Kommentar UmwG, 2009, § 131 Rz. 17; *Teichmann* in: Lutter/Winter, UmwG, 4. Aufl. 2009, § 131 Rz. 5 ff.

110 Pfandbriefgeschäfte (Verbindlichkeiten und Deckung) können im Rahmen einer Übertragungsanordnung nicht übertragen werden, für sie gelten gemäß § 36a Abs. 2 PfandBG die §§ 30 ff. PfandBG als *lex specialis*, s. Begründung RegE RestrG, BT-Drucks. 17/3024, S. 84.

111 Begründung RegE RestrG, BT-Drucks. 17/3024, S. 66 re. Sp.

ten, die Gläubigern, welche unterschiedlichen Gläubigergruppen angehören, geschuldet sind, grundsätzlich zwischen Brückeninstitut und Restbank aufgeteilt werden können, soweit sie teilbar sind.[112] Die Teilbarkeit stößt aber bei Anleihen an Grenzen, die dem Recht der Schuldverschreibung selbst innewohnen. Bei deutschem Recht unterliegenden Schuldverschreibungen aus einer Gesamtemission im Sinne des § 1 Abs. 1 SchVG[113] halten alle Anleihegläubiger inhaltsgleiche Stücke, die zur Sicherstellung der Umlauffähigkeit und Fungibilität nicht unterscheidbar sind und wegen ihrer kollektiven Bindung vom Schuldner jederzeit gleich zu behandeln sind (§ 4 Satz 2 SchVG). Die Auswechselung des Schuldners wäre zwar eine wesentliche Änderung der Anleihebedingungen. Da das Kreditinstitut als Schuldner aber im Rahmen einer Übertragungsanordnung nicht an der Ungleichbehandlung mitwirkt, die durch die Abtrennung eines Teils der Verbindlichkeit einer Anleiheserie eintritt, dürfte das Gleichbehandlungsgebot einer solchen Aufteilung auf zwei Rechtsträger nicht prinzipiell im Wege stehen. Die Ausgliederung eines Teils der Anleiheverbindlichkeit würde voraussetzen, dass der Kapitalbetrag der von den übergehenden bzw. zurückbleibenden Gläubigern gehaltenen Serie von Bonds angegeben wird. Wegen der fungiblen Ausstattung der Anleihe sind die auf der Grundlage festgelegter Gläubigergruppen eligiblen einzelnen Investoren nicht bekannt. Ihre Identifizierung könnte allenfalls unter Mitwirkung und Sperrung des Handels in der jeweiligen Serie über einen bestimmten Zeitraum erfolgen. Für ein solches Verfahren fehlen freilich die gesetzlichen Grundlagen. Daher wäre es allenfalls denkbar, dass die Investoren über die Clearingsysteme aufgefordert werden, ihren Anteil an der Anleihe auf ein Sperrdepot zu buchen und sich gegenüber dem Schuldner namentlich zu identifizieren. Die Durchführung eines solchen Verfahrens, das der Abwicklung eines Umtauschangebots für Schuldverschreibungen ähnelt, dürfte bei global plazierten Papieren einige Wochen in Anspruch nehmen und ist bei unmittelbarem Handlungsbedarf daher unpraktikabel. Selbst wenn ein solches Verfahren im Rahmen einer partiellen Rückübertragungsanordnung durchgeführt würde, bleibt es wegen der hohen Komplexität und verbleibenden Rechtsunsicherheit zweifelhaft, ob alle zu schützenden Finanzmarktteilnehmer mitwirken werden.

4. Anerkennung im Ausland und negative Transferfolgen

a) Gegenstände mit Auslandsbezug

Da größere, vernetzte Kreditinstitute typischerweise erhebliche Auslandsaktivitäten aufweisen, ist die Behandlung von Ausgliederungsgegenständen mit Auslandsbezug ein neuralgischer Punkt bei der Übertragungsanordnung wie schon bei der Abspaltung

112 Dies ist zum UmwG inzwischen anerkannt, s. *Simon* in: Kölner Kommentar UmwG, 2009, § 131 Rz. 28; *Hörtnagel* in: Schmitt/Hörtnagel/Stratz (Hrsg.) UmwG, 5. Aufl. 2009, § 131 UmwG Rz. 47; *Heidenhain* NJW 1995, 2873 (2877); *Schröer* in: Semler/Stengel, UmwG, 2. Aufl. 2007, § 131 Rz. 69 f.; a.A. (generelles Teilungsverbot bei Verbindlichkeiten) noch die Begründung des RegE eines Gesetzes zur Bereinigung des Umwandlungsrechts, BT-Drucks. 12/7265, zu § 126, 11./12. Abs.; *Rieble* ZIP 1997, 301 (310).

113 In der heutigen international üblichen Praxis kommt die Ausgabe effektiver Stücke (Einzelurkunden) kaum noch vor, s. *Bliesener* in: Perspektiven des Wirtschaftsrechts, Beiträge für Klaus J. Hopt 2009, S. 355 (363).

von Risikopositionen und nichtstrategienotwendigen Geschäftsbereichen auf bundesrechtliche Abwicklungsanstalten.[114] Der Bezug der Geschäftsaktivitäten zu ausländischen Rechtsordnungen kann durch das anwendbare Recht, einen Gerichtsstand im Ausland, ein im Ausland belegenes Aktivum oder Sicherungsobjekt, die Buchung oder Verwahrung von Vermögenswerten im Ausland oder eine eigene ausländische Niederlassung oder Buchungsstelle (*booking location*) hergestellt werden. Auch kann sich der Sitz oder die Niederlassung des Schuldners, Gläubigers oder der Gegenpartei im Ausland befinden.

b) Globale Wirkung der Ausgliederung nach deutschem Recht

Da die Rechtsfolgen der Übertragungsanordnung denen der Ausgliederung ausdrücklich nachgebildet sind (§ 48 g Abs. 2 Nr. 1 KWG) und das Gesetz die Übertragung – vorbehaltlich bestimmter Sondernormen – wie eine Ausgliederung zur Aufnahme behandelt, spricht aus Sicht des deutschen Rechts einiges dafür, die Ausgliederung durch Übertragungsanordnung und die Ausgliederung nach dem UmwG im Hinblick auf ihre Wirkungen auf Gegenstände mit Auslandsbezug gleich zu behandeln. Auch daraus, dass die Ausgliederung durch einen Verwaltungsakt der BaFin herbeigeführt wird, ergibt sich nichts anderes; denn mit den Sonderregeln des § 48 i KWG für dem ausländischen Recht unterliegende Gegenstände bringt der Gesetzgeber zum Ausdruck, dass er eine globale Wirkung der Ausgliederung anstrebt. Nach ganz herrschender Meinung im deutschen Internationalen Privatrecht ist bei Umwandlungsvorgängen wie der Ausgliederung das Gesellschaftsstatut der beteiligten Rechtsträger maßgeblich.[115] Die Anwendbarkeit des Gesellschaftsstatuts kann allenfalls aufgrund völkerrechtlicher Vereinbarungen mit einzelnen Staaten konkretisiert, modifiziert oder auch ausgeschlossen sein (Art. 3 Nr. 2 EGBGB).[116] Das Gesellschaftsstatut führt im Falle einer Ausgliederung aufgrund Übertragungsanordnung zur Anwendbarkeit des deutschen Rechts, weil sowohl das in Schieflage geratene Kreditinstitut als auch der übernehmende Rechtsträger nach deutschem Recht gegründet wurden bzw. werden und in Deutschland ihren tatsächlichen Verwaltungssitz unterhalten. Das auf die Ausgliederung anwendbare

---

114 Vgl. die Abspaltungen der WestLB-Gruppe auf die Erste Abwicklungsanstalt (EAA) in den Jahren 2009 und 2010 sowie die Abspaltungen der HRE-Gruppe auf die FMS Wertmanagement (FMS-WM) im Jahr 2010. S. auch *Binder* Bankenintervention und Bankenabwicklung in Deutschland: Reformnotwendigkeiten und Grundzüge eines verbesserten Rechtsrahmens, Sachverständigenrat Arbeitspapier 05/2009, S. 48, abrufbar unter: http://46.4.4.24/fileadmin/dateiablage/Arbeitspapiere/Bankenintervention_und_Bankenabwicklung_in_Deutschland.pdf.

115 S. nur *Kuntz* IStR 2006, 224 (229) m. w. N. An der Geltung des Gesellschaftsstatuts ändert auch die Europäischen Verordnung vom 11. Juli 2007 über das auf außervertragliche Schuldverhältnisse anzuwendende Recht („Rom II-Verordnung“) und die entsprechende Anpassung von Art. 3 EGBGB nichts, weil die Verordnung nicht für gesellschaftsrechtliche Schuldverhältnisse gilt (vgl. Art. 1 Abs. 2 lit. d der Verordnung).

116 Allgemein MünchKommBGB-*Sonnenberger* 5. Aufl., 2010, Art. 3 EGBGB Rz. 3 ff. Eine völkerrechtliche Vereinbarung mit den U.S.A. enthält Bestimmungen hinsichtlich des Anknüpfungspunkts für das Internationale Gesellschaftsrecht und sieht dazu insbesondere die sog. „Gründungstheorie“ vor, s. etwa MünchKommBGB-*Kindler* IntGesR, 5. Aufl. 2010, Rz. 359 ff. Im Übrigen bleibt es für die U.S.A. bei den allgemeinen Grundsätzen, i. E. ebenso *Kusserow/Prüm* WM 2005, 633 (635).

Recht bestimmt auch deren Rechtsfolgen einschließlich der im Rahmen der Ausgliederung erfolgenden Übertragung von Gegenständen im Wege der Sonderrechtsnachfolge.[117] Die Übertragung erfolgt somit aus deutscher Sicht auch bei Auslandsbezug nicht nach dem auf eine Einzelübertragung anwendbaren lokalen Recht (bei Waren und Grundstücken etwa das Recht des Belegenheitsorts), sondern nach deutschem Recht.[118] Die Sonderrechtsnachfolge erfasst – soweit keine Ausnahme eingreift – im Ausland belegenes ebenso wie inländisches (aktives und passives) Vermögen.[119] Die Diskussion in der Literatur über Ausnahmen und Einschränkungen der Geltung des Gesamtstatuts zugunsten des auf die Einzelrechtsnachfolge anwendbaren Rechts (Einzelstatut) dreht sich insbesondere um sachenrechtliche Fallgestaltungen, in erster Linie um die grundsätzlich nach dem Recht des Belegenheitsorts (*lex rei sitae*) erfolgende Übertragung von Grundstücken und am Rande auch von Mobilien.[120] Soweit durch die Ausgliederung Grundstücke und bewegliche Sachen übertragen werden, richten sich daher die Rechtsfolgen der Ausgliederung nach dem Recht des Belegenheitsorts.[121] Für Forderungen, Verbindlichkeiten und Verträge werden solche Ausnahmen von der alleinigen Geltung des Gesellschaftsstatuts – soweit ersichtlich – nicht diskutiert. Für Gegenstände des Passivvermögens (einschließlich Eventualverbindlichkeiten) werden Ausnahmen vom Grundsatz der ausschließlichen Geltung des Gesellschaftsstatuts für die Bestimmung der Spaltungsfolgen ebenfalls nicht diskutiert. Sie sind auch nach der Logik der diese Ausnahmen befürwortenden Literaturmeinung allenfalls dann begründbar, wenn die fremde Rechtsordnung die (partielle) Gesamtrechtsnachfolge aufgrund Spaltung als rechtliches Konzept nicht anerkennt. Innerhalb der Europäischen Union (EU) sind die Mitgliedstaaten grundsätzlich zur Anerkennung der Gesamtrechtsnachfolge im Rahmen der Spaltung verpflichtet.[122] Wenn Mitgliedstaaten nach der Öffnungsklausel des Art. 17 Abs. 3 der Spaltungsrichtlinie[123] die Übertragung bestimmter Vermögensgegenstände von „besonderen Förmlichkeiten“ abhängig machen und die Einzelrechtsübertragung verlangen, ist dies in der Regel mit der Anknüpfung an die *lex rei sitae* verbunden.[124] Unabhängig von der Öffnungsklausel bleibt es dabei, dass sämtliche

---

117 *Kusserow/Prüm* WM 2005, 633, 635; widersprüchlich *Stratz* in: Schmitt/Hörtnagel/Stratz (Hrsg.) UmwG, 5. Aufl., § 20 Rz. 33 f.

118 *Vossius* in: Widmann/Mayer, 117. Erg.-Lfg., September 2010, § 20 UmwG, Rz. 41; *Kollmorgen/Feldhaus* BB 2007, 2189 (2190).

119 *Marsch-Barner* in: Kallmeyer, UmwG, 3. Aufl., § 20 Rz. 5 (zur Verschmelzung); *Grunewald* in: Lutter, UmwG, 4. Auflage, 2009, § 20, Rz. 11 (zur Verschmelzung); *Racky* DB 2003, 923 (zur Verschmelzung); *Bungert* FS Heldrich, S. 527 (528) (zur Verschmelzung); *Vossius* in: Widmann/Mayer, 117. Erg.-Lfg., September 2010, § 20 UmwG, Rz. 41 (zur Verschmelzung); *Kübler* in: Semler/Stengel, UmwG, 2. Auflage, 2007, § 20 Rz. 10 (zur Verschmelzung); *Kuntz* IStR 2006, 224 (229); Palandt-*Thorn* BGB, 70. Aufl., 2011, Anh. Art. 12 EGBGB Rz. 18 (zur Verschmelzung).

120 *Vossius* in: Widmann/Mayer, 117. Erg.-Lfg., September 2010, § 20 UmwG, Rz. 42 will beispielsweise Ausnahmen „nur“ zulassen, soweit die Rechtsfolge der Universalsukzession mit dem „Sachenrecht“ des Belegenheitsortes unvereinbar ist.

121 Es finden sich in der Literatur keine Aussagen dazu, ob dies entsprechend auch für Sicherungsrechte an Grundstücken oder beweglichen Sachen gilt.

122 S. *Bungert* FS Heldrich, S. 527 (531).

123 Sechste Richtlinie 82/891/EWG des Rates vom 17. Dezember 1982 gemäß Artikel 54 Absatz 3 Buchstabe g) des Vertrages betreffend die Spaltung von Aktiengesellschaften, ABl. EG Nr. L 378 S. 47.

124 *Racky* DB 2003, 923, 924; richtigerweise sind damit aber nur „Formerfordernisse“ gemeint, s. *Bungert* FS Heldrich, S. 527 (531).

Mitgliedstaaten der EU auf der Grundlage der Spaltungsrichtlinie das Prinzip der partiellen Gesamtrechtsnachfolge im Wege der Spaltung anerkennen und damit ein Vorrang des Einzelstatuts sich jedenfalls innerhalb der EU nicht damit begründen lässt, die Gesamtrechtsnachfolge werde dort abgelehnt. Darüber hinaus lässt sich die Anerkennung der Ausgliederung durch Übertragungsanordnung innerhalb der EU auch auf die Sanierungs- und Liquidationsrichtlinie stützen.[125] Zwar gilt diese Richtlinie neben der Abwicklung von Banken nur für Maßnahmen, mit denen die finanzielle Lage eines Kreditinstituts gesichert oder wiederhergestellt werden soll, was auf die Übertragungsanordnung nicht unmittelbar zutrifft. Aber da eine Übertragungsanordnung zumindest den Geschäftsbetrieb oder einen Teil davon sichern und restrukturieren soll, könnte sie auch als Sanierungsmaßnahme aufgefasst werden. Aus Sicht des deutschen Rechts ist davon auszugehen, dass die Ausgliederung vorbehaltlich bestimmter Ausnahmen globale Wirkung entfaltet, so dass von der Gesamtrechtsnachfolge grundsätzlich § 48g Abs. 2 Nr. 1 KWG auch Ausgliederungsgegenstände erfasst sind, die ausländischem Recht unterliegen.[126] Da innerhalb der EU nur im Herkunftsmitgliedstaat des Kreditinstituts ein einheitliches Liquidations- oder Insolvenzverfahren durchgeführt wird,[127] ist davon auszugehen, dass der europaweiten Wirkung der Übertragungsanordnung auch im Rahmen eines deutschen Insolvenzverfahrens Geltung verschafft wird.

c) Fehlende Anerkennung in ausländischen Jurisdiktionen

Anders kann sich aber die Übertragungsanordnung aus der Sicht des ausländischen Rechts darstellen, insbesondere im außereuropäischen Ausland. Dort wird eine partielle Gesamtrechtsnachfolge möglicherweise nicht anerkannt, oder es gibt andere Transferhindernisse. Gerade in wichtigen Jurisdiktionen wie New York wird die partielle Gesamtrechtsnachfolge auf Grund von vertraglichen und anderen Übertragungshindernissen (etwa Zustimmungserfordernisse, Abtretungsverbote), Verboten im lokalen Aufsichtsrecht oder sektoralen Regelungen (öffentliche Sicherheit u. ä.) nicht anerkannt. Auch bei grundsätzlicher Anerkennung können in kontinentaleuropäischen Jurisdiktionen Ausnahmen für höchstpersönliche Rechtsverhältnisse, Aktiva, die garantiert oder versichert sind, oder Positionen, die im lokalen Recht eine Banklizenz voraussetzen, bestehen. Auch der Kündigungsausschluss des § 48g Abs. 7 KWG wird aus Sicht des ausländischen Rechts möglicherweise nicht anerkannt.[128] Im Falle der Nichtanerkennung der Sonderrechtsnachfolge durch die ausländische Rechtsordnung (oder bei Zweifeln bezüglich der Anerkennung, § 48i Abs. 4 KWG) statuiert § 48i Abs. 1 KWG die Pflicht des Kreditinstituts, auf eine Übertragung durch Einzelrechtsnachfolge nach den Vorschriften des ausländischen Rechts hinzuwirken.[129] Bis zur Übertragung stehen das Kreditinstitut und der übernehmende Rechtsträger in einem durch § 48i Abs. 2 KWG

125 Art. 3 Abs. 2 Unterabsatz 3 der Richtlinie 2001/24/EG des Europäischen Parlaments und des Rates vom 4. April 2001 über die Sanierung und Liquidation von Kreditinstituten, ABl. EG Nr. L 125, S. 15 vom 5. Mai 2001.

126 Zum UmwG *Kollmorgen/Feldhaus* BB 2007, 2189 (2190); *Kübler* in: Semler/Stengel, UmwG, 2. Aufl. 2007, § 20 Rz. 10 (zur Verschmelzung); *Marsch-Barner* in: Kallmeyer, UmwG, 4. Aufl. 2010, § 20 Rz. 5 (zur Verschmelzung).

127 Art. 9 Abs. 1 der Sanierungs- und Liquidationsrichtlinie.

128 S. auch *Schuster/Westpfahl* DB 2011, 282 (286).

129 S. dazu auch für Großbritannien Sec. 39(3) Banking Act 2009.

angeordneten Treuhandverhältnis, das das Kreditinstitut zur Verwaltung für den übernehmenden Rechtsträger verpflichtet (gesetzlich angeordnete "*fallback subparticipation*"). Gläubiger der betroffenen Gegenstände können ihre Ansprüche gemäß § 48i Abs. 3 Satz 2 KWG nicht gegen das Kreditinstitut geltend machen. Die im Rahmen des Treuhandverhältnisses getroffenen Handlungen sind nicht anfechtbar und die betroffenen Vermögensgegenstände gehören im Falle einer Insolvenz des Kreditinstituts nicht zur Insolvenzmasse.[130] Auch die Ausgliederung durch eine Übertragungsanordnung ist gemäß § 48h Abs. 2 KWG insolvenzfest und kann weder innerhalb noch außerhalb eines Insolvenzverfahrens über das Vermögen des übertragenden Kreditinstituts angefochten werden. Die Insolvenzfestigkeit gilt jedoch nur für das deutsche Insolvenzverfahren und wegen der Konzentration der Bankeninsolvenz im Herkunftsmitgliedstaat im Europäischen Wirtschaftsraum (EWR).[131] Kein Schutz besteht dagegen vor Partikularinsolvenzverfahren außerhalb des EWR (etwa in den U.S.A. oder Japan). Dort entfällt auch die Wirkung einer subsidiären wirtschaftlichen Übertragung aufgrund des vom deutschen Gesetz angeordneten, dort aber wahrscheinlich nicht anerkannten Treuhandverhältnisses. Im Hinblick auf die betroffenen Gegenstände besteht im Falle der Partikularinsolvenz ein erhebliches Risiko, dass sie das Brückeninstitut im außereuropäischen Ausland nicht erfolgreich beanspruchen und verwerten kann. Dies kann u. U. zu signifikanten Einbußen und erhöhtem Kapital- und Liquiditätsbedarf bei dem Brückeninstitut führen. Damit kann der Erfolg einer Übertragungsanordnung als Transferinstrument ebenso geschmälert werden wie im Fall einer Abspaltung bei der Befüllung der Abwicklungsanstalten.[132] Eine Lösung kann hier nur durch multilaterale Regulierung und Harmonisierung erreicht werden. In der Praxis ist zu erwägen, ob mit vertretbarem Aufwand in der zur Verfügung stehenden Zeit parallel zur Ausgliederung alternative Transferwege, die mit den jeweiligen vertraglichen Anforderungen in Einklang stehen, beschritten werden können.[133]

d) Negative Transferfolgen

Unter negativen Transferfolgen ist das Risiko zu verstehen, dass der Transfer von Vermögensgegenständen bzw. Verbindlichkeiten auf den übernehmenden Rechtsträger zwar in ausländischen Jurisdiktionen anerkannt wird, dort aber nach lokalem Recht negative Folgen für das Kreditinstitut oder den übernehmenden Rechtsträger auslöst. Die Minimierung der negativen Transferfolgen sollte daher bei der Selektion der Gegenstände möglichst berücksichtigt werden. Gravierende, nicht vermeidbare negative Transferfolgen können sich als faktische Transferhindernisse auswirken. Wird die Ausgliederung im ausländischen Recht überhaupt nicht anerkannt, drohen keine negativen Transferfolgen.

---

130 Die Ausgliederung durch eine Übertragungsanordnung ist gemäß § 48h Abs. 2 KWG insolvenzfest und kann weder innerhalb noch außerhalb eines Insolvenzverfahrens über das Vermögen des übertragenden Kreditinstituts angefochten werden.

131 S. Art. 16 ff. der Verordnung (EG) Nr. 1346/2000 des Rates vom 29. Mai 2000 über Insolvenzverfahren, Amtsblatt Nr. L 160/1 vom 30. Juni 2000 (EuInsVO).

132 Vgl. auch *Zimmer* Stellungnahme RestrG, S. 2, abrufbar unter http://www.bundestag.de/bundestag/ausschuesse17/a07/anhoerungen/2010/029/Stellungnahmen/35_Prof__Dr__Daniel_Zimmer.pdf.

133 Alternative Transferwege sind nicht vorgesehen, aber gleichwohl in § 48i Abs. 1 KWG als Hilfsmaßnahmen angelegt. Die gleichzeitige Vornahme von Einzelübertragungsakten ist damit nicht ausgeschlossen.

In diesem Fall findet keine Übertragung statt, so dass aus ausländischer Sicht auch keine rechtlichen Veränderungen stattgefunden haben, die bestimmte unerwünschte und unerkannte Folgen zeitigen. Negative Transferfolgen drohen auch dann, wenn die Ausgliederung in einen Einzelrechtstransfer umgedeutet wird. In diesem Fall könnten an die Einzelrechtsübertragung nachteilige Konsequenzen geknüpft sein.

Typische negative Transferfolgen sind etwa Sanktionen gegen den übernehmenden Rechtsträger mangels lokaler Banklizenz, Sonderkündigungsrechte des Schuldners/Gläubigers, Vertragsstrafen, Stamp Duties bei der Übertragung von Realsicherheiten, Schadensersatzansprüche gegen das Kreditinstitut oder den übernehmenden Rechtsträger bei Nachteilen der Gegenpartei aus der Übertragung oder negative steuerliche Folgen. So soll das Beendigungsverbot des § 48g Abs. 7 KWG zwar eine zwingende Vorschrift i. S. v. Art. 9 Rom I[134] darstellen, die unabhängig von dem auf das Rechtsverhältnis anwendbaren Recht Wirksamkeit entfaltet.[135] Es bestehen aber Zweifel, ob das Beendigungsverbot im Ausland anerkannt werden wird und ob nicht mangels Anerkennung der Ausnahmevorschrift die Übertragung von Verträgen auf ein anderes Institut zu einer automatischen Beendigung von Verträgen führt.[136] Anders als bei der Portfolioübertragung auf Abwicklungsanstalten nach § 8a Abs. 1 FMStFG steht als Lösungsansatz eine Vereinbarung von Unterbeteiligungen oder Back-to-back-Geschäften mit der Option späterer Rückübertragung nicht zur Verfügung.[137] Die Eliminierung negativer Transferfolgen wird der deutsche Gesetzgeber ebenfalls nicht allein lösen können. Es bedarf daher einer internationalen und europäischen Abstimmung, um Rechtsunsicherheiten und mögliche Schäden von einem Brückeninstitut und den übrigen Beteiligten fernzuhalten.[138]

e) Due Diligence

Eine Due Diligence-Prüfung und Bewertung von rechtlichen Transferrisiken ist gesetzlich nicht vorgesehen und vermutlich in Anbetracht der Kürze der zur Verfügung stehenden Zeit nicht oder nicht vollständig möglich. Für eine umfassend vorbereitete Entscheidung über die Übertragungsanordnung durch die BaFin wäre aber im Regelfall die Einschätzung der Transferrisiken sinnvoll, insbesondere im Falle der Übertragung von Portfolien mit Auslandsbezug. Sofern Gegenstände im Wege der Gesamtrechtsnachfolge nicht übergehen, ist dies entsprechend zur berücksichtigen; für die Auswahl ist entscheidend, dass die Gegenstände möglichst übertragbar sind.

---

134 Verordnung (EG) Nr. 593/2008 des Europäischen Parlaments und des Rates vom 17. Juni 2008 über das auf vertragliche Schuldverhältnisse anzuwendende Recht (Rom I), Amtsblatt Nr. L 177 vom 4. Juli 2008, S. 6.

135 Begründung RegE RestrG, BT-Drucks. 17/3024, S. 67 re. Sp.; zweifelnd *Zimmer* Stellungnahme RestrG, S. 2, abrufbar unter http://www.bundestag.de/bundestag/ausschuesse17/a07/anhoerungen/2010/029/Stellungnahmen/35_Prof__Dr__Daniel_Zimmer.pdf.

136 *Amend* ZIP 2009, 589 (596 f.); *Paech* WM 2010, 1965 (1970); *Zimmer* Was das Gesetz zur Rettung der Banken taugt, F.A.Z. vom 10. September 2010, S. 12.

137 S. dazu auch für Großbritannien Sec. 39(4) Banking Act 2009.

138 Allgemein dafür auch *Krahnen/Siekmann* Stellungnahme RestrG, HoF Policy Platform, S. 4, abrufbar unter http://www.hof.uni-frankfurt.de/component/option,com_docman/Itemid,288/gid,13/task,doc_download/; *Zimmer* Was das Gesetz zur Rettung der Banken taugt, F.A.Z. vom 9. September 2010, S. 12; kritisch *Rudolph* Bankregulierung nach der Finanzkrise, in: FS Hopt, 2010, S. 2407 (2411 f.).

5. Brückeninstitut

Als übernehmender Rechtsträger kommt ein Marktteilnehmer oder ein von der FMSA für den Restrukturierungsfonds gegründetes Brückeninstitut ("bridge bank") i. S. d. § 5 RStruktFG in Betracht. Auch wenn das Gesetz dies als Ausnahme ansieht, dürfte eine Übertragung auf ein Brückeninstitut oder eine andere geeignete staatliche Einrichtung aussichtsreicher sein als die unmittelbare Einbindung eines Marktteilnehmers als übernehmenden Rechtsträger. Im Rahmen der Abwicklung können dritte Markteilnehmer als potentielle Erwerber einzelner Portfolien oder des gesamten Geschäftsbetriebs angesprochen werden. Das Brückeninstitut dient dazu, Gegenstände des Kreditinstituts zu übernehmen und dann – sobald es im Interesse der Stabilität des Finanzsystems möglich ist – wieder dem privaten Sektor zuzuführen.

a) Rechtsform

Gemäß § 5 Abs. 1 RStruktFG kann der Restrukturierungsfonds durch die FMSA eine juristische Person gründen, die im Rahmen einer Übertragungsanordnung als Brückeninstitut fungiert. Auch die Übernahme von Anteilen an bestehenden Gesellschaften ist unter bestimmten Bedingungen gemäß § 5 Abs. 2 RStruktFG möglich. Die Rechtsform eines Brückeninstituts gibt das RStruktFG nicht vor, sondern legt nur fest, dass es sich um eine juristische Person handeln muss. In Betracht kommen zum Beispiel GmbH, Aktiengesellschaft oder Anstalt des öffentlichen Rechts.[139] § 48c Abs. 5 Satz 2 KWG bestimmt jedoch, dass, wenn das Kreditinstitut in der Rechtsform einer Kapitalgesellschaft verfasst ist, der übernehmende Rechtsträger in derselben Rechtsform organisiert sein soll. Die Ratio der Soll-Vorschrift des § 45c Abs. 5 Satz 2 KWG ist allerdings zweifelhaft. Für diese Soll-Vorschrift könnte sprechen, dass bei Übernahme des gesamten Geschäftsbetriebs die Kontinuität durch Wahl derselben Rechtsform befördert wird. Freilich dürfte ein Wechsel im Management und in der Corporate Governance auch beim Übergang von Geschäftsaktivitäten auf ein Brückeninstitut oder einen anderen Marktteilnehmer unvermeidlich sein. Hinzu kommt, dass eine nur partielle Übertragung der Geschäftsaktivitäten oder die Vollübertragung mit anschließender partieller Rückübertragung unweigerlich zu einem Bruch in dem bisherigen Geschäftsgang des Unternehmens führen wird. Da die Übertragung auf ein Brückeninstitut nach der Gesetzessystematik einen Sonderfall darstellt, bei dem auch die FMSA als Verwalterin des Restrukturierungsfonds eingebunden wird, sprechen gute Gründe dafür, dass in diesem Fall von dem gesetzlichen Regelfall der Rechtsformidentität abgewichen werden darf. Um die Struktur und Führung des Brückeninstituts unter der Ägide der FMSA möglichst effizient zu gestalten, bietet sich als Rechtsform eine Gesellschaft mit beschränkter Haftung (GmbH) an. Da eine GmbH als Rechtsträger allgemein an Vorgängen nach dem Umwandlungsgesetz beteiligt werden kann, dürfte sie der Rechtsform der Anstalt des öffentlichen Rechts vorzuziehen sein.

Da die Abstimmung der Gründung eines Brückeninstituts bei FMSA, Lenkungsausschuss und BMF gewisse Zeit in Anspruch nehmen kann, erscheint es sinnvoll, ein oder mehrere Brückeninstitute bereits vor der ersten Übertragungsanordnung zu gründen

139 Anders noch § 8a Abs. 1 Satz 1 FMStFG.

und vorzuhalten.[140] Mangels Geschäftsbetriebs, hinreichender Organisation und Finanzausstattung werden diese Vorratsinstitute noch nicht über eine Bankerlaubnis verfügen. § 5 Abs. 1 RStruktFG erlaubt – anders als § 8a Abs. 1 Satz 1 FMStFG[141] – ausdrücklich die Gründung eines Instituts ohne konkreten Anlass.

Der Ausstieg des Restrukturierungsfonds aus dem Brückeninstitut ist[142] nicht geregelt. Möglich sind der Verkauf der Beteiligung an dem Brückeninstitut, der Verkauf des Portfolios und die Liquidation des übernommenen Geschäftsbetriebs.

b) Refinanzierung

Das Brückeninstitut verfügt in der Regel nicht über ein eigenes Kreditrating. Da die übertragenen Unternehmensteile u. U. von einem Kreditinstitut in Liquiditätsschwierigkeiten abgetrennt werden, ist davon auszugehen, dass zusätzliche Refinanzierungsmittel vom ersten Tag an erforderlich sein werden. Da die Zusammensetzung der Aktiv- und Passivseite des Brückeninstituts jedenfalls bei einer partiellen Übertragung von der Bonität und wirtschaftlichen Lage des übertragenden Kreditinstituts erheblich abweichen wird, ist die Übernahme des Ratings des Kreditinstituts durch das Brückeninstitut höchstens eine vorübergehende Notlösung. Ob das Brückeninstitut in nennenswertem Umfang mit diesem Alt-Rating Refinanzierungsmittel aufnehmen kann, ist zweifelhaft. Daher wird das Brückeninstitut auf eine Garantie des Restrukturierungsfonds für neue Emissionen angewiesen sein. Da der Restrukturierungsfonds – wie der SoFFin (§ 5 Satz 2 FMStFG) – das Privileg der Bundeshaftung genießt,[143] dürften die von ihm garantierten Anleihen ein erstklassiges Rating erhalten. Zwar sollen Steuermittel nicht mehr für Liquiditätshilfen und andere Banksanierungsbeiträge haften. Allerdings kann der Fonds neben den regulären Beiträgen (ab September 2011) zur Deckung des Mittelbedarfs, der bei der Entscheidung über Maßnahmen nach § 3 Abs. 2 RStruktFG festzulegen ist, auch Sonderbeiträge erheben.[144] Sollte der Mittelbedarf nicht zeitgerecht durch Sonderbeiträge gedeckt werden, kann der Restrukturierungsfonds nach § 12 Abs. 6 RStruktFG Kredite beim Bund aufnehmen, deren Volumen auf maximal 20 Mrd. Euro beschränkt ist. Darüber hinaus ist das Garantievolumen auf das 20fache der angesammelten Mittel und maximal auf 100 Mrd. Euro begrenzt. Falls die Bundeshaftung tatsächlich in Anspruch genommen werden muss, soll die Kreditwirtschaft jedenfalls im Nachhinein an den Kosten beteiligt werden.

c) Kapitalausstattung

Das Anfangskapital jedes übernehmenden Rechtsträgers muss als Kreditinstitut mindestens 5 Mio. Euro betragen. Die Kapitalausstattung eines Brückeninstituts wird im Regelfall nicht durch die Alteigentümer der Restbank dargestellt werden, da Vermögensgegenstände und Verbindlichkeiten, nicht aber das Aktienkapital auf das Brückeninstitut übertragen werden. In Betracht kommt aber die Übertragung von stillen Einla-

140 So auch *Bachmann* ZBB 2010, 459 (469); *Schuster* Börsen-Zeitung vom 1. September 2010, S. 2.

141 Dazu *Wolfers/Rau* NJW 2009, 2401 (2404).

142 Anders in Großbritannien *HM Treasury*, Banking Act 2009, Code of Practice, 8.3.

143 § 10 Satz 2 RStruktFG.

144 § 12 Abs. 3 S. 2 RStruktFG.

gen und Hybridkapitalinstrumenten, wobei deren Inhalt ggf. an die Verhältnisse des Brückeninstituts anzupassen ist.

Falls in dem Brückeninstitut eine Eigenkapitallücke auftritt, kann sich der Restrukturierungsfonds an der Rekapitalisierung beteiligen und nach § 7 RStruktFG Einlagen gegen Anteile oder stille Beteiligungen am Brückeninstitut erwerben.

6. Ausblick

Mit einer Übertragungsanordnung wird in rechtlicher Hinsicht Neuland betreten. Das Instrument ist in den U.S.A. für die Abwicklung kleiner und mittlerer Regionalbanken mit überschaubarem Geschäftsbetrieb und ohne Auslandsaktivitäten entwickelt worden und wurde bisher noch nicht auf systemrelevante Institute angewandt. Bei der Umsetzung sind zahlreiche schwerwiegende praktische Hürden absehbar. Eine zentrale Anforderung an einen funktionierenden Bankbetrieb ist die Abbildung von Geschäftsvorfällen in separaten Buchungskreisen durch eine leistungsfähige Datenverarbeitung (IT). Es wird bei der Abtrennung von Unternehmensteilen darauf ankommen, dass das Brückeninstitut möglichst zeitnah in die Lage versetzt wird, über eine geeignete IT-Plattform die historischen Geschäftsvorfälle nachzuvollziehen und die künftigen Geschäftsvorfälle aufzuzeichnen. Die Übertragung und Fortführung des Geschäftsbetriebs setzt eine in der Regel aufwendige Datenmigration voraus. Dazu bedarf es entweder eines geeigneten IT-Systems beim Brückeninstitut, das jedenfalls nicht auf Abruf in der erforderlichen Konfiguration vorgehalten werden kann, oder eines geeigneten mandantenfähigen IT-Systems beim übertragenden Kreditinstitut.[145] Um die Konsequenzen, die Marktteilnehmer aus der Schieflage eines systemrelevanten Instituts ziehen, also insbesondere einen Bank Run, zu vermeiden, wird typischerweise sehr hoher Zeitdruck bei der Umsetzung einer Übertragungsanordnung bestehen. Dies stellt die Portfolioselektion und die technische Umsetzung (IT) vor erhebliche praktische Schwierigkeiten und stellt damit die Durchführbarkeit der Übertragung in Frage. Insgesamt wird es deshalb auf eine möglichst umsichtige, abgestimmte Kommunikation durch das Kreditinstitut, das Brückeninstitut, die BaFin und die FMSA ankommen, um alle Beteiligten – Gläubiger und Schuldner des Kreditinstituts, Derivatekontrahenten, Börsen und Handelsplattformen, Clearingsysteme, ausländische Aufsichtsbehörden, Arbeitnehmer[146] und Öffentlichkeit – zu einer konstruktiven Mitwirkung an der Umsetzung der beabsichtigen Übertragung zu bewegen.

145 Für das Kreditinstitut besteht bei der partiellen Übertragung gemäß § 48k Abs. 4 KWG die Pflicht, dem übernehmenden Rechtsträger die (Mit-)Nutzung von Gegenständen zu gestatten, die bei dem Kreditinstitut verbleiben, auf deren (Mit-)Nutzung der übernehmende Rechtsträger aber angewiesen ist, s. auch für Großbritannien Sec. 63(2) Banking Act 2009. Diese Pflicht besteht so lange, bis der übernehmende Rechtsträger die betroffenen Gegenstände ersetzen kann und wird mit einem angemessenen Entgelt vergütet. Die Verpflichtung oder entsprechende vertragliche Abreden sind anfechtungs- und insolvenzfest.

146 Wie bei der Ausgliederung nach dem UmwG führt die Sonderrechtsnachfolge durch eine Übertragungsanordnung zum Übergang der dem relevanten Geschäftsbereich zugeordneten Arbeitnehmer (§ 48g Abs. 5 KWG, § 613a BGB); s. hierzu *Otto/Mückl* NJW 2011, 91.

The Regulatory Responses to Bank Insolvencies in Germany and the United States – An Evaluation of the German KredReorgG and the U.S. FDICA Insolvency Regime from a Restructuring Perspective

Leo Plank, Wolfgang M. Nardi, Carl Pickerill, Matthias Raphael Prause

Table of Contents

I. Introduction
II. The German Credit Institution Reorganisation Act (Kreditinstitute-Reorganisationsgesetz – KredReorgG or the "Act")
  1. Restructuring Procedure (*Sanierungsverfahren*)
  2. The Reorganization Procedure (*Reorganisationsverfahren*)
    a) Requirements
    b) Initiation of the procedure
    c) The Reorganization Plan
    d) Main Instruments for Reorganization
      (1) Intervention Into the Rights of Creditors
      (2) Debt Equity Swap
      (3) Carve-Out and Takeover
    e) Voting of the creditors and shareholders
    f) Implementation of the Reorganization Plan
  3. Regulatory Competences of the BaFin
    a) Preventative and Interventional Mesures.
    b) Special administrator (*Sonderbeauftragter*)
    c) Transfer order (*Übertragungsanordnung*)
III. Statutory framework for bank insolvencies in the U.S.
  1. Bank holding companies and non-bank financial companies vs. regulated banks
  2. General framework of bank insolvency and receivership by the FDIC for regulated banks
    a) The goals of the bank insolvency vs. corporate bankruptcy procedure
    b) Core features of the FDIC bank insolvency regime
    c) Stages of the procedure
    d) Initiation of the procedure
    e) Conservatorship and receivership
    f) Purchase and assumption transaction (P&A)
IV. Roads out of the Crisis: The German and US bank insolvency regime – An analytical review
  1. Systemic causes for the financial crisis and bank insolvencies
    a) Deficiencies in corporate and financial governance
    b) Regulatory deficiencies

2. Regulatory strategies after the crisis
a) Structural differences between the KredReorgG and the FDIC rules
b) The German KredReorgG as a response to the crisis
(1) Only on the bank's initiative
(2) Potential reluctance of regulatory authorities
(3) Restructuring procedure allows only limited impairment of creditors' rights
(4) Possible limited impact of restructuring procedure
(5) Overly demanding requirements for a reorganization procedure
(6) No joint-entity procedure
(7) Blocking for close-out netting period too short
(8) Joint debtors
(9) Integration of voting of the creditors into the shareholder's meeting
V. Conclusion

I. Introduction

'*Systemic risk*',[1] '*too big to fail*' and '*safety net*'[2] were the buzzwords of the financial crisis in 2007 and 2008. In rapid succession, governments around the world undertook legislative action to prevent a collapse of global financial markets. Given the fact that German banks – or more precisely, such banks' off-balance sheet special purpose vehicles – were among the biggest purchasers of subprime mortgage bonds, it is no surprise that many German banks had to be bailed out as well. In light of these experiences, the German legislator (Gesetzgeber) took action to reshape German law with an aim toward preventing a repeat of events similar to those that occurred in the aftermath of the subprime crisis and Lehmann Brothers collapse. In particular German bank supervision rules were overhauled and powers of the *BaFin* were extended. In order to tackle the "too big to fail" dilemma and enable a meaningful contribution of the private sector in a bank restructuring, a new *restructuring and reorganization procedure* (*Sanierungs- und Strukturierungsverfahren*) for distressed banks outside insolvency through the *Credit Institution Reorganisation Act* (*Kreditinstitute-Reorganisationsgesetz, KredReorgG*, hereinafter, the *Act*), which – after a comparatively short legislative process of only nine months – was implemented and became effective on 1 January 2011[3]. The first part of this article takes a

---

1 *Systemrelevanz.*

2 *Rettungsschirm.*

3 The KredReorgG was part of larger omnibus package of financial regulatory reform laws approved by the German Bundestag on 28 October 2010 and by the Bundesrat on 26 November 2010. Article 2 Nr. 16 a (providing for certain amendments to the German Banking Act (*Kreditwesengesetz*)) as well as Articles 5 (providing for certain amendments to the German Financial Market Stability Act (*Finanzmarktstabilisierungsbeschleunigungsgesetz*)) and 7 (providing for certain amendments to the introduction to the German Stock Company Act (*Einführungsgesetz zum Aktiengesetz*)) became effective 15 December 2010. Article 3, which enacted the below-discussed German Bank Restructuring Funds Act (*Gesetz zur Errichtung eines Restrukturierungsfonds für Kreditinstitute*) as well as Article 4, which provided for certain amendments to the German Financial Market Stability Fund Act (*Finanzmarktstabilisierungsfondsgesetz*) became effective 31 December 2010. The remaining portions of the omnibus packge, including the Act, became effective 1 Ja-

closer look at the Act from the perspective of practitioners involved in the reorganization and restructuring of corporate groups. Subsequently, in a second part, we will contrast the legislation to comparable instruments available under U.S. law. The last part of the article contains an analytical comparison of both systems.

II. The German Credit Institution Reorganisation Act (Kreditinstitute-Reorganisationsgesetz – KredReorgG or the "Act")

The Act seeks stabilization of the financial markets through the restructuring and reorganization of credit institutions domiciled in Germany. The Act's new restructuring and reorganization procedure provides instruments that are designed to avoid involvency proceedings in the first place. However, recognizing that even best efforts cannot guarantee solvency, the Act provides the *Federal Financial Supervisory Authority* (*Bundesanstalt für Finanzdienstleistungsaufsicht*, in the following referred to in *short* as *BaFin*) with authority to file a petition for insolvency to the extent the subject credit institution later becomes insolvent during the course of a restructuring or reorganization. The Act does not explicitly suspend the rules of German insolvency law regarding the compulsory requirement to file for for insolvency in the event of illiquidity or overindebtness).[4] However, in practice, such a suspension may occur, as only BaFin (and not, for example, a bank's creditors or even the bank itself) may file such a petition.

The core elements of the Act are two new procedures: the *restructuring* procedure (*Sanierungsverfahren*) and the *reorganization procedure* (*Reorganisationsverfahren*).[5] Parties to such procedures are, in addition to the distressed bank, the *Frankfurt Court of Appeal* (*Oberlandesgericht Frankfurt*), *BaFin* and a *restructuring/reorganization consultant*.

1. Restructuring Procedure (Sanierungsverfahren)

The restructuring procedure is the first of two instruments provided by the Act. Importantly, the restructuring procedure is applicable even at relatively low levels of financial distress. The sole aim of the restructuring procedure is to *safeguard the ongoing liquidity of the bank*. Therefore, the restructuring procedure does not foresee interventions into the rights of the creditors. However, the bank is allowed to take on new loans and lenders

---

nuary 2011. See Entwicklungsgeschichte des Restrukturierungsgesetz *available at* gesetzgebung.beck.de/node/1002936.

4 See § 15 a German Insolvency Code (*Insolvenzordnung*, hereinafter InsO).

5 See for a comprehensive analysis of the Act also *Eidenmüller* Finanzkrise, Wirtschaftskrise und das deutsche Insolvenzrecht, Berlin 2009, page 57 et seq.; *Eidenmüller* Restrukturierung systemrelevanter Finanzinstitute, in: S. Grundmann et al. (Hrsg.), Unternehmen, Markt und Verantwortung – Festschrift für Klaus J. Hopt zum 70. Geburtstag am 24. August 2010, Berlin 2010, page 1713 et seq.; *Eidenmüller/Frebenius/Prusko* 13 NZI 545 (2010); *Kindler* 63 NJW 2465, 2468 (2010); *Lorenz* 13 NZG 1046 (2010); *Lorenz* 64 WM 1426 (2010); *Pannen* 13 ZinsO 2026 (2010); *Obermüller* 13 ZinsO 305, 313 et seq. (2010); *Riethmüller* 64 WM 2295 (2010); *Spindler* 55 AG 601 (2010); *Zimmer* 39 ZGR 597 (2010). For a comparison with the Swiss law for bank insolvencies See *Zulauf* 64 WM 1525 (2010).

extending such credit have priority over the bank's existing unsecured creditors. The Act grants priority ranking of those loans and other facilities only if:

- the loans were made in the course of a restructuring plan;
- a (subsequent) insolvency procedure was initiated within three years after the order to implement a restructuring plan; and
- the facility does not exceed 10% of the bank's own financial resources.[6]

The procedure is initiated by filing a restructuring plan with the BaFin by the bank itself. The bank may also propose a restructuring consultant (*Sanierungsberater*). In contrast to the reorganization procedure, as further described below, the restructuring procedure offers no means to non-consensually impair the rights of creditors or other parties. Arguably, the only significant advantage for the bank's access to liquidity is the priority ranking of restructuring loans (*Sanierungskredite*) vis-à-vis other unsecured claims. This privilege becomes effective immediately upon entry of the court order and therefore provides a fairly expeditious means of improving liquidity during periods of financial difficulty.[7]

Another potential issue concerning the ability of the court and the restructuring consultant to interfere or suspend shareholders rights. When considering filing a restructuring plan and initiating a restructuring procedure, the relevant bank's management will also take into account potential restrictions for the bank and its management resulting from orders of the court or the compulsory restructuring consultant. Banks and their owners may be reluctant to use the procedure because they fear that they will be deprived of shareholder rights or their managerial powers may be curtailed. Although the option to remove management ultimately was taken out of the final version of the Act, the Frankfurt Court of Appeals and the restructuring consultant have far-reaching competences which could curtail the control of the bank's managers and owners over the banks affairs.

The court may for instance take further measures at BaFin's suggestion if such measures are necessary for the bank's restructuring and if there is a risk that the bank may not otherwise fulfill its obligations to creditors. These measures may include *prohibiting management* or shareholders from exercising their functions, appointing a CRO (*Sanierungsberater*), prohibiting *withdrawal* or *distribution of profits*, reviewing management's *compensation and bonus scheme* or *substituting* its consent for that of the bank's board of directors.[8]

6 § 2 (2) KredReorgG.

7 The effectiveness of the restructuring procedure may be limited. In particular, restructuring loans, while superior to unsecured claims, rank behind any existing secured claims. This is, notably, in contrast to superpriority "debtor in possession" financing loans (i.e., so-called "DIP loans") often relied on by Chapter 11 debtors in the United States to fund the administrative costs and their operations during a Chapter 11 bankruptcy proceeding. See, e.g., 11 U.S.C. § 364(d) (allowing debtor in possession to obtain secured credit "secured by a senior or equal lien on property of the estate that is subject to a lien" to the extent the debtor is unable to otherwise obtain credit and the secured party is adequately protected). Under the German regime, while a bank with available unpledged assets likely will be able to obtain liquidity in the form of secured loans, banks with liens over all available assets (as often is the case) may find the restructuring procedure to be of limited use.

8 See § 5 (1) KredReorgG. If the court undertakes such measures, it must provide the bank and other interested parties (*Betroffenen*) the opportunity, either contemporaneously or immedi-

The restructuring agent on the other hand may enter the office premises of the bank and conduct investigations, inspect the account books and files and request the presentation of documents and the release of all necessary information, participate in all sessions of all boards and other bodies of the bank in an advisory capacity, give directives to the members of the management of the bank, initiate a special audit or a review of possible claims for damages against board members or former board members of the bank, and monitor the compliance with already imposed requirements according to the *Financial Markets Stabilisation Fund Act* (*Finanzmarktstabilisierungsfondsgesetz, FMStFG*).[9]

This aspect of the law may induce BaFin to put pressure on management of a bank in (potential) difficulty, and although BaFin has no authority to request commencement of a restructuring procedure, it may at any time turn to its regulatory toolbox pursuant to the German Banking Act (*das Gesetz über das Kreditwesen*, hereinafter, *KWG*), in particular: (a) § 45 KWG, allowing entry of a transfer order (*Übertragungsanordnung*);[10] (b) enabling appointment of a an agent of the *BaFin* (*Sonderbeauftragter*);[11] or (c) dismissal of management.[12]

---

ately thereafter, to have their concerns heard. See § 5 (2) KredReorgG. To the extent the court finds no reason to alternative measures taken, it can issue its judgement without a written order (*formlos*). See id.

9 See § 4 (1) KredReorgG. However, the restructuring agent is supervised by the Frankfurt Court of Appeals and the court as well as the BaFin can request information or a report about the current situation and about the management at any time. Furthermore the restructuring agent may be dismissed for cause by the court and may be liable for damages in case of breach of his duties, See § 4 (2), (3) KredReorgG.
As a result, management's decision to commence a restructuring procedure and file a restructuring plan creates a challenge to balance the tension between the needs of rapidly securing access to liquidity on the one hand and the danger of disempowerment and the commercial consequences of publicizing financial difficulties on the other. Notwithstanding potentially negative impacts, however, signs of early intervention followed by a controlled and well-supervised process may be interpreted positively by financial markets.
As further described below, the impact of the restructuring procedure (*Sanierungsverfahren*) may be limited given its protection of creditor rights. Accordingly, one instance where it may be beneficial for bank management to seek the protection of the reorganization procedure (*Reorganisationsverfahren*) may be in the case of recalcitrant shareholders (for example, aggressive hedge funds who seek to block a consensual reorganization). The bank could use the reorganization procedure to effectively shield itself from the shareholder under the protection of the court. Such strategic insolvency filings have been used in the past in Germany and it is conceivable that the reorganization procedure will be used accordingly, especially if ownership of banks by non-traditional investors increases.

10 See § 48 a KWG.

11 See § 45 c KWG.

12 As in the case of a *Reorganisationsverfahren*, as further set forth below, in order to impose a transfer order (*Übertragungsanordnung*) pursuant to § 48 a KWG, the *BaFin* is required to demonstrate both risk to the affected bank's future existence (*Existenzgefährdung*) and that failure of the bank poses a risk to the existence of the financial system (*Systemgefährdung*). See § 48 a KWG. Moreover, the *BaFin* must show that the *Systemgefährdung* cannot be overcome through any other means other than through a transfer order. Finally, it is important to note that *BaFin*'s authority to impose and implement a transfer order is limited to companies engaging primarily in banking activities (*Kreditinstitute*, See § 1(1) KWG), but does not extend to, for example, companies engaging in financing consulting, intermediary, equity and debt placement, portfolio management, and related activities (*Finanzdienstleistungsinstitute*, See § 1(1 a) KWG). As discussed in greater detail below, with the passage of the Dodd-Frank Act (as defined herein), and expansion of the U.S. FDIC's authority to administer failing "covered financial companies (which could be

The bank's ability to propose the restructuring consultant constitutes another positive aspect of the Act. Moreover, the restructuring consultant's status as a member of the bank's corporate body or bodies will not disqualify him from involvement in the preparation of the bank's restructuring plan.[13]

Conclusion: On first impression, the restructuring procedure appears to be a quick and simple means of addressing an impending liquidity crisis. However, a closer look reveals certain doubts with respect to its practical relevance. In particular, the restructuring procedure provides only very limited means for non-consensual impairment of the rights of creditors or other stakeholders. In addition, a priority ranking of new loans will only be of limited benefit to the extent all substantial assets of the bank already have been encumbered for existing or new debt (as often is the case for distressed companies). Furthermore, the reluctance of management to initiate a procedure due to potential negative publicity and possible interventions by the restructuring consultant should not be underestimated. In addition the court may take certain other measures to limit or negate the influence or control of shareholders over the bank's activities.[14]

2. The Reorganization Procedure (*Reorganisationsverfahren*)

The second and more comprehensive procedure established by the Act is the reorganization procedure. It is modeled after the *insolvency plan procedure* of the German Insolvency Act (§§ 217 et seq. InsO) and allows, in contrast to the restructuring procedure, impairment of the rights of creditors and owners without their consent.[15]

a) Requirements

The reorganization procedure functions as a second level of emergency measures to the extent a bank believes that an already existing restructuring procedure is *unlikely to succeed* or if a *preceding restructuring procedure has already failed.*[16] A reorganization procedure may not be commenced unless the continuing existence of the bank is endangered (*Bestandsgefährdung*) and that such endangerment causes a substantial systemic risk to the financial market (*Systemgefährdung*).[17] The substantial systemic risk for the continuing existence of the bank (*Bestandsgefährdung*) is defined by reference to § 48 a (1) 1 KWG as the risk of a breakdown of the bank due to insolvency if corrective measures are not

---

brokers, insurance companies and other related financial sector entities), the U.S. FDIC appears to now enjoy greater latitude than currently allowed for by KWG.

13 Here again, however, the benefits of the Act are limited. In particular, *BaFin* may nominate an alternative person to the Frankfurt Court of Appeal, and the Court of Appeal, in addition, has the authority to reject any proposed restructuring consultant if he is apparently not qualified.

14 Ultimately, the only real advantage of the procedure is the ability to obtain additional funding with priority over unsecured creditors. However, because existing security interests cannot be primed, a lender would be required to lend on an unsecured basis. As noted above, it is doubtful whether this is practical. Accordingly, either a distressed credit institution will choose to seek funding in the financial markets on its own (in which case it does not need to rely on the Act) or it cannot in which case no one will lend on a senior unsecured basis.

15 See §§ 8 (3), 12 KredReorgG.

16 § 7 (1) KredReorgG.

17 See § 7 (2) KredReorgG.

taken.[18] This risk is presumed if, *inter alia*, the core capital or the equity capital of the bank fall more than 10% below its statutory limits.[19] By contrast, the substantial risk for the proper functioning of the financial market (*Systemgefährdung*) is defined by reference to § 48 a (2) 2 KWG and must be caused by the risk to the bank's continued existence in order for the Act to apply.[20] The Act provides that the risk for the continuing existence of the bank must have a significant negative impact on other financial institutions, on the financial markets, or on the general confidence of investors and other market participants in the proper functioning of the financial system.[21] When evaluating the *risk for the financial system*, the type and extent of the debts of the bank, the amount of accepted deposits, the risks taken by the bank, its interdependence with other market players and the situation of the financial markets including the expected consequences of a breakdown of the bank must be taken into consideration.[22]

b) Initiation of the procedure

The reorganization procedure is initiated either by the *bank* or – if a prior restructuring procedure has failed – by the *restructuring consultant* with approval of the bank through *notification* of the BaFin and submission of a *reorganization plan*.[23] The BaFin, for its part, may apply for a reorganization procedure at the Frankfurt Court of Appeal if it considers the statutory requirements satisfied.[24]

c) The Reorganization Plan

The *reorganization plan* comprises the core of the reorganization procedure and is in structure and function comparable to the insolvency plan of the insolvency procedure.[25] Its goal is to allow a fair restructuring of the bank with the participation of its creditors and owners. The reorganization plan provides a flexible instrument and controlled environment for the bank to take self regulating measures, including its recovery or liquidation. The reorganization procedure does not assume a predetermined result and may, therefore, contemplate either a restructuring plan or a liquidation plan.

According to the Act, the reorganization plan must contain a *descriptive* and a *constitutive* part. The *descriptive part* serves to inform all participants of the factual basis and the consequences of the reorganization plan and to provide a basis to creditors and shareholders for their decision to approve or dismiss the plan.[26] The *constitutive part* determines how the reorganization plan will alter the legal rights of the participants. In contrast to an insolvency plan pursuant to the German Insolvency Code, interventions into the rights of third parties are not limited to creditors but may also include the

---

18 See id.
19 See § 48 b (1)&(2) KWG.
20 See § 7 (2) KredReorgG.
21 See § 48 b (2) KWG.
22 § 48 b (2) 1–5 KWG.
23 § 7 (1) KredReorgG.
24 § 7 (2) KredReorgG.
25 See the *explanatory memorandum* to the act, BT-Drs. 17/3024, p. 49 et seqq. (available at http://dip.bundestag.de/btd/17/030/1703024.pdf). Compare §§ 217 et seq. InsO.
26 § 8 (1) 2 KredReorgG. See for the voting decision § 16 et seq. KredReorgG.

shareholders. Accordingly, a reorganization plan may also provide for changes to the bank's corporate structure.[27] The plan *must* explicitly state in its constitutive part the extent to which and the means by which the plan will intervene with the rights of third parties (i.e. to what fractional amount creditors' claims will be reduced, how long they will be deferred, how they will be secured, etc.).[28]

d) Main Instruments for Reorganization

The Act provides for three main instruments to reorganize the bank's financial and corporate structure:

- *interventions* into the *rights of creditors and owners*
- *debt-equity-swap*
- *carve-out* and *takeover*

(1) Intervention Into the Rights of Creditors

A core element of the Act is that it allows interventions into individual rights of creditors through respective measures in the reorganization plan which include the *reduction*, *deferral* and the *assignment* of claims for security.[29] In contrast to the insolvency plan, the reorganization plan must state explicitly to what extent and in what way it intervenes with the creditors' rights including the fractional amount the claims of the creditors will be reduced or deferred.[30] A provision similar to § 225 *InsO*,[31] which provides that claims of subordinated creditors are, in cases of doubt, to be treated as released in order to simplify the insolvency procedure, likely would have been inappropriate at a potentially early phase of a liquidity crisis where the bank has not yet reached the state of insolvency. The Act, accordingly, contains no such provision.[32] The interventions within the scope of the reorganization procedure shall furthermore not affect the requirements provided by European law in respect to the recovery of collateral[33]. They are also not applicable to claims which are covered by deposit guarantee funds such as the *Einlagensicherungsfonds des Bundesverbands deutscher Banken*[34], to wage *claims* of employees and to claims for benefits of the *company pension scheme*.[35] These limitations correspond to the purpose of the reorganization procedure, which is the financial recovery of the bank through the participation of the principal creditors.[36] Employees and beneficiaries of a company pension scheme are not considered part of that group and therefore remain unaffected. Their claims are existential for their livelihood and furthermore not secured by insolvency payments or a *pension guarantee system*.[37]

---

27 *Explanatory memorandum*, p. 49 (supra note 25).
28 § 12 (1) KredReorgG.
29 See § 12 (1) KredReorgG.
30 See § 12 (1) KredReorgG.
31 For *InsO* See supra note 42.
32 See *explanatory memorandum*, p. 50 (supra note 25).
33 See § 23 KredReorgG.
34 See § 12 (2) KredReorgG.
35 See § 12 (3) KredReorgG.
36 See *explanatory memorandum*, p. 52 (supra note 25).
37 Ibid.

(2) Debt Equity Swap

The debt-equity-swap, in which a bank's creditors agree to cancel some or all of a bank's debts in exchange for equity in the bank, is considered by experts to be one of the core features of an attractive and effective restructuring procedure.[38] It has benefits for both creditors and the bank and is a suitable instrument to turn a risk into an advantage, thereby maximizing value: Creditors may exchange their claims (which may otherwise be difficult or impossible to enforce) for a share in the equity of the bank and thereby take control of the business as a going concern and capture the economic upside. This allows creditors to actively participate on a long term basis in the restructuring process. The bank, for its part, receives a reduction of its debts, an increase in its equity capital and is relieved from the insolvency risk of the respective debts. Naturally, this transaction, which is mutually beneficial for creditors and the bank,[39] is achieved at the price of dilution of existing shareholders' stake in the company. Such dilution is, however, the typical consequence of efforts to rescue a debtor in a restructuring outside insolvency.

Implementation by reduction and increase of share capital[40]

From a German legal-technical perspective, the debt-equity-swap is achieved by a reduction and subsequent increase in the bank's share capital through a contribution in kind

---

Despite the comprehensive regulations provided by the Act, two main questions remain unsolved: Will it be possible to terminate contracts and other obligations in the context of a reorganization procedure? And is there a temporary or factual limit to the scope of application for interventions into the rights of the creditors or is it for instance possible to include also future claims for damages into the reorganization plan?

38 See *explanatory memorandum*, p. 50 (supra note 25).

39 A Debt-Equity-Swap is usually mutually beneficial but this is not always the case and depends on the particular circumstances. See *Helpman* The Simple Analytics of Debt-Equity Swaps, 79 The American Economic Review 440, 443 et seq. (1989). See also Harvey R. Miller & Shai Y. Waisman, *Is Chapter II Bankrupt?*, 47 B. C. L.Rev. 129, 143 (2005) (arguing that prepackaged and prenegutiated debt-equity swaps and expeditions sales have undermined the focus on comprehensive operational restructurings, which should be the focus of rehabilitation measures).

40 As set forth in footnote 3 above, the omnibus financial reform package also enacted the German Bank Restructuring Funds Act (*Gesetz zur Errichtung eines Restrukturierungsfonds für Kreditinstitute*), which establishes a fund for distressed banks. It is unclear from the text of the Act and from the Act's legislative history (*Begründung*) whether public funds made available to a distressed bank must be included or excluded from any later valuation in the context of a "debt equity swap." The Act's *explanatory memorandum* states that the capital reduction portion of the "debt equity swap" must be undertaken in accordance with yearly report valuation principles (*Bewertungsgrundsätzen für den Jahresabschluss*). See *explanatory memorandum* at 50. The German Commercial Code (*Handelsgesetzbuch* or *HGB*) is silent on whether public subsidies are to be considered in valuation of a company. See HGB §§ 252 et seq. However, pursuant to the International Accounting Standards, public funds are considered in a company's balance sheet only if (a) the company receiving such funds will satisfy any applicable conditions and (b) the funds are actually provided. See IAS 20.7. However, such funds are not to be included in the company's equity (*Eigenkapital*). See IAS 20.12. In light of skepticism voiced by the European Union Commission regarding public subsidies for domestic companies, substantial discussion has taken place in the accounting community regarding proper treatment of such subsidies in a company's balance sheet. In particular, the Institute for Public Accountants in Germany (*das Institut der Wirtschaftsprüfer in Deutschland e.V.*) has published a draft set of accounting standards for assessing public subsidies, which relies on various factors including whether (a) there is risk that the

(*Sacheinlage*) and a prohibition on existing shareholders from exercising any subscription rights/options (*Bezugsrechtausschluss*).[41] For the increase of the bank's share capital, the value of the contributed claims against the distressed bank has to be determined which generally results in a significant reduction in the face value of the claim. New shareholders benefit from special *privileges* of the Insolvency Code in order to reduce the risks of the creditors in connection with the conversion of their claims into shares of the company.[42] Pursuant to § 9 (4) 1 KredReorgG, the *restructuring privilege* (*Sanierungsprivileg*) and the *minority shareholder privilege* (*Minderheitenprivileg*) set forth in the InsO are applicable to shareholder loans.[43] The *restructuring privilege* protects claims held by shareholders from subordination in a later insolvency proceeding as long as the shareholder acquired its shares with the intention of rehabilitating the company.[44] By granting such a privilege, the legislator sought to incentivize creditors to provide risk capital and engage actively in the restructuring process of distressed companies. Similarly, the *minority shareholder privilege* protects claims of shareholders in a later insolvency proceeding when such shareholders hold less than 10% of the equity of the debtor. Since the influence of a 10% shareholder on management decisions generally is limited, the legislator reasoned it would be inequitable to subordinate its claims notwithstanding shareholder status.[45]

No agreement of the owners necessary

The debt-equity-swap does not require the agreement of the existing shareholders and may, therefore, also be implemented against existing owners non-consensually. This is an important paradigm shift in German law since, historically, shareholders did not participate in a reorganization procedure, given the strict division between corporate law and insolvency law.[46]

However, owners must be *compensated* for their losses.[47] The adequacy of the compensation is determined by independent experts who are chosen and appointed by the court.[48] If a recovery of the bank through successful restructuring appears to be possible,

---

subsidy will be unwound, (b) such risks are appropriately described, (c) effects of any subsidy on share capital, etc. See IDW EPS 700 § 3 (Stand 23. 6. 2010). In light of the applicable accounting standards, it is possible that public funds would be included in the context of a valuation for a capital reduction (*Kapitalherabsetzung*) and subsequent capital increase (*Kapitalerhöhung*). However, any risks of repayment or obligations to unwind the subsidy would be assessed and, to the extent determined to exist, any public funds likely would be booked as a reserve (*Rückstellung*). See *also* HGB § 253(2) (discussing calculation of reserves with maturities over one year). If there risks were determined to be material, a corresponding obligation would need to be booked to cover any such repayment obligations.

41 See *explanatory memorandum*, p. 50 (supra note 25) and § 9 (1) 3 KredReorgG which sets forth the respective competences.

42 Pursuant to § 9 (4) 1 KredReorgG the privileges of § 39 (4) 2, (5) InsO are applicable (*Sanierungs- und Minderheitenprivileg*).

43 See §§ 39 (4) 2, (5) InsO.

44 See §§ 39 (4) 2 InsO.

45 See §§ 39 (5) InsO.

46 See *Simon* Der Debt Equity Swap nach dem Gesetz zur weiteren Erleichterung der Sanierung von Unternehmen (ESUG) Corporate Finance law 7/2010 at 448 ("German Insolveny law suffers a structural deficit rooted in the disunion of insolvency law and corporate law.").

47 See § 9 (2) KredReorgG.

48 Ibid.

the value of the existing shares must be determined according to the *going concern* principle. This is particularly the case if the distress is caused by mere temporary liquidity problems not otherwise indicative for a true depletion of a company's equity.[49] However, the shares must be evaluated according to the actual remaining value of the bank, adequately considering its current financial situation. Further, if public authorities participate financially in the reorganization, they benefit from a special privilege and are protected from insolvency claw-back.[50]

(3) Carve-Out and Takeover

In addition to the *debt-equity-swap* and the ability to impair creditors' rights, the Act also provides for the *carve-out of business units (Ausgliederung)* or the *takeover of the entire bank* as further core instruments for the reorganization of a bank. These procedures allow the complete or partial transfer of the bank's assets to an existing or newly created company.[51] The purpose of the *partial carve-out* is the separation of the healthy from the distressed parts of the bank such that those units which are crucial for the proper functioning of the financial market (and therefore systemically relevant) can continue to operate in a stable and healthy corporate environment and preserve access to liquidity, whereas the non-core parts of the bank can be liquidated within a regular insolvency procedure.[52] The company to which the carved-out business units can be transferred may either be (a) an existing bank, (b) a bank specifically created for the purpose of the particular carve-out, or (c) a state-run "bridge-bank," which in certain instances may be established by the German *restructuring fund* (*Restrukturierungsfonds*).[53] A *complete takeover* of the distressed bank might be considered if a strong and solvent bank well vested with capital and liquidity is available and willing to continue the operation of the distressed bank. In this instance, the restructuring fund may also provide financial assistance.

A partial carve-out or a full takeover of the distressed bank or its business units can only take place in exchange for participation of the existing shareholders in the acquiring bank.[54] The details of the carve-out or takeover, including the company's articles of incorporation in case of a transfer to a newly created company, and the consequence for the employees and the work councils, must be considered in the context of a reorganization plan.[55] The reorganization plan may also provide for the retransfer of individual assets so that the creditors have fewer incentives to make use of their option of termination.[56]

If the assets are transferred to an already *existing bank*, a notarized declaration of approval of the shareholders of that bank is necessary. Additionally, the existing bank

---

49 See *explanatory memorandum*, p. 50 (supra note 25).

50 See § 9 (3) KredReorgG. It remains to be seen whether this provision will have significant relevance – in most bank rescues, the equity will be substantially depleted.

51 See § 11 (1) 1 KredReorgG.

52 See explanatory memorandum, p. 3.

53 Pursuant to § 5 (1) Restructuring Funds Act (*Restrukturierungsfondsgesetz, RstruktFG*), the restructuring funds may create a pool of bridge banks without any particular cause which then are ready to be used as receiving entities in the case of partial or full carve-outs of distressed system-relevant banks or its parts.

54 See § 11 (1) 1 KredReorgG.

55 See § 11 (1) 3 KredReorgG, § 48 e (1) KWG.

56 See § 11 (1) 2 KredReorgG. For the creditor's termination option See § 13 KredReorgG.

must comply with the qualification standards applicable to the bank whose assets are being transferred.[57] If the assets are transferred to a newly-created bank, the governing documents of that bank must be modeled after those of the bank subject to the reorganization procedure. The transfer becomes effective with the approval of the reorganization plan by the court which initiates the entry of the respective changes into the commercial register *ex officio*.[58]

The assets are transferred in the course of universal or partial *universal succession*. Both banks, the transferring and the absorbing bank, remain liable as *joint debtors* (*Gesamtschuldner*).[59] Although the liability of the absorbing bank to any one creditor is limited to the amount such creditor would have received absent the carve-out or takeover of the transferred assets,[60] joint liability prevents an effective discharge and may impede access of the carved-out business to liquidity in the financial market.[61] Moreover, the possibility that the transferred bank division's new owners (*Rechtsträger*) could remain (partially) on the hook for liabilities occurring prior to the effective date of transfer may make the carve-out less appetizing for new investors.

e) Creditor and Shareholder Voting

In order to become effective, the reorganization plan proposed by the debtor pursuant to §§ 7 and 8 KredReorgG requires the *consent of the creditors and the shareholders*[62] as well as the *confirmation (Bestätigung) by the Frankfurt Court of Appeals (Oberlandesgericht)*.[63] In preparation for the voting, potential creditors have the right to file claims for outstanding obligations and liabilities.[64]

---

57 See § 11 (4) KredReorgG.

58 See § 21 KredReorgG.

59 See § 11 (4) KredReorgG.

60 See § 11 (4) 2 KredReorgG.

61 As further discussed below, practically, this may have the effect of enabling creditors, whose claims have been subjected to reduction in a *Reorganisationsverfahren*, to seek recourse against the new joint entity on account of their reduced claims. As a more effective alternative, the legislator could have chosen to completely release the new legal entity from the historic liabilities that brought about financial distress but preserved an obligation of the new legal entity to use its profits for the discharge of debts left behind. The benefit of the new entity continuing to exist and being released of historic debt arguably is sufficient compensation for the shareholders of the new entity who will participate in the profits of the new entity only after discharge of all debt left behind.

62 "Approval" of the plan by shareholders means that a majority of the actually voted shares have voted to approve the reorganization plan. See §§ 18(3) & 19(1)(1) KredReorgG. Approval by creditors means that a majority in number as well as a majority in amount of creditors actually voting have voted to approve the plan. See § 19(1) (2) & (3) KredReorgG. However, similar to the "cram down" (*Obstruktionsverbot*) procedures set forth in section 245 InsO (in the context of an insolvency plan procedure (*Insolvenzplanverfahren*)), and as further discussed below, a creditor group is deemed to accept a plan as long as (a) the creditors in such group are no worse off under the reorganization plan as without, (b) no creditor receives more than its allowed claims and no creditors subordinated to the group receive any recovery on account of their claims, and (c) the majority of all groups voting on the reorganization plan have voted to accept. See § 19(2) & (3) KredReorgG.

63 See §§ 19, 20 KredReorgG.

64 See § 14 KredReorgG.

Creditor Voting

Creditors are grouped for voting according to their legal status (i.e. secured or unsecured creditors) and their respective economic interests. For the adoption of the reorganization plan in each group of creditors, both an absolute majority of heads and a majority on the basis of the amount of the respective claims are necessary.[65] To avoid obstruction with an otherwise approvable and beneficial plan, the Act presumes acceptance of the plan by creditors if a) such creditors receive the same or better treatment they would have otherwise received without a reorganization plan, b) such creditors adequately participate in the economic value that ultimately will accrue to all parties according to the reorganization plan *and* c) a majority in number of all groups of creditors and shareholders taken together agrees to the reorganization plan.[66] Creditors adequately participate, if a) no other creditor receives assets which exceed the full amount of his claim *and* b) neither a creditor who but for the reorganization plan would be junior to the creditors of that group nor the bank or one of its shareholders receives any benefit *and* if c) no creditor who but for the reorganization plan would rank equally with the creditors of that group would be better off than these creditors.[67]

Shareholder Voting

For shareholder voting purposes, the reorganization consultant calls a general meeting in which the shareholders consent to the organization with its absolute majority.[68] However, intervening measures such as barring shareholders from exercising applicable subscription rights or reduction of share capital, requires a majority of 2/3 of the votes or of the represented equity.[69] An absolute majority is sufficient if at least half of the equity capital is represented in the general assembly.[70] The Act provides that any conflicting provisions in the company statute shall be disregarded.[71]

As is the case with the creditors, the consent of shareholders may under specific circumstances be presumed and dissenting shareholders may be forced to accept the terms of a plan. However, due to protection of property rights guaranteed by the German constitution (*Grundgesetz*), the requirements for a *fictional consent* are higher: in addition to the consent of the majority of voting groups with the required majorities it is also necessary that the measures provided for in the reorganization plan serve to defend against systemic risks and, therefore, are deemed to prevent the negative effects of the substantial risk for the continuing existence of the bank (*Bestandsgefährdung*) for other companies within the financial sector and to avoid an instability of the financial system.[72] Accord-

65 See § 19 (1) no. 2 and 3 KredReorgG.

66 See § 19 (2) KredReorgG; compare 11 U.S.C. § 1129(b) (setting forth standards for "cram down" procedures in U.S. Chapter 11, in which a dissenting class of creditors is presumed to the accept the plan as long as one other impaired class of creditors has accepted the plan and the plan satisfies the so-called "absolute priority rule" as to the dissenting class).

67 See § 19 (3) KredReorgG.

68 See § 18 (1), (2) KredReorgG.

69 See § 18 (3) 2 KredReorgG.

70 See § 18 (3) 3 KredReorgG.

71 See § 18 (3) 4 KredReorgG.

72 See § 18 (4) KredReorgG.

ingly, any interventions into the property rights of shareholders must be suitable, necessary and appropriate for that purpose.[73]

f) Implementation of the Reorganization Plan

The reorganization plan becomes effective with the approval by the Frankfurt Court of Appeals.[74] For its decision, the court schedules a special hearing within one month after the consent of creditors and shareholders to the reorganization plan.[75] The court will approve the reorganization plan if the statutory requirements have been satisfied.[76] Creditors may object to the reorganization plan with a written statement which under particular circumstances may allow the court to deny its approval.[77]

3. Regulatory Competences of the BaFin

In addition to the regime of voluntary measures of self-regulation provided by the restructuring and reorganization procedure of the Act, the *BaFin* may act on a regulatory level if it considers such measures necessary in order to avoid a destabilization of the financial system. In case of a risk to the stability of the financial system, BaFin has the authority to take all necessary measures if required also without the consent of the participants such as management, creditors and shareholders.[78]

The BaFin's authorities were significantly expanded by Article 2 of the *Restructuring Act* of 2010 (*Restrukturierungsgesetz*), which was passed in conjunction with the KredReogG (which comprised Article 1 of the *Restrukturierungsgesetz*). The *explanatory memorandum* makes clear that the BaFin's authorities under the *Restruktierungsgesetz* are in addition to the measures set forth in the Act, at least as to systemically important financial institutions. In other words, to the extent the Act is insufficient to combat a danger to the domestic financial markets, the BaFin may exercise its expanded authorities under the *Restrukturierungsgesetz* to take matters into its own hands.[79]

---

73 Ibid. However, whether the fictional consent of the shareholder's meeting complies with the second company law directive remains to be seen. However, the provision is meaningful and should be kept, even if that provokes a definite clarification by the ECJ. See *Bachmann* supra note 163, at page 5.

74 See § 21 (4) KredReorgG.

75 See § 20 (1) KredReorgG.

76 See § 20 (2), (3) KredReorgG.

77 See § 20 (3) KredReorgG.

78 *Explanatory memorandum*, at page 3 (supra note 25).

79 See *explanatory memorandum*, at pages 61–71 (supra note 25) (describing additional provisions and noting that the *Reorganisationsverfahren* pursuant to the KredReorgG is not always sufficient to address broader financial market disruptions, in particular where (a) management delays commencing a procedure under KredReorgG, (b) market uncertainty regarding the likelihood of success of a KredReorgG procedure demands more precise intervention, (c) no third party financiers are available to assist the distressed financial institution and such resources are necessary to enable the financial institution to survive and (d) doubt exists as to the viability of any proposed reorganization plan).

a) Preventative and Interventional Mesures

First, the BaFin may take a preventive measure in order to reduce the risk of failure if the financial situation of the bank suggests that it may not be able to fulfill the statutory requirements permanently. This may include:

- requesting a report of the bank's major business activities
- ordering specific measures for the reducing risks for the solvency
- ordering appropriate measures to increase equity capital
- requesting development of a concept for averting a particular existential danger to the bank[80]

Second, BaFin may intervene if it determines that the statutory minimum requirements are in fact not fulfilled. Therefore it may:

- prohibit or limit withdrawal from equity capital or distribution of profits
- prohibit specific accounting measures which aim to compensate for an annual deficit
- prohibit distribution of yields of equity capital if they are not covered by an annual net profit
- prohibit or limit the grant of loans
- request that the bank takes measures in order to reduce risks
- request a restructuring plan and to inform regular information about the progress of these measures
- prohibit or limit the distribution of flexible compensation and bonuses[81]

Third, to the extent BaFin determines a bank is on the verge of insolvency, the BaFin may take further measures, including:

- give specific orders to the bank's management
- prohibit the acceptance of deposits of the grant of loans
- prohibit management or shareholders from exercising their functions
- order a temporary freeze of sales and payments
- order the closure of the bank for transactions with customers
- prohibit the acceptance of specific payments which owns aimed to fulfill obligations vis-à-vis the Institute[82]

---

80 See § 45 (1) KWG.
81 See § 45 (2) KWG.
82 See § 46 (1) 2 KWG.

b) Special administrator (Sonderbeauftragter)

The BaFin may also appoint a special administrator with particular competences (*Sonderbeauftragter*).[83] The appointment of a special administrator is not an alternative for removal of the CEO but an independent regulatory instrument with preventive character.[84] The BaFin is at any time free to appoint a special administrator for specific tasks at the financial institution and to transfer the necessary competences to him. Particularly assume responsibilities or those of particular bank committees or organs. In addition, he may perform *specific tasks* tailored to the particular needs of regulatory intervention such as specific intervention for *restoring the regular business activities and reducing the risks* if the bank has severely and repeatedly violated statutory provisions, *monitoring the implementation of regulatory orders* of the BaFin, *reviewing possible claims* of the bank against current or former management and *preparing a restructuring plan* or a *transfer order*.[85] He is entrusted with all competences necessary to fulfill his tasks. He may also *request information* and *documents, participate* at all sessions and meetings of the management of it and advisory function, *enter the business facilities, review accounting books* and *conduct investigations*.[86] The management and the owners are obligated to fully cooperate with the special administrator.[87] The bank has to bear the costs for his activities including his compensation which is determined by the BaFin.[88] However the special administrator is liable for damages in case of negligence and intent.[89]

c) Transfer order (Übertragungsanordnung)

As a means of last resort the KWG, allows BaFin to order a partial carve-out or total transfer of a bank's assets (*Übertragungsanordnung*).[90] This allows the separation of the healthy from the distressed parts of the bank by transferring the healthy parts to a private bank or a state-run bridge bank. The transfer order allows such a transaction without the participation of management, shareholders and creditors. The requirements for such an order are basically the same as for a restructuring plan – substantial risk for the continuing existence of the bank *(Bestandsgefährdung)* and a substantial risk for the proper functioning of the financial market (*Systemgefährdung*) – except that the transfer order is only possible if no other equally effective measures are available.[91] The transfer order is subject to limited yet at least some level of judicial review. In particular, the administrative Court of Appeals is the first and the last court of resort.[92]

---

83 See § 45 c (1) KWG.

84 See *Explanatory memorandum*, at page 60 (supra note 25).

85 See § 45 c (2) KWG.

86 See § 45 c (1) 3 KWG.

87 See § 45 c (1) 4 KWG.

88 See § 45 c (6) KWG.

89 See § 45 c (7) 1 KWG.

90 See § 48 a (1) KWG.

91 See § 48 a (2) 1 KWG.

92 See § 48 r (1) KWG.

III. Statutory framework for bank insolvencies in the U.S.

Germany's Act to address German domestic bank insolvencies did not take shape in a legislative vacuum. One of the main inspirations came from the United States. Since the Great Depression of 1929, the United States has vested authority to address bank insolvencies – and, if necessary, liquidate insolvent banks – in the Federal Deposit Insurance Corporation (hereinafter, FDIC) and certain other regulatory agencies.[93] The FDIC's powers (as well as those of other U.S. financial regulators) have undergone significant alteration over the years. However, one key element of the U.S. statutory framework is the distinction it makes between (a) *bank holding companies* (BHCs) and *non-bank financial companies* (NBFCs) on the one hand and (b) traditional *regulated banks* on the other.[94]

This second part of the article will first address the key differences in treatment under U.S. law for the various U.S. domestic financial institutions. It will then discuss the powers and authority of the FDIC and other financial regulatory agencies to address bank insolvencies.

The U.S. regulatory regime remains in flux. Summer 2010 saw the passage of the *Dodd-Frank Wall Street Reform and Consumer Protection Act* of 2010 (hereinafter, the *Dodd-Frank Act*), which vastly altered the financial regulatory landscape.

Finally, the article will evaluate what Germany could or should have learned from the U.S. experience and how effective each regulatory regime is at averting financial crisis, addressing moral hazard, and ensuring predictability to participants.

1. Bank holding companies and non-bank financial companies vs. regulated banks

A *bank holding company* is an entity in control of one or more banks (or bank holding companies) which does not necessarily engage in the banking business itself. BHCs are subject to regulation by the *Federal Reserve Board of Governors* (FRB) and – if they have more than 300 shareholders – by the *Securities and Exchange Commission* (SEC). Compared to traditional regulated banks, BHCs have much easier access to liquidity and more flexibility in their investment activities. This comes, however, at the cost of high *levels of regulation* and *extensive administrational costs*.[95]

In contrast to regulated banks, which are further discussed below, *bank holding companies* and *non-bank financial companies* may commence voluntary bankruptcy proceedings under Chapter 11 of the U.S. Bankruptcy Code.

---

93 See *Gary Rice* An Overview of U.S. Regulation of Depository Institutions, A Guide to Banking and Financial Services Law and Regulation 2008, 1708 PLI/Corp. 11, 14 (2008).

94 See *Stanley V. Ragalevsky & Sarah J. Ricardi* Anatomy of a Bank Failure, 126 Banking L.J. 867, 868 (2009).

95 During the global financial crisis of 2008 many traditional independent investment banks (e.g. Goldman Sachs and Morgan Stanley) as well as other corporations in the financial sector (e.g. *American Express* and *GMAC*) converted to BHC status as a strategy to raise capital. *Lawrence A. Cunningham & David Zaring* The Three or Four Approaches to Financial Regulation: A Cautionary Analysis Against Exuberance in Crisis Response, 78 Geo. Wash. L. Rev. 39, 59–62 (2009).

Non-bank financial companies (hereinafter, NBFC's) are companies in the financial markets – such as large insurers, investment firms and hedge funds – which provide banking services but do not hold a banking license and are therefore subject to far less regulation than traditional regulated banks or bank holding companies. Particularly in light of the U.S. government's extension of credit to non-bank financial company American International Group, Inc. (commonly known and referred to as *AIG*), the U.S. Congress subjected certain systemically-important non-bank financial institutions to the Federal Reserve Board's supervisory umbrella in the *Dodd-Frank Act*. As a result, such companies must now comply with certain regulatory requirements to a similar extent as bank holding companies. In particular, the *Dodd-Frank Act* enables the FDIC to take control over certain "covered financial companies"[96] to the extent such company threatens to default, such default would have a significant adverse impact on U.S. financial stability, no alternatives from the private sector exist and the balance of interests weighs in favor of FDIC intervention.[97] Even if a particular NBFC has commenced Chapter 11 proceedings, the *Dodd-Frank Act* enables the FDIC to initiate receivership proceedings and unilaterally terminate the Chapter 11.[98] Moreover, the *Dodd-Frank Act* also requires banks and NBFCs with an asset value over $50 billion to provide periodic reports regarding their financial condition, risk management systems, transactions with subsidiaries and other activities that could have a disruptive effect on U.S. economic stability.

In contrast to regulated banks and similar to industrial corporations, non-financial companies and BHCs may commence voluntary bankruptcy proceedings under Chapter 11 of the U.S. bankruptcy code.[99] Chapter 11, in contrast to many civil law countries, provides a "debtor in possession" (cf. *Eigenverwaltung*) model and grants bankrupt debtors "breathing space" to restructure and rehabilitate their operations. Debtors in possession also have extensive authority to "reject" onerous contracts, "assume" advantageous contracts and challenge or avoid (cf. *anfechten*) certain fraudulent or preferential prepetition transactions.[100] In the wake of the 2008 global financial crisis, several BHCs and other NBFCs commenced Chapter 11 proceedings, including, notably, Lehman Brothers Holding, Inc., Washington Mutual Inc. and Corus Bankshares, Inc.

Regulated banks are fully governed by U.S. bank regulation law on both the federal and state level. Bank regulation law in the U.S. is highly fragmented compared to other countries (and especially to Germany). As a result, regulated banks may be subject to various federal and state banking regulators. Regulated banks which are supervised by the *Federal Deposit Insurance Corporation* (FDIC) or a similar authority are not allowed to file for bankruptcy.[101] Instead, in the case of a crisis they are taken over by the regulating

---

96 See Dodd-Frank Act §§ 201(a)(8) & 203(b).

97 See Dodd-Frank Act § 203(a).

98 See Dodd-Frank Act § 208(a).

99 However, with passage of the Dodd-Frank Act, the FDIC can intervene and suspend any such Chapter 11 proceedings to the extent it makes a determination that such NBFC or BHC constitutes a "covered financial company," whose failure would pose a risk to U.S. financial markets. See Dodd-Frank Act § 203(a).

100 See 11 U.S.C. §§ 305, 547 et seq.

101 Pursuant to § 109 (b) (2) U.S. Bankruptcy Code regular, cooperative and savings banks as well as other financial corporations such as domestic insurance companies, savings and loan associations, building and loan associations, homestead associations, New Markets Venture Capital

authority and come under forced administration. Their reorganization or liquidation organization is regulated by the *Federal Deposit Insurance Act* (FDIA) whose provisions differ significantly from the U.S. corporate bankruptcy code and which enables the FDIC to deal effectively and expeditiously with bank insolvencies.[102]

The differences between *corporate insolvencies* governed by the U.S. bankruptcy code on the one hand and *bank insolvencies* governed by the FDIA on the other reflect the U.S. Congress' assessment of the differing consequences of credit institution failure for the U.S. and global economy. Both the importance of financial institutions to financial and non-financial markets as well their inherent fragility cause bank insolvencies to produce substantial negative externalities in the domestic and international economy as compared to the failure of other (non-financial) corporations.[103] For that reason, the U.S. financial insolvency regime contemplates a fast and preemptive procedure, putting the FDIC as regulatory body in a position of strength to mitigate potential social costs.[104]

2. General framework of bank insolvency and receivership by the FDIC for regulated banks

The FDIC plays the central role in the regulation of the operation and the reorganization of banks: it serves as an *insurer, regulator* and, in case of insolvency, also as a *receiver*. As an *insurer* it guarantees the safety of deposits in member banks up to USD 250,000 per depositor and bank.[105] According to the FDIC, its deposit insurance "is backed by the full faith and credit of the United States government. This means that the resources of the United States government stand behind FDIC-insured depositors."[106] The deposit insurance system has worked well so far. The fact that "since the FDIC was established, no depositor has ever lost a single penny of FDIC-insured funds"[107] is prevalently referred to by member banks throughout the country. As a *regulating agency*, the FDIC examines and supervises banks to ensure they meet the statutory liquidity and reserve requirements and takes measures to the extent these requirements are not met. If a bank becomes undercapitalized, the FDIC issues a *warning* to the bank. It can also remove management and impose *corrective measures* if undercapitalization drops below specific limits. As a last step the FDIC has the authority to declare the bank insolvent and as a *receiver* to take over management of the bank. In recent years, that function has become increasingly important since the number of bank failures has risen dramatically and has reached its highest level since the *savings-and-loan crisis* in 1992.

---

companies, small business investment companies, credit unions, industrial banks are specifically exempted from the corporate bankruptcy code.

102 See Bliss, R.R/Kaufman, G.G., Corporate and Bank Insolvency Regimes: An Economic Comparison and Evaluation, WP 2006-01, the Federal Reserve Bank of Chicago, 2006 for a detailed analysis.

103 See *Bliss/Kaufmann* (2006), p. 3. (supra note 102).

104 Ibid.

105 See Dodd-Frank Act § 335(a).

106 See http://www.fdic.gov/deposit/deposits/insured/basics.html.

107 See i.e. http://www.capecodfive.com/home/per/fdic.

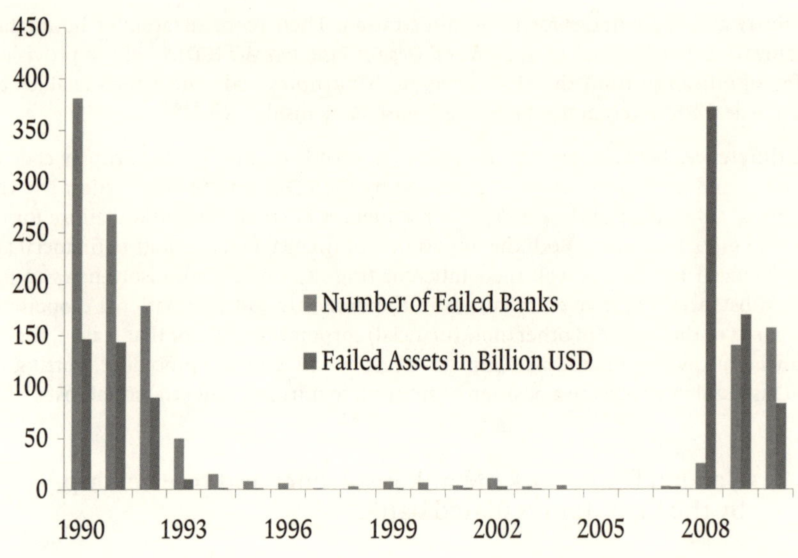

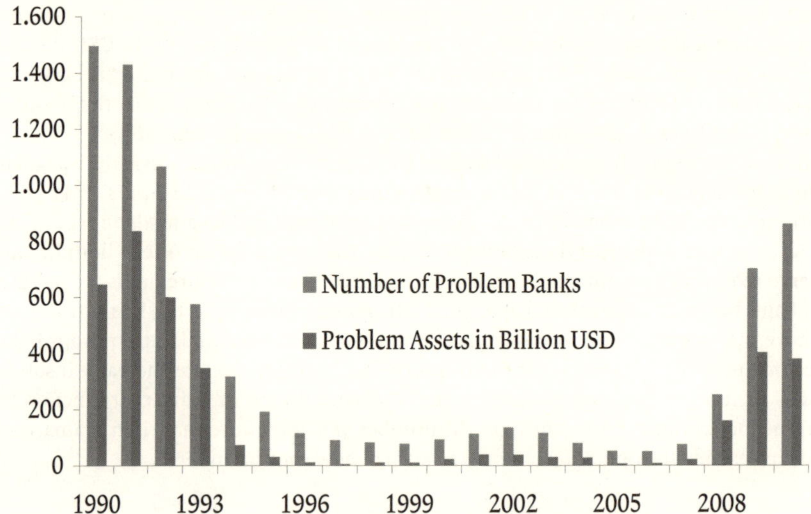

Source: FDIC statistics[108]

a) The goals of the bank insolvency vs. corporate bankruptcy procedure

The goals of the bank insolvency procedure under administration of the FDIC are substantially different from the goals of corporate bankruptcy under the U.S. bankruptcy

108 http://www.fdic.gov/bank/statistical/stats/index.html.

code. While corporate Chapter 11 proceedings are geared toward restoration of the bankrupt firm through renegotiation and impairment of creditors' claims, the goal of a *bank insolvency proceeding* is primarily to achieve a resolution that is the *least costly to the deposit insurance fund* (*least cost resolution*) and which therefore maximizes the net present value return from the sale of assets.[109] As a result, the *bank insolvency* proceeding strongly favors *depositors* over other creditors, whereas the *corporate bankruptcy procedure* favors *debtors* and in case of the Chapter 11 procedure, the *existing management* and the *survival* of the company.

The aim of the FDIC in the course of a bank administration is therefore not the revitalization of the bank consistent with its long-term going-concern value but to reduce the payments of the deposit insurance fund as much as possible and to recover effected payments to insured depositors to the largest possible extent.[110] In addition, the FDIC's strategy for stabilizing the financial markets is not solely to rehabilitate distressed banks but to prevent them sliding into a crisis in the first place through intense regulatory scrutiny and to relieve liquidity shortfalls by providing alternative liquidity from the deposit insurance fund.[111]

Certain other important guiding principles also inform the FDIC's course of action. Specifically, in addition to reducing systemic risk to financial markets and protecting depositors (up to the statutory maximum limit), the FDIC must adhere to certain cost savings directives contained in the FDIA itself. First and foremost is the so-called "least cost resolution" rule,[112] implemented by Congress in 1991, which requires the FDIC in any bank administration proceeding to implement measures that result in the lowest financial burden to the public fisc (exceptions exist to the extent adherence to the rule "would have serious adverse effects on economic conditions and financial stability and any action or assistance ... would avoid or mitigate such adverse effects"[113]). As further discussed below, the range of measures at the FDIC's disposal is broad, making careful and timely assessment critical.

b) Core features of the FDIC bank insolvency regime

In dealing with bank insolvencies, the FDIC has far-reaching competences. The U.S. bank insolvency regime allows a quick and complete takeover of the distressed bank for the purpose of minimizing losses to the deposit insurance fund and allows a maximum recovery of effected payments to insured depositors without regard to the position of management, creditors and shareholders. In contrast to the corporate bankruptcy procedure, the FDIC scheme comprises an administrative proceeding without supervision

109 See *Bliss/Kaufmann* (2006), p. 8. (supra note 102).

110 See *Bliss/Kaufmann* (2006), p. 9. (supra note 102).

111 See *Ravalevsky/Ricardi* (2009) at 868 ("The strategic goal of the law governing bank failures is to maintain public confidence in the banking system by bringing to depositors sound, effective and uninterrupted operation of the banking system with resulting safety and liquidate of bank deposits.").

112 See 12 U.S.C. § 1223(c)(4)(A); see also FDIC, Resolutions Handbook: Methods for Resolving Troubled Financial Institutions in the United States at 13 (1998) (hereinafter, Resolutions Handbuch).

113 12 U.S.C. § 1823 (c) (4) (G).

by a court with the FDIC as a sole actor. Once the process has started, the governing documents of the bank are revoked, senior management is removed and replaced by the FDIC in its role as receiver or conservator and shareholders' rights are terminated.[114] Management, creditors and shareholders do not participate and have no legal standing, representation or right of approval. In its role as receiver or conservator, the FDIC makes all necessary decisions unilaterally. Judicial review of the FDIC's actions is extremely limited: only some of the FDIC's decisions are subject to ex post judicial review and the only remedy consists of damages. With respect to the priorities of distribution, bank insolvency law differs significantly from corporate bankruptcy law. As a first priority, FDIC deducts its administrative expenses from the recovery. Insured depositors are then fully paid by the FDIC up to the statutory maximum. The residual accrues to general unsecured depositors, and then, to the extent of any excess, to shareholders.[115]

Core features of the FDIC insolvency proceeding

- **administrative proceeding**
- **far-reaching competences** of the FDIC
- FDIC is **solely in charge**, no separate oversight authority
- **no participation** of creditors, management and shareholders
- very **limited rights of claimants**
- only **ex post** judicial review of some FDIC decisions, only damages are available
- many decisions **subject to limited judicial review**

In summary, the FDIC insolvency regime may be characterized as follows:[116]

Objectives

- minimization of losses to the FDIC
- reduction of systemic risks to financial stability
- avoidance of excessive burdens to the public fisc

Procedure

- non-voluntary administrative procedure
- FDIC acts as statutory receiver or conservator & takes over management
- no supervision by a court but limited ex post judicial review
- preemptive measures are possible
- FDIC has the final word

114 See *Bliss/Kaufmann* (2006), p. 5 et seq., 14 (supra note 102).
115 See *Bliss/Kaufmann* (2006), p. 15 (supra note 102).
116 Following *Bliss/Kaufmann* (2006), p. 30 (supra note 102).

Priorities

- 1st: FDIC administrative expenses
- 2nd: insured depositors are fully paid by the FDIC
- 3rd: general creditors

deviation from priorities only in case of systemic risks and if consistent with least cost resolution

Rights of managers, creditors and shareholders

- very limited rights of managers, shareholders and creditors
- no participation & legal standing of managers, shareholders and creditors
- no right of approval for creditors
- shareholder interests are terminated
- very limited ex post judicial review with damages as only possible remedy

c) Stages of the procedure

The FDIC's bank insolvency regime follows a five step procedure:[117]

1. *Notification.* Once the regulated bank undergoes a crisis the overseeing regulating authority (e.g. Office of the Comptroller of the Currency for "National Associations" or "National Banks"; the Fed or the FDIC for "Federal Savings Institutions" or "Savings and Loan" Banks) issues a "failing bank letter" to the FDIC on the basis of a detailed opinion which comprehensively describes the cause for the insolvency.
2. *Examination.* The FDIC examines the facts (including extensive due diligence of the bank's books and records) and decides whether the bank should be sustained as "going concern", whether it should be sold to a different entity or whether it should be closed immediately.
3. *Marketing.* The FDIC utilizes the bank and its assets for the marketing and sale process. The FDIC evaluates potential offers to purchase the bank's assets as well as appropriate courses of action in accordance with the "least cost resolution" principle.
4. *Commencement.* The FDIC commences the receivership and seizes the assets and operations of the bank. Ideally the bank is immediately sold to a third party in order to limit losses.
5. *Distribution.* Creditors register their claims and the FDIC distributes the proceeds from the sale of the bank or its assets.

d) Initiation of the procedure

The involvement of the FDIC as receiver or conservator may be effected for any one of the following reasons:[118]

117 See *Ravalevsky/Ricardi* (2009) at 870–78, 881.
118 12 U.S.C. § 1821(c)(5).

- over-indebtedness and insolvency
- dangerous or unduly onerous credit terms and impermissible business conditions
- violation of a cease and desist order
- concealment of accounting records or refusal of supervision by the competent authority
- actual or impending losses posing a danger of exhausting the capital
- misdemeanor causing an insolvency, posing a threat to the financial position of the bank or impending a disadvantage to the depositors
- undercapitalization

Additionally the FDIC is statutorily required to close a bank within 90 days after the delivery of the notification of the bank of "prompt corrective action".[119] Normally the FDIC is involved far before the opening of the receivership process in order to decide about the bank's future.

e) Conservatorship and receivership

The FDIC has two options for the administration of a distressed bank – receivership and conservatorship.[120] *Receivership* leads to the immediate closure and liquidation of the bank or sale of the bank's assets and the subsequent distribution of the respective proceeds. By contrast, in a *conservatorship* the bank is taken over and operated by the FDIC until a more final resolution (such as a sale to a third party entity) is reached. In general, the FDIC acts as a receiver in the vast majority of cases.

In its administrative activities, the FDIC has far-reaching competences to operate and market the bank. As a conservator or receiver, it has the authority to take *all measures* which are in the interest of the bank, its depositors or the FDIC. Within 30 to 60 days before the initiation of the administration, the FDIC performs due diligence to assess the financial situation of the bank and evaluate its assets and liabilities.[121] All outstanding loans made to the bank are grouped according to their respective value and type and defaulted credits are separated from those not in default.[122] The FDIC then develops appropriate measures, markets the bank and tries to sell the bank in accordance with the above-discussed "least cost resolution" principle.[123] For that purpose, prospective purchasers may conduct a company auditing or due diligence. Bidders must agree to be bound by a pledge of confidentiality and fulfill certain qualification requirements. Offers are made approximately 10 days before bank closure. Importantly, all bidders must identify what they believe to the "collectable value" of the bank's assets, as well as any "franchise premium" contained in the offer.[124] The FDIC then reviews the offers with regard to the bank's liquidation value and the Board of Governors de-

119 12 U.S.C. § 1821 (c) (4).
120 See, e.g., 12 U.S.C. § 1821(c)(5).
121 *Ravalevsky/Ricardi* (2009) at 879.
122 See Id. at 872.
123 See Id. at 872–73.
124 See Id. at 874.

cides for a cost minimizing solution.[125] After the marketing, the FDIC is appointed as receiver.

f) Purchase and assumption transaction (P&A)

The FDIC can resort to a variety of measures as conservator or receiver in order to protect depositors and to preserve value by maintaining the distressed bank on a going concern basis. The method most frequently used (and the FDIC's preferred method) is the *purchase and assumption transaction* (P&A).[126] In a typical P&A, the FDIC and a healthy purchasing bank agree to a transaction in which the purchaser *assumes* a part or all of the *deposits* of the failed bank and *purchases* a part or all of its *assets*. All liabilities which have not been transferred remain within the administration of the FDIC and are liquidated separately (with distributions made to creditors in accordance with the distribution scheme discussed above).[127] The FDIC is authorized to litigate against third parties including former members of the board of directors and CEO's. From a historical perspective the FDIC prefers the P&A as an instrument for maintaining the value of the company and for avoiding harm to depositors as well as negative externalities for the domestic economy.

Generally, a P&A transaction is conducted either on a *whole bank* or on a *clean bank* basis. In a *whole bank P&A* (e.g. the sale of Washington Mutual to J.P. Morgan) all assets are sold "as is" at book value.[128] The purchaser assumes all deposit liabilities including those which are not insured by the FDIC. By contrast, in a *clean bank P&A*, the purchaser assumes only the core deposits. This transaction is the most frequently used if the timeframe for a due diligence is too short. The FDIC receives a premium for good will which corresponds to the core deposits. Good assets which are recoverable stocks, loans cash and liquid funds are transferred.[129]

The P&A transaction itself provides the FDIC a broad variety of mechanisms to maximize recoveries, reduce the risks to the purchaser and to motivate bidders to submit offers.

Loss sharing arrangement. Such an arrangement consists of three or more loss thresholds. The purchaser offers all losses up to the purchase price. From that first loss threshold upwards the FDIC compensates for 80% of all further losses and gets 80% of all proceeds refunded. If the losses reach a second loss threshold the FDIC compensates for 95% of all losses.[130]

Bridge bank. In case of a sudden and unexpected insolvency, the FDIC can create a bridge bank in order to buy more time for further interventions. The failed bank is transferred to the bridge bank and the FDIC administers the bank until a further transfer through a P&A transaction.[131]

---

125 See Resolutions Handbuch at 13.
126 *Ravalevsky/Ricardi* (2009) at 876.
127 Id.
128 Id. at 877.
129 Id. at 877–78.
130 Id. at 879.
131 12 U.S.C. § 1821(d)(2)(F); See also *Ravalevsky/Ricardi* (2009) at 880.

Government aid. In rare cases, the FDIC offers government aid in the form of an *open bank assistance program.*[132] The bank in crisis receives direct subsidies or a part or all of its liabilities are assumed by the FDIC. However, the FDIC is only authorized to provide government aid in case of a crisis of a *systemically important* bank and only in so far as the shareholders of the bank are not provided undue advantage.

If the FDIC fails to timely find a purchaser, it is obligated to close the bank, liquidate it and to use the proceeds for the repayment of the bank's liabilities. Deposits exceeding USD 250,000 are treated as simple (i.e., general unsecured) insolvency claims. After payment of secured claims and administrative costs, the FDIC repays deposits to depositors and receives payments for recovery which rank equal to unsecured deposits.[133] In general, liquidation of the failed bank is the most expensive method at the FDIC's disposal. As a result, it is one that the FDIC generally seeks to avoid.

From the beginning of the receivership, the FDIC assumes authority and control over all administrative tasks of the failed bank, including corporate headquarters and corporate books and records, without the supervision of a court or another authority.[134] The FDIC compiles a directory of assets and liabilities and determines the identity of insured depositors. Additionally the FDIC publishes a commencement notice.[135] The creditors have until 90 days after publication of the commencement notice to file their claims.[136] Within a period of 180 days the FDIC can assert or contest these claims.[137]

In order to ensure that enough funds are available to allow distributions to creditors, the FDIC sells the bank's assets as soon as possible. The FDIC may also commence foreclosure of nonperforming loans or change their terms and conditions in order to avoid foreclosure.

Similar to the Chapter 11 procedure, the FDIC can "reject" onerous contracts which would adversely affect the assets available for distribution among the unsecured creditors.[138] Importantly, this occurs without court approval. The "contract rejection" option is broader than that of a debtor within a chapter 11 proceeding. Specifically, the FDIC is authorized to refuse the execution of *every* contract, not only those that are not yet completely executed (i.e., so-called "executory contracts").[139] The contracting party can only claim actual damages, not lost profits.[140]

Likewise similar to a Chapter 11, the FDIC may challenge or "avoid" certain fraudulent transactions occurring within 5 years prior to commencement of the FDIC's receiver-

132 See Id. at 882.
133 12 U.S.C. § 1121(d)(11)(A).
134 12 U.S.C. § 1121(d)(2)(B).
135 12 U.S.C. § 1121(d)(3)(B)(i).
136 Id.
137 For example, in the insolvency of the U.S. bank Washington Mutual (in which the FDIC acted as receiver) Washington Mutual's BHC, Washington Mutual Inc., filed claims for several billion USD which have been contested in whole by the FDIC. Washington Mutual Inc. appealed that decision up to the District Court for the District of Columbia. Ultimately, the dispute was settled.
138 12 U.S.C. § 1121(e)(1).
139 Id.
140 12 U.S.C. § 1121(e)(3).

ship.[141] However the FDIC may not rescind merely *preferential (non-fraudulent) transfers*.[142] As a result depositors or other creditors may withdraw their loans prior to commencement of FDIC proceedings without being exposed to the risk of insolvency rescission.

Contracts whose termination has been effected by the insolvency of the bank can largely be transferred to the FDIC. Furthermore the contracting parties have to relinquish their termination rights within the first 90 days of the commencement of the FDIC's receivership (45 days in case of conservatorship).[143] The FDIC may also request a 90 day suspension of all lawsuits and demand the transfer of the law suits pending before state court up to the federal level.[144]

IV. Roads out of the Crisis: The German and US bank insolvency regime – An analytical review

The financial crisis of 2007–2010, considered by many to be the worst since the Great Depression of the 1930's, revealed both the *fragility* of global financial market and the *insufficiencies* of available regulatory responses to such a crisis. The collapse of venerable firms such as Lehman Brothers, Bear Stearns and AIG demonstrated that the crisis of systemically important, strongly connected financial institutions can cause dramatic shock waves to financial markets putting the stability of the global financial system at substantial risk.[145] Indeed, the spectacular liquidity shortfall in the U.S. banking system forced national governments into costly bailouts of banks in Germany and the United States alike. Widespread bank failure had far-reaching consequences for the economy including the crisis of key businesses, the decline of demand and, ultimately, a worldwide recession.

1. Systemic causes for the financial crisis and bank insolvencies

Although the U.S. banking market – which is dominated by special and investment banks rather than universal banks and is generally characterized by a much higher risk tolerance – appeared to be much more fragile than the European banking system, the crisis of the German bank HRE demonstrated to a great extent that the European and the U.S. financial markets, suffer from similar systemic faults (albeit in varying degrees).

a) Deficiencies in corporate and financial governance

A number of serious deficiencies in *corporate and financial governance* contributed to the global financial crisis: the lack of corporate liability on the side of mortgage banks seriously affected the quality of mortgage portfolios while business owners' skewed incen-

141 12 U.S.C. § 1121(d)(17).

142 *Ravalevsky/Ricardi* at 896–97.

143 12 U.S.C. § 1121(e)(13)(C)(i).

144 12 U.S.C. § 1819(6).

145 See *Explanatory memorandum*, p. 1 et seq (supra note 25).

tives shifted business risks to special purpose entities, encouraging irresponsible and highly risky behavior.[146] Incentives to maximize short term corporate profits and interest yields led to neglect of critical risks and failure to pay sufficient attention to long-term business interests.

The legislative history of the KreditReorgG stated that one of the principal causes of the crisis was the fact that management did not take personal responsibility for their actions.[147] As noted in the legislative history, compensation schemes – particularly short term bonuses which rewarded highly risky maneuvers while disregarding the consequences of a failed investment – arguably set the wrong incentives, allowing managers to neglect their managerial duties.[148] Ultimately, risky behavior of market participants in the interest of maximizing short-term gain undermined companies' long-term profit strategies. At the same time, companies' supervising bodies as well as government regulators had difficulty dealing with the intrinsic risks associated with particular business models. Indeed, these problems gained sufficient attention only when it was already too late for effective action.[149]

The dramatic consequences of not anticipating the potential effects of risky business activities and the reluctance of management to take prompt corrective measures had wide-reaching effect in the case of systemically important banks. Signals of a company's approaching liquidity crisis were not dealt with expeditiously and necessary measures, particularly the filing of insolvency, were delayed until a total breakdown of a bank was inevitable. That sort of behavior arguably was triggered partly by the *psychological mechanisms* of selective perception, especially overconfidence and the avoidance of acknowledging personal faults[150] on the one hand and the *moral hazard* of state bailouts on the other.[151] Collectively, this had the partial effect of setting improper incentives, which promoted excessive risk-taking at the expense of prudent market participation. Indeed, market participants made decisions based on the expectation that governments would not allow failure of a systemically important financial institution. Consequently, such market actors came to expect state-sponsored bailouts through use of public funds.[152] Furthermore in case of insolvency risk, management of an affected bank would be inclined to hide or sugarcoat the bank's fundamental problems and delay necessary measures in order to avoid *negative repercussions for its refinancing* and the likely *withdrawal of investors* if the liquidity crisis were to be publicized. The delay of crisis management therefore has become the norm.[153]

---

146 See *Hellwig* Stellungnahme, 5. 10. 2010, page 2 et seq. For (http://www.bundestag.de/bundestag/ausschuesse17/a07/anhoerungen/2010/029/Stellungnahmen/index.html); See *Explanatory memorandum,* at page 1 et seq. (supra note 25). For an overview of current reform efforts to improve corporate governance as a response to the financial crisis See *Wittig,* 64 WM 2337 (2010).

147 See *Explanatory memorandum,* at page 1 et seq. (supra note 25).

148 See *Explanatory memorandum*, p. 1 et seq (supra note 25).

149 See *Hellwig* supra note 146, at page 2.

150 See for the role of psychological biases in business life *Bühring-Uhle/Eidenmüller/Nelle* Verhandlungsmanagement, Analyse, Werkzeuge, Strategien, München, 2009, page 41 et seq.

151 See *Explanatory memorandum,* at page 1 et seq. (supra note 25) and *Samwick* Moral Hazard in the Policy Response to the 2008 Financial Market Meltdown, 29 Cato J. 131, 133 (2009).

152 See *Samwick* supra note 151, at page 133.

153 See *Hellwig* supra note 146, at page 5.

b) Regulatory deficiencies

This situation became more problematic due to the lack of efficient regulatory instruments, making it impossible for the government to adequately react to the dramatic failure of financial and corporate governance.[154] It reduced the state to a virtually powerless spectator, forced to helplessly watch the crisis progress. In the case of Germany, although the *BaFin* already had powerful instruments in §§ 45, 46 KWG, enabling early intervention, these instruments were more aimed at stabilizing the financial market rather than preemptive protection of a bank's assets. In particular, by halting the operation of a bank's business (including the contractual relationships to third parties) in reliance on §§ 45, 46 KWG, *BaFin* may have unwittingly brought about exactly these adverse systemic consequences it sought to avoid.[155] In practice, state regulators were (prior to financial market reform) to a large extent unable to intervene without risking a backlash. What was missing were instruments allowing early intervention without the risk of systemic counter reactions on the market. The conflict between the private interest in the protection of the creditors and the public interest in the protection of the financial system has so far been structured to heavily favor creditors.[156] In sum, the regulatory instruments in Germany were not prepared to effectively handle the crisis of systemically important financial institutions. As a result, the government was virtually forced to bailout distressed banks such as HRE in order to avoid adverse externalities to the stability of the financial market. Although such subsidizing interventions were suitable to effectively avoid the negative consequences for market stability, they created a moral hazard problem by incentivizing risky and reckless behavior by creditors, management and shareholders. Furthermore, they shifted the risks and costs for the resolution of bank failures to the taxpayer who ultimately bore the consequences of unwise and self-serving corporate decisions.

2. Regulatory strategies after the crisis

The deficiencies in corporate and financial governance and the lack of effective regulatory instruments urged governments to take legislative action to handle such crisis effectively. The strategies implemented in Germany and in the US were in their core elements the same: 1. resolution of distressed and systemically important banks *without incurring risks for the stability* of the financial system, 2. *early regulatory intervention*, 3. shifting the *risks and costs* from the public sphere to creditors and shareholders of the distressed bank.[157] Besides implementing more demanding regulatory requirements for banks and other financial institutions as a *preventive* strategy, the central parts of the regulatory response to the crisis consisted of instruments which will allow a restructuring or an orderly liquidation of the distressed bank as a *responsive* strategy. While Germany with the *Credit Institutions Reorganization Act* (KredReorgG) and its restructuring and reorganization procedure implemented a new framework to with bank

154 See *Explanatory memorandum,* at page 1 et seq. (supra note 25); *Hellwig* supra note 146, at page 2 et seq.

155 See *Explanatory memorandum,* at page 1 (supra note 25); *Hellwig* supra note 146, at page 3, 7.

156 See *Hellwig* supra note 146, at page 3, 9.

157 See *Explanatory memorandum,* at page 1 et seq., 40 et seq. (supra note 25).

insolvencies, the United States essentially expanded the regulatory regime for bank insolvencies to non-banks, bank holding companies and other financial institutions with the OLA procedure of the *Dodd-Frank Act* which was modeled after the FDIC receivership rules.

a) Structural differences between the KredReorgG and the FDIC rules

A closer look at the two regimes reveals that the implementation of strategies to deal effectively with the failure of major financial institutions differs to a certain extent. The German regime for bank insolvencies is similar to the pre-*Dodd-Frank Act* scheme in the United States. Indeed, prior to passage of the *Dodd-Frank Act*, non-bank insolvencies came within the scope of the *corporate bankruptcy code*. Similarly, the revised German scheme therefore now resembles (with certain important exceptions, as further noted above) the basic structure of Chapter 11 bankruptcy procedures rather than those of the FDIC rules: a self-regulating vs. a state regulated procedure; comprehensive participation by all stakeholders vs. their extensive disempowerment; self-management under supervision of a courts vs. unilateral administration by a principal creditor with superpowers and without court supervision; continuation of operating business as existing management vs. instant removal of senior management and revocation of company statute; preservation of shareholder's rights vs. termination by the regulating authority; going concern vs. liquidation; recovery of the bank or settlement of creditor's claims vs. minimizing losses to FDIC and maximizing its recovery; maximizing participation by all participants vs. maximizing speed of process; unlimited ex post and ex ante vs. unlimited judicial review ex post only.

The structural differences between both procedures may be roughly outlined as follows:

Objectives

KreditReorgG Rules	**FDIC Procedures**
• mostly going concern, otherwise liquidation	• mostly fast liquidation, otherwise going concern
• reduction of systemic risks to financial stability	• minimization of losses to the FDIC
	• maximization of recovery through optimal sale of assets
	• reduction of systemic risks to financial stability

Procedure

KreditReorgG Rules	**FDIC Procedures**
• voluntary mixed procedure	• non-voluntary administrative procedure by the FDIC as principal creditor with superpowers
• management normally remains in place	• FDIC acts as statutory receiver or conservator & takes over management
• central role of restructuring / reorganization agent	• preemptive measures are possible
• preemptive measures are possible	• FDIC has the final word
• participation of management, shareholders and creditors	• designed for speed
• designed for participation	

Rights of management, shareholders and creditors

KreditReorgG Rules	FDIC Procedures
• supervision by a court and ex ante and ex post judicial review	• no court supervision but limited ex post judicial review with damages as only possible remedy
• participation and legal standing	• no participation & very limited rights
• creditors cannot be forced into a shareholder position	• no right of approval for creditors
	• shareholder interests are terminated

Priorities

KreditReorgG Rules	FDIC Procedures
• special privileges for shareholders (restructuring and minority shareholder privilege)	• 1st: insured depositors are fully paid by the FDIC
• special privileges for public authorities if they participate financially (protection from insolvency rescission)	• 2nd: recoveries are shared equally by FDIC and unsecured depositors
	• 3rd: excess recoveries are distributed to general creditors and then to shareholders
	• deviation from priorities only in case of systemic risks and if consistent with least cost resolution

Apart from that basic structure, the KredReorgG already contains various instruments for the BaFin to take specific administrative measures such as the removal of the bank's management to deal with the reluctance of the participants to cooperate. Moreover, the option to substitute the consent of the owners and shareholders to the reorganization plan shows the increasing demand for effective administrative measures in an urgent crisis of a systemically relevant bank.

In addition to the regime of basically voluntary measures of self-regulation provided by the restructuring and reorganization procedure of the KredReorgG, the *BaFin* remains competent to intervene on an administrative level if it considers such measures necessary in order to avoid destabilization of the financial system. In particular, the *BaFin* may:

- order the partial carve-out or total transfer of the bank's assets as an instrument of *"Good-Bank/Bad-Bank" separation and a bridge bank solution* (*Ausgliederung und Übertragungsanordnung*)[158]
- appoint a special administrator with for the bank with particular competences (*Sonderbeauftragter*)[159]
- order specific measures to improve the equity capital and liquidity of the bank[160]

Essentially, the German procedure aims to continue the operating business of the distressed bank as far as possible under significant financial and managerial participation

158 See § 11(1) 1 KredReorgG; § 48(a) 1 KWG.

159 See § 45(c) 1 KWG.

160 See § 46(1) 2 KWG.

of all stakeholders (management, shareholders and creditors) and seems to consider the ordered liquidation of the bank only as an instrument of last resort. By contrast, the U.S. FDIC regime seems focused on the possibility of prompt closure of the bank (or prompt sale to or merger with a healthier financial institution) for the purpose of the maximum recovery of its assets in order to reduce losses for the depositors' insurance fund.

b) The German KredReorgG as a response to the crisis

The new German legislation – inspired by the U.S. Chapter 11 bankruptcy procedure[161] – provides a two-step procedure allowing coordinated collective negotiation among creditors, managers and shareholders and consensual solutions for the restructuring or orderly liquidation of a distressed bank. As set forth above, the procedure is designed as a self-regulating instrument and initiated by the distressed bank itself. Whereas the restructuring procedure (*Sanierungsverfahren*) initially contemplates preemptive action to address a bank's financial difficulties long before the bank becomes insolvent, it does not provide interventions into the rights of third parties. By contrast, the reorganization procedure (*Reorganisationsverfahren*), applicable once substantial risks for market stability are demonstrated and modeled after the insolvency plan procedure, allows not only interventions into the rights of creditors but also contemplates shareholder participation to avoid obstructive behavior. If stakeholders do not participate actively in the reorganization or if the procedure is unlikely to remedy the bank's financial crisis, the *BaFin* may appoint an administrative supervisor to take the necessary measures under the KWG.[162] The new legislation effectively provides a combination of regulatory measures meant to recognize that a systemic market crisis cannot be predicted and it therefore cannot be anticipated which instruments might be needed.[163]

(1) Only on the bank's initiative

As discussed above, the new procedures themselves also have certain deficiencies. One perceived weakness is the fact that it can only be initiated by the bank, thereby failing to address management's strong incentives to postpone necessary measure.[164] The reasons may have for management delaying necessary restructuring measures, as set forth above, generally are to preserve the bank's standing in capital markets and avoid the risk of massive withdrawal of investors upon disclosure of the bank's financial situation.[165] In addition, the prospect of management disempowerment and any potential CRO's influential position may deter management from commencing KredReorgG proceedings.[166] Moreover, any benefits with respect to ranking of claims – particularly the exceptions to subordination of particular claims – and the privilege of restructuring loans, as well as

---

161 See *Explanatory memorandum*, p. 50 (supra note 25).

162 See *Explanatory memorandum*, p. 2 et seq. (supra note 25).

163 See *Bachmann* Stellungnahme zum Restrukturierungsgesetz-E, 5. 10. 2010, page 1 et seq. (http://www.bundestag.de/bundestag/ausschuesse17/a07/anhoerungen/2010/029/Stellungnahmen/index.html).

164 See *Hellwig* supra note 146, at page 6 et seq. (http://www.bundestag.de/bundestag/ausschuesse17/a07/anhoerungen/2010/029/Stellungnahmen/index.html).

165 See *Bachmann* supra note 163, at page 3; *Hellwig* supra note 146, at page 2.

166 See *Bachmann* supra note 163, at page 2; *Hellwig* supra note 146, at page 7; *Eidenmüller* Finanzkrise, Wirtschaftskrise und das deutsche Insolvenzrecht, Berlin 2009, page 57 et seq.

the fact that illiquidity and over-indebtedness are not required to initiate the procedure are somewhat insignificant compensation for these disadvantages. For these reasons, the voluntary initiation of a restructuring or reorganization procedure by management of a distressed bank seems unlikely to be an effective instrument to deal with a financial crisis of a systemically significant bank.

Instead, the legislation may have been improved by vesting the *BaFin* with authority similar to that enjoyed by the U.S. FDIC by authorizing the *BaFin* to initiate a restructuring or reorganization procedure *ex officio* – such as, for example, Swiss Law already provides[167] – or to request a reorganization plan from the bank's management since it normally does not have the necessary information to provide a reorganization plan itself.[168] The legislator's explanation for its decision not to grant the *BaFin* such authority (i.e., that the goal of the procedure is a restructuring *with* the financial institution *not against its will*)[169] seems to be circular and does not justify the limited legislative action. In practice, the provision might be less severe than it might appear at first glance: although the BaFin has no actual legal rights to initiate a restructuring or reorganization procedure, the impending use of its regulatory competences might be sufficient to incentivize management to file a notice and thereby initiate the procedure.

(2) Potential reluctance of regulatory authorities

However, that alone might not be sufficient to safeguard prompt action, as the tendency to avoid drastic corrective action is not limited to corporate decision-makers but also is present within governments and regulatory agencies. Indeed, the possibility that a highly-publicized and potentially protracted restructuring process itself may threaten systemic stability may lead the government or the *BaFin* to avoid taking measures pursuant to the KredReorgG or the KWG and instead to resort to publicly funded bailouts.[170] Whether these considerations are also valid in practice are hard to tell. The FDIC on the other hand has not shown reluctance to make use of its administrative powers and the expedience of the FDIC procedure suggests that the systemic repercussions of U.S. public involvement might be limited. Moreover, because the FDIC is often not a financial institution's primary regulator, its first priority, as noted elsewhere herein, is to protect its fund. Accordingly, its incentive to forebear will inevitably be lower than that of a primary regulator. Nevertheless it has to be kept in mind that the FDIC so far mainly dealt with small, structurally simple banks with few known deposit liabilities whereas it still remains unclear how the FDIC procedure would prove itself in practice when dealing with the failure of a systemically-important bank with substantial non-deposit liabilities, international activities and non-traditional on and off-balance sheet activities.[171] This applies particularly to banks owned by holding company.[172]

---

167 See Art. 28 Swiss Banking Act (*Bankgesetz*). For a comprehensive comparisons of the German and Swiss special resolution regime for bank insolvencies See *Zulauf* supra note5.

168 The draft proposal of the German Federal Department of Economy included such a provision allowing the BaFin to request a reorganization plan. See also *Bachmann* supra note 163, at page 3 et seq.

169 See *Explanatory memorandum,* at supra note 25, at page 45.

170 See *Hellwig* p. 7.

171 See *Bliss/Kaufmann* (2006), p. 29 (supra note 102).

172 Ibid.

(3) Restructuring procedure allows only limited impairment of creditors' rights

One initial objection to the newly-enacted restructuring procedure (*Sanierungsverfahren*) is that it curtails attempts to impair third party rights, which is of particular relevance if parties consider undertaking a debt-equity-swap. While distressed banks and regulatory authorities may use the prospect of resorting to the more potent reorganization procedure (*Reorganisationsverfahren*) as a "carrot-stick" incentive to induce creditor participation in a restructuring procedure, the high hurdles necessary to initiate a reorganization procedure may hamper this approach.

(4) Possible limited impact of restructuring procedure

For these reasons, the KredReorgG restructuring procedure may have very little practical significance, particularly where the stress level of the bank or the risk posed by the distressed bank to financial markets is insufficient to meet the requirements for commencing a reorganization procedure. In addition to its limited-intervention instruments, the restructuring procedure is highly formalized and requires specific notification and reporting duties which arguably are superfluous, especially given the fact that the procedure does not allow interventions into third-parties' rights.[173]

(5) Overly demanding requirements for a reorganization procedure

These objections apply similarly (albeit to a lesser extent) to the KredReorgG reorganization procedure. Although it provides a much larger toolbox (including impairment of third party rights), its requirements for initiation are much higher, demanding a substantial risk for the proper functioning of the financial market (*Systemgefährdung*). Such high hurdles do not seem feasible and even seem to exceed those provided under German insolvency law for commencement of an insolvency plan procedure.[174] If the reorganization procedure is understood as a special procedure similar to the insolvency plan procedure and if we keep in mind that the requirement of substantial risk for the continuing existence of the bank (*Bestandsgefährdung*) does impose a requirement of similar level like the one of "Insolvency" according to InsO, then it is difficult to understand why the reorganization procedure (with the requirement of *Systemgefährdung*) should require a significantly higher hurdle.[175] It would therefore seem to be sufficient to limit the requirements for the initiation of the reorganization procedure to the *Bestandsgefährdung* and to refrain from a *Systemgefährdung.*[176] This likewise corresponds more appropriately to the goals set forth in the legislative history. Furthermore, if the reorganization procedure is only available to systemically significant financial institutions, then it is questionable whether the KredReorgG sufficiently addresses the moral hazard problems that partially gave rise to the financial crisis in the first place. Indeed, the

173 In that sense also *Bachmann* supra note 163, at page 2; *Eidenmüller* Finanzkrise, Wirtschaftskrise und das deutsche Insolvenzrecht, Berlin 2009, page 58; *Hellwig* supra note 146, at page 7 et seq.

174 See *Bachmann* supra note 163, at page 4.

175 Ibid.

176 Ibid.

option of publicly-funded state bailouts particularly applies to those banks that fulfill the requirement of *Systemgefährdung*. However, since the legislative practice of the *KredReorgG* was explicitly to limit the necessity of state bailouts, the existence of the reorganization procedure might also serve as a strong argument that the moral hazard problem does not exist anymore.

(6) No joint-entity procedure

Both KredReorgG instruments – the restructuring procedure and the reorganization procedure – are applicable to one entity only. In contrast to U.S. bankruptcy law, the KredReorgG does not contemplate a joint- or multiple-entity procedure. This limitation might impact the practical significance of the new instruments since not only one entity but also large corporate enterprises might be subject to restructuring and reorganization efforts.[177] This problem is partially mitigated, but not entirely solved, by the possibility of proposing one single restructuring process or one single reorganization agent for a multitude of corporations. Moreover, the *BaFin* serves as the sole regulatory authority and the *Frankfurt Court of Appeals* as the one forum with jurisdiction over any proceeding.

(7) Blocking for close-out netting period too short

The initiation of a reorganization procedure publicizing the liquidity crisis of a bank inevitably will disturb a bank's creditors. The Act therefore provides a protection mechanism which prohibits termination of all contracts vis-à-vis the bank for a period of one business day after the day of the bank's deliverance to the BaFin of a notice initiating the procedure.[178] Moreover, all other reasons for termination are delayed until that time. This provision is not, however, applicable to creditors secured by deposit insurance. Contrary to the statements made in the Act's legislative history, it has been argued that a period of one day is not sufficient to allow implementation of effective protective measures or to notify creditors. Also, negotiation and an agreement prior to the initiation of the procedure likewise does not seem feasible due to the risk of publicizing the liquidity crisis of the bank. Furthermore, as an analysis of the Lehman Brothers bankruptcy demonstrates, the exception for derivates and repro transactions might even *increase* the probability for insolvency of the distressed bank rather then remove the systemic risk as the legislator intended. Indeed, termination by derivatives counterparties of swap and other securities contracts (a carve-out from the otherwise applicable "automatic stay" applicable in Chapter 11) led to a massive liquidity drain from the Lehman Brothers estate. As a result, it inevitably will be necessary to preserve liquidity through use of a standstill or other creditor cooperation.

(8) Joint debtors

As set forth above, in the case of a partial carveout or complete transfer of assets of a company, the transferring and the absorbing bank are liable as *joint debtors* (*Gesamt-*

---

177 Indeed, the Chapter 11 cases of Lehman Brothers Holdings, Inc. involved 23 different debtor entities. See *In re Lehman Brothers Holdings, Inc.*, Case No. 08-13355 (Bankr. S.D.N.Y. Sept. 15, 2008).

178 See § 13 KredReorgG.

schuldner). Despite the limitation of that liability to the amount which creditors would have received absent the carve-out or the takeover, the entities' liability as joint debtors impedes the effective access of the new owners to liquidity. As suggested it would be preferable to release the new owners from liability for existing claims and to instead obligate them to use all future profits for the settlement of such outstanding claims. That would allow the new or absorbing bank a fresh start and create better conditions for the absorbing bank's operation and for the settlement of existing claims.

(9) Integration of voting of the creditors into the shareholder's meeting

The reorganization procedure is subject to the consent of both creditors and shareholders who vote in separate voting procedures. As demonstrated above, although desirable to integrate creditor voting into a general shareholders' meeting, a similar result can be reached by skillful setting the time and place of both voting procedures. Furthermore, the judicial competence to deal with all rescissions in the context of the reorganization procedure should be concentrated at the Frankfurt Court of Appeals.

V. Conclusion

The new legislation has significantly re-shaped the landscape of bank insolvency law in Germany. The legislative toolbox of available instruments to deal with the crisis of systemically relevant banks now largely corresponds to international standards as well as the instruments suggested by the proposed EU framework for bank insolvencies. However, certain doubts remain as to whether the self-regulating mechanisms established by the KredReorgG legislation will be effective in practice. [179]

1. In particular, the restructuring and reorganization procedure may not provide sufficient incentives for management to make use of these instruments. The advantages for the management to initiate the procedure essentially are limited to a higher priority for restructuring loans vis-à-vis unsecured claims and certain privileges of questionable importance, whereas the Act contains certain disincentives for management, shareholders and creditors (publicity of liquidity crisis, disempowerment of management, strong position of restructuring and reorganization consultant, interventions by the BaFin and the Court of Appeals, possible non-consensual approval of a restructuring plan over the dissent of creditors and shareholders). If the initiation of these procedures remains within the sole discretion of the bank, the probability that these procedures will have a significant practical impact may remain low. More preferable may have been authorization of the BaFin to initiate these procedures or to itself request a reorganization plan. Furthermore, the attraction of both procedures potentially could have been increased by modeling them more closely on the chapter 11 procedure. So far, the similarities in the Act to the U.S. Chapter 11 regime are limited.

179 In that sense also *Eidenmüller* Finanzkrise, Wirtschaftskrise und das deutsche Insolvenzrecht, Berlin 2009, page 58.

2. Furthermore it is questionable whether the reliance on a self-regulating model as a primary means for the resolution of the distressed and systemically relevant bank is feasible. In contrast to the US model, which provides state regulators with extensive "super powers" allowing complete takeover of a distressed bank's operations, removal of management and termination of shareholders' rights, the German approach relies mainly on self regulation. Administrative interventions only apply as a measure of last resort. At first glance this solution offers advantages: it is undisputedly in line with the principle of proportionality, it strengthens the self-regulating responsibility of market actors and leaves management of the bank (which generally has sufficient knowledge and experience in the bank's business) in place. It is a classic approach fostering private autonomy that attempts to avoid the moral hazard of spending public funds for state bailouts, a key objective of the legislation. Indeed, if management and the market have "caused the mess," it is arguably that they should be held responsible to resolve it with their own financial resources. Although the legal competences of the *BaFin* remain unaffected by the initiation of a restructuring or reorganization procedure, the direct intervention of state regulators such as the *BaFin* seems to be considered as a means of last resort only applying when a self-regulating strategy fails.

3. However, serious doubts remain whether this strategy will work in the face of a substantial crisis of a systemically relevant bank.[180] Delay in implementing corrective measures, the reluctance to recognize and remedy faulty decisions and the inclination to cover-up a bank's true financial situation can contribute significantly to the crisis of a bank. Whether it is wise to trust management (which, ultimately, contributed to the bank's crisis in the first place) to take prompt, decisive and transparent action is questionable. Although the *BaFin* remains free at any time to intervene (e.g. by requesting court-ordered removal of management, effectuating a transfer of part of the bank to an *existing bank* or to a *bridge bank* (*Übertragungsanordnung*), or other individual measures) the priority given to self-regulation in the current framework of the German bank insolvency regime may inhibit the *BaFin* from using the full range of administrative instruments at an early stage of crisis. Although the principle of proportionality generally requires a multi-step procedure of increasing intensity, the speed and manner with which financial crises often develop suggests that comprehensive and time-consuming restructuring and reorganization procedures may not be the most appropriate way to address a crisis. Against this background, the question remains whether the procedures set forth in the KredReorgG are functionally equivalent to the administrative measures set forth in the KWG and therefore adequately appropriate to deal with a bank failure. The impression remains that creditor protection tops system protection.

   However, optimally, given the acute risks posed by failure of a systemically relevant bank, it is important to ensure that financial stability is favored over protecting stakeholders' rights when attempting to strike a balance between protecting the public interest and protecting stakeholders. Reduced participation by shareholders

180 See *Eidenmüller* Finanzkrise, Wirtschaftskrise und das deutsche Insolvenzrecht, Berlin 2009, page 59 et seq.

and creditors is legitimized by the risks taken by many financial institutions and the resulting repercussions for the stability of the global financial system.

For these reasons, the U.S. regime for bank insolvencies explicitly prohibits traditionally regulated banks from commencing proceedings under the debtor-friendly U.S. chapter 11 bankruptcy regime (and now, with passage of the *Dodd-Frank Act*, effectively prohibits or, at the very least, undermines any attempt by certain systemically relevant "covered financial companies" to commence such proceedings)[181] and instead subjects such entities to FDIC supervision. The U.S. bank insolvency regime not only limits the participation of shareholders, management and creditors but also relieves these actors completely of their authority. This regulation is certainly driven by the idea that these participants are seen as obstacles rather than helpful participants able to contribute meaningfully to finding an effective resolution of the bank's crisis.

In light of the powers currently enjoyed by the FDIC, the German legislator may have been better advised top consider a receivership or conservatorship option for systemically relevant banks and other credit institutions, or even provisions allowing for partial or full nationalization. Indeed, as the coordination of different instruments for bank insolvencies is unfolding on an international and EU level, the current legislation may only be a first step towards a coordinated framework. Further legislation may improve these initial steps by allowing the *BaFin* to *initiate* a restructuring or reorganization procedure, by providing more *incentives* for the management to make use of these instruments (i.e. by granting super priority of new loans restructuring loans also vis-à-vis secured claims) and by vesting the BaFin with conditional competences.

181 See Dodd-Frank Act § 208(a) (providing for automatic dismissal of any bankruptcy proceeding or in the case of a broker-dealer, SIPA proceeding upon appointment of the FDIC as receiver for a "covered financial company"). Moreover, Dodd-Frank gives the FDIC power to act well before a "covered financial institution" is actually in default (i.e., even if there is "danger of default"). See Dodd-Frank Act § 203(b). Thus, assuming vigilant supervision on the part of the FDIC, the likelihood that a bankruptcy filing actually would be allowed to occur is remote.

Gläubigerschutz in einem Sonderinsolvenzrecht für Banken

Creditor Protection in Bank Resolution

Too Big to Fail: Do we need Special Rules for Bank Resolutions? The Treatment of Creditors in Bank Insolvencies[1]

John L. Douglas

Table of Content

Introduction: Who Should Bear the Losses?
The FDIC Receivership Process for Banks
The US Response to Systemically Important Financial Organizations
The Dodd-Frank Response
Concerns with the Dodd-Frank OLA
Other Alternatives
Summary, Conclusions and Questions

Introduction: Who Should Bear the Losses?

One of the critical issues in any bank insolvency is allocating the losses associated with the failure. There are strong public policy issues that would require the equity holders and creditors to suffer the losses of failure. Certainly there is moral hazard associated with any system where private investors reap the rewards of success but the public absorbs the losses of failure. If the creditors or equity holders of large institutions are to be protected, that protection will translate into a series of funding and other advantages. However, when our largest and most systemically important institutions have faltered, the costs of stabilizing those institutions have generally been absorbed by the government. The unknown costs of failure and the uncertain ramifications for our economies, businesses and communities have generally proven to be too daunting to risk a true failure. As the government has weighed the systemic effects of some form of insolvency scheme that would have creditors bear the losses of failure, almost invariably the government has chosen stability.

There was, however, great dissatisfaction with the governmental response to the latest crisis. In the United States, public funds were used to provide direct support a number of entities, including Fannie Mae and Freddie Mac, two privately owned enterprises supporting the residential mortgage market[2] and AIG,[3] and to facilitate the sale of Bear

---

1 The author acknowledges the contributions of *Pengyu Jeff He* and *Caroline Chan* in the preparation of this article. Unless otherwise noted, this article reflects legislative and regulatory developments as of December 2010.

2 Press Release, Federal Housing Finance Agency, Statement of FHFA Director *James B. Lockhart* at News Conference Announcing Conservatorship of Fannie Mae and Freddie Mac (Sept. 7, 2008). See Statement by Secretary *Henry M. Paulson, Jr.* on Treasury and Federal Housing Finance

Stearns to JPMorgan Chase.[4] Through the Troubled Assets Relief Program or TARP, direct equity investments were made in over 400 banks, including each of the nine largest institutions in the country.[5] The Fed,[6] Treasury[7] and FDIC[8] each instituted special liquidity programs to facilitate funding for banks, brokerage firms, money market funds and other financial entities. This type of action was repeated throughout the developed world, with unprecedented support to major institutions in the UK, Germany, France, Switzerland and elsewhere.[9]

At the same time, the United States embarked on a bold experiment with Lehman Brothers. In spite of official denials,[10] it is apparent that the government, had it wished,

---

Agency Action to Protect Financial Markets and Taxpayers (September 7, 2008), available at http://www.ustreas.gov/press/releases/hp1129.htm. See also Press Release, Fed. Housing Fin. Agency, Fact Sheet: Questions and Answers on Conservatorship (Sept. 7, 2008). Fannie Mae is the common name for The Federal National Mortgage Association and Freddie Mac is the common name for The Federal Home Loan Mortgage Corporation.

3 Am. Int'l Group, Inc., Annual Report (Form 10-K), at 3–5 (Mar. 2, 2009). See also Davis Polk & Wardwell LLP, Financial Crisis Manual 28–32 (2009). The Financial Crisis Manual is available at http://www.davispolk.com/files/Publication/d1ab7627-e45d-4d35-b6f1-ef356ba686f2/Presentation/PublicationAttachment/2a31cab4-3682-420e-926f-054c72e3149d/fcm.pdf, and is referred to herein as the "Financial Crisis Manual."

4 See Financial Crisis Manual 24–27.

5 See Office of the Special Inspector General for the Troubled Asset Relief Program, Quarterly Report to Congress (October 26, 2010), available at http://www.sigtarp.gov/reports/congress/2010/October2010_Quarterly_Report_to_Congress.pdf. See also Financial Crisis Manual 41–104.

6 See, e.g., *Madigan*, Bagehot's Dictum in Practice: Formulating and Implementing Policies to Combat the Financial Crisis (Aug. 21, 2009); *Bernanke*, The Federal Reserve's Balance Sheet, Speech at the Federal Reserve Bank of Richmond's 2009 Credit Markets Symposium (Apr. 3, 2009).

7 See Financial Crisis Manual 18–40. For a chart of the Federal Reserve's various emergency lending facilities, see Forms of Federal Reserve Lending to Financial Institutions (July 2009). See also *Randall D. Guynn*, The Global Financial Crisis and Proposed Regulatory Reform, 443–450, Brigham Young University Law Review, Vol. 2010, No. 2.

8 See Financial Crisis Manual 116–143. More information on the FDIC liquidity support programs is available at http://www.fdic.gov/regulations/resources/tlgp/index.html.

9 See generally An Assessment of Financial Sector Rescue Programmes, Bank for International Settlements (July 2009), available at http://www.bis.org/publ/bppdf/bispap48.pdf?noframes=1; 79th Annual Report, Bank for International Settlements (June 29, 2009), available at http://www.bis.org/publ/arpdf/ar2009e.pdf?noframes=1. See also *Randall D. Guynn*, The Global Financial Crisis and Proposed Regulatory Reform, 451–460, Brigham Young University Law Review, Vol. 2010, No. 2; *Ben Livesey* and *Jon Menon*, British Banks Get Unprecedented Government Bailout, Bloomberg, Oct. 8, 2008, http://www.bloomberg.com/apps/news?pid=newsarchive&sid=aeIqWGr5Vnkw; Lower House of German Parliament Approves Bailout, N.Y. Times DealBook, Oct. 17, 2008, http://dealbook.nytimes.com/2008/10/17/lower-house-of-german-parliament-approves-bailout/?scp=9&sq=germany%20bailout&st=Search; *Henry Samuel* Banking bail-out: France unveils 360bn package, The Telegraph, Oct. 13, 2008, http://www.telegraph.co.uk/finance/financetopics/financialcrisis/3190311/Banking-bail-out-France-unveils-360bn-package.html; *Nelson D. Schwartz* UBS Given an Infusion of Capital, N.Y. Times, Oct. 16, 2008, http://www.nytimes.com/2008/10/17/business/worldbusiness/17swiss.html?dbk; *Nelson D. Schwartz* Netherlands Takes Over Fortis's Dutch Operations, N.Y. Times, Oct. 3, 2008, http://www.nytimes.com/2008/10/04/business/worldbusiness/04fortis.html.

10 See *Scott Lanman* Bernanke Says He Wasn't "Straightforward" on Lehman, Bloomberg (Sept. 2, 2010); *Tom Bawden* Henry Paulson Claims He 'Lacked the Power' to Save Lehman Brothers, The Times (Oct. 24, 2008).

could have found a way to support Lehman, whether it was through the direct intervention along the lines of AIG or through asset support to facilitate a sale along the lines of the Bear Stearns/JPMorgan Chase transaction. Lehman was allowed, or forced, to go into bankruptcy, and the losses associated with the failure were immediately shifted to the equity holders and creditors of Lehman.

A general consensus appears to have arisen that the Lehman failure was a tremendous mistake, and that somehow if there had been a more efficient framework that would have allowed the government to intervene, preserve the systemically important elements of Lehman but still impose the losses on the equity holders and creditors of Lehman, we would have avoided many of the more pernicious elements of the financial crisis.[11] The argument is that bankruptcy was a messy and expensive undertaking and the government lacked control over the ultimate outcome of the bankruptcy proceeding, thus exacerbating systemic uncertainties. On the other hand, at the time, bailing out Lehman was viewed as an inappropriate public policy choice. Accordingly, governments have searched for some other way to put itself in control, allowing it to preserve the systemically important elements of the company while still shifting the costs to the equity holders and creditors. Hence, in the United States, we find the orderly liquidation authority provisions of Dodd-Frank.[12]

While we can certainly debate the proposition that the Lehman bankruptcy was a policy mistake, it appears that the new "middle way" between the bankruptcy process and bail outs incorporated in Dodd-Frank has become the new paradigm. Similar provisions are being enacted in Germany and are under consideration elsewhere.[13]

Dodd-Frank's orderly liquidation authority is modeled on the receivership provisions of the Federal Deposit Insurance Act.[14] These provisions have been used in thousands of bank failures in the United States over the years. Yet notwithstanding their wide use, they are poorly understood within the United States and even less understood elsewhere.[15] The provisions provide a very efficient framework for resolving community

11 See Too Big to Fail: The Role of Bankruptcy and Antitrust Law in Financial Regulation Reform: Hearing Before the Subcomm. on Commercial and Administrative law, H. Comm. on the Judiciary, 111th Cong. (2009) (testimony of Michael S. Barr, Assistant Secretary of the Treasury). There are also some notable dissenters. See, e.g., *Paul Mahoney /Steven Walt* Viewpoint: Treasury Resolution Plan Solves Nothing, Am. Banker, Nov. 20, 2009; *Peter J. Wallison/David Skeel* Op-Ed: The Dodd Bill: Bailouts Forever, Wall St. J., April 7, 2010; *John B. Taylor* Op-Ed: How to Avoid a 'Bailout Bill', Wall St. J., May 3, 2010.

12 Wall Street Reform and Consumer Protection Act of 2010, H.R. 4173, 111th Cong., 2nd Sess. (hereinafter Dodd-Frank Act), Title II (July 21, 2010).

13 See European Commission, An EU Framework for Cross-Border Crisis Management in the Financial Sector (October 2010); Crisis Management and Resolution for a European Banking System, IMF Working Paper (March 2010); Report and Recommendations of the Cross-border Bank Resolution Group, Basel Committee on Banking Regulation (March 2010).

14 Most of the resolution authority provisions are in Sections 11 and 13 of the Federal Deposit Insurance Act, 12 U.S.C. §§ 1821, 1823.

15 Unlike the extensive body of case law, legal commentary and other guidelines that exists with respect to reorganisations and liquidations under the U.S. Bankruptcy Code, only a very limited body of legal guidance supplements the bank resolution statute. As described by former general counsels to the FDIC and the Federal Home Loan Bank Board (the predecessor to the Office of Thrift Supervision) and the Resolution Trust Corporation, respectively: "This is a confusing

banks, and in a very ruthless fashion shift the losses of failure to equity holders and creditors. Because, however, it is now the model for the new resolution regimes, it is critical to understand how it works and what its limitations might be if applied to the larger, systemically important institutions.

The FDIC Receivership Process for Banks

Federal deposit insurance, first provided for banks in the United States in 1933,[16] now provides protection of up to $250,000 (US) for each depositor in each bank.[17] This deposit insurance reflects a public policy decision that depositors should not bear the risks of bank failure, as they are in little position to assess or monitor the solvency of the institutions in which they entrust their funds.[18] As a consequence, insured depositors do not bear the costs of failure. Rather, the government, through the deposit insurance fund, absorbs the costs of protecting these depositors, funding its obligations through a tax imposed on banks.[19] This deposit insurance provides a stable base of funding for banks, accounting in great measure for the large number of depositories in the United States.[20]

It should be noted that deposit insurance was adopted to provide systemic stability to the banking system in the United States.[21] Prior to the adoption of deposit insurance,

---

area. The challenge arises less because of the complexity of the rules than because of their ambiguity and obscurity. The Bankruptcy Code generally constitutes the starting point for rules governing the financial failure of companies in the United States. It contains a detailed set of rules that fill three volumes of U.S. Code Annotated, volumes of West's Bankruptcy Reporter, and over four linear feet of Collier's [on Bankruptcy]. But the statutes governing conservatorships and receiverships of federally insured banks and thrifts fill, at most, about 111 pages of the U.S. Code Annotated. Moreover, those 111 pages were fundamentally changed less than 18 months ago in the Financial Institutions Reform, Recovery and Enforcement Act of 1989 ("FIRREA")." Douglas, Luke & Veal, Introduction, Counseling Creditors of Banks and Thrifts: Dealing with the FDIC and RTC, PLI Order No. A4-4323 (Jan. 14, 1991).

16 Banking Act of 1933, ch. 89, § 8(l)–(n), 48 Stat. 162, 172–77.

17 The deposit insurance provisions are generally contained in Sections 5, 6, 7 and 11 of the Federal Deposit Insurance Act, 12 U.S.C. §§ 1815, 1816, 1817 and 1821. All federally chartered depository institutions and virtually all state-charted institutions are required to be FDIC insured. Currently, deposits are insured by the FDIC up to generally $250,000 per person per institution. Dodd-Frank Act, § 335.

18 See Public Policy Objectives For Deposit Insurance System, available at http://www.fdic.gov/deposit/deposits/international/guidance/guidance/publicpolicyobjectives.pdf.

19 Under the Dodd-Frank Act, the FDIC must base deposit insurance assessments on an insured depository institution's average consolidated total assets minus its average tangible equity, rather than on its deposit based. Dodd-Frank Act, § 331(b).

20 Between 1978 and 2005, the percentage of U.S. banks that were able to fund at least two-thirds of their total assets with core deposits (estimated as total deposits minus brokered deposits and other time deposits that are in denominations greater than $100,000) fell from nearly 91 percent to 59 percent. See *Christine M. Bradley/Lynn Shibut* The Liability Structure of FDIC-insured Institutions: Changes and Implications, FDIC Banking Review (2006), Vol. 18, No. 2.

21 See *John R. Walter* Depression-Era Bank Failures: The Great Contagion or the Great Shakeout? Federal Reserve Bank of Richmond, Economic Quarterly, Vol. 91/1, Winter 2005. Others have

depositors bore the losses of bank failures along with all other creditors. Because depositors were generally in a poor position to understand the financial condition of the bank, there were strong incentives to withdraw deposits at the first hint of trouble, regardless of the veracity of the hint. Failure or trouble at one bank would often lead depositors to withdraw funds at other banks, and the resulting contagion was severe. As banks failed, assets were liquidated precipitously at inopportune times, exacerbated problems at other institutions. Federal deposit insurance virtually ended bank runs. It did, however, represent a policy choice that one class of creditors – namely depositors – deserved protection for systemic reasons.

Milton Friedman once stated that federal deposit insurance:

> has succeeded in achieving what had been a major objective of banking reform for at least a century, namely, the prevention of banking panics. . . . [B]anking panics have occurred only during severe contractions and have greatly intensified such contractions, if indeed they have not been the primary factor converting what would otherwise have been mild contractions into severe ones. That is why we regard federal deposit insurance as so important a change in our banking structure and as contributing so greatly to monetary stability – in practice far more than the establishment of the Federal Reserve System.[22]

We should point out that the banking system in the United States is quite different from that found in Europe. There are over 7,500 FDIC-insured banking organizations in the United States, the overwhelming majority of which hold less than $2 billion (US) in assets and engage in relatively straightforward deposit taking and lending activities.[23] Only a relatively small number engage in sophisticated capital markets, derivatives, insurance or similar activities, and only a handful engage in international operations to any significant degree.

Further, the most common structure of a banking organization is to house the banking activities in a separately chartered bank that in turn is a subsidiary of a holding company. It is the holding company, through other subsidiaries, that will normally engage in insurance and many securities activities.[24] There are, simply, no true "universal banks" in the United States.

Hence, when the FDIC acts as the insurer of deposits in banks, in virtually every case it is backing the deposits of entities that are engaged only in relatively straightforward lending activities. The FDIC receivership process is designed to handle the failure of these institutions in a straightforward, efficient way.

---

argued that the primary reason was that it has the support of small banks that overrode the opposition of bigger banks. See *Nicholas Economides/R. Glenn Hubbard/Darius Palia* The Political Economy of Branching Restrictions and Deposit Insurance: A Model of Monopolistic Competition Among Small and Large Banks, Journal of Law and Economics 39 (1996).

22 *Milton Friedman/Anna Jacobson Schwartz* A Monetary History of the United States, 1867–1960, p. 440–442.

23 FDIC Quarterly Banking Profile (Third Quarter 2010), available at http://www2.fdic.gov/qbp/2010sep/qbp.pdf.

24 Thus there are no "universal banks" in the United States. Bank holding companies, on a consolidated basis, may engage in banking, insurance, securities and asset management businesses. Any insurance or securities activities conducted in the banks themselves are limited and relatively straightforward.

When an insured bank fails, the FDIC is appointed receiver.[25] As such, it steps into the shoes of the institution, and is granted by statute "all rights, titles, powers, and privileges of the insured depository institution, and of any stockholder, member, accountholder, depositor, officer, or director of such institution with respect to the institution and the assets of the institution."[26] Its statutory obligation is to assure that insured depositors are protected, and in that capacity will generally arrange for another insured bank to assume the insured deposit liabilities.[27] At the same time it will facilitate the sale of as many of the banking assets as possible to the acquiring institution, thus attempting to maintain the assets in an ongoing institution. As there are rarely sufficient "good" assets to cover the deposit liabilities assumed, the FDIC is generally called upon to provide cash or other assistance to facilitate the sale.[28] The FDIC, as receiver, is generally left with the other liabilities of the institution as well as the unwanted assets and, by virtue of having provided some form of assistance to facilitate the protection of depositors, is typically the largest claimant against the assets of the receivership. As receiver, it then will liquidate those assets and use the proceeds to satisfy the claims to the extent of available funds.

To minimize the public costs, the statutory provisions governing receiverships provide for a depositor preference regime.[29] That is, the proceeds of a receivership, after the FDIC recovers its administrative expenses, are first allocated to cover the claims of depositors (other than deposit liabilities payable solely outside the United States). Only after those claims are satisfied will there be funds available for general creditors. Only after the general creditor claims are satisfied in full will funds be available for subordinated creditors. Any residual funds are allocated to equity holders in the order of their priority.

---

25 Federal Deposit Insurance Act § 11(c)(2), 12 U.S.C. § 1821(c)(2).

26 Federal Deposit Insurance Act § 11(d)(2)(A)(i), 12 U.S.C. § 1821(d)(2)(A)(i).

27 See FDIC, Resolutions Handbook: Methods for Resolving Troubled Financial Institutions in the United States (2003), available at http://www.fdic.gov/bank/historical/reshandbook/, referred to herein as the "FDIC Resolutions Handbook." While the Handbook is a little dated, it provides significant insight into the receivership and resolutions process for failed institutions. Chapters include a review of the resolutions process, a discussion of purchase and assumption transactions, the FDIC's role as receiver and other significant public policy issues.

28 Federal Deposit Insurance Act § 13(c)(2)(A), 12 U.S.C. § 1823(c)(2)(A). See also FDIC Resolutions Handbook 29–35 (2003); FDIC, Managing the Crisis: The FDIC and RTC Experience 1980–1994, Volume 1, at 193–209 (1998); FDIC Staff Presentation, The Failing Bank Marketing Process: Whole Bank Transactions and Loss Share Transactions (American Bankers Association, Sept. 2, 2009); FDIC Staff Presentation, Resolutions: The Process of Bidding on Distressed Banks in the New Millennium (July 18, 2008). See also, e.g., Purchase and Assumption Agreement, Whole Bank, All Deposits, Among FDIC, Receiver of Colonial Bank, Montgomery, AL, FDIC, and Branch Banking and Trust Company, Winston-Salem, NC §§ 4.15A–4.15C (Aug. 14, 2009), available at http://www.fdic.gov/bank/individual/failed/colonial-al_P_and_A.pdf.

29 Federal Deposit Insurance Act § 11(d)(11), 12 U.S.C. 1821(d)(11). See also Marino & Bennett, The Consequences of National Depositor Preference, 12 FDIC Banking Rev. No. 2, 19; Thompson, The National Depositor Preference Law, Economic Commentary, Federal Reserve Bank of Cleveland (Feb. 15, 1994).

The FDIC, having protected the depositors, steps into the depositor class in the liquidation priority as subrogee.[30] Because deposits are the largest creditor class of these smaller banking entities, it is the FDIC, as the insurer of deposits that has the greatest interest in the receivership. And given the value of assets in most of these failed institutions, it is the rare receivership that has funds available to even satisfy the depositor class. Accordingly, general creditors of a failed bank rarely recover anything on their claims.[31]

As a result of the statutory receivership framework, the losses of bank failures are shifted to the creditors and equity holders of the institution. The losses that might otherwise be suffered by the depositor class are (i) mostly assumed by the FDIC and (ii) minimized by the depositor preference framework.

Perhaps the simplest way to understand the FDIC's resolution process is to walk through the failure of a hypothetical bank. In our very simplified example set forth below, the bank has assets of 130, but liabilities of 150, with a negative equity of 20.

PROBLEM BANK				
Assets			**Liabilities**	
Cash and Securities	30		Insured Deposits	100
Good Loans and Assets	50		Uninsured Deposits	20
Bad Loans	40		Secured Creditors	10
Other Assets	10		Unsecured Creditors	20
Total Assets	**130**		**Total Liabilities**	**150**
			Shareholders Equity	(20)

Upon failure, the FDIC is appointed receiver, and the FDIC assumes this entire balance sheet. As the rights of secured creditors are generally unimpaired as a result of the bankruptcy,[32] in our example we remove 10 in assets and 10 in secured liabilities from the balance sheet, leaving assets of 120, liabilities of 140, and again a negative equity of 20.

30 Federal Deposit Insurance Act § 11(g), 12 U.S.C. § 1821(g).

31 The FDIC website, www.fdic.gov, contains substantial information on bank failures. At http://www2.fdic.gov/divweb/index.asp bottom, the FDIC has set forth the results of its receivership activities on failures since 2000. Of the over 300 banks that have failed, the FDIC has been able to satisfy the claims of depositors in only three instances, and in only one of those have those claims been paid in full. In every other instance, the depositor class has suffered a loss, meaning that the FDIC has had to absorb a loss in the deposit insurance funds as a result of the failure.

32 Federal Deposit Insurance Act § 11(d)(11)(A), 12 U.S.C. 1821(d)(11)(A).

PROBLEM BANK (SECURED CREDITORS PROTECTED)				
Assets			**Liabilities**	
Cash and Securities	20		Insured Deposits	100
Good Loans and Assets	50		Uninsured Deposits	20
Bad Loans	40		Secured Creditors	0
Other Assets	10		Unsecured Creditors	20
Total Assets	**120**		**Total Liabilities**	**140**
			Shareholders Equity	(20)

The FDIC will then attempt to arrange a transaction where the insured deposit liabilities are assumed by a purchaser. At the same time, the purchaser will typically purchase the "good" assets of the failed bank. In the prototypical "purchase and assumption" transaction, a relatively clean bank will be sold by the FDIC as receiver, normally to another insured financial institution.[33] Because the liabilities assumed will typically exceed the value of the assets purchased, the FDIC is required to contribute cash to the transaction to provide a "balanced" balance sheet. Indeed, in most transactions, the bidding process revolves around how much cash the FDIC must provide in order to induce a purchaser to acquire the institution.

THE "CLEAN" BANK PURCHASE & ASSUMPTION				
Assets			**Liabilities**	
Cash and Securities	20		Insured Deposits	100
Good Loans and Assets	50		Uninsured Deposits	0
FDIC Cash	30		Secured Creditors	0
			Unsecured Creditors	0
Total Assets	**100**		**Total Liabilities**	**100**
			Shareholders Equity	0

The FDIC is left with the problem assets and the unassumed liabilities. There is now a new creditor of the receivership: the FDIC, who in our example was forced to contribute 30 of its own funds to induce the purchaser to acquire the bank. The FDIC will liquidate

33 FDIC Resolutions Handbook 19–35 (2003). See e.g. Purchase and Assumption Agreement, Whole Bank, All Deposits, Among FDIC, Receiver of Horizon Bank, Bellingham, WA, FDIC and Washington Federal Savings and Loan (Jan. 8, 2010), available at http://www.fdic.gov/bank/individual/failed/horizon-wa_P_and_A.pdf.

the assets of the remaining receivership estate, applying them to creditors in the order of priority provided by statute.

THE REMAINING RECIEVERSHIP ESTATE				
Assets			**Liabilities**	
			Uninsured Deposits	20
Bad Loans	40		Unsecured Liabilities	20
Other Assets	10		FDIC Advance	30
Total Assets	**50**		**Total Liabilities**	**70**
			Shareholders Equity	(20)

As noted above, the priorities are (i) administrative expenses, (ii) depositor claims (other than deposit liabilities payable solely outside the United States), (iii) any other general creditors, (iv) subordinated creditors and (v) equity holders in order of preference.[34]

Interestingly, the FDIC controls the process of determining which claims will be recognized in the receivership.[35] Creditors and claimants must file an administrative claim with the FDIC, much like a proof of claim in a bankruptcy.[36]

The following chart demonstrates the allocation of the proceeds. Note in our example, only if the FDIC recovers the full 50 on the remaining assets will it recover its costs associated with the failure. And only if the recovery exceeds 50 will there be any funds available for general creditors.

	Recovery							
Claimant (Amount)	**10**	**20**	**30**	**40**	**50**	**60**	**70**	**80**
Uninsured Depositors (20)	4	8	12	16	20	20	20	20
FDIC (30)	6	12	18	24	30	30	30	30
Unsecured Creditors (20)	0	0	0	0	0	10	20	20
Equity Holders (remainder)	0	0	0	0	0	0	0	10

Note that our example is extremely simplified. The FDIC may provide some form of loss protection on the bad assets in order to induce the purchaser to acquire more of the

34 Federal Deposit Insurance Act § 11(d)(11), 12 U.S.C. 1821(d)(11).

35 Federal Deposit Insurance Act § 11(d)(4), 12 U.S.C. § 1821(d)(4).

36 Federal Deposit Insurance Act authorises the FDIC to conduct the claims process without any court supervision. Federal Deposit Insurance Act § 11(d)(13)(D), 12 U.S.C. § 1821(d)(13)(D). The FDIC's decision to disallow a claim is unreviewable by any court, but the validity of a claim is subject to de novo judicial consideration following completion of the administrative claims process. Federal Deposit Insurance Act § 11(d)(5)(E), (d)(6)(A), 12 U.S.C. § 1821(d)(5)(E), (d)(6)(A).

assets.[37] This may minimize its up front costs, but will likely result in payments to the acquirer as the losses in the assets are realized. The acquirer often elects to assume the uninsured deposits as well. There are special rules for certain types of assets, such as swaps, derivatives and other securities contracts,[38] and there are special rules that have the effect of limiting certain types of claims against the receivership.[39] Nonetheless, the example provides a reasonable illustration of the process.

The receivership process for these relatively straightforward organizations is quick and efficient. The FDIC will commence its process of evaluating the assets, selecting a preferred disposition strategy and contacting potential acquirers in advance of the failure.[40] In a typical transaction the bids will be submitted a week prior to the anticipated failure date, the bids will be opened on a Wednesday, the institution will be closed on a Friday afternoon, and the winning bidder must open the bank on Monday morning without interruption to the depositors and customers.

Some useful data points: Since the crisis began in the summer of 2008, the FDIC has closed approximately 400 banks.[41] The aggregate cost to the FDIC exceeds $75 billion. Of the failed banks, there has only been one where funds are currently available to general creditors; in every other failure the FDIC is anticipated to suffer a loss, meaning the recoveries on the assets will not exceed the amount of deposits of the failed institution. The Deposit Insurance Fund has plummeted from a positive $55 billion to a negative $8 billion, although it has substantial assets as a result of requiring banks to pre-pay three years of deposit insurance premiums, and will replenish itself through continued assessments on the banks.[42]

One of the critical points to remember regarding the bank resolution process is that it is designed to foster stability.[43] While general creditors and shareholders bear the losses of failure, insured depositors are always protected. Losses that would have otherwise been

---

37 FDIC Staff Presentation, The Failing Bank Marketing Process: Whole Bank Transactions and Loss Share Transactions (American Bankers Association, Sept. 2, 2009); FDIC Staff Presentation, Resolutions: The Process of Bidding on Distressed Banks in the New Millennium (July 18, 2008). These presentations are available from the FDIC. Davis Polk maintains copies on file.

38 Qualified financial contracts, including swap agreements, repurchase agreements, forward contracts, commodities contracts and securities contracts, etc., are a special class of contracts that receives preferential treatment in a receivership. In a receivership, counterparties have the right to exercise any contractual rights to terminate, liquidate, close out, net or resort to security agreements upon the appointment of the FDIC as receive, subject to one business day cooling-off period. Federal Deposit Insurance Act § 11(e)(8), 12 U.S.C. 1821(e)(8).

39 E.g., 12 U.S.C. 1821(e) allows the receiver to repudiate contacts it determines to be burdensome, and limits damages to actual, direct compensatory damages determined as of the date of the receivership, and excludes claims for lost profits, punitive or exemplary damages or damages for pain and suffering.

40 See generally FDIC Resolutions Handbook (2003).

41 See www.fdic.gov/bank/individual/failed/banklist.html. Data is as of September 9, 2011.

42 These statistics are available through the quarterly reports provided by the FDIC available at www.fdic.gov. See FDIC Quarterly Banking Profile (Third Quarter 2010), available at http://www2.fdic.gov/qbp/2010sep/qbp.pdf.

43 A useful history of the FDIC is found in Federal Deposit Insurance Corporation: The First 50 Years, published by the FDIC in 1984, available at http://www.fdic.gov/bank/analytical/firstfifty/.

borne by the insured depositors are absorbed by the FDIC, that in turn is funded by assessments on the banks. However, the risks of bank runs are minimized and there is little systemic instability as a result of the failure of a community banking organization in the United States.

The US Response to Systemically Important Financial Organizations

The bank receivership process outlined above did not apply to bank holding companies during the crisis, nor did it apply to securities firms, investment banks, asset management companies, insurance companies or other non-bank financial institutions. Such institutions, to the extent they become insolvent, are generally relegated to the Bankruptcy Code's liquidation or reorganization procedures, although insurance companies are subject to state-run liquidation schemes. As these organizations suffered during the crisis, a policy decision was made that bankruptcy was not an appropriate option (other than Lehman Brothers).[44] Instead, the government adopted a variety of measures designed to provide liquidity, equity support and other forms of assistance. The most important of these included:

- TARP.[45] Originally designed as a means whereby banks could sell troubled assets, it quickly evolved into a program where the Treasury purchased preferred stock in banking organizations. Each of the nine largest institutions was basically required to participate,[46] and approximately 400 other institutions of varying sizes also engaged in the program. All of the large institutions have repaid the TARP funds with interest. Several of the smaller institutions have failed or otherwise had to restructure their TARP capital in connection with recapitalizations; however, the TARP program will likely result in minimal costs to the government.

- FDIC Liquidity Support.[47] The FDIC raised the deposit insurance limit to $250,000 from $100,000 and provided unlimited insurance for low- and non-interest bearing transaction accounts. It also provided a guarantee for certain bank and bank holding company debt. The guarantee program proved to be both quite useful and quite prof-

---

44 See Too Big to Fail: The Role of Bankruptcy and Antitrust Law in Financial Regulation Reform: Hearing Before the Subcomm. on Commercial and Administrative law, H. Comm. on the Judiciary, 111th Cong. (2009) (testimony of Michael S. Barr, Assistant Secretary of the Treasury).

45 See Office of the Special Inspector General for the Troubled Asset Relief Program, Quarterly Report to Congress (October 26, 2010), available at http://www.sigtarp.gov/reports/congress/2010/October2010_Quarterly_Report_to_Congress.pdf. See also Financial Crisis Manual 41–104.

46 *Joe Weisenthal* Documents Reveal How Paulson Forced Banks to Take TARP Cash, Bus Insider, May 13, 2009, available at http://www.businessinsider.com/uncovered-tarp-docs-reveal-how paulson-forced-banks-to-take-the-cash-2009-5; see also *Joanna Ossinger* Report: Paulson Told Banks They Must Take TARP Money, Fox Bus., May 13, 2009, available at http://www.foxbusiness.com/story/report-paulson-told-banks-tarp-money/; For one version of the events leading up to the meeting where the regulators announced to the nine largest bank holding companies that they had no choice but to accept such capital, see *David Wessel* In Fed We Trust 236–241 (2009).

47 See Financial Crisis Manual 116–143. More information on the FDIC liquidity support programs is available at http://www.fdic.gov/regulations/resources/tlgp/index.html.

itable for the FDIC. There have been no defaults on the guaranteed debt, and the FDIC's charges substantially exceeded its administrative expenses.

- Federal Reserve Liquidity Support.[48] The Federal Reserve engaged in a variety of liquidity measures designed to provide funding to banks and other firms, including term funding, liquidity guarantees and support for money market mutual fund assets.
- For Bear Stearns, the Federal Reserve backstopped $30 billion in assets to facilitate the acquisition of Bear Stearns by JPMorgan Chase.[49]
- For Fannie Mae and Freddie Mac, the Treasury, through the Federal Housing Finance Agency, placed the institutions into conservatorship and under the control of the government,[50] and has provided over $150 billion of direct assistance to facilitate their continued operation.[51] There is little prospect of those funds being repaid. Indeed, the estimates are that the assistance required will ultimately exceed $400 billion.[52]
- For AIG, the Treasury purchased substantially all of the equity of AIG to facilitate its continued operation.[53] While the government has provided substantial assistance, it is likely that much of the assistance will be repaid.[54]
- For Citigroup, Treasury, the FDIC and Federal Reserve guaranteed a pool of assets, providing much needed capital relief to Citigroup.[55] Citigroup and the government have terminated the guarantee, and Citigroup has repaid the costs of the guarantee.[56]
- For Bank of America, in order to facilitate the acquisition of Merrill Lynch, the Treasury and the FDIC were prepared to guarantee a pool of assets. Ultimately Bank of America concluded not to accept the assistance.[57]

---

48 See Financial Crisis Manual 18–40. For a chart of the Federal Reserve's various emergency lending facilities, see Forms of Federal Reserve Lending to Financial Institutions (July 2009), available at http://www.ny.frb.org/markets/Forms_of_Fed_Lending.pdf.

49 See Financial Crisis Manual 24–27.

50 See Statement by Secretary *Henry M. Paulson, Jr.* on Treasury and Federal Housing Finance Agency Action to Protect Financial Markets and Taxpayers (September 7, 2008), available at http://www.ustreas.gov/press/releases/hp1129.htm. See also Press Release, Fed. Housing Fin. Agency, Fact Sheet: Questions and Answers on Conservatorship (Sept. 7, 2008).

51 See Data as of November 9, 2010 on Treasury and Federal Reserve Purchase Programs for GSE and Mortgage-Related Securities, available at http://www.fhfa.gov/webfiles/19475/TreasFED 11052010.pdf.

52 See The Future of Housing Finance: A Progress Update on the GSEs, Statement by *Edward J. DeMarco*, Acting Director, Federal Housing Finance Agency before the U.S. House of Representatives Subcommittee on Capital Markets, Insurance and Government-Sponsored Enterprises (September 15, 2010), available at http://www.fhfa.gov/webfiles/16726/DeMarcoTestimony 15Sept2010final.pdf.

53 Financial Crisis Manual 28–32.

54 See Press Release, U.S. Department of the Treasury, Treasury Update on AIG Investment Valuation (Nov. 1, 2010), https://ustreas.gov/press/releases/tg936.htm.

55 For more information on the Asset Guarantee Program, please visit http://www.financialst ability.gov/roadtostability/assetguaranteeprogram.htm.

56 The termination agreement is available at http://www.financialstability.gov/docs/Citi%20AGP %20Termination%20Agreement%20-%20Fully%20Executed%20Version.pdf

57 On September 21, 2009, Bank of America announced that it had reached an agreement with regulators to pay a $425 million fee to terminate guarantee program. Bank of America Press Re-

- For Citigroup, the Treasury and FDIC were prepared to guarantee a pool of assets to facilitate Citibank's acquisition of Wachovia Bank.[58] Ultimately that transaction was not concluded as Wells Fargo elected to purchase Wachovia without direct FDIC or Treasury assistance.[59]

These stabilization programs should generally be judged to be a success in spite of the political unpopularity. The major institutions survived, and other than Fannie Mae and Freddie Mac, have repaid the assistance and have resumed their roles within the financial system. The system itself survived. And while equity holders in these institutions generally saw a substantial diminution in value,[60] they remain owners and continue to participate in the profits of the enterprises in which they invested. Creditors were generally protected.

As noted, however, there was no assistance provided to Lehman Brothers. In spite of official denials that it lacked the authority to do so, it would appear that the same authority used to provide support to AIG could have been used for Lehman had the government been so inclined. Notwithstanding, Lehman was allowed to fail and to fall into bankruptcy proceedings. Many have pointed to the failure as a mistake, exacerbating the crisis.

The general response of the United States to support its large, systemically important institutions was repeated elsewhere.[61] Governments have become the largest shareholder of many large financial institutions, and to assure funding stability, have provided blanket guarantees to depositors and other creditors. These reactions are entirely understandable, for during a time of crisis, there is little appetite for inducing greater uncertainty into the financial system. And for better or worse, most of the supported institutions were in fact extremely important to the overall economies of the affected nations.

The costs of this support, however, have given rise to a substantial public outcry, and politically it has become imperative to find another way to deal with these systemically

---

lease, Bank of America Terminates Asset Guarantee Term Sheet (Sept. 21, 2009), available at http://newsroom.bankofamerica.com/index.php?s=43&item=8536. See also *Margaret Popper/ David Mildenberg* Bank of America to Pay $425 Million for Merrill Aid (Update 1), Bloomberg, Sept. 22, 2009, available at http://www.bloomberg.com/apps/news?pid=20601087&sid=a2c5hYE7Uv.Y.

58 Press Release, FDIC, Citigroup Inc. to Acquire Banking Operations of Wachovia: FDIC, Federal Reserve and Treasury Agree to Provide Open Bank Assistance to Protect Depositors (Sept. 29, 2008).

59 Wells Fargo Press Release, Wells Fargo's Merger with Wachovia to Proceed as Whole Company Transaction with All of Wachovia's Banking Operations (Oct. 9, 2008).

60 In Fannie Mae and Freddie Mac, the shareholders were essentially wiped out. On June 16, 2010, Fannie Mae and Freddie Mac were delisted from the New York Stock Exchange by an order from the Federal Housing Finance Agency. See Press Release, Federal Housing Finance Agency, FHFA Directs Delisting of Fannie Mae and Freddie Mac Stock from New York Stock Exchange (June 16, 2010).

61 See generally An Assessment of Financial Sector Rescue Programmes, Bank for International Settlements (July 2009), available at http://www.bis.org/publ/bppdf/bispap48.pdf?noframes=1; 79th Annual Report, Bank for International Settlements (June 29, 2009), available at http://www.bis.org/publ/arpdf/ar2009e.pdf?noframes=1.

important institutions without the overt use of public funds yet while still avoiding the uncertainties and attendant risks of bankruptcy.

The Dodd-Frank Response

The Dodd-Frank Wall Street Reform and Consumer Protection Act of 2010 represents the first major legislative attempt to address the problems associated with the potential failure of large, systemically important financial firms.[62] There are two underlying themes contained in Dodd-Frank. First, there is an effort to assure that these institutions do not fail in the first instance. Embodying this first theme are the new Financial Stability Oversight Council, designed to designate systemically important institutions, identify risks and mandate remedial action; higher capital standards; centralized clearing and reporting of swaps; a swaps "push-out" rule for larger banks; and the new "Volcker Rule" limiting proprietary trading and investing in hedge funds and private equity funds. Second, and relevant for this discussion, is the new orderly liquidation authority, providing for a non-bankruptcy resolution of systemically important institutions.[63]

Orderly liquidation authority ("OLA") is modeled on the FDIC receivership provisions discussed above. In order to be subject to OLA, the Secretary of the Treasury must make a series of determinations that liquidation under OLA will promote financial stability upon the recommendation of two-thirds of the governors of the Federal Reserve Board and two-thirds of the members of the FDIC board, after consultation with the President.[64] The very nature of this process indicates that the decision is as much a political decision as an economic or financial decision.

If the OLA procedures are invoked, tremendous pressure will be put on the affected institution to consent to OLA.[65] The board of directors is not liable if it acquiesces or consents to the appointment of the FDIC as receiver.[66] If the institution does not consent, the Secretary of the Treasury is empowered to seek a court order invoking the

---

62 Wall Street Reform and Consumer Protection Act of 2010, H.R. 4173, 111th Cong., 2st Sess. (hereinafter Dodd-Frank Act) (2010). For more information on the Dodd-Frank Act, see Davis Polk Client Memorandum, Summary of the Dodd-Frank Wall Street Reform and Consumer Protection Act, Enacted into Law on July 21, 2010 (July 21, 2010), available at http://www.davispolk.com/files/Publication/efb94428-9911-4472-b5dd-006e9c6185bb/Presentation/PublicationAttachment/efd835f6-2014-4a48-832d-00aa2a4e3fdd/070910_Financial_Reform_Summary.pdf.

63 Dodd-Frank Act, Title II (July 21, 2010).

64 If the financial company is a securities broker-dealer or its largest U.S. subsidiary is a securities broker-dealer, the designation must be approved by 2/3 of the Securities and Exchange Commission and 2/3 of the Federal Reserve Board, provided that the FDIC is consulted. If the financial company is an insurance company or its largest U.S. subsidiary is an insurance company, the designation must be approved by the Director of the new Federal Insurance Office and 2/3 of the Federal Reserve Board, provided that the FDIC is consulted. Dodd-Frank Act, § 203(a).

65 The Treasury Secretary is not required to obtain court authorization if the financial company's board of directors, or body performing similar functions, "acquiesces or consents" to the FDIC's appointment as receiver. Dodd-Frank Act, § 207. Because the statute protects directors against any liability for acquiescing or consenting to the FDIC's appointment in "good faith," it is likely that the Treasury Secretary will put intense pressure on boards to acquiesce or consent in order to avoid judicial review of the appointment decision.

66 Dodd-Frank Act, § 207.

procedure, and the court must rule on the petition within 24 hours.[67] If denied, the Secretary may appeal, but the appeal will not stay the effect of the process invoked.[68]

The FDIC will assume control of the institution, again assuming "all rights, titles, powers, and privileges of the covered financial company and its assets, and of any stockholder, member, officer, or director of such company."[69] The FDIC is instructed to engage in a liquidation of the enterprise, attempting to maximize its value and maintain stability within the financial system, yet still imposing the losses associated with the failure on equity holders and creditors.[70] The FDIC is empowered to transfer assets and liabilities to other entities or to a bridge company, notwithstanding contractual provisions to the contrary.[71] There is a special claims process, where claims of creditors are first considered by the FDIC in an administrative process,[72] and there are special rules for the treatment of swaps, derivatives and other securities contracts similar to that provided in the FDIC bank resolution statutes.[73] The FDIC has broad contract repudiation powers, and once again there are specific rules limiting damage claims against the institution.[74]

There was a general attempt to harmonize the treatment of creditor claims with that provided under the Bankruptcy Code. In most instances the drafters of the legislation did so, although there are important differences in creditor treatment remaining in the two regimes.[75] Notwithstanding, each creditor is entitled to at least the recovery it would have received had the institution been liquidated under Chapter 7 of the Bankruptcy Code.[76] As with the bank receivership powers, the resolution process is handled by the FDIC alone, and there are no provisions for creditors' committees. Likewise there is very little judicial oversight as the FDIC administers the process.

Losses are to be imposed on shareholders and creditors. To the extent public funds are required to facilitate the liquidation of a systemically important institution, the FDIC may borrow from the Treasury.[77] The FDIC is required, to the extent possible, to recover the advances from the creditors of the institution that received more than they would have received had the institution been liquidated.[78] To the extent it is unable to do so, it is required to recover the costs through assessments on the systemically important institutions.[79]

---

67 Dodd-Frank Act, § 202(a)(1)(A).
68 Dodd-Frank Act, § 202(a)(2).
69 Dodd-Frank Act, § 210(a)(1)(A).
70 Dodd-Frank Act, § 206.
71 Dodd-Frank Act, § 210(a)(1)(G).
72 Dodd-Frank Act, § 210(a)(2).
73 Dodd-Frank Act, § 210(c)(8).
74 Dodd-Frank Act, § 210(c)(1).
75 See Davis Polk Client Memorandum, Summary of the Dodd-Frank Wall Street Reform and Consumer Protection Act, Enacted into Law on July 21, 2010, 27–31, (July 21, 2010).
76 Dodd-Frank Act, §§ 210(a)(7), (b)(4), (d)(4) and (h)(5)(E).
77 Dodd-Frank Act, § 210(n).
78 Dodd-Frank Act, § 210(o).
79 Unlike federal deposit insurance, which is an ex-ante system, to the extent Treasury funds are expended in the orderly liquidation authority and not recouped from creditors, the assessment

An important aspect of Dodd-Frank is that many of the tools used to get the United States through the current crisis have been prohibited. The Federal Reserve cannot use its 13(3) authority to facilitate the sale of an institution like Bear Stearns to JPMorgan Chase, and may only use the powers in connection with a "program or facility with broad-based eligibility" and only after receiving approval from the Secretary of the Treasury.[80] The FDIC may not provide the type of asset guarantees that facilitated the survival of Citigroup.[81] Only broad based programs of general applicability are to be used, and then only with the concurrence of the Secretary of the Treasury, and the approval of two-thirds of both the FDIC board and the Federal Reserve Board.[82] Congress must provide a maximum amount of debt that can be guaranteed by joint resolution. These restrictions inject a political element into the decision-making process and limit the agencies from exercising the very important flexibility that allowed the systemically important firms to survive.

Concerns with the Dodd-Frank OLA

Dodd-Frank can properly be viewed as a series of political statements.[83] There are to be no more bailouts. Shareholders and creditors must suffer losses. Financial stability is best preserved by allowing the government to control the resolution process rather than entrusting it to a bankruptcy court. These principles will eliminate moral hazard, take away the funding advantages previously enjoyed by the larger institutions and impose greater discipline on institutions and their creditors. Notwithstanding the attractiveness of these statements, serious concerns surround OLA.

As a preliminary matter, there is uncertainty surrounding which institutions will be subject to OLA. The determination is made in part by administrative agencies with responsibilities for financial institutions and financial system stability, but at the end of the day it represents a political determination. There will be no pre-identified list of entities that would be handled under the OLA procedures.[84]

---

are ex-post. Congress adopted the ex-post system as a means of discouraging the use of a pool of funds to bail out creditors or shareholders in systemically important institutions.

80 Dodd-Frank Act, § 1101.

81 Until recently, the FDIC had the authority, under Section 13(c) of the Federal Deposit Insurance Act, to provide "open bank" assistance to troubled banks or thrifts to prevent them from failing or facilitating the resolution of a failed institutions, such as in the case of Citigroup. This authority was eliminated by the Dodd-Frank Act. Dodd-Frank Act, § 1106.

82 Dodd-Frank Act, §§ 1105–1106.

83 See e.g., Remarks by FDIC Chairman Sheila C. Bair, "Ending Too Big to Fail: The FDIC and Financial Reform," 2010 Glauber Lecture at the John F. Kennedy, Jr. Forum, Harvard University (Oct. 20, 2010).

84 Unlike almost any other statute, the OLA is not limited to a fixed category of persons, determinable in advance, such as all systemically important financial companies. Instead, it could apply to any "financial company" if certain determinations are made. Dodd-Frank Act, § 201(a)(11). The required determinations depend as much on general market conditions as they do on the systemic importance of a particular firm in a vacuum. The conditions for coverage are more likely to be found during a financial panic. They are less likely to be found during periods of relative calm.

Importantly, an institution need not be a bank or bank holding company, or even have been previously designated a "systemically important financial institution" under Dodd-Frank to be subject to OLA. The only requirement is that the company be predominantly engaged in financial activities and that the regulatory authorities make the proper determinations.[85] A company, and its creditors, may be quite surprised to find that rights and powers are dramatically different if it becomes subject to OLA.

There are also remaining discrepancies between treatment of creditors under the Bankruptcy Code insolvency proceedings and OLA.[86] These differences, however slight, will create uncertainties in creditors of large institutions. In a time of stress, when OLA is designed to provide systemic stability, these uncertainties may exacerbate funding difficulties, thus increasing the risks of necessary government intervention.

Importantly, the stated purpose of OLA is to impose losses on creditors. While there were certainly many causes of the current crisis, its primary manifestations were frozen credit markets and a lack of liquidity. In a time of crisis, explicit policies designed to punish creditors would seem to have the logical effect of drying up credit markets for these larger institutions. One can legitimately question the wisdom of tying the government's hands so tightly before a crisis.

Indeed, in October 2010 the FDIC promulgated proposed rules to implement OLA.[87] Those rules emphasized that equity holders, subordinated debt holders and long term creditors would never be transferred to a new institution following insolvency, but rather would be left behind in a receivership. The FDIC assured that these parties would ultimately receive no less than they would have received in a Chapter 7 liquidation of the company. However, it seems anomalous that in the context of attempting to resolve a large, systemically important institution the FDIC would wish to limit its options. Systemic problems in a crisis may demand flexible responses. And if creditors are going to be treated as if there were a bankruptcy, it is hard to see how many of the systemic liquidity issues will be avoided in a time of crisis.

The very nature of the OLA process would likely exacerbate these concerns. Unlike a bankruptcy procedure, where the process is public, under the supervision of a judge and here creditors may form committees to participate directly in the process and have their views considered, the resolution process of OLA is modeled on the FDIC's bank receivership process. There is little transparency. Claims are adjudicated administratively. Creditors and claimants generally await the FDIC's efforts to realize on the assets of the failed institution and are entitled only to distributions to the extent provided by law. There is little opportunity for creditors to influence or evaluate the FDIC's actions.

There is, of course, the substantial question of whether any governmental agency has the capacity to resolve a large, complex interconnected institution in a time of crisis. While there would be little other logical choice in the United States for a liquidation

85 Dodd-Frank Act § 203. And, of course, unless the company acquiesces, the courts must agree with the regulatory determinations. The judicial review process, however, is quite expedited, and the standard for review is quite limited. Dodd-Frank Act § 202.

86 See Davis Polk Client Memorandum, Summary of the Dodd-Frank Wall Street Reform and Consumer Protection Act, Enacted into Law on July 21, 2010, 27–31, (July 21, 2010).

87 75 Fed. Reg. 64173–64182 (October 19, 2010).

agency than the FDIC, in truth the FDIC has little experience with large complex institutions. The largest failure was the $400 billion Washington Mutual Bank, at its heart a relatively simple thrift institution engaged in the business of making residential mortgage loans. The FDIC handled Washington Mutual by transferring all of its assets and businesses to JPMorgan Chase.[88]

Further, the large, systemically important institutions generally have substantial international activities. There is no provision in Dodd-Frank that gives the FDIC authority to override the actions of regulators in other jurisdictions as they act to preserve and protect stability within their own countries.[89] While Dodd-Frank encourages international cooperation, there is no body with authority to mandate that cooperation.

At the same time, Dodd-Frank restricts the use of many of the tools used by the government to address systemic problems associated with liquidity crises in larger, systemically important institutions. The Federal Reserve's Section 13(3) authority to provide credit to non-banking institutions is substantially restricted.[90] The FDIC's asset guarantee and backstop programs for specific institutions are limited.[91] These tools were critical in facilitating transaction involving Bear Stearns, Merrill Lynch and in supporting Citigroup during some of the most critical moments in the crisis, all of which occurred without ultimate cost to the government. The government seems to have placed its faith in an untried and untested process, and tied its hands with respect to some of its most useful tools.

Thus while the bank resolution model works quite well with the relatively simple community banks and does an excellent job of imposing losses on creditors and equity holders, systemic stability is provided through the explicit protection of depositors. It is not clear how well this system will work with the larger, complex, interconnected institutions.

Other Alternatives

Certainly the goals of enhancing systemic stability while shifting losses associated with insolvencies are a laudable goal. To achieve these goals, there has been widespread interest in other mechanisms.

---

88 Press Release, FDIC, JPMorgan Chase Acquires Banking Operations of Washington Mutual: FDIC Facilitates Transaction that Protects All Depositors and Comes at No Cost to the Deposit Insurance Fund (Sept. 25, 2008); Purchase and Assumption Agreement Among FDIC, Receiver of Washington Mutual Bank, Henderson, NV, and JPMorgan Chase Bank, N.A. §§ 2.1, 3.1 (Sept. 25, 2008), available at http://www.fdic.gov/about/freedom/Washington_Mutual_P_and_A.pdf.

89 The Dodd-Frank OLA has only one sentence that deals with international coordination: "The Corporation, as receiver for a covered financial company, shall coordinate, to the maximum extent possible, with the appropriate foreign financial authorities regarding the orderly liquidation of any covered financial company that has assets or operations in a country other than the United States." Dodd-Frank Act, § 210(a)(1)(N).

90 Dodd-Frank Act, § 1101.

91 Dodd-Frank Act, §§ 1105–1106.

Some of the most intriguing proposals regard processes that would convert debt instruments in the capital structure to equity.[92] Contingent convertible capital, or so-called "co-co's," would be subordinated debt instruments that would be converted to common equity upon certain designated circumstances. These circumstances could include falling below certain designated capital levels or upon certain regulatory actions such as a determination of the need for additional capital. Defining those circumstances would appear to be a significant challenge; leaving the determination to the regulators would seem to inject a substantial degree of uncertainty into the instruments. It seems likely that holders of such instruments would demand a premium to compensate for the enhanced risk of becoming an equity holder. While certain holders may prefer becoming an equity holder rather than a creditor in an insolvency proceeding, it would seem that some might well prefer retaining a more senior position even in the event of insolvency.

The "bail-in" proposals would seem to present many of the same difficulties. In the bail-in concept, the regulator would have the unilateral power to convert debt to equity. There have been discussions with the FDIC as to whether the OLA provisions could be used to effect a bail-in regime through the resolution process. In essence, the assets of the institution would be transferred to a new bridge company. Short-term credit might be transferred to the new bridge, but the subordinated and long term debt might be given the equity of the new bridge company in exchange for some or all of their debt claims.

These debt-to-equity regimes may ultimately provide useful tools for dealing with larger institutions, but many unanswered questions remain. There remain the practical issues of whether the markets will support such instruments on a widespread basis and, if so, at what price? Would a conversion, voluntary or involuntary, trigger defaults in other instruments? Are there residual "takings" issues if done on an involuntary retroactive basis?

Summary, Conclusions and Questions

The potential failure of large, systemically important, interconnected financial institutions presents difficult public policy choices. Certainly it is important at many levels to have the equity holders and debt holders of those institutions suffer upon insolvency. However, the very nature of these institutions means that how the insolvencies are handled will affect systemic stability. No government will wish to destroy its economy

---

92 See, e.g., The Association for Financial Markets in Europe (AFME), The Systemic Safety Net: Pulling Failing Firms Back from the Edge (August 2010); British Bankers Association (BBA), Resolution and Unsecured Creditors (October 2010); *Suresh Sundaresan/Zhenyu Wang* Design of Contingent Capital with a Stock Price Trigger for Mandatory Conversion, Federal Reserve Bank of New York Staff Reports (June 2010); Squam Lake Working Group on Financial Regulation, An Expedited Resolution Mechanism for Distressed Financial Firms: Regulatory Hybrid Securities (April 2009); *Calello/Ervin* From Bail-out To Bail-in, The Economist (January 30, 2010); *Charles Plosser* Convertible Securities and Bankruptcy Reforms: Addressing Too Big to Fail and Reducing the Fragility of the Financial System, Speech at the Conference on the Squam Lake Report: Fixing the Financial System (June 16, 2010); *Jones/Klutsey/Christ* Speed Bankruptcy: A Firewall to Future Crises (January 10, 2010).

or financial system simply to make a point about how shareholders and creditors are treated.

The FDIC receivership procedures for banks have proven to be an effective and appropriate tool for addressing the insolvency of relatively simple financial institutions. One wonders, however, how well that model will translate in connection with the larger systemically important institutions.

There may well be no easy way out of this dilemma. Some institutions may well be too big to fail. However, they should not be too big to assure that equity holders and creditors suffer the consequences of insolvency. It is not clear that Dodd-Frank provides the final solution, and it is apparent that there remains much work to do.

Gläubigerschutz in einem Sonderinsolvenzrecht für Banken

*Christoph Thole**

Gliederung

I. Einleitung
II. Ziele des Sonderinsolvenzrechts
III. Verfahrensrechtlicher Gläubigerschutz
1. Antragstellung
2. Beteiligung bei Insolvenzverwalterauswahl
3. Reorganisationsverfahren und Rechtsschutzmöglichkeiten
4. Zwischenfazit
IV. Materieller Gläubigerschutz
1. Privilegierung von Zahlungsverkehrssystemen
2. Lösungs- und Beendigungsklauseln und Netting
3. Insolvenzanfechtung
a) Die Geltung der Anfechtung im Allgemeinen
b) Anfechtung bei Zahlungsverkehrssystemen
c) Anfechtung der Übertragung von Risikopositionen
4. Debt-Equity-Swap
5. Hoheitliche Übertragungsanordnungen
V. Grenzüberschreitungen
VI. Fazit

I. Einleitung

Das hier gewählte Thema hat jedenfalls als Querschnittsthema bisher kaum Beachtung gefunden, und zwar weder in der insolvenzrechtlichen Literatur noch, soweit ersichtlich, im Bankrecht. Offenbar herrscht im Bankrecht der Eindruck vor, die Instituts- und die Einlagensicherung würden Fragen des Gläubigerschutzes in der Bankeninsolvenz apriorisch erledigen. Das ist zweifellos nicht der Fall, wenn man sich den begrenzten praktischen wie rechtlichen Anwendungsbereich der Sicherungssysteme vor Augen führt. Umgekehrt hat sich die Insolvenzrechtswissenschaft den spezifischen Fragen der Bankeninsolvenz kaum gewidmet. Die spezielle Frage des Gläubigerschutzes ist also eine Frage, bei der wir auf weitgehend unbestelltem Terrain wandern; allgemeine Prinzipien und Leitlinien für die Ausgestaltung des Gläubigerschutzes in einem Sonderin-

* Die Vortragsform wurde beibehalten.

solvenzrecht für Banken sind bisher nicht entwickelt. Die folgenden Überlegungen können daher nur vorläufiger Natur sein. Die weitere Diskussion bleibt abzuwarten.

Wenn man sich über Gläubigerschutz im Sonderinsolvenzrecht verständigen will, muss man sich zunächst darüber klar werden, wie der Begriff des Sonderinsolvenzrechts überhaupt belegt ist. Das ist nicht nur eine begriffliche Klarstellung, sondern eine elementare Grundlegung im Hinblick auf die jeweils anzulegenden Wertungsprinzipien. So stellt anerkanntermaßen erst die Eröffnung des Insolvenzverfahrens die entscheidende Zäsur dar, bei deren Eintritt der Schuldner zwingend seiner eigenständigen Verwaltungs- und Verfügungsbefugnis zu entledigen ist. Der Grundsatz der Gläubigergleichbehandlung, der das Insolvenzverfahren beherrscht, ist grundsätzlich – auf Vorwirkungen wie beispielsweise bei der Insolvenzanfechtung komme ich noch zu sprechen – erst im eröffneten Insolvenzverfahren oder jedenfalls nicht vor Eintritt der Insolvenzreife beachtlich und nicht schon in einem diesem Zeitpunkt vorgelagerten Stadium.

Wenn man indessen die gegenwärtige Diskussion recht überblickt, wird der Begriff des Insolvenzrechts im Kontext des hiesigen Themas meist sehr weit verstanden. Mit ihm wird nicht nur das förmliche Insolvenzverfahren nach Maßgabe der InsO verbunden, das innerhalb *eines einheitlichen Verfahrens* nach Eintritt der Zahlungsunfähigkeit oder Überschuldung[1] entweder auf Liquidation oder eine Sanierung des Schuldners hinauslaufen kann.

Mit dem Hinweis auf das Insolvenzrecht oder Sonderinsolvenzrecht der Banken wird vielmehr auch die Diskussion um ein dem Insolvenzverfahren vorgeschaltetes Reorganisationsverfahren (*bank resolution*) erfasst, das mit dem Restrukturierungsgesetz vom 28. 10. 2010 nunmehr in Gesetzesform gegossen worden ist.[2] Dieses Verfahren ist zwar an das Insolvenzplanverfahren angelehnt. In der Sache zielt es aber gerade auf die Vermeidung eines Insolvenzverfahrens, also eine vorinsolvenzliche Sanierung, und vielleicht auch – etwas ketzerisch formuliert – vor allem auf die Vermeidung des bösen Wortes „Insolvenzverfahren“. Wenn wir also von Sanierung und Restrukturierung im Insolvenzrecht sprechen, kann damit entweder die Sanierung im Insolvenzverfahren, namentlich im Insolvenzplanverfahren, gemeint sein oder eine „freie“ Sanierung zur Insolvenzvermeidung oder aber ein vorinsolvenzliches Reorganisationsverfahren, wie es im RestrukturierungsG vorgesehen ist.

Darüber hinaus werden mit dem Begriff des Bankeninsolvenzrechts häufig auch das Aufsichtsrecht und namentlich die Eingriffsbefugnisse der BaFin nach §§ 45 ff. KWG verknüpft.[3] Diese Aufsichtsbefugnisse können beispielsweise, wiederum vor Eintritt von Zahlungsunfähigkeit und Überschuldung, zu einem Moratorium und damit zu

1 Vgl. allerdings die Möglichkeit des Eigenantrags bei drohender Zahlungsunfähigkeit bzw. durch die BaFin mit Zustimmung des Instituts, § 46 a Abs. 1 S. 5 KWG.

2 BGBl. I 2010, 1900.

3 Umfassend *Pannen* Krise und Insolvenz bei Kreditinstituten, 3. Aufl. 2010, Kap. 1, S. 6 ff.; aus dem neueren Schrifttum *Linden* ZInsO 2008, 583; *Grabau/Hundt* DZWIR 2003, 275; *Weber* ZInsO 2009, 628; *Ruzik* BKR 2009, 133; zur Insolvenz von Schuldverschreibungsemittenten *Delhaes* FS Metzeler, 2003, S. 39.

einem weitgehenden Verlust der Verwaltungs- und Verfügungsbefugnis des Kreditinstituts führen.

Wenn man aber dies alles mit in den Begriff des Sonderinsolvenzrechts einbezieht, also darunter ein irgendwie geartetes Verfahren versteht, das bereits an eine Krise anknüpft, ohne dass ein förmlicher Insolvenzgrund gegeben sein muss, dann kann die Frage dieser Tagung eigentlich schon beantwortet werden; denn es bedarf dann keines Sonderinsolvenzrechts, sondern es besteht schon eines. Demnach wird Insolvenzrecht im Rahmen der Bankeninsolvenz erweiternd verstanden.[4]

Nun muss und kann man indessen über die Frage streiten, ob dieses Sonderinsolvenzrecht ausgedehnt und stärker verselbständigt werden soll. Das erscheint im Grundsatz richtig: Banken sind anders. Um ein Problem kommt man dabei indessen nicht herum. Damit ist die Abstimmung mit dem allgemeinen Insolvenzrecht und dessen Wertungsprinzipien, und insbesondere mit dem Ziel des Gläubigerschutzes angesprochen, das das kollektive Haftungsverwirklichungsverfahren prägt. Dieser „insolvenzrechtliche" Blickwinkel soll im Folgenden dominieren. Das Ziel des Gläubigerschutzes kann auf drei Ebenen relevant werden: einmal bei der Formulierung eines übergeordneten Ziels des Sonderinsolvenzrechts, zweitens im Hinblick auf die verfahrensrechtliche Stellung von Gläubigern und drittens auf materiell-rechtlicher Ebene bei der Ausgestaltung des Inhalts des Sonderinsolvenzrechts im Einzelnen.

Dabei ist stets im Blick zu halten, dass ein umfassendes Sonderinsolvenzrecht für Banken sowohl das echte, förmliche Insolvenzverfahren als auch das – aus bankrechtlicher Sicht stärker diskutierte – Sanierungs- und Reorganisationsverfahren (*bank resolution*) im Blick behalten muss; daher sollen die folgenden Überlegungen auch beide Verfahrensarten einbeziehen.

II. Ziele des Sonderinsolvenzrechts

Wenn wir von Gläubigerschutz sprechen, so muss es zunächst darum gehen, den Stellenwert dieses Schutzzwecks zu verdeutlichen. Ist Gläubigerschutz nur ein Aspekt unter vielen oder ist es der primäre Zweck des Verfahrens?

In dem Papier der Europäischen Kommission über einen EU-Rahmen für das grenzüberschreitende Krisenmanagement auf dem Banksektor, das Ende 2009 veröffentlicht wurde, wird beispielsweise die Möglichkeit in Betracht gezogen, dass in einem Sonderinsolvenzrecht auch andere Ziele als die Gläubigerbefriedigung Priorität genießen könnten, wie etwa fiskalische und öffentliche Interessen.[5] In der Tat ist auch in der deutschen Reformdiskussion angemahnt worden, statt des Gläubigerschutzes den Schutz vor systemischen Risiken in den Vordergrund zu stellen.[6] Obwohl die systemischen Gefahren in der Tat Beachtung finden müssen, sehe ich gleichwohl eine Öffnung

4 Vgl. auch ausdrücklich *Flessner* ÖBA 2010, 655, 656 f.

5 Mitteilung der Kommission: „Ein EU-Rahmen für das grenzübergreifende Krisenmanagement auf dem Banksektor", vom 20. 10. 2009, KOM (2009) 561 endg., Abs. 4.2.

6 *Hellwig* Gutachten zum 68. DJT, 2010, S. E 53 f.

des Insolvenzrechts für fiskalische, politische und letztlich außerrechtliche Interessen mit einer gewissen Sorge, weil damit die *floodgates* auch mit Blick auf die Ziele des allgemeinen Insolvenzrechts zu weit aufgestoßen werden könnten. Man sollte sich vergegenwärtigen, dass die Gläubigerbefriedigung in der Tat das primäre Ziel eines Insolvenzverfahrens und eines Insolvenzrechts sein muss. § 1 S. 1 InsO erhebt die gemeinschaftliche Befriedigung der Gläubiger zum Verfahrenszweck. Das ist die klassische exekutorische Funktion des Konkurses: Das Insolvenzverfahrensrecht stellt sich als ein Recht der Vermögenshaftung dar, das die Aufgabe wahrnimmt, zugunsten der Gläubiger die Haftung des Schuldners zu verwirklichen.[7] Eine individuelle Rechtsverfolgung muss dem Kollektivverfahren weichen. Die rechtspolitische Aufgabe ist es, das Insolvenzrecht so auszugestalten und zu praktizieren, dass das Schuldnervermögen den Gläubigern den höchsten Ertrag einbringt.[8]

Die kollektive Haftungsverwirklichung zugunsten der Gläubiger muss also im Vordergrund stehen; das, was sonst durch Einzelzwangsvollstreckung erreicht wird, soll das Insolvenzverfahren durch Gesamtvollstreckung erreichen. Es ist daher beispielsweise erfreulich, dass auch das BMJ in seinem jüngsten Regierungsentwurf eines Gesetzes zur weiteren Erleichterung der Sanierung von Unternehmen vom 23. 2. 2011 an dem Hauptzweck der bestmöglichen Befriedigung der Gläubiger festhält.[9] Das gilt für die Bankeninsolvenz nicht minder. Eine Sanierung um jeden Preis muss und sollte es nicht geben. Unwirtschaftliche Unternehmen sollen vom Markt genommen werden. Die Filterfunktion des Insolvenzrechts, die durch Abschottung insolventer Unternehmen vom Markt – im Sinne des großen Ökonomen Joseph Schumpeter[10] – eine schöpferische Zerstörung offenlegt, gilt es zu bewahren.[11]

Das heißt nicht, dass sich das Insolvenzrecht, insbesondere ein Sonderinsolvenzrecht für Banken, gegenüber öffentlichen und Gemeinwohlinteressen blind stellen sollte. Selbstverständlich ist gerade bei systemrelevanten Banken die Vermeidung eines Zusammenbruchs häufig eine vorzugswürdige Strategie, um in der Summe größere Nachteile für alle Verkehrsteilnehmer zu vermeiden. Die volkswirtschaftliche Dimension eines Zusammenbruchs ist ungleich größer und damit das Sanierungsinteresse höher. Zudem mag man die Vorwirkungen des Schutzzweckes des Gläubigerschutzes für umso geringer halten, je weiter vor der eigentlichen Insolvenzreife ein Bankeninsolvenzrecht (im oben skizzierten weit verstandenen Sinne) ansetzt. Nur muss die Sanierung des Kreditinstituts jedenfalls nach Eintritt in das Insolvenzverfahren unter dem Postulat der Gläubigerbefriedigung stehen. Das gilt gleichermaßen für das Reorganisationsverfahren, jedenfalls soweit man es gewissermaßen bewusst als äquivalentes Surrogat an die Stelle des Insolvenzplanverfahrens setzt und es an einen finanzwirtschaftlichen Zustand des Kreditinstituts anknüpft, der eigentlich eine Insolvenzeröff-

---

7 Dazu *Thole* Gläubigerschutz durch Insolvenzrecht, 2010, S. 51 ff.

8 *Thole* Gläubigerschutz durch Insolvenzrecht, 2010, S. 52 m.N.

9 Veröffentlicht unter www.bmj.de/SharedDocs/Downloads/DE/pdfs/RegE_ESUG_23022011.pdf?_blob=publicationFile, hier S. 25.

10 *Schumpeter* Kapitalismus, Sozialismus und Demokratie (Capitalism, Socialism and Democracy, Harper & Brothers, New York, 1942), hier 5. Aufl., 1950, 134 ff.; vgl. *ders.* Theorie der wirtschaftlichen Entwicklung, 6. Aufl., 1952, 318 ff.

11 *Eidenmüller* ZIP 2010, 649, 650.

nung erlauben würde. Wenn, und nur wenn es für die Gläubiger vorteilhaft ist zu sanieren, ist dieser Weg zu beschreiten.

Es geht mir also um die grundlegende Zielrichtung, die auch in einem Insolvenzverfahren über das Vermögen einer Bank beachtlich bleiben sollte. Der Schutz zielt auf die Gläubiger ab. Einen Erhalt des Bankinstituts als solches muss es nicht zwingend geben, wenn sich systemrelevante Risiken anders abfedern lassen. Dieser Schutzzweck prägt die Auslegung der Gesetzesinhalte und -instrumente.[12]

Eine zweite vorweg zu schaltende Überlegung muss dem Grundsatz der Gläubigergleichbehandlung gelten (par conditio creditorum). Dieser Grundsatz prägt jede herkömmliche Insolvenzordnung. Nur gesicherte Gläubiger werden bevorrechtigt, die ungesicherten, einfachen Gläubiger müssen sich das knappe Vermögen des Schuldners teilen. Das par conditio-Prinzip muss spätestens dann eingreifen, wenn der Schuldner sich in einem förmlichen Insolvenzverfahren befindet und überschuldet oder zahlungsunfähig ist, weil dann die Gläubiger um die knappen Ressourcen des Schuldners konkurrieren.[13]

In einem diesem Stadium vorgelagerten Sanierungsverfahren müsste der Grundsatz indessen noch nicht seine volle Wirkung entfalten, solange man dieses Verfahren nicht als echtes Surrogat zum Insolvenzverfahren versteht. In jedem Fall sollte das Prinzip aber nicht leichtfertig überspielt werden, wie es beispielsweise durch die soeben erfolgte partielle Wiedereinführung des sogenannten Fiskusprivilegs in das Insolvenzrecht geschehen ist.[14] Die Gläubigergleichbehandlung hat Vorteile: Sie gewährleistet eine geordnete Abwicklung und verhindert eine Zerfledderung der Masse durch Zugriff einzelner Gläubiger.[15] Daher gilt es auch in einem Sonderinsolvenzrecht die Gläubigergleichbehandlung möglichst durchzuhalten. Ungleichbehandlungen von Gläubigern und Eingriffe in Rechte einzelner Gläubiger- oder Gläubigergruppen müssen stets sachlich begründet sein und sie sollten zugleich auch verfahrensmäßig durch entsprechende Beteiligungen abgesichert sein.

III. Verfahrensrechtlicher Gläubigerschutz

Damit bin ich auch schon bei den zwei Säulen, auf denen ein Gläubigerschutz in einem Sonderinsolvenzrecht für Banken aufbauen kann. Angesprochen werden müssen zum einen die verfahrensrechtliche Beteiligung der Gläubiger, und zum anderen der „materielle" Gläubigerschutz. Ich werde diese Punkte im Folgenden abarbeiten, und dabei jeweils versuchen zu ermitteln, ob Besonderheiten des Bankwesens zu Abweichungen von allgemeinen Regeln zwingen.

---

12 *Pawlowski* DZWIR 2001, 45.

13 *Thole* Gläubigerschutz durch Insolvenzrecht, 2010, S. 61.

14 Vgl. die Änderungen durch das HBeglG 2011; BGBl. I, 2010, 1885.

15 *Thole* Gläubigerschutz durch Insolvenzrecht, 2010, S. 61 m. zahlr. Nachw.

1. Antragstellung

Der verfahrensrechtliche Gläubigerschutz setzt zunächst bei der Einleitung des Verfahrens an. Im allgemeinen Insolvenzrecht steht das Recht, die Eröffnung des Insolvenzverfahrens zu beantragen, mit Recht neben dem Schuldner auch dem Gläubiger zu. Das Kollektivverfahren ist für ihn eine Fortsetzung der Zwangsvollstreckung mit anderen Mitteln. Obwohl natürlich die Beantragung eines Insolvenzverfahrens für den Gläubiger in praktischer Hinsicht ein zweischneidiges Schwert ist, darf man dem Gläubiger das Recht zur Antragstellung nicht einfach aus der Hand schlagen.

Im Bereich der Bankeninsolvenz ist ein Antragsrecht der Gläubiger natürlich mit offenkundigen Schwierigkeiten befrachtet. Der Domino-Effekt eines im Ergebnis vielleicht unbegründeten Insolvenzantrags kann sich verheerend auswirken. Es ist daher gerechtfertigt und erscheint plausibel, wenn das Gesetz in § 46b Abs. 1 S. 4 KWG das Recht zur Antragstellung allein auf die BaFin überträgt, die zur Verhinderung von Angstreaktionen immer auch das Systemvertrauen der Allgemeinheit sowie die hohe Nervosität im Interbankengeschäft im Blick behalten kann.[16] Die BaFin wird die Verfahrenseröffnung im Rahmen ihrer Ermessensentscheidung vor allem beantragen, wenn die Maßnahmen im Rahmen des Moratoriums keinen Erfolg gehabt haben.

An diesem alleinigen Antragsrecht der BaFin sollte man im Ergebnis festhalten, um die nachteiligen und unkontrollierbaren Folgen eines Gläubigerantrags zu vermeiden; und aus dem gleichem Grund ist mit Recht auch im Restrukturierungsgesetz für das Reorganisationsverfahren kein Antragsrecht der Gläubiger vorgesehen.[17] Man muss sich nur darüber verständigen, dass die BaFin insoweit auch in einer Treuhänder-Funktion tätig wird. Das Antragsrecht der BaFin für das echte Insolvenzverfahren ersetzt die nach allgemeinem Insolvenzrecht und im Übrigen nach Verfassungsrecht (Recht auf effektiven Rechtsschutz) geforderte Antragsberechtigung der einzelnen Gläubiger. Das ist eine wichtige Erkenntnis. Sie hat Bedeutung für die Frage, ob einzelne Gläubiger von der BaFin die Beantragung des Insolvenzverfahrens verlangen können, wenn die BaFin davon ausnahmsweise einmal nach gescheitertem Moratorium absehen wollte. Hier war die Literatur bisher eher zurückhaltend und hat offenbar angenommen, dass man die BaFin nicht im Wege des Verpflichtungsantrags zur Stellung des Antrags zwingen könne.[18] M.E. ist das so nicht haltbar. Man wird – wiederum der Filterfunktion des Insolvenzverfahrens Rechnung tragend – annehmen können, dass die BaFin im Interesse der Gläubiger ggf. klageweise zur Antragstellung verpflichtet werden kann, wenn alle Sanierungsbemühungen gescheitert sind.[19]

16 *Flessner* ÖBA 2010, 655, 658.

17 Vgl. auch *Flessner* ÖBA 2010, 655, 657.

18 Zur Diskussion *Stürner* Die Sicherung der Pfandbrief- und Obligationengläubiger vor einer Insolvenz der Hypothekenbank, 1998, S. 39; *Binder* Bankeninsolvenzen im Spannungsfeld zwischen Bankaufsichts- und Insolvenzrecht, S. 577.

19 *Stürner* Die Sicherung der Pfandbrief- und Obligationengläubiger vor einer Insolvenz der Hypothekenbank, 1998, S. 40.

2. Beteiligung bei Insolvenzverwalterauswahl

Der Schutz der Gläubigerinteressen muss sich darüber hinaus bei der Auswahl des Insolvenzverwalters niederschlagen, soweit es um ein förmliches Insolvenzverfahren nach Eintritt von Zahlungsunfähigkeit und Überschuldung geht. Nochmals: Bei Vorliegen dieser Insolvenzgründe muss der Zweck der Gläubigerbefriedigung das Ruder übernehmen, und der werbende Zweck des Schuldners umschlagen in den Zweck, die Gläubiger bestmöglich zu befriedigen, sei es durch Sanierung, sei es durch Liquidation. Nun ist allerdings die Auswahl des Insolvenzverwalters häufig gar nicht in die Hände der Gläubiger gelegt. Nach deutschem Insolvenzrecht bestellt zunächst das Insolvenzgericht den ihm als geeignet erscheinenden Kandidaten; die Gläubiger dürfen erst in der Gläubigerversammlung einen anderen Insolvenzverwalter wählen (§ 57 InsO). Doch dann ist es häufig zu spät, um mit dem Wechsel des Verwalters noch etwas bewirken zu können. Der Gläubigereinfluss ist also bisher gering.

Was darüber hinaus das Restrukturierungsgesetz angeht, so ist für das Sanierungsverfahren vorgesehen, dass der Schuldner, d. h. das Kreditinstitut selbst, einen Sanierungsberater vorschlagen darf, der dann grundsätzlich vom Gericht zu bestellen ist (§ 2 Abs. 2, § 3 Abs. 1 RestruktG); auch insoweit besteht kein rechtlich bindender Gläubigereinfluss.

In diesem Fall einer Sanierung vor dem Insolvenzverfahren mag man das noch für unschädlich erachten. Hier geht es ja zunächst zu Beginn weniger um ein echtes Haftungsverwirklichungsverfahren als vielmehr um ein vorgeschaltetes Sanierungsverfahren auf Eigeninitiative des Schuldners.

Demgegenüber ist der fehlende Gläubigereinfluss im echten Insolvenzverfahren mehr als misslich. Das Problem stellt sich indessen nicht nur in der Bankeninsolvenz, sondern berührt ein allgemeines Problem des Insolvenzverfahrens, das schon lange in der rechtspolitischen Diskussion ist.[20] Jedenfalls insoweit besteht kein Bedarf für von den allgemeinen Prinzipien abweichende Regeln im Bankinsolvenzrecht. Mittlerweile liegen einige Vorschläge auf dem Tisch, nach denen die Auswahl der Verwalter reformiert und den Gläubigern bereits in einem früheren Stadium ein Mitspracherecht eingeräumt werden soll.[21] Die Schwierigkeiten liegen hier vor allem in der praktischen Abwicklung und der Eilbedürftigkeit. Ohne dass ich hier auf Details eingehen kann, so sollte hier jedenfalls auch mit Blick auf Bankeninsolvenzen die allgemeine Insolvenzentwicklung abgewartet werden. Darüber hinaus mag es ein gangbarer Weg sein, ähnlich wie bei der Verfahrenseinleitung auch der BaFin ein mit Großgläubigern abgestimmtes Vorschlagsrecht einzuräumen, das sozusagen an die Stelle von Vorschlagsrechten einzelner Gläubiger tritt.

3. Reorganisationsverfahren und Rechtsschutzmöglichkeiten

Ein weiterer wichtiger Problembereich des Gläubigerschutzes betrifft die Beteiligung der Gläubiger im Insolvenzverfahren selbst.

---

20 Vgl. z. B. die Empfehlungen der Uhlenbruck-Kommission, ZIP 2007, 1432.

21 Fn. 20; ferner das Detmolder Modell, *Busch* DZWIR 2004, 252. Zum Ganzen jetzt auch § 56 InsO-RegE im Entwurf des ESUG (Fn. 9).

Hier geht es vor allem um die Möglichkeiten von Gläubigern, auf die Verwertungsentscheidung Einfluss zu nehmen. Insoweit dürften jedenfalls bei den Verfahren, in denen eine Sanierung nicht mehr in Betracht kommt, die allgemeinen insolvenzrechtlichen Beteiligungsmöglichkeiten ausreichen und keine Abweichungen erforderlich machen. Über ihr Stimmrecht in der Gläubigerversammlung und über den Gläubigerausschuss wirken die Gläubiger auf die Entscheidungen im Verfahren ein.

Problematisch ist allein die Beteiligung der Gläubiger im Insolvenzplanverfahren, und in dem neu eingeführten Reorganisationsverfahren. Hier geht es vor allem um das Gruppenprinzip bei der Abstimmung über den Plan und damit verbunden auch um die letztlich materiell-rechtliche Frage, inwieweit durch einen solchen Sanierungsplan in die Rechte der Gläubiger eingegriffen werden kann. Insgesamt ist ein Insolvenzplanverfahren als privatautonome Gestaltung gerade sinnvoll und mit dem Schutzzweck der Gläubigerbefriedigung vereinbar. Die Gefahren liegen nicht so sehr in der Missachtung der Gläubigerbelange durch den Schuldner als vielmehr in der Konkurrenzsituation der Gläubiger untereinander, die unterschiedliche Interessen haben können. Der Grundsatz der Gleichbehandlung muss auch insoweit berücksichtigt werden, was allerdings im geltenden Insolvenzrecht geschieht, weil innerhalb der verschiedenen Gläubigergruppen jeweils keiner bevorzugt werden darf, sofern sich nicht alle Beteiligten besser stellen als ohne den Plan. Zudem ist in jeder Gruppe von Gläubigern die Kopf- und Summenmehrheit zur Annahme des Plans erforderlich, was mir als ein tauglicher Kompromiss erscheint.

Das bisher geltende Insolvenzplanverfahren leidet stattdessen vor allem daran, dass recht große Obstruktionsmöglichkeiten bestehen und dass der Plan erst ab rechtskräftiger Bestätigung durch das Gericht Wirkungen entfaltet. Minderheiten können sich beispielsweise auch dann noch auf § 251 InsO und die dort verankerte Prüfung nach einer Schlechterstellung im Vergleich mit einer hypothetischen Lage ohne Plan berufen, wenn sie im Abstimmungstermin nur unsubstantiiert widersprochen haben. Dazu kommt vor allem das Blockadepotential von Altgesellschaftern, das nicht nur einen Debt-Equity-Swap, sondern auch eine sonstige Übertragung von unveräußerlichen Rechten an einen Investor unmöglich machen kann;[22] hier drückt der Schuh offenbar am meisten.

Die Mängel des Insolvenzplanverfahrens haben neben anderen dazu geführt, dass das Insolvenzplanverfahren als schwerfällig gilt und bisher kaum genutzt worden ist. Allerdings sind Reformbestrebungen im Gange. Der Regierungsentwurf des Gesetzes „zur weiteren Erleichterung der Sanierung von Unternehmen" will die Rechtsschutzmöglichkeiten reduzieren und Möglichkeiten eines Debt-Equity-Swaps einführen, der in den letzten Jahren auch unter deutschem Recht an Bedeutung gewonnen hat;[23] der Minderheitenschutz wird davon abhängig gemacht, dass Einwände bereits im Abstimmungstermin glaubhaft geltend gemacht werden.[24]

Da das Reorganisationsverfahren des Restrukturierungsgesetzes dem Insolvenzplanverfahren nachgebildet ist, sollte es die Mängel des Insolvenzplanverfahrens möglichst

22 Näher *Eidenmüller* ZIP 2010, 649 ff.; *ders.* Finanzkrise, Wirtschaftskrise und das deutsche Insolvenzrecht, 2009, S. 35 ff.

23 Zu den Gründen hierfür *Ekkenga* ZGR 2009, 581, 587.

24 § 251 Abs. 2 InsO-RegE.

vermeiden. In der Tat will das RestruktG die Rechtsschutzmöglichkeiten begrenzen.[25] Zugleich wird in § 12 der Eingriff in Gläubigerrechte ausdrücklich zugelassen, indessen anders als nach allgemeinem Insolvenzrecht davon abhängig gemacht, dass schon im darstellenden Teil des Insolvenzplans deutlich gemacht wird, wie dieser Eingriff (durch Stundung, Kürzung etc.) aussehen soll.

Wenn ich die materiell-rechtliche Seite zunächst außen vor lasse, so scheinen mir hier insgesamt drei Gesichtspunkte der Erwähnung wert:

1. Der erste betrifft die Beschränkung der Rechtsschutzmöglichkeiten. Insgesamt halte ich insoweit eine maßvolle Reduktion von Rechtsschutzmöglichkeiten für vertretbar. Die zunehmende Verrechtlichung in alle Richtungen und auch im hier relevanten Bereich hat zwar ihre Meriten, aber die wirtschaftlichen Zwänge und die Eilbedürftigkeit dürfen nicht unberücksichtigt bleiben. Darüber hinaus ist zu berücksichtigen, dass die Forderungen der Gläubiger bereits durch die Krise des Instituts erheblich entwertet sind, so dass vor diesem Hintergrund ein Zurücktreten der Belange der Gläubiger in verfahrensrechtlicher Hinsicht insoweit vertretbar erscheint. Die größeren Schwierigkeiten liegen beim Blockadepotential der Altgesellschafter, deren Schutzbedürftigkeit indessen noch viel geringer ausfällt. Ist der Gesellschaftsanteil entwertet und die Gläubigerbefriedigung gefährdet, müssen sich die Gesellschafter/Anteilseigner dem Postulat der Gläubigerbefriedigung beugen. Eingriffe in die Rechte der Gesellschafter erscheinen daher – entgegen den Unkenrufen von der vermeintlichen Enteignung – allemal gerechtfertigt.

2. Eine zweite Bemerkung betrifft die Abstimmungserfordernisse. Insoweit denke ich, dass die geltenden Mehrheitserfordernisse in der Sache wohlbegründet sind: Kopf- und Summenmehrheit und die Unterscheidung nach den verschiedenen Gruppen von Gläubigern, also namentlich zwischen absonderungsberechtigten und Insolvenzgläubigern. Das ist ein plausibler Kompromiss, der einer Übervorteilung einzelner Gläubiger vorsorgt, aber zugleich dem wirtschaftlich stärker exponierten Gläubiger ein größeres Stimmrecht einräumt.

3. Die dritte Bemerkung ist grundsätzlicher und rechtspolitischer Natur. Es bleibt natürlich bei allem die Frage, ob man zwingend ein eigenes Restrukturierungsverfahren braucht, wie es das Restrukturierungsgesetz nunmehr vorsieht. Es ist nicht Aufgabe dieses Referats, die Frage abschließend zu beleuchten. Notwendig ist nur der Hinweis, dass mit einem Quasi-Insolvenzplanverfahren für Banken im Grunde die Einheitlichkeit des Insolvenzverfahrens aufgegeben wird. Bisher galt ja für das Bankenwesen auch die übliche Vorgehensweise, dass noch bzw. erst im Insolvenzverfahren über Sanierung oder Liquidation bzw. übertragende Sanierung entschieden wird. Dieses Modell gibt man, wie bereits eingangs angedeutet, partiell auf, wenn man das Reorganisationsverfahren gleichsam vorgeschaltet an die Stelle des Insolvenzplanverfahrens setzt. Es besteht dann die Gefahr, dass sich die Maßstäbe von Reorganisationsverfahren einerseits und Insolvenzplanverfahren andererseits auseinanderentwickeln, vor allem, wenn über streitige Rechtsfragen beim BGH nicht der IX. Zivilsenat, sondern der Bankensenat, also der XI. Senat zuständig sein würde. Andererseits kann man sagen, dass mit den Maßnahmen nach KWG schon

25 Vgl. u. a. § 1 Abs. 3 RestruktG.

bisher eine gewisse Verselbständigung des Bankeninsolvenzrechts erreicht wurde, die dann nur fortgesetzt würde. Diese Frage bleibt also auf der Agenda.

4. Zwischenfazit

Damit komme ich zu einem Zwischenfazit:

Der Gläubigerschutz und der Gedanke der kollektiven Gläubigerbefriedigung müssen sich auch in der Verfahrensgestaltung niederschlagen. Tiefgreifende Abweichungen von den allgemeinen insolvenzrechtlichen Prinzipien sollte es hier nicht geben.

IV. Materieller Gläubigerschutz

Ein Kernpunkt des Gläubigerschutzes in der Bankeninsolvenz von noch weitaus größerer Bedeutung ist die Frage nach dem „materiellen Gläubigerschutz". Damit meine ich die Auswirkung des Insolvenzverfahrens auf die Rechtspositionen einzelner Gläubiger oder Beteiligter unter dem Blickwinkel einer Förderung des Wohls der Gesamtheit der Gläubigerschaft. In der Sache geht es hier vor allem um die Auswirkungen des Insolvenzrechts auf schuldvertragliche Gestaltungen.

Ich möchte einige Punkte aufgreifen, die in einem Sonderinsolvenzrecht für Banken Beachtung finden sollten. Wiederum bleibt auch hier die Frage latent im Hintergrund zu berücksichtigen, ob und in welchem Umfang Abweichungen von allgemeinen insolvenzrechtlichen Prinzipien angezeigt sind.

Ein sensibler Bereich ist dabei sicher die Auswirkung eines Insolvenzverfahrens auf den Zahlungsverkehr und namentlich auf Teilnehmer von Zahlungsverkehrssystemen, weil sich durch die Insolvenz eines Systemteilnehmers „Ansteckungsgefahren" ergeben können. Hier besteht ggf. ein Zielkonflikt. Einerseits muss vermieden werden, dass Gläubiger, die im Rahmen eines solchen Systems vorgeleistet haben oder noch Ansprüche wegen eines Guthabens auf dem Verrechnungskonto haben, gegenüber gewöhnlichen Gläubiger privilegiert werden, andererseits muss aber das System als solches geschützt werden.

1. Privilegierung von Zahlungsverkehrssystemen

Allerdings sind die Gefahren jedenfalls im deutschen Recht schon dadurch begrenzt, dass das deutsche Recht eine automatische Rückwirkung der Verfahrenseröffnung im Sinne eines sog. relation-back grundsätzlich nicht kennt, wie beispielsweise in anderen Ländern, wo die Insolvenzeröffnung oder -beantragung auf Null Uhr des jeweiligen Tages zurückwirkt.[26] In Deutschland besteht daher jedenfalls insoweit nicht die Gefahr,

26 Dazu *Binder* Bankeninsolvenzen im Spannungsfeld zwischen Bankaufsichts- und Insolvenzrecht, S. 340.

dass bereits abgewickelte Zahlungsaufträge o. ä. mangels Wegfall der Verfügungsbefugnis des betroffenen Instituts kassiert werden.

Darüber hinaus sind im europäischen Recht wegen der Finalitätsrichtlinie und der Finanzsicherheitenrichtlinie bereits Regelungen zum Schutz von Zahlungsverkehrssystemen umgesetzt worden.[27] In Deutschland wird zum Beispiel nach Verfahrenseröffnung die Verrechnung von Ansprüchen und Leistungen aus Zahlungsaufträgen oder Wertpapierübertragungsaufträgen geschützt, wenn sie in das System eingebracht wurden, § 96 Abs. 2 InsO. Zahlungsaufträge erlöschen bei Insolvenzeröffnung nicht automatisch, § 116 S. 3 InsO. Darüber hinaus werden Sicherheiten weitgehend geschützt, wenn sie im Rahmen von Zahlungssystemen erworben wurden, § 166 Abs. 2 S. 3 InsO; hier ist nicht der Insolvenzverwalter zur Verwertung berechtigt, sondern der Sicherungsnehmer selbst, ohne dass er die sonst notwendige Kostenbeteiligung zugunsten der Masse leisten muss.

Insgesamt erscheint mir hier kein akuter Bedarf für eine weitergehende Privilegierung von Zahlungsverkehrssystemen zu bestehen, umgekehrt aber auch keine Notwendigkeit, die bisherigen Privilegierungen einzuschränken. Die bestehende Privilegierung der Zahlungssysteme führt zwar zur Begünstigung der Teilnehmer, ist aber erstens gerechtfertigt durch das Ziel eines effizienten Zahlungssystems im öffentlichen Interesse und zweitens eingebettet in eine allgemeine Sicherung beispielsweise der Einlagensicherung, von der die dadurch ggf. benachteiligten Insolvenzgläubiger profitieren.[28] Freilich tritt eben doch eine gewisse Sonderbehandlung ein, und daher sollte man bei weiteren Ausnahmen vorsichtig sein.

Was allerdings nicht übersehen werden darf, ist die Frage, wie sich diese Regelungen zu einem Sonderinsolvenz- bzw. Restrukturierungsgesetz verhalten. § 46 a I 6 KWG ordnet heute an, dass die Vorschriften der Insolvenzordnung zum Schutz von Zahlungs- sowie Wertpapierliefer- und -abrechnungssystemen sowie von dinglichen Sicherheiten der Zentralbanken und von Finanzsicherheiten auf das Moratorium entsprechend Anwendung finden. Das führt allerdings zu Abstimmungsproblemen und wird im Schrifttum kritisiert, weil beispielsweise der eben genannte § 96 Abs. 2 InsO oder der für Sicherheiten geltende § 166 Abs. 2 InsO oder § 116 S. 3 InsO eigentlich erst ab Verfahrenseröffnung gelten.[29]

Daher hätte sich auch der Gesetzgeber eines Restrukturierungsgesetzes darum bemühen sollen, die Zusammenhänge zu den bereits vorhandenen insolvenzrechtlichen Vorgaben nicht aus den Augen zu verlieren. Insbesondere mag es sein, dass das RestruktG auch insoweit zu undifferenziert vorgeht, wenn es in § 23 wieder nur pauschal auf die Vorschriften zum Schutz von Zahlungssystemen in der InsO verweist.[30]

---

27 *Obermüller* FS Uhlenbruck, 2000, S. 365 ff.; umfassend zu Bankgeschäften in der Insolvenz der Bank *Pannen* Krise und Insolvenz bei Kreditinstituten, 3. Aufl. 2010, Kap. 5, S. 175 ff.

28 *Binder* Bankeninsolvenzen im Spannungsfeld zwischen Bankaufsichts- und Insolvenzrecht, S. 407.

29 *Binder* Bankeninsolvenzen im Spannungsfeld zwischen Bankaufsichts- und Insolvenzrecht, S. 371, 375 f., 389 et passim.

30 Vgl. *Binder* Bankeninsolvenzen im Spannungsfeld zwischen Bankaufsichts- und Insolvenzrecht, a. a. O.

2. Lösungs- und Beendigungsklauseln und Netting

Das gilt gleichermaßen für die Frage, ob schuldvertragliche Beendigungs- und Lösungsklauseln in der Insolvenz Bestand haben. Solche Klauseln, die entweder automatisch oder kraft Gestaltungserklärung zu einer Beendigung der vertraglichen Bindung mit der Bank führen, können vielgestaltig sein; im Bankwesen begegnen sie insbesondere in Form des Netting.[31]

Lösungs- und Saldierungsklauseln können je nach Sachlage für die insolvente Bank und ihre Gläubiger misslich sein, wenn Vertragspartner sich also bei Insolvenz vom Vertrag lösen können, andererseits haben solche Klauseln ex ante, vor Insolvenz – also auch aus der Sicht der damaligen Gläubiger – auch Vorteile, weil sie die Gegenpartei schützen und es dieser damit erleichtern, überhaupt mit dem später insolventen Institut Geschäfte zu machen, so dass sich Vertragsmodalitäten für das insolvente Institut verbessern mögen.

Entsprechende Klauseln für Netting-Verträge, also Klauseln im Rahmen eines Master Agreements, werden heute in § 104 InsO weitgehend geschützt, da der InsO-Gesetzgeber durch die Abkehr vom rechtlich sanktionierten „cherry picking" des Insolvenzverwalters bei beidseitig unerfüllten Verträgen den Finanzplatz Deutschland zu stärken beabsichtigte.[32] Es ist klar auszusprechen, dass darin eine wirtschaftspolitische Entscheidung liegt, Finanzinstitute in der Insolvenz zu bevorzugen, da die meisten anderen Gläubiger keine Nettingabreden mit dem insolventen Institut treffen werden.[33]

Dogmatisch ist hier einiges unklar. Allgemeine Lösungsklauseln außerhalb dieser Netting-Verträge werden von der h. M. nach § 119 InsO für unwirksam gehalten, soweit sie jedenfalls an die Eröffnung des Insolvenzverfahrens und nicht an einen vorgelagerten Umstand anknüpfen.[34]

Im Restrukturierungsgesetz wird jetzt in § 13 eine differenzierende Lösung vorgesehen. Anders als noch im DiskE des BMJ vorgesehen, wird eine vertraglich vereinbarte Beendigung eines Vertrags auf der Grundlage der Anzeige der Sanierungsbedürftigkeit an die BaFin bzw. der Einleitung des Sanierungs- und Reorganisationsverfahrens nicht mehr gänzlich untersagt. Vielmehr soll die Ausübung solcher Rechte möglich; sie bleibt allerdings gesperrt bis zum Ablauf des auf die Anzeige folgenden Geschäftstages.

M.E. ist das jedenfalls im Grundsatz ein guter Kompromiss: Die Lösungsklauseln werden nicht gänzlich untersagt; insofern gilt in dubio pro libertate. Das ist dogmatisch stimmig. Auch im allgemeinen Insolvenzrecht wird die Frage der Wirksamkeit von Beendigungsklauseln allein mit Blick auf die an die Eröffnung des Verfahrens geknüpften Klauseln diskutiert; aus Sicht des Insolvenzrechts sind also vertragliche Beendigungsrechte, die an einem dieser Zäsur vorgelagerten Umstand anknüpfen, unbedenklich, weil dann der Konflikt mit den insolvenzrechtlichen Prinzipien und dem Erfüllungswahlrecht des Verwalters nicht virulent wird.[35]

---

31 Umfassend im Kontext des Derivatenhandels *Ehricke* FS Kümpel, 2003, S. 77.

32 Zur Entstehungsgeschichte der Norm *Zimmer/Fuchs* ZGR 2010, 597, 623 f.

33 *Paech* WM 2010, 1965, 1967.

34 *Thole* in: Jahrbuch Junger Zivilrechtswissenschaftler, 2008, S. 267 ff., 274 ff.

35 *Thole* aaO; vgl. auch *K.-P. Berger* ZIP 1994, 173, 181 ff., 182; *Blank/Möller* ZInsO 2003, 437, 443.

3. Insolvenzanfechtung

Die Insolvenzanfechtung ist das insolvenzrechtliche Gläubigerschutzinstrument par excellence. Es zielt hier vor allem auf den Schutz vor einer Bevorzugung einzelner Gläubiger und damit auf die Wahrung des Prinzips der par conditio creditorum.[36] Mit der Anfechtung können Rechtshandlungen, die vor der Einleitung des Insolvenzverfahrens erfolgt sind und die Masse benachteiligen, wieder rückgängig gemacht werden; der Zuwendungsempfänger muss das Erlangte an die Masse zurückführen. Insofern muss in der Vertragspraxis stets im Blick behalten werden, ob im Falle der späteren Insolvenzeröffnung vielleicht eine Anfechtung droht.

a) Die Geltung der Anfechtung im Allgemeinen

Im Allgemeinen ist die Insolvenzanfechtung in der Bankeninsolvenz unproblematisch. Es bedarf hier keiner grundlegenden Anpassung. Das gilt insbesondere auch für Fälle des Interbankenverkehrs. Der Umstand allein, dass eine Bank, die mit der insolventen Bank kontrahiert hatte, das Erlangte wieder herausgeben muss, rechtfertigt – auch nicht unter Hinweis auf übergeordnete Interessen – eine Sonderbehandlung der Banken als Anfechtungsgegner nicht. Die Anfechtungstatbestände enthalten jeweils Abstufungen nach subjektiver Kenntnis und weiteren Voraussetzungen, so dass die Schutzbedürftigkeit des Anfechtungsgegners implizit berücksichtigt wird.

b) Anfechtung bei Zahlungsverkehrssystemen

Auch im Rahmen eines Zahlungsverkehrssystems ist eine Anfechtung grundsätzlich denkbar, die Finalitäts- und Finanzsicherheitenrichtlinie und die Umsetzungsgesetze schließen das nicht aus. Denkbar ist zum Beispiel die Anfechtung der Bestellung von Sicherheiten oder einer Verrechnungsabrede oder der vorgenommenen Verrechnung von Positionen selbst. Da allerdings die Anfechtungstatbestände inhaltlich sehr ausdifferenziert sind, würde ich dafür plädieren, es bei diesen Grundsätzen zu belassen. Wenn im Einzelfall eine Anfechtung durchschlägt, dann ist das zu verkraften und in der Sache gerechtfertigt. Grundsätzlicher Bedarf für eine Sonderregelung im Bereich der Bankeninsolvenz oder im Bereich des Zahlungsverkehrswesens besteht mE nicht, und dies wäre auch dogmatisch nicht wünschenswert, weil es die Anfechtung zu Unrecht vom allgemeinen Insolvenzrecht abkoppelte und aus normativen oder politischen Gründen eine Ausnahme statuierte, die sich mit den Wertungen der Insolvenzanfechtung nicht verträgt.

c) Anfechtung der Übertragung von Risikopositionen

Obwohl also kein Bedarf für eine weitreichende Ausklammerung des Anfechtungsrechts besteht, sind einige Sonderprobleme natürlich zu berücksichtigen.

---

36 Näher und differenziert *Thole* Gläubigerschutz durch Insolvenzrecht, 2010, S. 287 ff.

Das gilt zunächst für die Übertragung von Risikopositionen an Dritte wie beispielsweise an den Soffin oder an andere Brückenbanken oder eine Bad Bank. Darüber hinaus bildet die Ausgliederung von Unternehmensteilen eine relevante Baustelle.

In allen diesen Fällen handelt es sich um die Übertragung von Vermögensgegenständen der später insolventen Bank, auch wenn deren Wert im Einzelfall gering ist und die Realisierbarkeit der Position – eben weil es eine Risikoposition ist – zweifelhaft sein mag. Es ist jedenfalls nicht per se ausgeschlossen, dass im Falle einer Insolvenzeröffnung der Insolvenzverwalter die weggegebenen Vermögenspositionen unter Berufung auf die eingetretene Gläubigerbenachteiligung zurückfordern möchte, so dass der Erwerb durch den Erwerber anfechtungsrechtlich gefährdet ist.

Der Gesetzgeber des Finanzmarktstabilisierungsgesetzes und der Ergänzungsgesetze hatte darauf reagiert. § 18 FMStBG lautete:

„Rechtshandlungen, die im Zusammenhang mit Stabilisierungsmaßnahmen stehen, können nicht zu Lasten des Fonds, des Bundes und der von ihnen errichteten Körperschaften, Anstalten und Sondervermögen sowie der ihnen nahe stehenden Personen oder sonstigen von ihnen mittelbar oder unmittelbar abhängigen Unternehmen nach den Bestimmungen der Insolvenzordnung und des Anfechtungsgesetzes angefochten werden."

Gleiches gilt nach § 9 Abs. 3 RestruktG für den Debt-Equity-Swap und ähnlich ist es jetzt vorgesehen in § 48g RestruktG für die Ausgliederung; hier ist ein gänzlicher Anfechtungsausschluss gleich gegenüber welchem Empfänger vorgesehen.

Ich stehe diesen Regelungen mit einiger Sorge gegenüber. Auch im Kommissionspapier der EU wird darauf hingewiesen, dass bei der Übertragung von Vermögenswerten ggf. Schutzmaßnahmen zugunsten der Gläubiger geschaffen werden müssen.[37] Nach Lage der Dinge kann das insbesondere die Insolvenzanfechtung bieten. Die Insolvenzanfechtung greift ja ohnedies nur dann ein, wenn eine Gläubigerbenachteiligung festgestellt ist und das Insolvenzverfahren tatsächlich eröffnet wird, also die vorinsolvenzliche Sanierung offenbar gerade nicht funktioniert hat. Nach allgemeinem Anfechtungsrecht sind Sanierungsversuche aber nicht grundsätzlich der Anfechtung entzogen, sondern im Wesentlichen ist der sichere Ausschluss der Anfechtung davon abhängig, dass die Sanierung auf einem schlüssigen, nachvollziehbaren und erfolgversprechenden Konzept beruht; entsprechendes ließe sich eigentlich auch bei Stabilisierungsmaßnahmen denken. Ich gebe allerdings zu, dass eine Anfechtung natürlich die Komplexität erhöht und der Rechtssicherheit abträglich ist. Daher kann man hier ausnahmsweise einen gänzlichen Anfechtungsausschluss rechtfertigen. Es bleibt allerdings die Frage, ob es Sinn ergibt, nach Anfechtungsgegnern zu unterscheiden und nur die öffentliche Hand vor einer Anfechtung zu schützen; ganz konsequent scheint mir diese Differenzierung nicht zu sein.

M.E. sollte man sich jedenfalls davor hüten, die Anfechtung auch außerhalb der genannten Rechtshandlungen gänzlich aus einem Sonderinsolvenzrecht zu verbannen,

37 Mitteilung der Kommission: „Ein EU-Rahmen für das grenzübergreifende Krisenmanagement auf dem Banksektor", vom 20. 10. 2009, KOM(2009) 561 endg., Abs. 4.1.

weil sie eine wichtige Kontrollfunktion vorinsolvenzlicher Rechtshandlungen im Interesse der par conditio creditorum wahrnimmt.

4. Debt-Equity-Swap

Gerade der Debt-Equity-Swap wirft im Hinblick auf den Gläubigerschutz einige Fragen auf. Er führt zur Umwandlung von Fremdkapital in Eigenkapital nach Vollzug einer Kapitalerhöhung der Schuldnerin mit der Ausgabe von neuen Anteilen gegen die in der Einbringung der Forderung liegende Sacheinlage.[38] Die Sacheinlage wird entweder im Wege der Forderungsabtretung mit der Folge des Erlöschens der Forderung im Wege der Konfusion vollzogen, oder durch Abschluss eines Erlassvertrages.[39] Diese Strategie kann für Gläubiger Sinn machen, wenn sie, jedenfalls auf lange Sicht, bessere Ergebnisse erwarten lässt als eine übertragende Sanierung.

Schwierigkeiten entstehen freilich mit Blick auf den Schutz der verbleibenden und neuen Gläubiger. Kontrovers diskutiert wird die Frage, in welcher Höhe die beim Debt-Equity-Swap als Sacheinlage einzubringenden Forderungen anzusetzen sind: in der Höhe ihres augenblicklichen, verminderten wirklichen Wertes[40] oder in der Höhe ihres Nennwertes.[41] Damit angesprochen ist das System der Werthaltigkeitskontrolle im Rahmen der Kapitalaufbringung. Freilich handelt es sich dabei um ein allgemeines, gesellschaftsrechtliches Problem, das nicht genuin bankrechtlicher Natur ist, sondern in der Reform des Insolvenzplanverfahrens generell auf der Agenda steht.[42] Das Sonderinsolvenzrecht für Banken sollte sich an diese Entwicklung anpassen. Für eine Veranschlagung der eingebrachten Forderung in Höhe des Nennwertes bei einem Debt-Equity-Swap im Verfahren lässt sich insoweit anführen, dass auf Seiten des Schuldners beim Debt-Equity-Swap eine Verbindlichkeit in Höhe des Nennwertes erlischt und nicht lediglich in Höhe des wirklichen Wertes, wohingegen das Eigenkapital um den Nennbetrag der eingebrachten Forderung steigt.[43] Auch die übrigen Gläubiger sind bei einer Nennwertbetrachtung insofern besser gestellt, als die am Swap partizipierenden Insolvenzgläubiger hinter die einfachen und nachrangigen Insolvenzgläubiger zurücktreten, was diese übrigen Gläubiger besser stellt.[44] Die weitere Diskussion sollte auch dem Bankeninsolvenzrecht Impulse geben.

5. Hoheitliche Übertragungsanordnungen

Ein Punkt, der noch besondere Beachtung verdient, ist die in § 48a RestruktG ermöglichte hoheitliche Übertragungsanordnung von Vermögen und Verbindlichkeiten der

38 *Ekkenga* ZGR 2009, 581, 586.
39 *Priester* DB 2010, 1445.
40 H. M.: BGH NZG 2002, 1172, 1174; *Priester* DB 2010, 1445; *Ekkenga* ZGR 2009, 581, 599.
41 *Cahn/Simon/Theiselmann* CFL 2010, 238.
42 S. dazu § 225a Abs. 2 S. 1 InsO-RegE; *Simon* CFL 2010, 448, 450.
43 *Simon* CFL 2010, 448, 452.
44 *Cahn/Simon/Theiselmann* DB 2010, 1629, 1631; *Simon* CFL 2010, 448, 452; a. A. *Priester* DB 2010, 1445, 1449.

Not leidenden Bank auf eine Brückenbank. Der BaFin soll es erlaubt sein, das Vermögen eines Kreditinstituts einschließlich seiner Verbindlichkeiten auf einen bestehenden Rechtsträger im Wege der Ausgliederung zu übertragen, wenn das Kreditinstitut in seinem Bestand gefährdet ist und es dadurch die Stabilität des Finanzsystems gefährdet. Diese Initiative orientiert sich an entsprechenden Gesetzesänderungen in Großbritannien und den USA, hinter denen sie jedoch nach Umfang und Reichweite zurück bleibt.[45] Um dem Vorwurf der Enteignung von verfassungsrechtlich garantiertem Eigentum zu entgehen,[46] sieht § 48d RestruktG vor, dass das Kreditinstitut eine Gegenleistung in denjenigen Fällen erhält, in denen der Wert der zu übertragenden Gegenstände positiv ist, und zwar grundsätzlich in Form von Anteilen an dem übernehmenden Rechtsträger. § 48h KWG sieht eine Haftung des Kreditinstituts nur in der Höhe vor, in der ein Gläubiger im Falle einer Abwicklung Befriedigung erfahren haben würde, wenn es nicht zur Ausgliederung gekommen wäre, und auch nur dann, wenn der Gläubiger von dem übernehmenden Rechtsträger keine Befriedigung erlangen konnte.

Die letztgenannte Regelung erscheint mir eher unbedenklich, denn ohne die Übertragung hätte der Gläubiger mit dem übernehmenden Rechtsträger keinen neuen, zusätzlichen Schuldner gewonnen.

Mit der Übertragungsanordnung sind freilich einige Fragen aufgeworfen. Die Gläubiger derjenigen Verbindlichkeiten, die nicht übertragen werden, können sich nur noch an das ggf. entleerte alte Institut halten. Zu dessen Vermögenswerten gehören dann zwar auch die Anteile am Übernehmer, doch ob sich daraus wirklich äquivalente Befriedigungschancen ergeben, ist eher fraglich. Es könnte daher die Schwierigkeit aus Gläubigerschutzgesichtspunkten darin bestehen, zu unterscheiden, welche Verbindlichkeiten übergehen sollen und welche Gläubiger damit einen neuen Schuldner bekommen. Das kann eine Ungleichbehandlung der Alt- und Neugläubiger bedeuten. In der Sache wäre es konsequent, sich am übergeordneten Ziel der Vermeidung der System- und Bestandsgefährdung zu orientieren und damit die Ungleichbehandlung zu rechtfertigen. Nur solche Verbindlichkeiten dürfen übertragen werden, die system- und bestandsgefährdend sind; um die Abgrenzung vorzunehmen, wird man wohl der BaFin ein recht weites Ermessen einräumen müssen.

VI. Grenzüberschreitungen

Es ist bei allem nicht zu verschweigen, dass auch im Sonderinsolvenzrecht für Banken eine europäische Lösung sinnvoll ist, und zwar nicht oder nicht nur deshalb, weil das politisch opportun wäre, sondern gerade auch „rechtlich" gesehen. Immerhin hat schon die Richtlinie 2001/24/EG über die Sanierung und Liquidation von Kreditinstituten vom 4. 4. 2001 zu einer Harmonisierung des Insolvenzrechts für Banken geführt,

45 Dazu *Flessner* ÖBA 2010, 655, 659.

46 Zu der Debatte *Flessner* ÖBA 2010, 655, 659 m. w. N.

die sich allerdings im Wesentlichen auf kollisionsrechtliche Fragen beschränkt.[47] Daran ließe sich eine Fortentwicklung anknüpfen.

Auch in grenzüberschreitenden Insolvenzen – welche Bankeninsolvenz ist das nicht – ist dem Postulat der gleichmäßigen Gläubigerbefriedigung Rechnung zu tragen. Hier scheinen mir die Weichen noch nicht völlig richtig gestellt. So ist es zweifelhaft, wenn nach den Vorgaben der Richtlinie und jetzt nach § 46e Abs. 2 KWG Sekundärinsolvenzverfahren über Niederlassungen von Banken zugunsten eines strengen Universalitätsprinzips am Heimatsitz der Bank ausgeschlossen sind. Damit kann die Gläubigergleichbehandlung schnell zur Ungleichbehandlung werden, weil einige Gläubiger nicht an dem Ort, an dem sie mit der Bank in Kontakt traten, im Insolvenzverfahren ihre Forderungen geltend machen können, sondern sie gezwungen sind, im für sie fremden Herkunftsstaat der Bank ihre Forderungen anzumelden. Auch über dieses Bedenken wäre daher trotz aller Vorzüge des strikten Universalitätsprinzips ggf. noch weiter nachzudenken.[48]

Wie dem auch sei, wenn man sich die Überlegungen der Kommission ansieht, dann soll in der Bankenkonzerninsolvenz der Trend zu einer stärkeren Integration der Insolvenzverfahren gehen und Regelungen geschaffen werden, die eine Durchführung des Sanierungs- oder Liquidationsverfahrens aus einer Hand erlauben. Angedacht ist zum Teil auch an Lösungen wie *substantive consolidation*.[49] Daran ist sicher richtig, dass angesichts der Verflechtung der Konzerngesellschaften und Auslandsniederlassungen ein nationales Klein-Klein nicht sinnvoll ist. Aber ich gebe zu bedenken, dass sich der Gläubigerschutz hier stets an dem jeweiligen Schuldner orientieren muss und dass das Prinzip der beschränkten Haftung nicht leichtfertig überspielt werden darf. Die Gläubiger einer rechtlich selbständigen Niederlassung dürfen nicht ohne weiteres mit Gläubigern anderer Konzerngesellschaften vermengt werden.

Jeder Gläubiger hat andere berechtigte Erwartungen, was die Aussicht auf Befriedigung angeht, weil er sich an dem Vermögen seines Schuldners orientiert. Eine Lösung wie die *substantive consolidation* läuft auf eine Umverteilung zwischen Gläubigern hinaus. Daher kann es allenfalls um eine bessere verfahrensmäßige Koordination von Insolvenzverfahren über die jeweiligen Tochtergesellschaften gehen, nicht um eine materielle Zusammenfassung von Gläubigeransprüchen.

VII. Fazit

Damit komme ich langsam zum Schluss. Wie wir gerade gesehen haben, gibt es eine Menge Bezugspunkte des Gläubigerschutzes, die sowohl in einem vorinsolvenzlichen

47 ABl. EG L 125/15. Näher *Paulus* ZBB 2002, 492; *Gottwald* FS Georgidades, S. 823; *Pannen* Krise und Insolvenz bei Kreditinstituten, 3. Aufl. 2010, Kap. 56, S. 233 ff.; *Wimmer* ZInsO 2002, 897.

48 *Binder* Bankeninsolvenzen im Spannungsfeld zwischen Bankaufsichts- und Insolvenzrecht, S. 700 f.; weniger kritisch aber *Maucher* Die Europäisierung des Internationalen Bankeninsolvenzrechts, 2010, S. 50 ff.

49 Mitteilung der Kommission: „Ein EU-Rahmen für das grenzübergreifende Krisenmanagement auf dem Banksektor", vom 20. 10. 2009, KOM(2009) 561 endg., Abs. 4.3.

Sanierungs- und Restrukturierungsverfahren als auch in einem echten Insolvenzverfahren herkömmlicher Prägung relevant werden. Insgesamt muss man wohl konstatieren, dass der Bedarf für wirkliche Einschränkungen oder Erweiterungen des Gläubigerschutzes in einem Sonderinsolvenzrecht für Banken eher gering ist. Man muss m.E. aufpassen, die Sonderregelungen nicht zu weit zu treiben und damit den Anschluss an die allgemeinen insolvenzrechtlichen Entwicklungen aus den Augen zu verlieren.